Does Psychoanalysis Work?

ROBERT M. GALATZER-LEVY, M.D.
HENRY BACHRACH, Ph.D.
ALAN SKOLNIKOFF, M.D.
SHERWOOD WALDRON, JR., M.D.

Does
Psychoanalysis
Work?

Yale University Press
New Haven &
London

Set in Sabon type by Keystone Typesetting, Inc. Printed in the United States of America.

Library of Congress Cataloging-in-Publication Data
Does psychoanalysis work? / Robert M. Galatzer-Levy . . . [et al.].
        p.   cm.
Includes bibliographical references and index.
ISBN 0-300-06527-2 (alk. paper)
1. Psychoanalysis — Evaluation.   2. Psychotherapy — Outcome assessment.
3. Psychoanalysis — Research.   I. Galatzer-Levy, Robert M., 1944–
RC506.D62   2000
616.89'17 — dc21   99-36079

A catalogue record for this book is available from the British Library.

The paper in this book meets the guidelines for permanence and durability of the Committee on Production Guidelines for Book Longevity of the Council on Library Resources.

10 9 8 7 6 5 4 3 2 1

Contents

Introduction

During the first half of the twentieth century, psychoanalysis and its derivatives enjoyed a unique position: they were the only rational psychotherapies supported by a coherent theory of psychological function and psychopathology. This position, combined with the clinical experiences of successful treatments, convinced many people — mental health professionals and nonprofessionals alike — that psychoanalysis was a procedure that could effectively relieve many forms of psychological suffering.

Analysts did observe analytic failures, which they tended to attribute to misdiagnosis, faulty psychoanalytic technique, or the misapplication of psychoanalysis to forms of psychopathology that are inherently unresponsive to such treatments. Following World War II, therefore, deliberate efforts were made to correct these sources of failures. One approach was an attempt to diagnose psychopathology more precisely, in the hope of ensuring that patients suffering from analyzable disorders would be adequately treated and that those patients for whom analysis was not indicated could receive other intervention without the painful and sometimes harmful experience of failed analysis (Zetzel and Meissner, 1973). Psychologists developed tests designed to diagnose psychiatric conditions differentially and compare them to normal states as an aid in making therapeutic decisions (Rapaport, Gill, and Schafer, 1945).

A second line of approach tried to remedy psychoanalytic failures by working to improve psychoanalytic technique (Eissler, 1953). And finally, attempts were made to adapt analytic technique and thinking so as to address forms of psychological illness previously believed to be unresponsive to such measures — that is, forms of illness that were thought not to originate in neurotic conflict. In what was known as the widening scope of psychoanalysis (Stone, 1954; A. Freud, 1954), a range of ideas and techniques, including much of what was later called object relations theory (Kernberg, 1976) and self psychology (Kohut, 1971, 1984), was developed.

Except for psychological testing, all these activities involved extensive but unsystematic observations by psychoanalytic clinicians. Proceeding much as other physician-researchers had done before World War II, they collected and summarized clinical experience. They seldom had clear methods for exploring the data they collected or for assessing the validity of the conclusions they drew.

In general medicine, the development of increasingly potent pharmacological interventions after the war led to ever higher expectations of therapeutic interventions and higher standards for the methods used to determine their efficacy. Before the war physicians had a tiny group of truly effective drugs with which to work. By the end of the war, starting with antibiotics, an amazing array of effective medication became available. Researchers increasingly recognized that case reports and summaries of clinical experience could yield false impressions: investigators could overestimate the efficacy of an intervention, for example, on the basis of reports of enthusiastic patients or physicians. They could mistake positive findings that resulted from the general care of the patient, the natural history of the condition, or random variation in the course of the illness for treatment effects. Seemingly impressive results could be shown to arise from a chance difference between patients who were treated in the new way and those who were not. To a lesser extent, problems arose from the underestimation of therapeutic results because significant therapeutic effects were sometimes hard to discern against a background of variation resulting from extraneous factors. For example, when similar but distinct conditions are lumped together, a treatment effective for one of them can easily be missed if it fails to affect the other disorders.

Medical scientists developed sophisticated ways of dealing with these problems. Borrowing statistical methods originally developed to study agriculture and manufacture, they designed experiments that isolated the effects under study from other determinants of outcome and also quantified the credibility of research findings. These methods, which usually involved the comparison of groups within a population, gained enormous prestige and became the normative way to do medical investigation. Sometimes their prestige exceeded their usefulness.

In the social sciences during the same period, quantitative methods also gained popularity. Researchers saw them as a way to counteract personally motivated distortions in the study of people. In addition, they served to make the social sciences more like the hard sciences. Statistical and quantitative methods, combined with a positivistic stance that ignored elements of a situation that could not be measured reliably, became pervasive. Often the price was failure to explore the meaning of the phenomena to the people involved.

Psychoanalysis has had a peculiar and complex relation to normative science throughout its history. Freud labored to wed his radical clinical findings to the prestigious ideas of nineteenth-century quantitative science (Sulloway, 1979; Jones, 1953; Galatzer-Levy, 1976; Cohler and Galatzer-Levy, 1991; Kitcher, 1992). Many psychoanalysts maintain allegiance to this ideal even today, despite clear indications that Freud's efforts to treat clinical psychoanalytic findings like those of the biological sciences and to establish a psychological theory modeled on physical sciences did not stand up to scrutiny. Although psychoanalysts wished to claim the prestige of science, few of them have attempted to meet evolving standards of scientific investigation. In particular, most psychoanalytic discourse about therapy ignored the newer methodologies used to study effectiveness of other therapeutic activities.

As we shall show throughout this book, the systematic study of psychoanalysis is intrinsically difficult. Psychoanalysis is a complex, subtle, difficult-to-observe activity that extends over many years; the assessment of its effects may take decades. Second, those who choose to become psychoanalysts are generally most interested in understanding individual psychology in depth, not in quantitative methodologies. Third, the long history of psychoanalytic claims to scientific status has interfered with systematic exploration. In order to undertake such exploration a first painful step is to recognize that many of these claims are ill founded. Finally, the initial criticisms of psychoanalysis based on statistical analysis of studies of efficacy (Eysenck, 1952) were so clearly hostile and unfair that many analysts equated quantitative studies with negative attitudes toward psychoanalysis, and many continue to do so.

For all these reasons, despite the vast clinical experience of the past century, there have been few systematic studies that address vital questions about the efficacy of psychoanalysis. As psychoanalysis enters its second century, such questions have become urgent in view of increasing external pressure to prove the value of psychoanalysis in the marketplace of mental health services. Even if such pressure did not exist, many analysts, as well as patients and potential patients, would value more systematic and reliable knowledge of the circumstances in which analysis is (and is not) likely to be effective.

Over the past thirty years psychoanalysis has lost much status. No longer the sole rational therapy for psychological distress, today it competes with many other treatments. Some of these have solid conceptual bases, some are supported by systematic empirical research, and most claim to relieve psychological distress more quickly and at less cost than psychoanalysis. As many of the insights of psychoanalysis became clichés in American society, the prestige of psychoanalysis fell. Insurance companies increasingly refused to pay benefits for psychoanalysis because of the supposed absence of data supporting its clinical claims. And this development, analysts feared, might presage similar policies under health care reform legislation. All these broad issues affected the practice of psychoanalysts. Many noted a steady decline in the number and proportion of patients seeking psychoanalytic treatment, and many institutes experienced a decline in candidates seeking training.

One obvious approach to these problems is to provide data in support of the claim that psychoanalytic treatment is effective. In 1988 the president (Richard Simons) and president-elect (Homer Curtis) of the American Psychoanalytic Association asked the association's Committee on Scientific Activities to do just that. The committee, founded in 1976 under the guidance of Heinz Kohut and Robert Wallerstein, prides itself on critical scholarship and independence from political and institutional influence. Under the leadership of George Klumpner, the committee assumed the task of critically reviewing the existing literature on psychoanalytic outcomes.

The four authors of this book were selected as a subcommittee to conduct the review and draft the report to the association based solely on scientific principles. We proceeded cautiously, resisting pressure for quick or favorable findings. With helpful feedback from the Committee on Scientific Activities, we completed our report and condensed it into a paper (Bachrach, Galatzer-Levy, Skolnikoff, and Waldron, 1991). We began our study and we begin this book by attempting to formulate what we, as psychoanalysts, hope empirical investigations can teach us about our work.

We start with a question that absorbs a surprising amount of psychoanalytic time: what is psychoanalysis? Only when this question is clarified and some means provided for deciding whether an activity is or is not psychoanalysis can we ask meaningful questions about the efficacy of psychoanalysis. Sometimes analysts talk of psychoanalysis in terms of the most manifest of its arrangements — for example, frequency of sessions or whether the patient uses the couch. Sometimes they define analysis in terms of depth-psychological processes. How do these different descriptions of psychoanalysis relate to each other? This question is subject to empirical investigation.

Similarly, it is essential to establish what the relevant measures of outcome are for psychoanalysis. If we limit ourselves to measures that do not tap central psychoanalytic goals, research cannot be fruitful. Yet it is difficult to clearly specify the goals of psychoanalysis and their interrelation.

In analytic case conferences and similar discussions, analysts commonly debate which theory best explains the patient's psychopathology. On the basis of their understanding of the patient, they make recommendations about appropriate psychoanalytic technique. Currently these discussions, if they come to any resolution, do so though rhetorical persuasion (Spence, 1994) or authority. It is seldom possible for the discussants to marshal more than anecdotal evidence to support their views. Systematic empirical studies that relate theory, technique, and psychoanalytic outcome would be of great value in such discussions. Similarly, data that address the relation of the course of treatment to its outcome would be of practical significance. What sort of alliance is necessary for analytic success? How central must the analyst become in the patient's psychological life? Is a transference neurosis or any other specific aspect of analytic experience, such as a termination phase, necessary for good psychoanalytic outcome?

Finally, we want to know what qualities in the analyst and the analytic setting are needed for analysis to be effective.

In the second part of the book we ask what empirical research has taught us so far about psychoanalysis as therapy. We describe our methods of assessing modern research on psychoanalytic outcome and the criteria we have established. We then apply these methods and criteria to the four major studies on the outcome of analysis for populations of adult psychoanalytic patients. Although each of these studies has limitations, all represent monumental efforts. Their convergent findings support the belief that psychoanalysis is an effective treatment for appropriate patients.

In addition to these four major studies, we looked at contributions to the systematic study of child and adolescent analysis. Recent studies from the Anna Freud Center demonstrate a uniquely sophisticated approach. Other studies of child analysis, including one that compares child analysis and child psychotherapy and another that shows the results of child analysis through later analysis of the same individuals, are important for both their findings and their methods.

Several researchers have examined small groups of patients. Some of these studies are based on common methods of investigation, such as follow-up interviews. Some are based on common features of the patients, such as diagnosis or age. In reviewing these studies we again focus on their methodological strengths and weaknesses as well as their findings. Taken together these studies show that psychoanalysis is an effective treatment for many patients. They also show that some of our cherished assumptions about psychoanalysis are probably wrong.

Each study reviewed had significant methodological failings. This does not mean that the studies should not be taken seriously or that the findings are not credible. It simply means that appropriate care is necessary in interpreting the findings and that further work remains to be done.

However, these methodological failings were not the central problem with the studies. As we completed our review we realized that most of the studies we had considered failed to address central psychoanalytic issues, such as indications for psychoanalysis, the methods of analysis appropriate to different types of patients, and the results of psychoanalysis. With few exceptions, the studies we reviewed focused on other issues.

Reviewing the available empirical studies of psychoanalysis, we wondered why they had so little to say about the central controversies of psychoanalysis. All the studies were conducted by sophisticated analysts. Why were the questions that interest us most so often unaddressed or addressed unsatisfactorily? Retrospectively, it appears that the tools these investigators used were inadequate to the task. Psychoanalysis is an enormously complex activity based on the interaction of two people over an extended period. What means are necessary to capture the important elements of this situation? What methods are likely to provide answers to the questions we pose?

In the final part of this book we ask how we can learn what we want to know about psychoanalytic outcome. We begin by describing the broad issues of doing research in psychoanalysis, including framing research problems in ways that are psychoanalytic and empirically meaningful, finding contexts that support psychoanalytic research, conducting research ethically, and recognizing that some questions cannot be answered empirically. We then ask how data can be collected about psychoanalysis. Contrary to our first intuition, there is no single best way to collect psychoanalytic data. Data about analyses can vary from simple ratings of aspects of an analysis, to videotapes of the treatment, to deep exploration of past analytic experience. What we learn from our research is contingent on how the data are gathered. We discuss the various types of data that can be collected about psychoanalysis and show how different aspects of analysis can be investigated by focusing on aspects of the analytic work, the participants, and the course of the treatment. Psychoanalytic research often seems trapped between discarding vital information and being overwhelmed by the sheer volume of available data. We examine ways to make psychoanalytic investigation more tractable to research and to ways of selecting data for study.

How should analytic processes be described and measured? Several researchers have devised ways to describe the psychological events underlying manifest content. We illustrate several of these methods, in each instance exploring how the method relates to psychoanalytic ideas, how useful it is likely to be, and how it has been used. These developments are among the most promising in psychoanalytic research; they represent the kind of investment in methodology that has proved so fruitful in the development of other disciplines. Each of these methods give us snapshots, of varying quality, of aspects of analyses. Putting the resulting information together into a coherent picture of analytic process and outcome is another daunting task.

Fortunately, many other investigators of complex situations have faced similar problems, and we can learn from their experience. Those trained in the sciences are likely to believe that controlled clinical trials are the best means of establishing the effectiveness of a treatment. Indeed, this is the logic of design of many systematic investigations in psychoanalysis, although these investigations usually do not study an actual control group because the researchers believe that the developments observed in the treated group would almost certainly not occur spontaneously. Unfortunately, the controlled clinical trial is not a practical way to investigate psychoanalytic outcome. This is not an artifact of insufficiently careful research design but a difficulty intrinsic in attempts to apply methods developed to study simple, discrete interventions to complex treatments like psychoanalysis. In Part III we show why traditional clinical trial approaches can supply only limited results when applied to psychoanalysis.

This does not mean that it is impossible to investigate psychoanalysis empirically. In the past quarter-century the methodology of the single-case study has emerged as an important tool for studying complex situations over time. It is an extremely promising candidate for studying psychoanalysis. Single-case study methods should not be confused with the traditional single case reports. Case reports do not require that data be systematically collected and reported. They do not require that the logic connecting the case description to the conclusion be investigated. Single-case studies are a means of rigorously drawing inferences from the detailed study of a single case. We describe the logic and methods of the single-case study in enough depth for the reader to see how clear inferences can be drawn using this method, what limitations the method has, and how it may be applied to psychoanalysis.

Our exploration of how the therapeutic efficacy of psychoanalysis can be studied has been filled with surprises. What started as a seemingly simple job of summarizing a small scientific literature turned into a major study. We realized that to answer questions about psychoanalytic outcome we had to explore issues ranging from psychoanalytic conceptualization to research methodology and the practicalities of studying patients. The effort has led us to appreciate how difficult and multifaceted such studies must be. It has also led us to appreciate the work of the colleagues who have conducted the investigations we examine here. We believe that continued exploration of the issues can move psychoanalysis forward practically and conceptually. We hope to share some of the excitement and pleasure of our experience with our readers.

PART I

*What Psychoanalysts Want to Know About the
Therapeutic Effects of Psychoanalysis*

Despite the extensive advances in psychotherapy research during the past quarter-century (Garfield and Bergin, 1994; Roth and Fonagy, 1996), there have been few systematic efforts to address questions about psychoanalysis as therapy. Psychotherapy research, as a distinct and largely independent discipline, not to be confused with the practice of psychotherapy, involves systematic and empirical studies of psychotherapy process and outcome. It has gradually moved from fledgling attempts at empirical investigation, through a period of attempts to approximate a model of then-current medical research, to an increasing focus on interactive, subjective, and humanistic aspects of study (Orlinsky and Russel, 1994). Psychoanalysts tend to value complexity (Schafer, 1970b), while psychotherapy researchers work to produce quantitatively meaningful measurements. Questions important from a psychoanalytic viewpoint are often unexplored in psychotherapy research, which has tended to focus on briefer forms of treatment and to assess variables that can be measured reliably over short time periods. Most of the results of the massive research effort in psychotherapy are therefore not methodologically and conceptually comparable or translatable to psychoanalysis (Bachrach, 1989; Edelson, 1992).

Several currents in psychotherapy research have led psychoanalytic investigators to be overly wary about the applicability of the methods and strategies of general psychotherapy research to the study of psychoanalysis. Further, general psychotherapy research has traditionally been committed to methods favored by experimental psychology that entail a strong preference for measures that are operationally defined[1] — such as behavioral measures and symptom checklists — over less-operational measures that explore what psychoanalysts want to know. This does not mean that psychoanalytic concepts are inevitably imprecise or unreliable. But in the trade-off between precise measurement and the study of interesting matters, psychotherapy research has tended to favor precision over complexity, while analysts have been reluctant to abandon the richness of their material, even at the cost of being uncertain of the validity of their findings.

Adding to these difficulties is the historical discord between psychotherapy

---

1. Membership in a category is operationally defined when a specific procedure determines whether an entity belongs to a category — for example, if we define resistance as present when the patient manifestly disagrees with or makes no reference to an interpretation (Bridgmen, 1927, p. 5). When category membership is determined in any other fashion, even if one actually uses specific procedures to perform measurements, the concept is not operationally defined. When a concept is operationally defined one can be very clear about whether or not a particular happening is an instance of the concept.

researchers and psychoanalysts. Eysenck's (1952) oft-cited study of the allegedly failed outcome of psychoanalysis and psychotherapy was part of a polemic in which supposedly normative concepts of scientific method were used to fault the conceptual, therapeutic, and scientific merit of psychoanalysis. Authors working in this tradition then made wide-ranging statements about the failings of psychoanalytic psychotherapy and psychoanalysis, even though their research efforts have had limited bearing upon psychoanalysis (see, for example, Fisher and Greenberg, 1977; or Smith, Glass, and Miller, 1980).

For these reasons and others, we believe that it is more productive to explore studies of outcome and efficacy from a point of view native to psychoanalysis.

Within this context, we consider what psychoanalysts and others seriously interested in psychoanalysis would like to know about psychoanalytic outcome and efficacy, outlining a wish list of questions and topics for study.

I

What Is Psychoanalysis?

A first step in studying whether psychoanalysis is effective is to delimit the treatments that will be called psychoanalysis. Freud (1904) defined psychoanalysis as the *interrelated* methods of observation, a conceptual system, and a therapeutic procedure. But the details of this interrelation are unclear. What boundaries of technique and theory usefully set off psychoanalytic ideas and processes from other activities? How are various ways of thinking about psychoanalysis interrelated? The question of what activities and theory are legitimately called psychoanalytic pervades the history of the field, often resulting in discord (see, e.g., Freud, 1914b, 1924; Oberndorf, 1953; Roustang, 1976; Turkle, 1978; Wallerstein, 1995). As one approach to this question, we might ask what the components of psychoanalysis are and how they are related to one another.

Psychoanalysis is widely taken to refer to a point of view about psychological events that includes unconscious processes as its major focus. In this view psychoanalysis as therapy is defined by psychological occurrences. There is a continuum of views about the range of psychological events in the purview of psychoanalysis. Within the mainstream of contemporary American psychoanalysis these views range from a position that the proper focus of psychoanalysis is intrapsychic conflict (Arlow, 1969a,b; Brenner, 1976; Kris, 1951) to views that psychoanalysis properly addresses all psychological life (Gedo,

1979; Hartmann, 1939a,b; Loewenstein, Newman, Schur, and Solnit, 1966). These different theoretical views about the extent of the field have direct clinical implications. For example, the view that psychoanalysis properly addresses all aspects of psychological life suggests that analysts should be able to design therapeutic intervention for distressing conditions resulting from deficits in developmental experiences needed to achieve satisfactory psychological functioning. Based on psychoanalytic understanding, the analyst could provide educational experiences to compensate for earlier lacks in development. This is inconsistent with views that draw the boundaries of psychoanalysis around the study of intrapsychic conflict. Work on developmental deficits, however therapeutic, is not part of psychoanalysis as understood by those who adhere to a paradigm exemplified by Brenner's (1976) elaboration of Freud's ideas about psychic conflict. Most contemporary American psychoanalysts take an intermediate position. Outside this American mainstream, followers of theorists like Harry Stack Sullivan (1940, 1953, 1956, 1964) and Carl Jung (1933, 1954a, 1968) take interpersonal and transpersonal approaches to understanding psychology. Although they describe these ideas as psychoanalytic, we shall not pursue this group of positions in this book. Some psychoanalysts (Reed, 1987b) would exclude from psychoanalysis investigations like Kohut's that employ very different conceptual frameworks from Freud's, even though they retain important aspects of his clinical method (Wallerstein, 1988, 1990). Others hold that Freud's heritage includes two distinct, if easily confused, types of theorizing—one that attempts to extend nineteenth-century physical science to the study of mind (metapsychology) and another that arises from the understanding of meanings and motives as manifested in the clinical encounter (Klein, 1976). They tend to regard the latter as far more important and closer to the core of psychoanalysis (Galatzer-Levy and Cohler, 1990) and therefore include those who follow Freud's clinical methods within psychoanalysis, even when theories differ widely.

Controversies about which viewpoints should be included and excluded from psychoanalysis have plagued the field from its earliest days. This partly reflects the greater ease of forming an exclusive identity—saying what psychoanalysis is not—than describing inclusively what it is. As we proceed we shall include those theoretical outlooks that seek to explain human psychology on the basis of meanings and motives that are involved in psychological transformations intended to maximize psychological gratification and minimize psychological unpleasure. Even these extremely broad limits are arbitrary. They reflect what analysts within the mainstream of American psychoanalysis are interested in studying. Our questions are not about arbitrary definitions. Rather, we want to look at how, in fact, psychoanalysts, psychoanalytic institutions, and analysands use the term and how the various view-points sometimes labeled psychoanalytic relate to one another. Toward this goal we examine several aspects of psychoanalysis — its means of collecting data, its analytic technique, and its theory — to see how these aspects of the field can be used to delimit the boundaries of psychoanalysis.

Psychoanalytic Data

A central aspect of any discipline is its means of collecting data. Psychoanalysis can be characterized in this way. However, there is a spectrum of opinions among psychoanalysts about the best means of collecting analytic data. We can highlight these opinions by describing some sharply formulated positions. Most psychoanalysts do not function exclusively in any of these modes, but there is often a strong tilt in one direction and a view that a particular mode is preferred.

One widespread position, most evident in ego psychology, holds that the psychoanalyst's basic approach to the patient's psychological life is that of an external observer (Hartmann, 1927, 1959) who ascertains the relation between the components of compromise formation by inference from the repetitions and patterning of the analysand's associations in the psychoanalytic situation (Arlow, 1979; Rangell, 1969, 1984a). The analyst should focus primarily on the pattern of free association. In this view, insofar as the analyst follows the special insights available by virtue of psychological similarities and redundancies and uses empathy to grasp the subject's psychological state immediately, a clearer picture of the analysand's meanings and how her mind works is likely to emerge. However, empathy in particular may be subject to distortion resulting from countertransference. The analytic patient, in this view, is approached similarly to a patient suffering from organic illness. Although compassion and tact are always desirable, the physician's fundamental expertise lies in detailed knowledge of pathophysiology and therapeutics. This is the same type of knowledge one brings to the study of the physical world. This approach to psychoanalytic study, sometimes referred to as experience distant by those who object to it, has been the subject of wide controversy in the past quarter-century.

Some analysts suggest that the basic method of psychoanalytic investigation is precisely opposite to that of the external observer of the physical sciences. Most vigorously represented within self psychology and the intersubjective approach (e.g., Kohut, 1959; Atwood and Stolorow, 1984; Stolorow and Atwood, 1992), these analysts assert that the basic data of psychoanalysis are derived from empathy, defined as vicarious introspection. The empathic listener comprehends global psychological states by attempting to understand as precisely as possible what it is like to be in the analysand's shoes. The psychoanalytic enterprise is in this view the exploration and extension of subjectivity (Stolorow and Lachmann, 1980; Stolorow, Brandchaft, and Atwood, 1987).

Psychoanalysts operating in this mode have increasingly recognized that the resulting picture of the analysand's psychological world is changed through the process of investigation. The analyst's psychological world is also likely to be transformed by the psychoanalytic experience. Thus the picture of a stable objective reality of psychological life independent of the process of observation and the analyst cannot be simply extended to empathic observation (Goldberg, 1988).

Analysis as the Activity of Psychoanalysts

Both the external and the empathic points of view about psychoanalytic data characterize the psychoanalytic collection of data according to the method used by the analyst. Another approach looks in a different direction. Rather than thinking of psychoanalytic data collection as defined by its processes, some psychoanalysts regard it as principally defined by a psychoanalytic attitude that has become part of the analyst's personality. An unusual but interesting view, advanced by Donald Winnicott (1977), holds that psychoanalysis is what psychoanalysts do. In essence, Winnicott believed that the psychology of the psychoanalyst develops in such a way that a fundamentally psychoanalytic position becomes central to clinical interactions and also to the way he thinks about a wide range of issues. If accepted, this view leaves the thorny problem of defining who is an analyst, an enormously difficult task when addressed from a depth-psychological point of view.

Glover (1955) addressed this issue in his survey study of British psychoanalytic practice. His most striking finding was that even within this single society, practitioners varied markedly in how they conducted analyses. This variation did not merely reflect the major theoretical differences that existed within the British Society but seemed to be more importantly related to personal idiosyncrasies of the analysts.

Psychoanalysis as Theories

Psychoanalysis has been equated with its theories. Though most psychoanalysts include a range of theories in psychoanalysis, there is marked variation in views about the boundary between psychoanalytic and nonpsychoanalytic theories (Appy, 1989; Cooper, 1984; Wallerstein, 1988). Many analysts regard their technique as a logical consequence of the theory they embrace. For example, the therapeutic efficacy of catharsis was a logical consequence of the idea of dammed libido. Taking theory as central, psychoanalysis as therapy may be defined as the application of psychoanalytic theory to patients appropriately chosen for the psychoanalytic situation. Interpretation, in this view, is largely application of known psychological facts to particular patients. For example, many analysts believe that true hysteria originates in oedipal conflicts and is resolvable only through the development and analysis of a transference neurosis (Gann, 1984). The specific configuration of the Oedipus complex may vary, and with it the details of the transference neurosis, but the fundamental situation is given by preexisting knowledge. To be accepted as psychoanalysis, some analysts believe, the treatment must conform to the theory (Sachs, 1939). This view is held so strongly that many psychoanalytic organizations require candidates to prove the theory by specific structural changes — such as the resolution of oedipal conflicts within the transference neurosis — excluding or minimizing other outcomes in order to be certified as psychoanalysts (Abend, 1986b; Reed, 1987a).

Psychoanalytic Technique

The views described above characterize psychoanalysis by what happens psychologically in the patient, the psychoanalyst, or both (Abrams and Shengold, 1978). Psychoanalytic technique may facilitate or impede the work, but it is significant only insofar as it affects the psychology of the participants. Thus, for example, Gill (1982, 1988) described a once-a-week treatment as psychoanalysis because the focus of treatment was the analysis of transference, which, for him, as for many analysts (Strachey, 1934; Bird, 1972), is the psychological core of psychoanalysis.

A simpler, more easily operationalized approach is to describe psychoanalysis in terms of such issues as the frequency of session, the use of the couch, instructions to the patient, the duration of the analysis, and the nature of the analyst's intervention (Eissler, 1953; Gill, 1984; Panel, 1970, 1992a,b, 1993; Rangell, 1954, 1981b). Convincing arguments can be made that differentiate fundamentally different processes based on the analyst's technique (Wallerstein, 1989b). Unfortunately, there is no uniform concept of what technique or range of activities should properly be called psychoanalysis.

From this technical point of view, psychoanalysis is defined by the psychoanalytic setup. Many psychoanalysts feel reasonably comfortable calling a process psychoanalysis if the patient is seen four or more times per week for periods of forty-five minutes to an hour, reclines on a couch, and attempts to free-associate, and if the analyst's interventions consist predominantly in interpretation of these associations. Skolnikoff (1990) points to the form, not the substance, as currently defining psychotherapy and psychoanalysis. He suggests that the goals of psychoanalysis involve the patient and analyst achieving a mutual understanding of the patient's conflicts through the study of the transference-countertransference situation, which does not correlate well with these details of the analytic setup. In special cases the definition might be widened. In particular, many of these elements of technique are not followed in the psychoanalysis of children (Freud, 1965), though many child analysts contend that the core process of psychoanalysis is the same in children and adults. But overall this technical view is not far from what we mean by psychoanalysis from a procedural point of view. This is the least psychological characterization of psychoanalysis.

Psychoanalytic Process

In recent years many analysts have come to regard the presence of a psychoanalytic process as defining psychoanalysis (Arlow and Brenner, 1990; Vaughan, Spitzer, Davies, and Roose, 1997). If the term is used meaningfully, it avoids reducing psychoanalysis to potentially meaningless superficial dimensions or to any one of its component parts. Efforts to define analytic process have proved challenging. Attempts to reach consensus about the matter have foundered on issues of whether analytic process is principally in the psychology of the patient or in the interaction of patient and analyst, as well as on emphasis with regard to various elements of process (Abend, 1990). Vaughan et al. (1997), reviewing the discussion upon which Abend based his conclusions, suggest that analytic process includes free association, interpretation, and working through.

Unfortunately, showing empirically that an analytic process is present has proved difficult. Jones and Windholz (1990), using a Q-sort method (see Chapter 17), found a means for reliably describing the processes occurring within session. However, their method is very time-consuming and does not delimit analytic process from other processes within session. Vaughan and coworkers observe that while reliable means are available for assessing free association and interpretation, no such means are available for studying working through. They were unable to devise a measure differentiating sessions involving analytic process from other sessions because the underlying concept is not agreed upon by members of a fairly homogenous analytic community (individuals trained and practicing during the same period at a single analytic institute).

Sorting Out the Competing Views

How do these views of psychoanalysis relate to one another? That is the important empirical question. The recommendation of the standard analytic setup reflects the analyst's conviction that the psychological events of the analysis will derive, in significant measure, from its mechanics. But to what extent does the psychoanalyst's theory affect the psychoanalytic process (Pine, 1988; Wallerstein, 1990)? We know that the words patient and analyst use to describe what has happened vary markedly with the analyst's theory.[1] But we do not know the extent to which theory makes a difference in the psychology and process of analysis. It has been asserted that analysts with different theoretical orientation conduct analyses in similar ways (Wallerstein, 1988, 1989c). (Conversely, analysts who avow similar ideas may behave quite differently with patients.) All employ a few types of interventions (Basch, 1989). But the evidence for such assertions has neither been made public nor been fully accepted by the general psychoanalytic community.

This leaves the question of how and to what extent variations in technique alter the underlying psychological processes in psychoanalyses. Eissler (1953) argued that many variations in technique so obscure the transference neurosis as to make psychoanalysis impossible. His view, as presented, lacks empirical grounding. Under the influence of his work, North American analysts adopted a normative technique that is more abstinent and limited in its intervention than Freud's way of working with patients (Lipton, 1977a, 1979). Although systematic research about Eissler's view is lacking, his point must to some extent be correct. Certain activities of the psychoanalyst so disrupt the psychoanalytic process that its nature is altered. But what are these activities, with what kinds of patients, under what circumstances? How much does it matter if the analysand is not recumbent (Rangell, 1981; Gill, 1988; Stolorow, 1990)? Is there a significant qualitative difference between the process that emerges in once, twice, three, four, five and six times per week analysis, and if so, with what kinds of patients and analysts and under what kinds of circumstances is the effect of analytic frequency likely to be significant (Panel, 1997)? To what extent is the apparent qualitative difference between twice-weekly treatment

---

1. It is for this reason that detailed discussion of individual cases may be helpful in moving psychoanalytic discourse forward. A Kleinian psychoanalyst and a self psychologist who believed that their theories were at odds discovered in the course of a case discussion that, at least for the particular patient, their ideas converged markedly. However, one participant in the discussion called the psychological configuration being spoken of as the breast, while the other referred to it as a selfobject.

and four-times-a-week treatment a function of the experience of continuity? To what extent does the analyst's conviction that analysis cannot be done at the lesser frequency result in a self-confirming prophecy? And to what extent does a patient's willingness to be seen intensively reflect a capacity for analysis?

Such questions are routinely asked and answered in diagnostic consultation on the basis of clinical experience (Panel, 1987; Cramer and Flournoy, 1976; Panel, 1970; Wallerstein, 1969). But reliable empirically based answers are not fully known. Systematic investigations into the relation between the processes of psychoanalysis and various psychoanalytic arrangements and conceptual models offer one avenue for answering these questions.

Conclusion

The boundaries of psychoanalysis remain blurred. Although analysts commonly concur on many elements of analysis, sufficient divergence is present that we cannot conclude that a defining consensus exists in the analytic community. The attempt to find the common ground of analysis needs to continue. The absence of such a consensus means that we need to remain aware of the ambiguities implicit in statements about analysis generally. In discussing particular studies we need to clarify how the investigators characterized analysis, and in generalizing from those studies we must be constrained by the ambiguity of our use of the term *analysis*.

2

What Are the Relevant Measures
of Psychoanalytic Outcome?

Answers to questions about the outcomes and efficacy depend on the goals of psychoanalysis. Some people believe psychoanalysis should be judged by its ability to relieve symptoms, while others hold that it is successful to the extent that the patient achieves insight or develops self-analytic capacities (Ticho, 1967). A range of intermediate views are discussed elsewhere in this volume.

Other studies, such as those by Firestein (1978), Pfeffer (1959), and Wallerstein (1986), explore outcomes in terms of multiple aspects of psychological function, such as the ability to love, work, and play, and the development of self-analytic capacities, but the interrelations among the various measures of outcome are unclear.

One cannot define a unitary goal for psychoanalysis because of the variety of reasonable goals espoused. Wallerstein (1965), surveying earlier analytic discussions of psychoanalytic goals, notes that psychoanalysis is more ambitious than other therapies in that it hopes to affect fundamental personality organization. He quotes Strachey (Symposium, 1937): "What distinguishes the results of psychoanalysis from those produced by other methods seems to be depth and permanence. In so far as changes are produced by analysis, they seem in some sense or other to be real changes in the patient's mental functioning." The goals include not only improvement of present function but at least significant protection against future dysfunction. Consistent with these ambitious goals, analyst and patients commonly find the outcome of analysis includes accomplishments not anticipated at its outset.

Freud's informal characterization of analytic goals in terms of the capacity "to love and work" (Erikson, 1963) was elaborated by Reich (1924) and other prewar analysts in terms of orgastic capacity. Knight (1941–42) characterized the desirable results of psychoanalysis more broadly (see Table 2.1).

With the development of the structural theory Freud (1933) reconceptualized the goals of psychoanalysis as the extension of the dominance of the ego over both id and superego (a theory-based result). Subsequently many analysts came to think of the goal of psychoanalysis principally in terms of modification in the severity and irrationality of the superego (Alexander, 1925, 1930; Strachey, 1934). At the Marienbad Symposium (Symposium, 1937) several speakers emphasized the harmonious interplay of the three psychic agencies in normal development and psychoanalytic cure.

Beginning with the work of Balint (1936), analysts increasingly spoke of the hoped-for outcome of analysis in terms of increased capacity for new experiences both inside and outside the analysis.

Criteria for psychoanalytic outcome were formulated in terms of process goals, factors within the analysis itself. These range from goals of content, such as the resolution of the Oedipus complex or prosecutory and depressive anxiety (Klein, 1948b), to goals of observable change in the analytic process, such as the capacity to sustain and resolve a transference neurosis (Macalpine, 1950), the capacity to free-associate (Loewenstein, 1963), and the capacity for a "good analytic hour" (Kris, 1956), characterized by free movement between the analytic transference, the patient's life outside the analysis, and the patient's past.

Analytic outcome was also described in terms of the fate of the analytic work following termination. A good outcome was associated with the patient's self-analysis, supported by the patient's identification with the analytic functions of the analyst (Hoffer in Symposium, 1950) or the development of an autoanalytic function (Kramer, 1959).

Patients undertake psychoanalysis for a variety of reasons and are often well satisfied with achievements that might not please others. We would do better to outline several of the positions on psychoanalytic outcomes, because research that is insufficiently explicit about goals cannot answer the question of whether goals have been achieved, nor can it be compared to other research about the same questions. Hence we will describe a variety of goals carefully because of the surprising frequency with which outcome research in psychoanalysis has failed to be explicit about the appropriate measures of outcome (Bachrach and Leaff, 1978).

Psychoanalysis and the Relief of Suffering

Psychoanalysis first emerged as a clinical intervention for the treatment of neurosis. Like other clinical interventions, it may be judged by its capacity to ameliorate or cure those illnesses to which it is applied.[1] In thinking about the efficacy of psychoanalysis as a clinical procedure, it is useful to use the traditional medical distinction among symptoms, signs, and laboratory findings. *Symptoms* are the complaints of patients, what distresses them and leads them to seek treatment. Abdominal pain or painful dystonic worrying are symptoms. *Signs* are observable indications of illness, like a cardiac murmur or obsessional speech. *Laboratory findings* are the result of specific test procedures. Examples include elevated glucose levels, electroencephalogram abnormalities, or overly inclusive Rorschach test responses. Various combinations of return to normality (of symptoms, signs, and laboratory findings) have been taken as measures of outcome in medicine.

Although symptoms, signs, and laboratory findings represent different aspects of an underlying pathological process, their correlation is imperfect. Indeed, premature symptom relief may interfere in psychoanalysis or represent a resistance. If psychoanalysis is to relieve something, it is necessary to specify whether it is to be symptoms, signs, or laboratory findings and how they are related.

To evaluate change, it must be decided from what point in the treatment change is to be measured. Patients commonly initiate treatment because of fairly specific symptoms. Often it becomes apparent after a period of analysis that the structure of the patient's character is a far more important matter to address analytically than the presenting symptoms (Reich, 1933; Brenner, 1976; Baudry, 1983, 1984, 1989). Because diagnostic evaluation is an ongoing part of the psychoanalytic process, researchers must clearly specify the temporal point of comparison for the relief of difficulties if symptom relief is to be used as a measure of psychoanalytic outcome. The assumption that the presenting difficulties represent the patient's central problems is contrary to much clinical psychoanalytic experience, and the extent to which the formulation of the patient's difficulties changes in the course of an analysis requires systematic evaluation.

1. Clinical researchers are becoming increasingly sophisticated about the goals and procedures for efficacy research. In addition to the eradication of disease, issues like the overall quality of life, expense, and personal experience of patients are coming to be regarded as important. The urgency of placing effective treatments in the hands of practitioners has encouraged the development of research methods that produce findings about outcome rapidly, often at the expense of attention to clinical and human complexity (Greening, 1989).

Table 2.1 *Overview of Early Statistical Studies*

Diagnosis	No. of cases	Broken off	Six months or longer	Apparently cured	Much improved	% AC+MI	Improved	No change or worse	% I+NCW
Anxiety and conversion hysteria	216	62	154	59	35		49	11	
Anxiety state	6	–	6	2	2		1	1	
Compulsion neurosis	138	37	101	27	36		29	9	
Depression	51	14	37	10	13		12	2	
Hypochondria	8	7	1	1	–		–	–	
Inhibitions	87	24	63	23	20		15	5	
Traumatic neurosis	3	0	3	1	0		1	1	
Neurasthenia and anxiety neurosis	25	7	18	2	11		3	2	
All psychoneuroses						63.2			36.8
Unclassified sexual disorder	21	7	14	5	3		3	3	
Homosexuality	12	4	8	2	0		3	5	
Transvestism	1	–	1	–	1		–	–	
Impotence	8	0	8	3	0		5	0	
Enuresis	5	3	2	2	0		–	–	
All sexual disorders						48.5			51.5
Character disorders	111	28	83	13	32	56.6	25	11	43.4

Peptic ulcer	7	4	3	1	1	1	—
Gastric ulcer	4	2	2	1	1	—	—
Colitis	7	2	5	4	1	—	—
Chronic constipation	6	1	5	2	1	2	—
Bronchial asthma	13	7	6	1	3	2	—
Hay fever	1	0	1	1	—	—	—
Skin conditions	2	0	2	1	—	—	1
Female disorders	2	0	2	1	1	—	—
Endocrine disorders	3	3	0	—	—	—	—
Essential hypertension	3	1	2	0	1	1	—
Tics	4	2	2	2	—	—	—
Unclassified	3	1	2	1	1	—	—
All organic neuroses and organic conditions				72.7			27.3
Epilepsies	10	5	5	1	1	0	3
Migraine	1	0	1	1	—	—	—
Stammering	15	3	12	3	3	7	5
Chronic alcoholism	28	9	19	3	4	7	5
Psychopathies	31	19	12	1	0	4	7
Manic depression	44	7	37	6	5	14	12
Paranoia	6	1	5	0	2	1	2
Schizophrenia and schizoid	70	32	38	3	6	18	11
Total psychoses		30.2	55.9				69.8
Totals	952	292	660	183	186	201	90	44.1

Source: Knight, 1941. In some cases, the data seem to be in error.

Researchers should also carefully specify who judges the outcome of psychoanalytic treatment. Analysts tend to be more reserved than their patients or outside observers in evaluating the outcome of their work (Klein, 1960; Pfeffer, 1959; Weber, Bachrach, and Solomon, 1985b), as are psychotherapists generally (Luborsky et al., 1988). Outside observers may be unable to get a clear picture of what occurred. It may be that it is essentially impossible to track psychoanalytic work without reference to the analyst's subjective experience (Spence, 1982; Schwaber, 1983; Gardner, 1983; Jacobs, 1983, 1986; Meissner, 1989; Klumpner and Frank, 1991). As a result, the evaluation of outcome is likely to be profoundly affected by the nature of the observer.

Studies of psychoanalytic outcome commonly imply high degrees of perfectionism. Careful reading of the psychoanalytic literature reveals that analysts often equate "normality" with an ideal or optimal state of psychological functioning (Offer and Sabshin, 1974). For example, in a 1987 collection of papers on psychoanalysts' functioning in extreme situations, several authors equated the level of functioning they expected from well-analyzed colleagues with what, in any other context, would be called heroism (Chasseguet-Smirgel, 1987). It could be argued that the ubiquity of a disturbance should not interfere with the recognition of it as pathology. But it should raise serious questions if our criteria for health are achievable only by a very few people.

Freud (1937a) referred only to the "hypothetically normal ego." In thinking about outcomes of psychoanalysis, perfectionism will practically guarantee systematically negative evaluations. In a study of termination Firestein (1978) found that analysts tended to consider many outcomes incomplete in the sense that they failed to fulfill a long list of criteria, which amounted to a description of total mental health from a psychoanalytic perspective.

Similarly, the extent to which an analysand's psychological resources may be tested by the chance vicissitudes of life varies greatly. How different would the Wolfman's (Freud, 1918) later life have been had it not been for the Russian Revolution? Even here matters are complex. Differentiating accidental elements of external experience from unconsciously arranged events can often be achieved only by thorough psychoanalytic investigation. On the other hand, a patient who does well after analysis may have avoided undue stress because of good fortune, adaptedness, or neurotic constriction.

A different image of the desired results of psychoanalysis includes the capacity to seek assistance, including psychoanalytic assistance, when it is needed. Ritvo (1966) observed that Bornstein's patient Franky, whose first analysis was during his sixth year, recalled little of the content of his psychoanalytic experience when he returned to analysis in his twenties. But he did remember and value Bornstein's view that problems could be solved through talk. When he found himself in further difficulty as a young adult, he returned for further analysis. The capacity to seek and use assistance reflects an acceptance of the primitive and irrational aspects of one's personality. Heller's (1990) personal experience was similar.

In a clinical model, psychoanalytic efficacy is measured by enhancement of psychological functioning and symptom amelioration. However, the assessment of enhanced psychological functioning requires long-term follow-up. It is not enough to ask whether problems recurred. More sophisticated questions explore the intensity and type of stress that precipitate problems, the rapidity with which problems are addressed, and how intense and incapacitating they are. An agoraphobic patient who arranges and constricts her life to avoid incomprehensible panic attacks is in a very different position from the same patient who, after analysis, suffers rare manageable attacks in response to psychologically comprehensible stimuli. When, as in the case of transient neurotic symptoms, a clinical finding is common in the population, demonstrating prophylactic effects can be difficult.[2]

Some analysts expect even more of psychoanalysis — that it should provide a way to deal with future difficulties. Freud (1937a) recognized that conflicts that did not emerge spontaneously in the analysis could not be analyzed, even though they may leave the patient vulnerable to later difficulty. However, as a psychoanalytic view of the life course has begun to emerge, the interrelation among difficulties at various times in life is being clarified (see Galatzer-Levy and Cohler, 1993a,b; Gutman, 1987; Nemiroff and Calarusso, 1990). For example, midlife depressions (crises) and adolescent identity diffusion often share common dynamics, and midlife difficulties commonly result from premature and unsatisfactory closure of adolescent developmental issues (Galatzer-Levy, 1984a). Certainly, parents are commonly motivated to support psychoanalytic work with children and adolescents by their concern about the consequences of developmental failure. Evidence supports their concern (Waldron, 1976; Caspi, Elder, and Herbener, 1990; Farrington, Loeber, and Van Kammen, 1990; Robins and McEvoy, 1990).

In most therapeutic endeavors the recurrence of symptoms indicates a failure of therapy or at least an unfortunate coincidence. The patient's return to the physician suggests a failure or limitation of the previous therapy. In psychoanalysis the situation is more complex. Though the patient may be

2. Fortunately, much of the statistical methodology for studying effects of an intervention when there is a high prevalence of evidence of a disease was worked out in the course of studying polio vaccines when infection with polio virus was extremely common (Meier, 1985).

angry that her previous analysis failed to solve her current problems, her return for more analysis often reflects the belief that the previous analysis was useful. After all, she could have sought an alternative therapy. The patient may now be faced with new stresses either through external exigencies or new developmental demands (Gutman, 1987; Benedek, 1950, 1959). She may feel ready to address issues that earlier seemed intractable. As discussed above, the capacity to recognize the need for and appropriately seek further analysis can be a desirable result of psychoanalysis. Because psychoanalysis is inevitably incomplete (Freud, 1937a) and most analysts believe that ongoing self-analysis indicates a favorable psychoanalytic experience, a patient's return for more analysis has different implications than does return for other forms of treatment.

Beyond Symptom Relief: Structural Change

Without discarding the clinical view that psychoanalysis should provide symptom relief and ameliorate psychopathology, psychoanalysts generally look for broader changes in psychological functioning. Structural change has long been regarded as the most important factor differentiating psychoanalysis from other psychotherapies (Rangell, 1989).

Structural change refers to enduring changes in personality functioning, as opposed to those that are fluctuant. The term derives from the idea that the structures of the psyche as described by Freud (1926) are modified in the course of psychoanalysis. In this view psychopathology arises from faulty psychological structures or faults in their interrelation (Hartmann, 1939a; Hartmann, Kris, and Loewenstein, 1946; Hartmann and Loewenstein, 1962; Rapaport, 1951a,b, 1954; Rapaport and Gill, 1958). Historically, differentiation of structural from temporary or functional change has been closely tied to the concepts of ego psychology. However, the association of the concept of structural change with elaborate metapsychological theories of ego function is not logically necessary. It is perfectly possible to discuss structural change without recourse to complex metapsychological theories (Brenner, 1987).

One reasonable approach to the problem of structural change is to recognize the highly complex nature of psychological structures and to carefully explore the many factors that contribute to them. There have been many attempts to do this, especially in terms of ego function. The Hampstead Psychoanalytic Index and its associated Developmental Profiles provide thorough metapsychological descriptions of patients and their development that go far beyond the status of the three psychic agencies (Freud, 1965; Bolland and Sandler, 1965; Brinich, 1981; Burlingham, 1975; Kestenberg, 1980; Laufer, 1965; Meers, 1966; Thomas, 1966; W. Freud, 1968, 1971; Wills, 1981).

However, as yet, these profiles have been of little practical value in systematically exploring psychoanalytic process and outcome. The fifty-one scales of psychological capacities elaborated and tested by Wallerstein (1986a) represent a promising development in the systematic psychoanalytic description of patients, which eliminates the obfuscating effect of referring to psychoanalytic structural theory as if it provided explanations of disturbances in psychological functioning in terms of some underlying entity, psychic structure.

The structural approach is particularly appealing because it describes psychoanalysis in terms of its significant psychological dimension rather than its external features. However, as an approach to the study of outcome it has proved disappointing. Long-term studies (e.g., Wallerstein, 1986a; Horwitz, 1974; Kantrowitz, Katz, and Paolitto, 1990a,b,c; see Part 2 of this book) show a lack of clear relation between other characteristics of treatment and structural change.

The transformation of ego functions during analysis is widely used as a criterion of successful analysis. If analysis goes well, defensive operations become more mature and adaptive (Gray, 1973), and anxiety functions as a signal more regularly and reliably (Rangell, 1979). Although most analysts regard gross disturbances in reality testing and substantial thought disorders as contraindications to unmodified analysis, subtler distortions in reality processing and circumscribed archaic thinking are not uncommon among analytic patients (Abend, 1982b; Arlow, 1985; Bley, 1983; Gediman, 1985; Goldberg, 1984; Harris, 1989; Kantrowitz et al., 1987a; Novey, 1966a; Winnicott, 1960). Successful analysis would be expected to result in more effective reality processing, along with easier access to more archaic modes of thinking when those modes of thought were valuable to the person (Kris, 1952; Noy, 1979a). By following the status of ego functions through the course of analysis and afterward, researchers can also address inherently important psychological matters that are typically considered in evaluating psychoanalytic outcomes (Bellak and Smith, 1956; Greenspan and Cullander, 1975; Greenspan, 1989). The recent recognition that intelligence is most usefully thought of not as a unitary entity but rather a group of (not necessarily intercorrelated) capacities (Gardner, 1983; Gould, 1981; Hatch and Gardner, 1986) suggests that improvements in reality processing should be explored in a multidimensional fashion to see whether specific areas of intelligence are affected in analysis.

The Discovery of "Truth" and Self-Knowledge

Psychoanalysis may also be regarded as a way of discovering oneself and psychological truth. In Freud's view of psychoanalysis, the pursuit of truth took its most obvious form as a mode of scientific investigation with methods comparable to the methods of the natural sciences (Freud, 1913, 1925). The power of unconscious mental processes, the transformation that comes from making the unconscious conscious, and the awareness of resistance to knowledge of the unconscious are among the truths that patients and analysts are expected to rediscover in the course of successful analyses. This aspect of psychoanalysis arises from the modern belief that the accurate perception of reality will, in itself, liberate people from the pain that ignorance and irrationality impose on them (Toulmin, 1990).

Kohut (1984) asserted that the search for truth is a moralistic position imposed by the analyst. Other analysts (e.g., Gedo, 1989) believe that, although the nature of the truths to be discovered through psychoanalysis may differ from those that are commonly accepted, the defining quality of psychoanalysis lies in its truth seeking. American psychoanalysts appear to be more concerned with therapeutics than with finding "truth" for its own sake, while many French and Italian analysts value psychoanalysis principally as a mode of psychological investigation (Turkle, 1992).

Freud and many later psychoanalysts have equated the desirable outcome of psychoanalysis with the adoption of a worldview that values "reality" over the avoidance of psychological distress. This goal places a high premium on rationality and a scientific outlook as roads to personal freedom. It reflects Freud's adoption of the Germanic nineteenth-century scientific ideal (Bernfeld, 1941, 1949, 1951; Sulloway, 1979; Weber, 1905). These views led psychoanalysts to focus on change through one's own internal development and adaptation to material reality as opposed to transformation by mystical or supernatural means (Gay, 1989). Critics of this point of view maintain that it represents a form of moralistic judgment about the value of "reality" (Kohut, 1984) and a now-outmoded epistemology (Galatzer-Levy and Cohler, 1990).[3] However, the capacity to tolerate and process both external and psychological realities remains a reasonable goal for psychoanalysis. The outcome of psychoanalysis could thus be measured in terms of the enlargement of reality testing and processing (Hartmann, 1939a,b, 1950).

3. Rationality, the attempt to achieve some defined goal, is commonly explained as an inevitable feature of nature and equated with following a natural tendency to minimize or maximize some quantity—for example, "pleasure." Freud (1911a) clearly followed this view in his explanation of psychological economics. He was following a widely accepted program in equating this form of rationality with the processes of physics and economics. It is interesting to note that the program itself has a complex history in which the "rationality" of social actions was likened to psychological rationality, economic rationality, the rationality of deity, and the rationality of physical laws, in a circle of reference in which each form of rationality was used to bolster the other (Galatzer-Levy, 1976; Mirowski, 1989).

Freud (e.g., 1918) and most of his immediate followers believed that the stories reconstructed in psychoanalysis described the actual past situation of the patient, albeit filtered through the patient's fantasies, experience, and interpretations of material reality. For other analysts truth of analytic findings is their historical description of currently operative narratives of the past as these narratives affect the present rather than accurate reconstructions of past material or psychological events (Modell, 1990; Spence, 1982, 1991). Some analysts advocate that the emergence of a more coherent, enriched internal narrative, one that makes more sense of personal experience, regardless of its relation to "historical" reality, should be a central goal of psychoanalysis (Schafer, 1992). Others assert that the reality reconstructed in the analytic situation should have a closer relation to historical truth. (For discussions of these matters see Eagle, 1984; Freeman, 1985a,b; Galatzer-Levy and Cohler, 1990; Goldberg, 1984; Leary, 1989; May, 1990; Ricoeur, 1977; Sass and Woolfolk, 1988; Schafer, 1982, 1985, 1987; Sharpe, 1987; Spence, 1982, 1983b, 1986, 1989a,b; Wetzler, 1985). Depending on which views of the relation to reality is hoped for, change in this relation to reality measures psychoanalytic success. In this context an analysis is effective insofar as it results in a more coherent, inclusive, and meaningful life story for the analysand.

The Promotion of Growth, Development, and Values

Psychoanalysis may be regarded as a method of promoting development. From this view its goal is the resumption of development, and its successful outcome is the resulting reengagement in the developmental process.

This viewpoint first emerged in the study of child analysis. Anna Freud (1965) observed that age-related norms of development were not useful in diagnosing neurotic range psychopathology in children. Pathology is not accurately assessed by comparing the child's function to such norms. Instead, she proposed, the appropriate question is whether development is ongoing. When the child is moving forward vigorously, analysis is not indicated; failures to move ahead in development are indications for psychoanalysis. Because development is not expected to be completed in childhood, the goal of child analysis is not definitive psychological maturity but an actively developing psyche.

Early psychoanalysts believed that personality was essentially formed with the resolution of the Oedipus complex. Later researchers (e.g., Erikson, 1968, 1963; Blos, 1967) found that the evolution of personality continues through the life course (Nemiroff and Calarusso, 1985, 1990; Galatzer-Levy and Cohler, 1993a). Anna Freud's view that the task of analysis is the resumption of development can thus be extended and applied to adults.

Both psychoanalysts and developmental psychologists have long believed that there is a normal path of psychological development (Kagan, 1980, 1988). Development is seen as an epigenetic unfolding of various positions along developmental lines (Freud, 1965; Erikson, 1963; Piaget and Inhelder, 1969). The line of development of the libido laid out by Freud (1905) is the ideal type. Similar sequences have been described for various ego functions, moral development, cognitive development, and the development of object relations. Although there are various ideas about the sequence of development and what is centrally important in development, all these views share the idea of normative sequences that may go awry. Psychopathology may be described in terms of abnormalities and irregularities in the sequence of phases of development, and the effectiveness of interventions in terms of the restoration of the normal sequence.

Recent developmental research suggests that this promising perspective may have serious limitations. The concept of phase is often assumed and then imposed on data rather than being a generalization and abstraction from empirical findings (Karmiloff-Smith, 1986; Feldman, 1986). Ordinary psychological development may not be so orderly or so independent of the individual as once believed (Rutter and Rutter, 1993). Insofar as it is not, the idea that analysis should result in the resumption of development along ordinary lines would not be reasonable. According to another view, development per se, not necessarily the unfolding of specific normative developmental lines, is indicative of mental health (Galatzer-Levy, 1988b). In this view analysis could be regarded as a process that leads to reengagement of development in general.

The idea that the resumption of development is a major hoped-for result of psychoanalysis is implicit in the idea of the capacity for continued self-analysis. Self-analysis is not equivalent to conscious rumination about one's psychology, though this may be part of it. An unconscious process of analytic work and continued development are closer to what is meant by the self-analysis seen in successfully analyzed people (Weiss, 1981).

In all these developmental views the outcome of psychoanalysis is appropriately measured by the capacity to develop throughout the life course and to do significant self-analytic work when necessary to support that development. From this point of view psychoanalysis can be viewed as effective insofar as development that was previously blocked is resumed and development after termination of work with the analyst continues.

The Transformation of Internal Object Relations

For analysts who view object relations as central to psychology (e.g., Fairbairn, 1963; Kernberg, 1975, 1980, 1983, 1988b; Spruiell, 1979b; Panel,

1980; Joseph, 1988; Modell, 1988; Settlage, 1989; Greenberg and Mitchell, 1983; Blatt et al., 1991) the quality of internal objects is the most appropriate measure of psychoanalytic outcome. Assessing the status of object representations is challenging both because it is difficult to measure and because analysts disagree about the normative development of object relations. Freud's early (1911b) view that relations to objects progress along a line from autoeroticism to narcissism to object relations (in the sense of objects that are experienced as independent sources of initiative) was soon modified to include a differentiation between primary and secondary narcissism (Freud, 1914a). Contemporary ideas about normal object relations include the notion that the separation-individuation of the toddler years is a lifelong process (Panel, 1973a,b; Pine, 1979; Blatt and Behrends, 1987), that infants experience others as distinct and interesting independently of the functions they perform (Stern, 1985), and that narcissistic object relations are ordinary and healthy throughout the course of life (Kohut, 1971, 1976; Galatzer-Levy and Cohler, 1993a). Because the ordinary developmental line of object relations is a matter of contemporary controversy, application of the status of objects to the assessment of psychoanalyses is challenging and should be undertaken cautiously.

Outcomes in Relation to Analytic Process

Many analysts assess whether an analysis has proceeded well by the extent to which certain processes have occurred. Analysts' views of the central processes of psychoanalysis have evolved and diverged over the past century (Cooper, 1989).

In Freud's (1892) earliest conception, cure came through catharsis. Without abandoning the value of catharsis, Freud discovered that defenses stood in its way, so psychoanalysis evolved to include the systematic analysis of defensive operations that blocked discharge (Freud, 1895). By the late 1920s and mid-1930s the analysis of defense was regarded in theory, if not in practice, as a central psychoanalytic activity (A. Freud, 1936; Reich, 1933).

Also in the first quarter of the twentieth century the use of transference for therapeutic purposes rose to great importance. Transference was seen as playing a triple role: as resistance to remembering, as a source of insight about unconscious processes (archaic, repressed experiences were revivified in the transference), and, in its positive dimension, as a support for continuing analysis despite distress. Strachey (1934) asserted that the analysis of transference occupied a unique place in the psychoanalytic process; only in interpreting the transference do the object of transference and the interpreter become unified. Only transference interpretation could be "mutative" — that is, could alter superego function.

Object relations theorists (see Greenberg and Mitchell, 1983; Bacal and Newman, 1990) hold that the transformation of internal objects (including the self) is central to psychoanalytic change. In this context many analysts believe that the "holding" or "facilitating" environment that results from steadfast interest, benign neutrality, forgoing expected retaliation, the maintenance of integrity despite attacks and seductions, curiosity, and interpretation of what the patient does are central to the analytic process (Khan, 1983; Modell, 1976, 1978; Winnicott, 1965). This view emphasizes the possibilities for emotional experiences whose significance can be explicitly understood in the context of a holding environment.

In another group of views, experiences with the analyst induce the resumption of development. The patient, regressed in the transference, is able to experience appropriate parenting, which had not occurred earlier, and to learn from the new experience. The theories of treatment of Weiss, Sampson, and colleagues (1986) and Kohut (1971, 1984), which are otherwise different, both see psychoanalysis as an opportunity for new, more satisfactory developmental experiences. Kohut (1984) suggested that change in psychoanalysis, at least in disorders of the self, results in "transmuting internalizations." Transmuting internalization is a process by which — through optimal frustration (and gratification) of selfobject needs in tolerable nontraumatic experiences of selfobject failure — the patient takes on some functions for himself that could previously be performed only by the analyst (that is, the patient's fantasy of the analyst). Weiss, Sampson, and associates (1986) believe that psychoanalysis proceeds by addressing the false and terrifying systems of belief and expectation that determine pathological responses to the world. They hold that it is not the patient's unconscious gratifications through these views that lead to the belief's continued shaping of current experience. Rather, these ideas provide a sense of safety, and so the patient holds on to them. At the same time, the patient hopes to discover new possibilities. She arranges to test the analyst to see whether her feared expectations will be met. The analyst's neutrality supports development because it disconfirms the patient's neurotic expectation. These views of the psychoanalytic process stand in marked contrast to the evolution of Freud's (1926) structural model, in which the interpretation of intrapsychic conflict leads to normalizing shifts in pathological compromise formations.

Depending on which of these views of the analytic process seems cogent, a researcher might view their presence or absence as indicators of the quality of psychoanalytic outcome. This is not a circular position. It is how many analysts in fact judge whether an analysis is progressing satisfactorily. Insofar as a psychoanalytic process has been adequately engaged, the treatment is regarded as proceeding well by those who view analysis in these terms.

Transference

Transference provides a depth-psychological picture of unconscious wishes, object representations, fantasies, and defenses. It also shows how the patient works with conscious manifestations of unconscious processes. It is generally regarded as the most important focus of psychoanalysis.

Descriptions of the state of transference during and after analysis provide the most psychoanalytically significant measures of the status of the personality. The description of transference is more than a way to assess the various dimensions of personality. Pfeffer (1959, 1961, 1963) and Schlessinger and Robbins (1983) observed that in follow-up interviews transferences are rapidly reestablished and (if treatment has gone well) rapidly resolved.

One problem in using the state of the transference as a measure of psychoanalytic outcome is the difficulty of accurately appraising it. Many patients seen at follow-up by Schlessinger and Robbins (1983), for example, clearly were engaged during their analyses in transferences that the treating analysts failed to diagnose. Several coding systems for transferences have been proposed (Dahl, 1988; Gill, 1979; Hoffman and Gill, 1988; Luborsky and Crits-Christoph, 1988, 1990; see Chapter 17), but they have not found wide acceptance among clinicians. How well they represent the issues of interest to analysts is an open question. These measures all rely on relatively small segments of analyses. As a result they tend to emphasize the presenting surface of the transference at the expense of more deeply disguised issues.[4] For example, as occurred in a case studied by Schlessinger in follow-up, a characterologically compliant patient produced a wide range of associations and transference manifestations that corresponded to what he believed his analyst wanted to hear. Coding displaced referents from such a session would probably provide much data supporting the transference theme that the patient believed the analyst wished to hear about, whereas the need to be compliant, though far less apparent in the material, even in disguised form, is of much greater psychological significance.

Systematic study of countertransference as a measure of psychoanalytic

---

4. The hope that the careful studies of small samples of psychoanalytic material may capture the essence of the larger analytic process has recently received the support of an unexpected source. The study of fractal geometry (Barnsley, 1988; Mandelbrot, 1982) has shown that many natural phenomena have the characteristic that arbitrarily small fragments on the structure contain images of the whole. The Mandelbrot set, for instance, contains in its every segment, no matter how small, images of structures essentially like its entirety, and this property has been observed in a wide range of naturally occurring phenomena. This quality of "self similarity" thus makes it possible, in appropriate situations, to study a small fragment of empirical data in order to discover the overall structure (see Galatzer-Levy, 1995).

outcome is consistent with the views of analysts who regard countertransference as the most accurate way to understand patients' psychologies (Racker, 1968; Jacobs, 1983, 1986; Tyson, 1986). Kernberg (1988b) suggests that countertransference is more useful for gaining an understanding of severe psychopathology than for understanding neurosis. The use of countertransference to learn about analysis and psychotherapy has been discussed by Fleming and Benedek (1966), Ekstein and Wallerstein (1972), and Koff (1989), among others, as it is manifest through the "parallel process" in supervision, where the analyst's unconscious responses to the patient find representation in unconscious responses to the supervisor. It seems reasonable to explore the status of analyses in terms of the fate of the countertransference (Tyson, 1986). It may well be that it is the status of countertransference we tap as the major measure of psychoanalytic process and outcome in informal discussions. The systematic use of countertransference could provide a measure of the outcome of psychoanalysis (Windholz and Skolnikoff, 1985).

Thus practicing psychoanalysts use a range of measures to assess the effects of clinical psychoanalysis. Consistent with the view that psychoanalysis is directed at changing the depth of the personality, most analysts assess change in terms of broad stable changes in important chronic psychological functioning (structural change) and/or in terms of changes in major configurations in relation to objects, as manifest especially in transference and countertransference. They also assess analyses by the extent to which certain processes have occurred in the analysis. For systematic investigators to address questions important to analysts they must speak to these questions. As is appropriate for any intervention, the effectiveness of psychoanalysis is properly gauged against its intended goals. However, it is also appropriate to examine its effectiveness in terms of the various contexts in which people turn to analysts.

Other Factors in Assessing the Effectiveness of Psychoanalysis

Up to this point we have considered psychoanalysis only in terms of its effects as viewed in its own terms. It is also appropriate to examine psychoanalysis in terms of its place among the interventions available for relieving psychological distress and in relation to its costs, financial and otherwise.

THE COSTS OF PSYCHOANALYSIS

Psychoanalysts often cringe at discussions of the costs of psychoanalysis because we live in an environment in which the language of cost-benefit analysis is widely abused by insurance companies and review organizations to avoid payment of benefits to patients. This abuse should not stop us from asking whether psychoanalysis is, in fact, cost-effective.

What is the relation of the cost of psychoanalysis to its benefits? As with any cost-benefit analysis, answers to this question are contingent on the value placed on various outcomes. For example, how many hours of work missed to attend analytic sessions are to be equated with the capacity to form relatively unconflicted, lasting relationships? What is the value of enhanced creativity and productivity for patients whose difficulties are manifested in work inhibitions? How does one compare the value of analyses on two patients, one who gains the ability to marry and have children who contribute to society, another who develops a satisfying relationship that supports pleasurable personal endeavors that have little impact on the external world? How does one compare the psychoanalytic alleviation of chronic depression that also leads to an enriched life with the symptomatic alleviation of the same disorder by quicker, pharmacologic treatments that may even constrict the richness of lived experience? At what point do repeated returns to short-term therapies because of "relapses" outweigh the potential long-term gains of self-reliance that are among the goals of psychoanalysis? In essence, what value does one place upon the quality of life and enhanced abilities to love, work, and solve one's problems over the immediate alleviation of symptoms? Analysts and potential patients who must decide whether to undertake analysis face such issues in each individual case. Commonly these questions are not faced squarely, partly because they cannot be answered with assurance, and partly because other motives support or interfere with the beginning of treatment. Yet they are reasonable questions for both individuals and society.

Among the costs of psychoanalysis are untoward effects in some situations, effects that have negative impact on the patient or those around him. Analysts seldom discuss these effects. Psychoanalysis may disrupt current adjustments. For example, it is not rare that psychoanalysis contributes to the disruption of a neurotically based marriage. This disruption may hurt not only the analysand but also the spouse and children. More generally analysis of an individual may disturb the equilibrium of a previously stable family and social configurations, causing distress and harm to others than the analysand. It is not rare that the analysis of a child or adolescent disrupts a stable family system, sometimes with considerable negative effect on other family members (Galatzer-Levy, 1984a). Almost all evaluations of the effects of analysis focus exclusively on the individual, but many other people are commonly affected by an individual's analysis.

We must include in a cost-benefit calculation the rare serious situations in which negative therapeutic reactions, acting out of the transference, and transference psychosis leave the patient clinically worse. Psychoanalysis with impaired analysts who grossly or subtly abuse their patients may contribute to the patient's distress and worsen her condition. All this needs to be weighed in the context of the reasonable likelihood of various analytic outcomes, including interruptions and stalemated analyses.

Assessing the overall value of an intervention in terms of its effects on the entirety of the patient's life is difficult for any form of treatment. In recent years physicians have begun to pay closer attention to the effects of medical intervention on the "quality of life" (Greenfield, 1989; Parfrey et al., 1989; Reizenstein, 1986). They are asking not only whether interventions relieve symptoms, change laboratory values, or otherwise affect a pathological process but also how the patient's overall experience of life and the lives of those around him are affected. At least as applied to individuals, the "quality of life" approach is highly consistent with many psychoanalytic visions of health that emphasize people's overall psychological functioning rather than particular, isolated areas of function (A. Freud, 1979; Hartmann, 1939a,b; Kohut, 1982, 1984). These considerations are often important in the informal discussions of psychoanalysts, yet they are seldom addressed systematically in discussing analysis as therapeutics.

THE RELATION OF THEORY, TECHNIQUE, AND OUTCOME

In addition to knowing under what circumstances, to what extent, and in what ways psychoanalysis works, analysts would like to identify those elements in the psychoanalytic situation and process that contribute to its therapeutic efficacy. It is possible for a procedure to be efficacious but for very different reasons than practitioners believe. For example, until they were systematically studied, many medications with profound placebo effects were assumed to have a primarily pharmacological effect. In a complex procedure such as psychoanalysis, empirical identification of factors that have specific consequences is extremely difficult. As we will discuss, procedures designed to separate therapeutic factors from nontherapeutic factors run into difficulty simply because of the large number of possibilities and the small number of cases available for study, so that new research methods must be developed to achieve this differentiation. Because the measure of analysis as therapeutic is not a unitary concept, the question becomes even more complicated — what elements of the psychoanalytic procedure affect which measures of outcome?

THEORIES OF PSYCHOANALYSIS AS THERAPY

In this area the findings of psychotherapy research provide challenge. A recurrent finding from systematic investigations of psychotherapy is that, with minor exceptions, there is little difference in the benefits patients receive from a wide range of psychotherapeutic interventions (Luborsky et al., 1993; Luborsky, Singer, and Luborsky, 1975; Meltzoff and Kornreich, 1970; Smith, Glass, and Miller, 1980; Svarberg and Stiles, 1991; Lambert and Bergin,

1994).[5] A large proportion of patients benefit from treatment, and these effects are specific to psychotherapy — different from the effects of no treatment, pharmacotherapy, and the combination of drug and psychotherapy. Only a few disorders (psychosomatic disorders, panic attacks, mild phobias, schizophrenia, and suicidality) have been shown to respond differentially to different forms of psychotherapy. These findings may partly reflect deficits in the study designs (Auerbach and Johnson, 1979; Berman, 1989; Kazdin and Bass, 1989; Luborsky et al., 1993; Shadish and Sweeny, 1991; Smith, Glass, and Miller, 1980). But the finding is so recurrent that it must be taken seriously.

These findings strongly suggest that psychotherapies have many common elements that benefit patients (Rosenzweig, 1936; Frank and Frank, 1991; Strupp and Hadley, 1979). It may be that these common elements, rather than the theory-driven variations in treatment, account for much of the therapeutic effect of a wide range of psychotherapies, including psychoanalysis. A generic model of psychotherapy constructed from a massive review of the psychotherapy research literature proposes that five active elements — therapeutic contact, therapeutic intervention, the therapeutic bond, self-relatedness, and therapeutic realizations — account for the effects of psychotherapies (Orlinksy and Howard, 1986, 1987; Kolden and Howard, 1992). Psychoanalysts, who may disagree about what elements of the analytic situation are therapeutic and who increasingly view noninterpretive elements as important to therapeutic progress (Meissner, 1991), nonetheless tend to conceptualize the effective elements of psychoanalysis as highly specific. The generic-model hypothesis is the principal contender against all of the specific hypotheses about what is effective in psychoanalysis. We would like to know whether the specific elements of any form of psychoanalysis are important in its effects or whether the impact of these elements is minor in comparison with the generic elements present in most psychotherapies as well as psychoanalysis.

Psychoanalysts have generally assumed that the impact of psychoanalysis is highly specific and have debated what these specific effects are. There are many theories about which elements of psychoanalysis are effective, including theories of catharsis, defense, amelioration of the severity of the superego, reworking of psychic conflict, transformations of pathological internalized object relations, new developmental experiences, transformation of the self, and the abandonment of maladaptive modes of psychological function. We begin by reviewing these theories.

Freud's view of how psychoanalysis effected cure changed over time

---

5. It should be noted that these comparative studies do not include psychoanalysis and with rare exceptions also exclude other long-term and intensive psychotherapies of all kinds.

(Cooper, 1989). His early view was that neurosis was cured by catharsis of warded off noxious affects through a process that "transforms[s] what is unconscious into what is conscious" (Freud, 1915, p. 194). This view assumes the centrality of trauma in neurosogenesis and psychic conflict (Freud, 1896). A corollary of this view was that uncovering previously unconscious memories is indispensable for full recovery. Freud's (1926) later structural view of therapeutics is summarized in the maxim, "Where id was, there ego shall be" (Freud, 1933, p. 80). This transformation was to be achieved through redistribution of psychic energies between the three mental agencies. This was accomplished by talking (that is, the free association method), which led to new psychic attitudes and changes in the superego (Freud, 1926).

New ideas about alteration in the superego were formulated from work with the transference (Strachey, 1934). Strachey held that the patient displaces both superego functions and infantile representations onto the analyst. The analyst, by consistently behaving in accordance with his concept of reality and through interpretation of the transferences, enables the patient, through identification with the analyst, to differentiate infantile fantasy from current reality. "Mutative interpretation" alters a vicious cycle of hostile introjection and projection that supports neurosis. This is achieved by interpretively making id impulses conscious and thus making the patient aware that his hostile impulses are directed toward archaic fantasy objects, not contemporary objects. In this model, only the interpretation of the transference is expected to effect psychoanalytic change. Following Strachey, Gill (1979) emphasized that the curative factor in psychoanalysis is intense emotional experience examined within the transference. The analyst clarifies the existence and nature of the transference so that the patient may be fully and directly engaged in it.

Another view is that analysis cures by interfering with chronic defensive operations that make the patient unable to find more mature solutions to psychological problems (Freud, 1926; A. Freud, 1936; Reich, 1933; Gray, 1973). The analyst repeatedly demonstrates the nature and motives of defensive operations, particularly as they occur in the transference. Because defense is manifest in analysis as resistance, the curative factor in analysis, from this point of view, is the analysis of resistance (Schafer, 1971; Gray, 1972, 1982; Weinshel, 1984).

These views differ in important respects from Freud's (1926, 1937) structural model of therapeutics. This view has evolved by way of the contributions of Hartmann, Kris, and Loewenstein (1974), among many others, and takes its most contemporary form in the idea that the analysis of the components of compromise formations, as expressed in transference and resistance, lead toward ameliorating shifts in the structure of pathological compromise formations (Arlow and Brenner, 1964; Brenner, 1983; Boesky, 1989). In this view, the components of intrapsychic conflict include drive derivatives, anxiety and/or depressive affect; and defense, superego, and reality considerations that are linked to the cardinal danger situations of childhood (i.e., object loss, loss of love, castration, and guilt). Conflicts come alive in the transference. The analytic situation is unique in that it permits systematic analysis of these situations. When the analyst interprets conflicts in all their aspects and the patient works through the conflicts anew, pathological compromise formations change. More than a change in the structure of defense has been achieved (Brenner, 1982).

Consistent with the idea that the mind pivots on internal object relations, object relations theorists believe that the central curative activity of analysis is the transformation of object representation (Bacal and Newman, 1990; Fairbairn, 1952b; Greenberg and Mitchell, 1983; Winnicott, 1965). Several technical procedures are consistent with this outlook, including purely interpretive stances. However, many object relations theorists emphasize the importance of the analyst's actual good functioning as central to the establishment of new object relations (Bacal, 1985; Bacal and Newman, 1990; Balint, 1949, 1968; Guntrip, 1968; Little, 1987; Winnicott, 1962). This "good" functioning consists primarily in an ordinary psychoanalytic attitude. If the analyst believes that the difficulties in internalized object relations result principally from forces within the patient, such as intense aggressive drives or a tendency to use primitive defenses, then the actualities of the analyst will be less centrally important to conceptions of therapeutic effects, and his position will combine interpretation of impulses and defenses manifest within the transference (Kernberg, 1988b).

Loewald (1960) emphasized the central role of new experience with the analyst that induces a resumption of development by appropriately parenting the patient. In particular, the analyst communicates that the patient is an integrated human being with a past and an expectable future. The relationship of the analyst and patient is modeled on the parent-child relationship. The humanity of the analyst and the humanistic terms of the interaction between analyst and patient are seen as the major vehicle of therapeutic change.

Self psychologists believe that psychoanalysis cures by optimal frustration and optimal gratification (Kohut, 1984). In this view, cure occurs within selfobject transferences. The analyst inevitably fails in his selfobject function. The patient then experiences anxieties of an endangered self. However, if the analysis goes well, the patient's experience is nontraumatic, largely because of the analyst's empathic understanding of the patient's distress. In these situations, the patient builds a more coherent, invigorated self and assumes for himself functions the analyst had previously performed. The analyst does *not* perform these functions through enactments. He simply does not interfere with the patient's construction of the needed selfobject. For example, when the patient expresses manifest idealization of the analyst, this is not interpreted as a defense against other, less acceptable sentiments unless there is strong evidence to support this interpretation. Instead, the transference is allowed to flourish and the effects of its interruption are the major focus of analytic intervention (Kohut, 1991). The analyst's only active function is interpreting, understanding, and explaining. Cure, from the vantage point of self psychology, results not in abandonment of the use of selfobjects but in the emergence of more mature selfobject functions (Basch, 1991).

Weiss, Sampson, and colleagues (1986) believe that change results when the patient abandons false and terrifying beliefs and expectations, which were once adaptive and are currently continued to provide safety. Cure results from bringing these beliefs into the transference so that the patient, who unconsciously wants to overcome them, subjects them to repeated tests in the analysis. The patient's experiential discovery of his error leads to change. When the analyst frustrates the patient's manifest transference wishes, the patient is reassured because anticipated fantastic dangers do not materialize.

Each of these views about how psychoanalysis works finds varying degrees of support from the theories in which they are embedded, clinical experience, and in some instances systematic empirical studies (Sampson and Weiss, 1986; Goldberg, 1988). Some of these ideas have been the object of vigorous controversy largely because their technical implications are at odds with existing practice. Thus, for example, most analytic theories predict that progress will be associated with distress in the patient, whereas Weiss and Sampson's (1986) work predicts the opposite. It may well be that different factors contribute to analytic cure for different types of patients or even for the same patient at different times during an analysis. Still, analysts would like to be able to systematically study the different ways analysis effects change. Finding ways to explore these possibilities empirically would be a major step forward.

The relation of process and outcome is the implicit issue in most discussions of psychoanalytic technique. How do varying qualities of the analytic process relate to the overall effect of the psychoanalysis? A related question is how the psychoanalyst's technique affects the analytic process in its psychological depth. The relationship between analyst and patient has emerged as the central focus of study of how psychoanalysis works.

THE RELATIONSHIP OF ANALYST AND PATIENT

Consistent with the focus of Freud and later analysts on the relationship between analyst and patient as the center of the psychoanalytic situation, a complex group of ideas has emerged regarding this relationship. These ideas have proved particularly fruitful in conceptualizing the therapeutic action of psychoanalysis.

Having seen that analyses often went badly when little agreement and cooperation existed between analyst and analysand about important elements of the analytic work, analysts came to recognize those aspects of the relationship between analyst and analysand characterized as "alliance" (Greenson, 1965, 1967; Zetzel, 1958a,b; Meissner, 1996). The patient and analyst may be allied for some purposes and not allied for others. For example, an analysand may be allied with the analyst to produce symptom relief but uncommitted to an effort to understand his own psychology. Analysts would like to know how the various forms of alliance affect the outcome of the analyses (Curtis, 1979), and how and under what conditions they may change over time.

What is the effect of transferences on an analysis? Transferences and their analyses are universally regarded as the bedrock of psychoanalysis. But questions about the elements of transference to be analyzed, the depth of their analysis, and their effect on the course and outcome of analysis have not been systematically empirically validated. Such studies would be particularly valuable because of the widespread disagreement among psychoanalysts about the nature of transferences and the appropriate management of many forms of transference.

In particular, the place of the "transference neurosis" in psychoanalysis is in need of much clarification (Blum, 1971; Calef, 1971a,b; Cooper, 1987; Chused, 1988; Harley, 1971; Kern, 1987; Loewald, 1971; London, 1987; Nacht, 1957; Panel, 1991, 1993; Reed, 1987a, 1990; Weinshel, 1971). Although many analysts regard transference neurosis as the sine que non of psychoanalysis, the term is used in several not necessarily congruent ways. For example, it is sometimes used to refer to the clinical phenomenon in which the analyst becomes the central point in the patient's psychological life and pathology so that "it may be said that the earlier neurosis has now been replaced by a fresh 'transference neurosis'" (Freud, 1920a). It has been equated with the reactivation in analysis of the infantile neurosis (Kepecs, 1966). Without reviewing the long, complex discussions about the nature of the transference neurosis, it is clear that psychoanalysts would like to know whether the analyst must become the central focus for the patient's neurosis for the analysis to have a satisfactory outcome. If so, what does this mean, and under what circumstances and in which types of patients is this necessary (Anthony, 1986; Chused, 1988; Harley, 1971)? Must this engagement involve oedipal derivatives or any other specific developmental issues (for example, adolescent development, separation-individuation, selfobject functioning)? Are there classes of patients for whom various kinds of transferences must be engaged?

What is the optimal intensity of transference configuration so that psychoanalytic work progresses, and how does this depend on the patient's psychology? The clinical literature often leaves it unclear whether transference intensity or failures of the alliance account for the difficulties associated with "stormy" analyses. Are certain difficulties manifested as problems of alliance best conceptualized as aspects of transference?

The Unfolding of Analysis

Analysts have written extensively about the various phases of analysis (Freud, 1913, 1938; Gitelson, 1962; Glover, 1955; Sandler, 1988). Following Freud (1913), analysis is often conceptualized as a chess game in which common opening configurations are well understood, as are common endings, but a long middle phase is more idiosyncratic and less generally described. Clinical investigation of these phases of analysis could be enhanced by more-systematic empirical studies. This is particularly true of termination, whose timing, content, and technical management are all subjects of considerable discussion (Blum, 1989; Firestein, 1969, 1974, 1978; Pedder, 1988). Many questions remain open about termination. What are the indications for termination (Gillman, 1982; Firestein, 1978; Shane and Shane, 1984; Ticho, 1972)? Some analysts contend that the entire analytic process is termination (Blanck and Blanck, 1988); others observe phenomena unique to this period in the analysis (Oremland, 1973). Although analysts generally agree that specific work is mobilized in prospect of termination, the need for special technique during this period is a matter of controversy (Loewald, 1988; Shane and Shane, 1984). For example, it is widely held that setting a date for termination at least several months in advance mobilizes important issues and provides an opportunity for their analyses (Orens, 1955). But setting a date may be viewed as a procedure that artificially shapes the transference rather than allowing it to emerge in the context of an ongoing analytic investigation. It brings issues into awareness through the manipulation rather than analysis of resistance. If the date of termination is not set in advance, how does this affect the termination process and its outcome (Goldberg and Marcus, 1986)? What are the effects of incomplete and inadequate termination processes (Martinez, 1989; Mikkelsen and Guthiel, 1979)? Some analysts believe that scheduling termination dates that correspond to beginnings of the analyst's ordinary absences from the office, like summer vacations, dilutes the termination process. What is the optimal nature of postanalytic contact (Hartlaub, Martin, and Rhine, 1986)? Is termination the same process in various age groups, or are there age-specific aspects to termination that depend on the patient's current development (Burgner, 1988; Kohrman, 1969; Laufer and Laufer, 1989; Novick, 1976, 1982; van Dam, Heinicke, and Shane, 1975)?

Many specific elements of the psychoanalytic situation are believed to be associated with the outcome of analyses. However, few data are available to support these beliefs. For example, the role of dreams in psychoanalysis raises a large number of important, specific questions. The vast literature of dreams in analysis, as summarized by Altman (1975a), includes a wide variety of clinical observations, but little of this clinical information has been subject to systematic investigation. Some analyses seem to center around the interpretation of dreams, and some analysts and patients treat dreams as not only the royal road to the understanding of the unconscious but as the only one. Analysts and patients vary in their approach to dream material, from a position that dream interpretation is commonly the center of analytic work (Freud, 1905) to the position that dreams are associative material that differ little from other associations (Brenner, 1983; Arlow, 1979). Is this difference in attitudes to dreams merely idiosyncratic, or are some approaches consistently more effective, and/or more effective with certain types of patients? Is the presence or absence of dreams, their complexity, analyzability, frequency, or level of affect prognostic for the analyses in general, and if so in what ways?

Similarly, the prognostic significance of specific defensive constellations, character styles, and their technical implications has been the subject of extensive investigation (Fenichel, 1945; Rapaport, Gill, and Shafer, 1945; Zetzel and Meissner, 1973), but systematic study of these issues is not available.

Several commonly occurring special arrangements for analysis and special psychoanalytic situations seem to modify analyses in ways that have been discussed in the literature but have not been studied beyond providing clinical instances of these modifications. It would be useful to the practicing analyst to understand the effects of these factors on the course and outcome of analyses. How different are training analyses from "ordinary" analyses (Blum, 1986; Calef, 1972; Gitelson, 1954; Pfeffer, 1974; Shapiro, 1976) and to what extent does the reporting or nonreporting of the analyst to the institute affect the analysis (Calef and Weinshel, 1973; Lifschutz, 1976; McLaughlin, 1973)? How do insurance payments and the processes involved in collecting the payments influence analyses (Halpert, 1972, 1985; Rudominer, 1984)? How is the analysis affected when someone other than the patient pays? When fees are reduced or the patient is seen in a clinic, does it significantly alter the analytic course (Eissler, 1974; Allen, 1971; Epstein, 1990)? How does the analytic candidate's supervision affect the psychoanalytic process? To what extent and in what way are supervised and unsupervised analyses dissimilar?

In our enthusiasm for studying questions about psychoanalysis we must not forget to ask to what extent the very process of investigation alters the object of investigation. The analyst who wishes to do research wants to know the effect of the research on the analysis and the patient for both intellectual and ethical reasons. What are the effects of being a "research" case, or having one's analysis tape-recorded (Gill, 1982; Offenkrantz and Tobin, 1973)? We know that for at least two of Freud's analysands, Dora (Freud, 1905) and the Wolfman (Freud, 1918), having been contributors to psychoanalytic research had lifelong and probably negative effects (Deutsch, 1957; Erikson, 1962; Gardiner, 1971). On the other hand, Offenkrantz and Tobin (1973) discuss how exploration of the fantasies about the analyst's research enriches analysis. Similarly, Gill and Muslin (1976) have argued that tape recording interferes with analysis only to the extent that fantasies about recording remain unanalyzed. The effects of recording on psychoanalysis is of critical interest both for the ethical reason that no analyst would willingly introduce research tools that negatively affect the work and because the meaning of data collected from tape-recorded analyses becomes clear only with a knowledge of the effects of recording. Freud's (1915–17) assertion that analysis brooks no observers may be mistaken. Yet the analytic consequences both of being a research subject and of being tape-recorded have not been fully studied.

3

Predicting the Course and Outcome of Analysis

Every psychoanalyst of some clinical experience is aware of apparently unpromising analytic situations that turned out well and of analyses that began favorably but ended badly. Often, with benefit of hindsight, it is possible to identify sources of strength or weakness that were not recognized at the outset. Examples of such situations include barely mentioned but psychologically lifesaving relationships in the patient's early childhood, or disturbances of thinking not manifest in the initial consultation. The analyst's particular unresolved conflicts that lead to countertransference interferences may impede the ability to work with otherwise promising patients. Sometimes the reasons for unexpected outcomes remain mysterious. Our lack of understanding is often hidden by pseudoexplanatory references to nonspecific "congenital" or "biological" factors. Freud's (1937a) concept of the adhesiveness of the libido is an instance of such a pseudoexplanation.

As with any form of therapeutics, psychoanalysis can never be guaranteed to be effective (or ineffective). Still, analysts would like to be able to predict the likely outcome and course of analyses, if only to be able to answer their patients' reasonable questions about undertaking analytic treatment. In fact, many analysts believe that they can make reasonable predictions about analyses. Many of these predictions boil down to the expectation that the patient's character, whose many manifestations the analyst is only able to adumbrate from the history and initial presentation, is likely to shape the analytic course. Stormy, dramatic people have stormy, dramatic analyses; people who deal with anxiety through action use action-oriented defenses once in analysis; severely obsessional people are likely to have long analyses; people who do well in other aspects of life usually do well in analysis, and so on. Yet the refinement of our predictive capacities could save analysts or patients much time, effort, and misery when analysis is likely to be unsuccessful, and it could lead to encouraging analysis for patients who might seem unsuitable.[1]

Because the data required to determine analyzability are unavailable outside the analytic situation, some analysts believe that the only adequate test of analyzability is analysis itself. Is this the case, or have we not yet come upon systematically developed sources of data or means for effectively predicting analyzability? Certainly a trial of analysis does provide a clearer picture of how the analysand responds to the analytic situation and how analyst and patient work together than can be achieved on the basis of history and initial interview data.

Possibly we are placing unreasonable demands on ourselves in expecting to become good predictors of outcome. The limited predictive showing in the studies we shall review may say less about psychoanalysis than about complex systems in general. The image of science that commonly informs our thinking derives from eighteenth-century physics. In this view the universe is a giant mechanism governed by laws that can be embodied in a very complex set of differential equations. The French physicist Pierre Simon Laplace envisaged a complete set of equations whose solution would predict the course of the universe for all time (Kline, 1972). The only problem, as he saw it, was to discover and solve the correct equations. He regarded this problem as technically challenging but neither inconceivable nor necessarily impossible. Certainly on a small scale a clockwork universe should allow prediction that is as good as investigators desire, providing that they are willing to carry out the computation. Application of these ideas to psychology is implicit in Freud's regulatory principle of mental functioning (Galatzer-Levy, 1976), and a few

---

1. The clinical experience of failure to predict analytic outcomes is mirrored in the systematic studies discussed elsewhere in this volume. As with these studies it should be recognized that the attempt at clinical prediction is often an attempt to make differential judgments within a very narrow range of psychological situations. The analyst is generally attempting to make judgments about the analyzability of people who are functioning well enough to be considered for analysis and who are sufficiently interested that the question of analysis arises. Differentiating unanalyzable from analyzable patients in this narrow range is far more difficult than making a similar judgment for the populations as a whole.

analysts have actually tried to carry out a program of reducing psychological phenomena to the interaction of forces and solving problems in terms of those forces (e.g., French, 1952, 1954, 1958).

The likelihood of ever achieving such prediction in psychoanalysis is small, not only because of the technical difficulties but also because of the intrinsic nature of the effort. Following Freud (1920b), Waelder (1963) observed that analysts' capacities to describe coherently, after the fact, how psychological states arise is much greater than their predictive capacity. The multiple, quantitative factors that affect psychological outcomes, and the impossibility of measuring the initial state of variable without changing them in the process of measurement, were given as reasons that psychoanalytic prediction was unlikely to be fruitful. Rapaport (1960) and Wallerstein (1964) adopted a different point of view. They continued to recognize the inherent difficulty of prediction in the complex psychoanalytic situation, but they attributed some of the limitations of predictive effectiveness to inadequately developed theory and some of it to failure to attempt prediction. They observed that clinicians routinely make informal predictions. In the Menninger study systematic predictions were undertaken in the spirit that predictive capacity is central to what is commonly meant as science.

However, the nature of prediction, even in the physical world, is vastly more difficult than Laplace and many generations of physical and social scientists believed. For a predictive theory of the type they conceived to work, small changes in initial conditions must lead to small changes in final states. If a ball is thrown slightly harder, we expect it to go slightly farther, not to follow an entirely different course. The mathematics employed by classical physical scientists, linear differential equations, had precisely these qualities. In deriving descriptions of even simple physical systems, nonlinear differential equations often emerged. Because very satisfactory means of manipulating linear differential equations are available and because nonlinear equations are very difficult to handle mathematically, nonlinear equations were reduced to linear approximations. These approximations seemingly served well, although the assertion that they were adequate may have been an attempt to make the best of necessity. In the twentieth century the study of nonlinear differential equations moved forward. This led to the surprising discovery not only that they were technically difficult to manage but that nonlinearity in differential equations leads to qualitatively different phenomena from those found in linear differential equations (Hale and LaSalle, 1963). These differences are particularly distressing for prediction. Nonlinear equations commonly produce predictions in which arbitrarily small changes in initial conditions result not only in slight changes in the systems but in qualitatively different outcomes. Over the past two decades mathematical researchers have evolved an entirely new vision of physical reality, encompassed in terms like *fractal geometry, chaos theory,* and *catastrophe theory* (Galatzer-Levy, 1995; Mandelbrot, 1982; I. Stewart, 1989; Thom, 1975). These outlooks share an appreciation that ordinary natural systems occur where future evolution is not even qualitatively predictable (though the range of possibilities for such systems often does have a significant structure). For example, it has become clear that precise long-term weather prediction is fundamentally impossible because tiny changes in conditions at any given moment rapidly lead to dramatic changes in outcome over relatively short periods of time. This does not mean that the systems are in any sense nondeterministic or that fantastic additional mechanisms are needed to explain their behavior. Rather, it seems that the intuitions we have been educated to about determinism have been ill-founded.

In psychoanalysis it is likely that, as with other complex systems, detailed predictions are inherently impossible. In particular, it is probable that in the areas where change is most likely and where we want most to predict what will happen, our predictive capacities are least accurate. Confronted with extremely rigid and intractable personality structures, we can almost always reliably predict the outcome of analysis: little change. It is precisely among those patients who demonstrate some flexibility in their personalities that prediction becomes particularly difficult.

Lest the appreciation of the difficulty of prediction in complex situations lead to nihilism, it is worth underlining that people are instances of self-organizing systems (Nicolis and Prigogine, 1977), which attempt to preserve the cohesiveness and continuity of function and experience. They are therefore much more likely to be predictable in certain ways than other systems without similar systems that have evolved to achieve this end. In any case, the working analyst would welcome as rich a knowledge as possible of factors that predict the course and outcome of psychoanalysis.

What Information Is Needed to Predict the Outcome of Analysis?

Issues of importance include questions of when adequate predictions of outcomes and course are possible and which variables manifest during the diagnostic assessment might predict course and outcome, as well as a host of specific questions about populations of patients and situations that may be relevant to outcome.

The prediction of the course and outcome of analyses depends in part on the point in the process from which predictions are made. Some analysts believe that they have a good sense of how things will go in the first few minutes of their encounter with a patient: a sense of hitting it off, of dealing with a substantial person, or an overall negative impression or sense that there is little in the patient that the analyst can relate to. In very short periods of time people present huge amounts of information about themselves.

A second point at which the course and outcome of analyses might be predicted is when the analyst comes to a formal diagnostic impression. The popularity of systematic diagnosis in psychiatry originated from the hope that psychiatric diagnosis would serve the same function as medical diagnosis classically has — that is, in the ideal case a correct diagnosis carries a comprehensive description of the signs and symptoms associated with an illness, its natural history (course without treatment), specific therapeutic interventions with the associated course of the illness in this circumstance, and an understanding of the etiology of the condition (Goodwin and Guze, 1984; Ryle, 1948). Although this comprehensive picture of a condition is rarely available in medicine and hardly ever available for psychiatric disorders, especially those seen as appropriate for psychoanalytic treatment, attempts to approximate this ideal are the ordinary way diagnosis is used in medicine and psychiatry.[2] Much of the research on the course and outcome of psychoanalysis, and many of the customary ways of formulating clinically relevant questions, address the relation between diagnosis and the course and outcome of psychoanalysis.

A third point at which many analysts expect to be able to predict the analytic process is after the characterologic (or defense) transference has emerged. By character defense we mean the patient's typical modes of managing anxiety. Because in many analysts' views the tractability of the analysand and the major issue supporting the continuation of pathology are found in character defenses, the possibility of their clear evaluation early in the analysis may constitute a point of great prognostic significance.

A fourth point at which analysts have a sense of where the treatment is headed is the firm establishment of the transference.

At termination the manifest course of the analysis is clear, but what its course has been in depth is often less certain. Reanalyses that include analysis of the previous psychoanalytic experience and follow-up studies that explore earlier psychoanalyses both demonstrate that patient's and analyst's assessments at the time of termination may be highly inaccurate (Schlessinger and Robbins, 1974, 1975; Grossman and Cohler, in press). Even at follow-up,

---

2. When diagnostic criteria with the power of medical diagnoses have emerged for psychiatric disorders, as in general paresis, myxedema, and various vitamin deficiencies, these disorders have become the province of other medical specialties.

substantially after treatment has ended, assessment is difficult, and considerable work may be necessary to understand what has occurred. The natural history of the postanalytic period is little explored (Hoffs, 1972; Kantrowitz, Katz, and Paolitto, 1990a,b,c; Schachter, 1990). How the transformations achieved through analysis are ordinarily affected by later ordinary and extraordinary developments is particularly unclear.

Systematic empirical investigation might address the interrelation of assessments at various points in analyses. The early assessments are useful in deciding whether to initiate analysis. Such studies could test the idea that the only adequate test of analyzability is a trial of analysis. If a trial analysis is the only reliable test of analyzability, we want to know how long that trial should be with each kind of patient. Making decisions about altering the clinical approach could be informed by knowledge of the times in analyses when the assessment of treatment is likely to remain unchanged as the analysis moves forward.

Systematic empirical knowledge would be most useful during the diagnostic period. We would like to be able to answer the classical question posed by Oberndorf (1943) and elaborated by later researchers, "What treatment, by whom is most effective for this individual with that specific problem under which set of circumstances?" (Paul, 1967, p. 111). The predicament facing the analyst is that he knows that the basic processes of psychoanalysis occur deep within the personality and that the association between the manifest and latent parts of the personality is often obscure. Yet each analyst must make a reasonable assessment in a short time and advise patients on the basis of that assessment.

The cumulative wisdom of psychoanalytic practice has been brought to bear on the question of analyzability and transmitted through clinical supervision, study groups, scientific panels, a substantial clinical literature augmented by critical summaries and evaluations of the existing knowledge, and the reports of formal, systematic research efforts. The fruits of these efforts have sharpened the issues, but the main questions remain only partially answered. Much is known, and we would refer the reader to many of the excellent discussions about what is known (Diatkine, 1968; A. Freud, 1968; Guttman, 1968; Kuiper, 1968; Panel, 1973c; Rosenthal, 1988; Savitt, 1977; Shapiro et al., 1977; Sklansky, 1972; Tyson and Sandler, 1971; Valenstein, 1968; Waldhorn, 1968), but we have not yet reached a point where systematic answers are available.

The most obvious data about a patient are demographic. Higher educational experience may, for example, provide evidence of intellectual abilities, ego syntonic capacities to examine matters from multiple perspectives, or intellectualizing defenses. It may enrich the patient's discourse in ways that engage the analyst and provide a richer metaphoric range to communicate or avoid communicating.

Ethnic backgrounds may or may not affect analyzability. Traditional pessimism about analyzing people from religious backgrounds, especially those who remain committed to their religion, seems to have been ill-founded (Meissner, 1984a). On the other hand, people from backgrounds in which psychological issues and affect are normatively avoided may find analysis particularly difficult. The effect of common ethnic or cultural backgrounds between analyst and patient is unclear (Schachter and Butts, 1968). Shared backgrounds simplify communication, but culturally accepted defensive operations may remain unexplored. One colleague recommended, only half-jokingly, that analysts should never practice in their native culture. In doing so, they fail to question many of the irrationalities of analysands' thoughts (B. Kamm, personal communication, 1976). It has sometimes been advocated that only analysts not belonging to an oppressing majority can work well with oppressed minority group members because of the analyst's need to avoid the meaning of being a member of the oppressing group. (This is distinct from the idea, advocated from a distinctly psychotherapeutic viewpoint, that in order to be a useful object for identification the therapist must belong to the same minority group as the patient [Martin, 1982].)

To what extent does the patient's current external situation affect the analytic process? It both reflects the patient's psychology and constitutes an independent variable. Financial wherewithal affects the availability of analysts. Patients who do not pay for analysis themselves often present clinical problems in which it is hard to differentiate the payer's realistic difficulties in paying fees from resistances — that is, the analysand's inducing the payer not to pay or to pay slowly. The patient's work situation may also introduce issues about times for analytic hours. When major life decisions, such as choice of profession or spouse, have strong neurotic bases, the analytic work may meet opposition from affected third parties, as well as difficulties imposed on the patient who recognizes the neurotic nature of past choices.

Analysts would like to know how and when family configurations limit or enhance analytic possibilities. The differential recommendation of psychoanalysis versus family therapy, for example, should depend on the diagnostician's assessment of the extent to which intervention with other family members is necessary to relieve the suffering of the designated patient. Especially when people are strongly involved with their family of origin, family commitments and pathology may form an important issue in the analysis. This can be an issue not only for children and adolescents but also for young adults who far more commonly remain engaged with their families of origin than many analysts realize (Cohler and Grunbaum, 1981).

As we have mentioned, the correlation of course and outcome of treatment with diagnoses has been used in medicine and psychiatry in selecting appropriate therapeutics. The American Psychiatric Association's diagnostic and statistical manuals, DSM-III, DSM-III-R, and DSM-IV, adopted a "phenomenological" point of view, which attempted to classify psychiatric disorders on the basis of reliably observable features without reference to inferred underlying mechanism of pathogenesis. As a consequence, the classification abandons etiology-focused terminology so that, for example, "neurosis" or "psychoneurosis" — the entities for which psychoanalysis has classically been the therapy of choice — do not appear in the last two editions of the manuals. Because psychoanalysts believe symptoms are not tightly linked to underlying structures in the sense that the deeper structure cannot accurately be inferred from the symptoms, and that the pathogenesis of similar psychological illnesses can result in a wide variety of overt signs and symptoms, most analysts view classificatory systems such as DSM-IV as providing poor guides to the etiology and mechanism of pathogenesis. In fact, the manual was carefully designed to exclude major psychoanalytic concepts (Bayer and Spitzer, 1985). Some correlation between DSM-IV categories and analyzability doubtless does exist, but it seems unlikely that any specific relation will be found between descriptive diagnoses and analyzability beyond the relation between overall pathology and analyzability.

Can more-subtle diagnostic categories be developed that are specifically informative to prognostication of psychoanalytic outcomes? Alternative diagnostic systems, such as a systematic approach to the overall organization of psychopathology within ego-strengths and characterological contexts (Menninger, Mayman, and Pruyser, 1962), or to dynamic formulations (Sampson and Weiss, 1986; Perry, Cooper, and Michaels, 1987; Shapiro, 1989b,c), are much more closely aligned with psychoanalytic concepts and so might be expected to be more predictively reliable regarding psychoanalytic outcomes. More-elaborate diagnostic frameworks, like the Hampstead Index for the diagnostic assessment of children (Freud, 1965) and its extension to adolescents (Laufer, 1965), infants (W. Freud, 1967, 1971), and adults (Freud, Nagera, and Freud, 1965), and the database forms for description of potential and current psychoanalytic patients under development at several psychoanalytic institutes, reflect predominantly psychoanalytic thinking. But these methods, whatever their other intellectual merit, assess patients in a multidimensional fashion and thus do not categorize patients into discrete, mutually exclusive categories; as a result, they lose much of the intellectual power of diagnostic categorization. If possible, analysts would like to find a system equivalent to descriptive diagnosis that speaks to psychoanalytic questions.

Psychological testing was used widely in the past as part of the diagnostic assessment for psychoanalysis. Through the standardized procedures of such an examination, especially when formulated and psychoanalytically conceptualized, as at the Menninger Foundation, it was hoped to achieve a comprehensive picture of the patient's psychological functioning that would include psychoanalytically relevant matters — that is, the influence of predominant unconscious fantasies and the resilience of psychic structure, which are difficult to ascertain in initial clinical examinations. Unfortunately, most efforts to correlate psychological test results with treatment were neither psychoanalytically conceptualized nor informed. The more informed and sophisticated approaches did succeed in providing valuable data about treatment planning and the organization of psychic conflict and structure. However, they have not to date substantially increased our ability to predict the course of analytic treatment. The refinement or development of psychological testing to help predict psychoanalytic efficacy for particular patients would be a major step forward.

Another group of data available at the time of diagnostic evaluation involves the interview process. The evaluation of the interview process, including the interviewer's subjective responses to the patient, provides a window to many of the functions and qualities that will further or impede psychoanalytic work. Matters like transference readiness, capacity to modulate the intensity of transference, capacity to associate freely, rigidity of defenses, capacity to use interpretation, "psychological mindedness," richness of association, and the capacity for controlled regression may all be partly ascertained through the interview process. Many aspects of the diagnostic interview were explored by Deutsch and Murphy (1955), but they did not explore the relation of their findings with therapeutic process. Practicing analysts would find most useful systematic studies of how and to what extent these important functions manifest in the initial interviews are predictive of their status in future psychoanalytic work.

Our current knowledge about the predictive value of these kinds of information varies markedly. There are also marked differences in the extent to which analysts rely on one or another of these measures. The measures themselves are not independent. Each may reflect certain aspects of personality and analyzability in a different way. How do these various measures correlate at the beginning of analysis? To what extent does one or another of these measures emphasize particular qualities of the personality? To what extent may they be used interchangeably? These are but a few of the questions we could ask about the predictability of psychoanalytic outcomes.

Specific Questions About the Analyst and Other Issues

A recurrent question in psychoanalytic circles is whether some analysts do better with certain patients than do others (Fleming, 1961; Silverman, 1985a; Cooper, 1986; Baudry, 1991; Kantrowitz, 1992). Much psychotherapy research indicates that the match between therapist and patient is an important factor in the treatment's outcome (Luborsky et al., 1988; Beutler, Crago, and Arizmendi, 1986). But whether and to what extent the same is true for analysis remains unclear. Because the goal of most psychoanalytic procedures is to identify and work through impediments to further analytic work, properly conducted analyses should presumably be dependent only on the analyst's skill. Yet clinical experience suggests that some patients seem to fare better with certain analysts. Many analysts have a sense of what sorts of patients they do well or poorly with, but this area has received little investigation.

It would be helpful to know what can be predicted about the course of analyses based on a knowledge of the psychoanalyst's character style, training, experience, technical procedures, and theoretical orientation. Such questions could be asked with respect to groups of patients as categorized in any of the ways we have discussed in this part of the book. We would like to know whether an analyst can analytically engage issues that he has not explored in himself. Does theoretical orientation make a difference in the course and outcome of analysis? How do analysts' ways of working change across their careers?

However, these matters are difficult to study for two reasons. First, analysts at various levels of experience draw specific types of patients, the sickest patients generally going to the least experienced (Knapp et al., 1960). On the other hand, clear differences that one might expect between the effectiveness of highly experienced and inexperienced psychotherapists are not regularly found by investigators studying psychotherapy (Beutler, Crago, and Arizmendi, 1986).

It would be helpful to have systematic data about the effect of the "match" between analyst and analysand. *Match* may refer to similarity, complementarity, or the analyst's likelihood of inviting transferences that need to be analyzed. This can be far more complex than simple questions of shared ethnicity or capacity to collaborate in or avoid character defenses. For example, certain transferences, which Weiss (1981) has called "hidden transferences," are commonly misdiagnosed. Weiss's experience is that although most male psychoanalysts find it easy to experience themselves in the transference as the pre-oedipal mother, they usually do not recognize maternal oedipal transferences directed toward them. For this reason, as well as its greater syntonicity to the patient, maternal oedipal transferences come into sharper focus and may be better analyzed with female than male analysts.

Other Specific Questions

There are many additional pieces of analytic lore that might assist analysts in their daily work. Bits of clinical wisdom are usually held impressionistically and may be correct or not. Many of them are never even published but are passed on verbally among analysts. Others have been formally proposed. For example, Gitelson (1962) asserted that if the analyst appeared "undisguised" in the patient's first analytic dream, the prognosis was poor. Systematic investigation showed that this was wrong (Bradlow and Coen, 1975). On another level, not only was the clinical impression that the analysis of "hysterics" either went very well or very poorly confirmed in Zetzel's (1968) classic study, but a highly informative differentiation between the two populations emerged through that systematic study.

The practicing psychoanalyst has many small-scale questions and impressions about analyses that are currently answered on an impressionistic basis. Analysts would value more-systematic investigations. Incidentally, these less grand investigations are precisely the type of questions that occupy most of the publications in highly successful sciences. It is rare to see the grand, very large questions, like those that are the focus of most psychoanalytic publications, addressed in the research literature of other disciplines. We should encourage investigations of small-scale, answerable questions about psychoanalysis.

Conclusion

Psychoanalysis has reached a stage where it has a rich collection of naturalistic observations, many clear impressions, and areas of controversy. In this part of the book we have offered a brief list of questions that might be answered through systematic investigation. Such a list of questions is by no means static. Scientific investigations characteristically raise new questions as they unfold. Good studies raise as well as resolve questions. Furthermore, every analyst could add or subtract particular questions. But the clarification of what it is we hope to learn through efficacy and outcome studies is a first step toward producing more-useful investigations.

Many questions are absent from our list that might appear on a similar list prepared by a psychotherapy researcher, general psychiatrist, or clinical psychologist. This is deliberate. We believe that psychoanalytic research can move the field forward only by answering questions of interest to psychoanalysis. Defensively conceived investigations designed to refute external critics of psychoanalysis distract us from the central task of developing our field. Our advocacy of systematic, empirical research should not be mistaken for a wishful substitute for the tolerance of uncertainty required of psychoanalytic practice. There are far too many questions about psychoanalytic processes and outcomes that have not yet been answered by our traditional methods of investigation. Among many others, Fenichel (1945), Rapaport (1954), Arlow (1972), Arlow and Brenner (1988), and Rangell (1979, 1984b, 1988) have supported the need for a systematization of psychoanalytic theory and empirically derived knowledge. Our efforts remain in concert with such aspirations, and, in addition, it is our hope that systematic investigations will raise fresh questions about matters of psychoanalytic import.

PART II

*Empirical Studies of Psychoanalytic
Outcome and Efficacy*

4

Historical Background

Psychoanalytic investigators have repeatedly tried to answer Obern-dorf's (1943) classic question: what type of treatment is best suited to what kind of patient, suffering from what kind of illness, at what point in life, when treated by what kind of analyst, in what manner? A century of clinical experience has taught us much about the fate of different kinds of cases, the clinical management of the array of patients who consult psychoanalysts, the scope and limitations of the psychoanalytic method, and the qualities of patients that make them suitable or unsuited for psychoanalysis. Over the years there have been many critical reviews of the accumulated clinical wisdom.[1] But as a discipline matures, clinical and naturalistic observations must be supplemented, clarified, and extended by more-systematic investigations. This process has started in psychoanalysis.

Specific terms are used to designate various kinds of investigation. Empirical investigations are studies that attempt to derive conclusions from observations, as opposed to deriving them as logical consequences of accepted propositions.

---

1. E.g., Freud, 1937; A. Freud, 1954; Stone, 1954; Waldhorn, 1967; Tyson and Sandler, 1971; Bachrach and Leaff, 1978; Firestein, 1978, 1984; Erle and Goldberg, 1979; Bachrach, 1983; Schlessinger, 1984; Panels (e.g., 1953, 1958, 1960, 1963, 1964, 1968, 1976, 1977, 1979); Symposia (e.g., 1937; Oberndorf et al., 1948, 1950a,b, 1956).

For example, a study showing that avoiding libidinal gratification of the analysand promotes the emergence of an analyzable transference is empirical if the conclusion is supported by data that trace the results of providing and not providing such gratification in actual analyses. It is nonempirical if its conclusions come from abstract principles such as the presumption that "if libido is dammed it will find an alternate route of discharge."[2] A study is systematic if the author specifies and attends to the methodology of the study. An analyst who describes her impressions based on work with several patients of a certain type is doing empirical but not systematic research. If the analyst specifies how the data were collected and how her conclusions relate to those data, the study is systematic. Population studies generally involve directly observing a subpopulation (or sample) and generalizing the findings to a larger population. For example, "Obsessive-compulsive patients benefit from analysis" or "Most borderline patients benefit more from a supportive than an interpretive approach" are typical population-study conclusions if they are based on observing analyses of patients and if the investigator concludes that these observations can be generalized to all patients of this type. Often the generalization is achieved and its validity assessed using statistical methods. In case studies, by contrast, conclusions are drawn about the individual or individuals studied. Conclusions from case studies may or may not be generalized. Quantitative studies express and explore data numerically. When data are not explored in this way but are presented in narrative or discursive form, the study is qualitative.

These terms — *empirical, systematic, statistical, quantitative, qualitative,* and so on — are descriptive; they do not imply any assessment of the quality or value of the study. If they are done poorly, systematic quantitative empirical studies will yield meaningless results. Findings based on nonsystematic investigation can be of great value. It is, however, useful in thinking about the truth claims of psychoanalytic propositions to be aware of the nature of the evidence that supports them.

Systematic empirical investigation is not in opposition to the traditional reporting of clinical experience but complementary to it. The aims and significance of the two forms of study differ in terms of the uses to which they are legitimately put. Many clinical writings are not intended as empirical statements; rather, the authors want to alert other analysts about clinical phenomena. Sometimes clinical reports principally illustrate theoretical proposi-

2. Unfortunately, when investigators express clinical findings and generalizations in metapsychological language, readers often find it difficult to determine whether claims are based theoretically or empirically.

tions. At other times, a summary of a clinical experience is an early stage of systematic investigation in which the clinician-investigator puts forward hypotheses for refinement and testing. Occasionally, clinical reports reflect findings whose special nature — for example, limited applicability to a small group of patients — makes it unlikely that they will be subjected to more-systematic study. Similarly, those who conduct systematic investigations, though they make strenuous efforts to ensure that whatever conclusions they draw are rigorously supported, usually achieve this result by limiting the richness of their conclusions.

Our focus on systematic empirical studies in this section is not meant to suggest that they are of greater intrinsic value than other types of studies. We do believe, however, that considerable care should be taken in psychoanalytic writing to characterize the epistemic status of findings. Valuable clinical studies showing that a patient or small group of patients benefited from a particular technique become less valuable when they inaccurately claim to prove a wider finding. For example, a clinical study that clearly shows that some children with reading difficulties overcome those difficulties through analysis becomes less valuable if the author concludes that all poor readers would benefit from analysis. Likewise, when empirical studies fail to measure analytically important variables, it is not surprising that they find less effect than clinicians believe exist. For instance, a study of analytic outcome that does not explore changes in interpersonal relations would fail to note a significant effect of analysis noted by most clinicians.

In this part of the book we review findings from systematic studies of psychoanalytic outcome. These fall into two major categories. In the first, general analytic patient populations were studied in an attempt to discover correlations between features of the patient's presentation, treatment, and outcome and various aspects of the clinical situations (diagnosis and outcome, treatment method, overall psychological well-being at termination, and so on). The second group of studies collect several cases with similar features (patient age, analytic technique, diagnosis) to reach clinical generalizations about certain types of patients and their analytic treatment.

We begin by reviewing some early studies of groups of analytic patients. Then we consider how such studies can be evaluated. Using these criteria, we describe the published systematic studies of populations of psychoanalytic patients. Next we describe studies of multiple case histories designed to reach conclusions about populations of patients. Finally we describe what these studies have taught us about psychoanalysis, the methods of study themselves, and their limitations.

Early Studies of Psychoanalytic Outcome

Most of what we know about psychoanalytic processes and outcomes comes from the crucible of psychoanalytic practice. This knowledge has only partly been preserved in print. Much of it is passed on through supervision, teaching, and conversation. During the first fifty years of psychoanalysis, all discoveries came from the clinical psychoanalytic method. No studies were conducted using control groups, independent observers, or other means of systematic observation, in part because useful methodologies had not yet been developed. Nor were there any comparative treatment studies, because there were few other rational treatments with which to compare psychoanalysis. In this regard psychoanalysis was like other medical specialties before World War II. Although most medical investigations were carried out unsystematically until after the war, observant doctors paid attention to the effectiveness of what they did. Freud, for example, noted the ineffectiveness of electrotherapy and the transient results of hypnosis (Jones, 1953). In the introductory lectures he wrote, "Under favorable conditions we achieve successes which are second to none of the finest in the field of internal medicine; . . . they could not have been achieved by any other procedure" (1917, p. 458).[3] Some early investigators, however, attempted to provide statistical information about the efficacy of psychoanalysis.

Six years after the formation of the American Psychoanalytic Association, and fifteen years before formal institutions for training were established in America, Theodore Coriat reported on the therapeutic results in ninety-three cases based on his personal investigation and experience (1917, p. 209); he claimed that 46 percent were recovered, 27 percent much improved, 11 percent improved, and 9 percent not improved. Improvement rates were nearly equal for all fourteen of his diagnostic categories, which ranged from the anxiety hysterias to dementia praecox. However, more severe cases (for example, dementia praecox, manic depressive illness) required longer treatment — from four to six months! In analyzing his results, Coriat stressed consideration of the type of case best suited to psychoanalysis, the establishment of diagnosis-specific criteria for recovery, the duration of treatment, and the method of analyzing results.

The next survey of results appeared in 1930, in a Festschrift for the first ten years of the Berlin Psychoanalytic Institute. Fenichel (1930) reported that

3. Not only psychoanalytic but most medical investigations were carried out unsystematically until after the Second World War. Freud's claim may not have been far from true when it was made. The internists of his time had an extremely limited armamentarium, consisting principally of digitalis to treat heart failure and opiates to relieve pain.

between 1920 and 1930, the institute conducted 1,955 consultations and accepted 721 patients for psychoanalysis. The patients represented a wide range of occupations and were divided approximately equally between the sexes. Their modal age was sixteen to thirty-five. Diagnoses ranged from psychoneuroses (68 percent) to psychoses (14 percent). Sixty percent of the psychoneurotic cases and 23 percent of the psychotic cases were judged to have received substantial therapeutic benefits from treatment; 22 percent of the neurotic cases and 24 percent of the psychotic cases were judged unchanged or worse. It is not clear what standards were used to judge therapeutic benefit.

In 1936 Jones reported on the activities of the London Psychoanalytic Clinic from 1926 to 1936. During this time 738 patients applied to the clinic and 74 were taken into psychoanalysis; 80 percent of them (59) were considered neurotic and 20 percent psychotic. Forty-seven percent of the neurotic cases (28) were judged to have received substantial therapeutic benefits, and 10 percent (6) were judged unimproved or worse; all but one of the 15 psychotic cases (all treated as outpatients) were failures. In discussing the findings, Jones (1936) expressed concern about the comparability of statistical reports, because different analysts used different criteria in compiling their findings.

In the United States, Kessel and Hyman (1933) reported on twenty-one psychoneurotic and eight psychotic cases treated by medical psychoanalysts in New York. Nineteen of the neurotic cases received substantial benefit (10 percent were unchanged or worse), and all of the psychotic patients were unchanged or worse.

At about the same time, Alexander (1937) reported on the Chicago Psychoanalytic Clinic from 1932 to 1937. He discussed the difficulties of evaluating results, emphasizing the problems of record keeping and diagnostic nomenclatures, the multifaceted manifest and latent changes occurring in psychoanalysis, and the danger of the post hoc ergo propter hoc fallacy (the possibility, that is, that relief from symptoms might result from changes in life situations). Of the 157 cases included in Alexander's report, 22 percent were classified as psychoneurotic and 5 percent as psychotic; the rest received varying psychosomatic diagnoses. Sixty-three percent of the psychoneurotic cases, 40 percent of the psychotic, and 77 percent of the psychosomatic cases were judged as having substantial therapeutic benefit, with less than 10 percent of all being unchanged or worse.

Knight (1941) reported on 100 cases treated at the Menninger Clinic between 1932 to 1941. Twenty-five (81 percent) of the 31 neurotic cases and 15 (39 percent) of the 38 psychotic cases were judged to have received substantial therapeutic benefit. Only one of the neurotic cases and sixteen of the psychotic cases were unchanged or worse. Knight then combined the findings of the

Fenichel, Jones, Kessel, and Hyman report with that of Alexander and Knight into a composite tabulation of 952 cases. He preserved the classifications of the earlier reports as closely as possible. As can be seen from Table 2.1, the combined rate of substantial therapeutic benefit is in the 56–63 percent range for nonpsychotic cases, 78 percent for psychosomatic cases, and 25 percent for psychoses. About one-fifth of both the neurotic and the psychotic cases were unchanged or worse.

Knight (1941) described several pitfalls to evaluation in addition to those already recognized by these early students of psychoanalysis. He addressed the need to evaluate the work of well-trained, experienced analysts who treat types of cases for which they are especially suited by temperament and by specific experience, and he observed that any report of therapeutic results of psychoanalysis is a composite of the results of various individual analysts of varying degrees of experience and skill with cases of varying degrees of severity (p. 435). Reviewing all these reports, Fenichel (1945) echoed Knight's concern about the lack of standardized operational definitions.

In 1952 a Central Fact-Gathering Committee was established by the American Psychoanalytic Association, charged with designing a method of pooling psychoanalytic practice data. The committee developed a questionnaire which was completed by hundreds of association members on thousands of cases. But the responses were difficult to interpret because of long-recognized ambiguities in diagnosis, in nomenclature, and in judgments of effectiveness (Hamburg et al., 1967, pp. 841–42).

Another committee, appointed in 1961, was charged with reexamining available data, clarifying the methodological problems for future research, and exploring findings that might be stimulating to future investigators. An experience survey was sent to the membership of the American Psychoanalytic Association, focused on the sociology of analytic practice, analysts' opinions regarding the diagnoses of their patients, and analysts' opinions regarding the therapeutic results achieved (Hamburg et al., 1967, pp. 842–43). Approximately 10,000 questionnaires were returned by 350 members and 450 senior candidates. The final results were based on 3,019 reported cases. The patients were largely middle-class and well educated. Approximately half were in psychoanalysis, half in psychotherapy. About half received neurotic-level diagnoses, and about 10 percent psychotic-level diagnoses. Overall, 97.3 percent of the patients were judged improved in total functioning by their therapists, and 96.6 percent reported feeling benefited by their treatments. However, it is unclear at which point in treatment these assessments were made. Only about half of the patients completed treatment. This unlikely success rate probably reflects the study's methodological limitations, such as sampling biases, lack of operationalized definitions, and unsystematic means of analyzing individual, qualitative data about the cases.

These early statistical reports provide a valuable historical picture of psychoanalytic practice, but they are essentially opinion polls of questionable reliability. In assessing these studies it is important to remember when they were done. The studies summarized by Knight were at a higher level of statistical and methodological sophistication than most clinical studies in medicine conducted at that time. Close reading of these studies also shows that even early psychoanalytic investigators were aware of the importance of objectivity, reliability, and independence of observation. The main difference between these and more contemporary studies is in the development and employment of more-variegated and reliable methods for the study of psychoanalytic processes and outcomes.

Criteria for Evaluating Research on Treatment Outcomes

In the current era of accountability and comparative treatment research, there is much talk of randomization, matched control groups, double-blind strategies, complex, large-scale statistical designs, and statistical methodology as fundamental criteria for the design and conduct of research dealing with the efficacy of treatments. These buzzwords and concepts often obscure more-fundamental questions about efficacy studies. In any case, they refer to tools of empirical research, not to its essence.

In what follows we first describe criteria that we believe are meaningful for evaluating research about psychoanalytic treatment outcomes. Using these criteria, we then critically review the published systematic research about the outcomes of psychoanalysis and the factors influencing these outcomes. The basic criteria are as follows:[4]

1. Has the treatment to be evaluated taken place? The mere statement that a particular treatment was studied is insufficient. Criteria must be established for making explicit the major parameters of treatments (for example, terms and interventions), and means must be developed for independently determining that the intended treatments took place, such as treatment manuals, monitoring of the process (as happens automatically in supervised cases), and indications that the treatment conforms to standard practice (frequency of sessions, use of the couch). For a

---

4. The small number of studies we review and their varied methodologies make the use of formal meta-analytic methods inappropriate for our purposes.

complex treatment with important psychological dimensions like psychoanalysis, it may be extremely difficult to determine whether the treatment has actually occurred. Nonetheless, the meaningfulness of studies of purported psychoanalyses must be evaluated with reference to the likelihood that patients were in fact treated through psychoanalysis.

2. Has the treatment studied been conducted by practitioners of sufficient training, knowledge, and experience, in accordance with the accepted standards of practice? Obvious as this criterion may seem, the overwhelming majority of studies of psychotherapies have used inexperienced therapists such as psychiatry residents, psychology interns, and psychoanalytic candidates in the process of learning their craft (Garfield and Bergin, 1986a). Therapists-in-training are readily available, virtually captive subjects for research. But to rely on the work of novices in evaluating the results of psychoanalysis is like evaluating the results of heart transplants by examining the outcome of a surgeon's first few efforts at this procedure.[5]

3. Was analysis used to treat appropriate clinical conditions? Psychoanalysis, like any treatment, is not a panacea. Its effectiveness can be evaluated only in relation to the extent that one might reasonably expect a clinical condition to be ameliorated at a given state of therapeutic knowledge. For example, some conditions, such as autism, are not known at present to be systematically amenable to any form of treatment. Other conditions, such as certain affective disorders or schizophrenias, may be arrested or stabilized by pharmacologic or psychotherapeutic means, though the underlying pathology is not known to be alterable. Certain borderline disorders may be amenable to treatment only with difficulty, while others, such as certain depressive states and character neuroses, may respond to treatment more readily. Viewed in this light, the issue of efficacy becomes the extent of reasonably expectable influence rather than cure, and the degree and quality of change in comparison with that achievable by other treatment methods. The question of efficacy must always specify which conditions were treated and whether the conclusions of the investigators were sufficiently specific to those conditions.

5. Actually, the highly confusing data on the impact of therapist training on effectiveness suggest an even more complex and unpredictable significance to the use of student therapists for study on effectiveness (Beutler, Machado, and Neufeldt, 1994). It may be, for example, that some analysts do their best work while in training and benefiting from close supervision. In any case, generalization from student therapists to experienced ones risks significant errors.

4. Is the patient a suitable candidate for the treatment? All forms of treatment require patients to do certain things, and all forms thus assume that the patients have the ability to do these things. Traditional psychoanalysis of adults, for example, assumes that patients will be able to attempt to associate freely, think self-reflectively, and contain impulsive action in the face of strong feeling. Some cognitive-behavioral therapies require patients to construct precise hierarchies of conditions surrounding the appearance of symptoms. Patients who cannot do so are not candidates for this treatment. In general, all forms of expressive psychotherapy require that patients be able to participate actively in the treatment process and to entertain the possibility that their lot is at least in part a function of their attitudes, desires, perceptions, and values. Therefore, no matter what the indications are for any given form of treatment, the efficacy of that treatment depends on the patient's ability to engage in the process.

5. Are germane variables adequately specified conceptually, operationally, and reliably, and are they studied systematically? If not, it is impossible to understand what different investigators mean or to replicate findings. For example, a study showing that good analytic alliance correlates with satisfactory analytic outcome is meaningful insofar as these terms have been clearly defined, investigators have means to measure them that produce reliable findings, and these means of measurement are regularly employed. This does not mean that all variables must be systematically studied. In enterprises as complex as psychoanalysis, it is never possible to study systematically everything that might vary in a situation. It is essential only to study the factors central to the investigation. However, the assessment and description of the situation must be clear enough for the reader to evaluate the status of pertinent variables in order to determine for herself whether they affect the findings. For example, the question of whether the analyst has manifestly acted in compliance with certain of the patient's wishes might not be the focus of a particular investigation. Yet given the controversy about the impact of the analyst's behaving in this way, the reader should be informed of the status of this variable.[6]

6. We are not advocating a parody of scientific investigation, in which every possible variable is explicitly specified and the reader acts as though he can assume nothing. For example, it seems unnecessary to state that analyses take place in a private, reasonably quiet room, with no one but analyst and analysand present. However, it is our impression that both systematic investigations and case-reports analysts, in fact, err in the opposite

It is only after these questions have been answered about a study that more subtle questions of method can properly be addressed. We will return to many of these issues later. In the following chapters we examine the major contemporary studies of psychoanalytic outcome in populations of patients. Each study will be seen to have significant strengths and limitations, even by these simple criteria.

---

direction, leaving far too much implicit. This creates misimpressions. For example, most child analysts concur that meetings with children's parents affect the process of child analysis. There is wide variation among child analysts about the type and extent of interaction they have with parents. Yet many reports of child analyses omit any reference to this important variable. This is the kind of information that should be included in studies, even though the variable itself may not be the object of research in the particular study.

5

The Menninger Foundation
Psychotherapy Research Project

Systematic, methodologically informed research about psychoanalytic outcomes began with the Menninger Foundation Psychotherapy Research Project. This project is by far the most comprehensive published systematic study of psychoanalytic outcomes. In addition, it is a landmark in-depth study of the adult lives of disturbed individuals and is one of the most thorough studies of development in any adult population. It began in 1954, under the leadership of Lewis Robbins and Robert Wallerstein, as a naturalistic, longitudinal, prospective study. Its aim was to discover what kinds of changes take place in psychoanalysis and psychoanalytic psychotherapy, and how these changes come about. The influence of patient, analyst, and environmental factors on clinical outcomes were studied, along with the basic postulates of the psychoanalytic theory of therapy. New methods were developed, and scores of investigators, as well as distinguished consultants from around the world, were enlisted in the project. In its thirty-year history it produced more than sixty papers and five books, many of lasting value.

Methods

The initial outpatient evaluation, routine for the foundation, was comprehensive, consisting of ten psychiatric interviews, interviews with family members, a complete battery of psychological tests anchored in psychoanalytic ego psychology, and a complete physical examination. Treatment was recorded regularly and in detail as part of the routine practice of the foundation. These recordings included regular process notes, monthly treatment summaries, and supervisory records. It was therefore possible for teams of experienced analysts to review these records and come to independent assessments without influencing the ongoing treatments.

For the purposes of the study, all information about treatments was collected at termination of treatment, at which time patients were comprehensively reevaluated by research teams composed of senior clinicians. The patients were evaluated again after two years, and the research group continued to collect information about many of the patients for nearly thirty years.

Forty-two adult cases (twenty-two analyses and twenty psychotherapies) were randomly selected for study. The patients were evenly divided between the sexes and ranged in age from seventeen to fifty at the start of treatment. Patients who came to the foundation primarily for hospitalization and those who were overtly psychotic, organic, or mentally defective were excluded from the study. Nevertheless, because of Menninger's international reputation, many patients came there after having failed in other treatment efforts. Consequently, as a group they were more severely ill than is typical for psychoanalytic patients in most communities. One-third of the analytic patients in the study required hospitalization at some point in their treatment. Drug and alcohol abuse and many types of narcissistic and borderline psychopathology were present in the study group. Table 5.1 illustrates how disturbed these patients were perceived initially, as measured by the hundred point Health-Sickness Rating Scale (HSRS) developed by the project (Luborsky, 1962).[1]

Because the average HSRS ratings for the psychotherapy patients were only five points below those of the analytic patients (a difference that is not statistically significant), the psychotherapy patients are combined with the analytic patients in Table 5.1 to provide an overview of the level of illness for all the patients. The average in the study was under 50, indicating more severe ego weakness than is usually associated with neurosis.

Descriptions of three patients from the study indicate the range of the treat-

---

1. The HSRS is a widely used measure of psychological well-being. It consists of eight graphic hundred-point scales. The scales measure global mental health, capacity for autonomy, severity of symptoms, subjective distress, effect on the environment, utilization of abilities, quality of interpersonal relationships, and depth of interests. The global scale is derived from the judges' assessment of the other seven scales and comparison of the case to thirty ranked case descriptions. The scale's reliability and validity have been demonstrated in many studies (Luborsky and Bachrach, 1974; Luborsky, Crits-Christoph, Mintz, and Auerbach, 1988).

*Table 5.1 Menninger Project: Distribution of
Initial Health-Sickness Scale Ratings*

Initial HSR	Cases	%
1 to 10	0	0
11 to 20	0	0
21 to 30	5	11.9
31 to 40	14	33.3
41 to 50	8	19.0
51 to 60	8	19.0
61 to 70	7	16.7
71 to 80	0	0
81 to 90	0	0
91 to 100	0	0
Total	42	100.0

ment population. The "healthiest" patient in the sample, as measured by his HSRS score (70), was a vocationally successful man with a phallic-level, narcissistic personality disorder. He came to treatment because he felt insecure and had difficulties maintaining intimate relations with women. He prematurely terminated his four-year analysis but subsequently returned to his analyst for once-a-week psychotherapy for one year. He was unable to overcome major character resistances, and an analytic process was not considered to have developed. However, he acquired intellectual insights, which he used productively in his subsequent marriage and other areas of his life. Aspects of the analyst's style and defenses interdigitated with those of the analysand, possibly contributing to the patient's failure to come to grips with the core issues. The patient was judged "moderately improved," a result attributed to his ability to use elements of the psychoanalytic situation supportively.

The "sickest" patient in the sample, HSRS score 25, was a housebound, phobic woman. She was brought to treatment in a severe toxic state superimposed on a chronic brain syndrome that resulted from fourteen years of a withdrawn, constricted, lonely life, marked by severe, constantly increasing barbiturate addiction. Initially she was treated by psychoanalysis (by two analysts, for a total of more than 1,300 hours). Ultimately she became a therapeutic "lifer," who continued in once-monthly psychotherapy. Though her life remained constricted, she developed more expansive ways, became able to travel, and stopped using drugs. While considered a "transference cure," the long-term clinical result was considered "very good."

The case of an alcoholic physician (HSRS score 40) who was taken into analysis for "heroic" reasons (Ticho, 1970) represents one of the least favorable outcomes of the analytic cases in the study. He came to treatment after ten years of heavy alcoholism and managed to conceal his paranoia and his symbiotic attachment to his mother in the initial evaluation. His seven-year attempt at analysis, which included psychotic transference reactions, ended with his death from aspiration-pneumonia acquired while drinking.

Such disturbed patients were included in the study for several reasons in addition to the attraction of the Menninger Clinic to the severely ill. In the 1950s the idea of a "widening scope" of indications for psychoanalysis (Stone, 1954; A. Freud, 1954) became popular. The Menninger Foundation, with its unique facilities, was willing to accept patients who were not deemed suitable for psychoanalysis under more ordinary circumstances. The effectiveness of psychotropic medications, especially for major affective disorders, had not yet been established. Therefore, both because of optimism about the possibilities for analytic treatment of severe psychopathology and because of the absence of other effective therapeutic approaches, analysis was attempted with patients for whom it would be unlikely to be used today, at least as an exclusive means of treatment. The findings concerning these heroic interventions, while important in themselves, cannot properly be generalized to the psychoanalytic treatment of severely disturbed individuals as it is practiced today. Currently, even if such patients were taken into analysis, medication would probably be used to manage some of their more disrupted states.

Exclusion criteria had an important impact on the study. Patients were excluded if they were connected with Menninger's or the mental health field, were well known, or were in a training analysis. Because such patients were typically treated by training analysts, these criteria excluded most patients of senior analysts. As a consequence, most of the analyses studied were conducted by candidate-analysts, while most of the psychotherapies were conducted by more-experienced clinicians.

The study's findings are based on massive amounts of data. Hundreds of pages of information were collected for each patient. An impressive array of variables were specified, quantified, assessed, and correlated. The study explored changes from initial evaluation to termination and follow-up. The variables explored included patient (for example, ego strength, motivation), therapist (for example, skill), treatment (for example, degree of expressiveness), and situational factors (for example, extent of interpersonal support). The reliability of the clinical data was established by a method of paired comparisons.[2] On the basis of these data, teams of researchers made contingency

---

2. Clinicians were asked to assess two cases on a given dimension — for example, ego strength — and state which was higher on each dimension. Through a series of such

predictions of the treatment's course. (The predictions were of the form "if a particular event occurs, we predict that the patient will react in a particular way.") Horwitz (1974) describes the outcome of more than 1,700 individual predictions made on the basis of the initial case record. No attempt to summarize these findings would do justice to their complexity. Generally, however, despite the careful and elaborate design efforts, attempts to predict specific clinical developments were disappointing. Still, certain well-known clinical precepts were confirmed, such as the relation between initial ego strength and improvement.

Findings

The Menninger study revealed that most of the very ill patients who were taken into psychoanalysis — often for heroic reasons, and treated by student-analysts — did not do well. Six of the twenty-two patients who started in analysis had to be switched to psychotherapy because of unmanageable transferences. Most of the analyses had to be modified to some degree. As judged by Wallerstein (1986a), six of the twenty-two analyses were counted as failed, and another three showed equivocal improvement. In contrast, five showed moderate improvement and eight "very good" improvement. This rating was not shown to be reliable, but it correlated well with changes in the HSRS, a measure with established reliability. Furthermore, when one studies the extensive clinical data provided by Wallerstein (1986), his assessments seem meaningful and balanced.

For purposes of studying the efficacy of psychoanalysis we are especially interested in the ten cases in which analysis took place without very great modification. The results were not significantly different from those of the other cases. (Two patients had a "very good" result, four a "moderate" improvement, and the rest were equivocal or failed cases.) In view of the small number of cases, it seems unwarranted to draw conclusions from any quantitative finding.

For the entire sample the average improvement, as measured by the change in HSRS ratings from the initial ratings to the ratings at follow-up, was substantial for both analytic and psychotherapy patients, averaging almost thirteen points. But, as can be seen in Table 5.2, there was considerable variability.

---

comparisons, it was possible to evaluate the reliability of these comparisons, not only in comparing one rater to another but also in terms of the stability of the rating as used by one rater. For instance, if a rater rated patient A as higher than B on a given dimension, B higher than C, and C higher than A, then the rating of this variable is clearly unreliable.

*Table 5.2 Menninger Project: Distribution of Gain or
Loss in HSR from Initial to Follow-up*

HSR Change	No. of cases	% of cases
−49 to −40	0	0
−39 to −30	1	2.5
−29 to −20	0	0
−19 to −10	3	7.5
−9 to 0	2	5
1 to 10	13	32.5
11 to 20	10	25
21 to 30	6	15
31 to 40	5	12.5
41 to 50	0	0
Total	40	100

The patient who fared worst showed a 33-point drop, and the patient with the best outcome showed a 40-point improvement. In evaluating these findings it should be remembered that the degree of improvement reflects the difference between initial and final ratings. A stabilized psychotic patient might be considered more improved than a neurotic patient in whom less change occurred, though the functioning of the neurotic patient after treatment might be much better than that of the former psychotic patient. With this caveat in mind, patients treated by psychotherapy (more supportively and by more experienced clinicians) sometimes did better than patients treated by psychoanalysis. On the whole, the results of psychoanalysis were not distinguishable from the results of psychotherapy. However, in Wallerstein's (1986a) clinical retrospective, only ten of the twenty-two patients taken into analysis initially seemed suitable for psychoanalysis. Six of these cases were undertaken on the basis of heroic indications, and all of these analyses failed.

The Menninger study findings were surprising in view of the then-current theory of psychoanalysis as therapy (Wallerstein, 1986a). At the time of the study, it was widely believed that insight was the major curative factor in analysis and that the analyst's major activity was interpretation. The patient's affective expression of previously unconscious material was regarded as central to the cure. Many analysts recognized that supportive elements occur in psychoanalysis (Gill, 1951; Bibring, 1954), but these elements were regarded as at best adventitious or even as threats to the analytic process (Eissler, 1953). Supportive elements in psychoanalysis were viewed in terms of either specific actions of the therapist (for example, suggestion and manipulation) or an overall approach that strengthened the patient's adaptive defenses by encouraging them or by discouraging maladaptive defenses. Wallerstein identified additional supportive elements of treatments in the Menninger cases, including the use of the positive dependent transference to support the patient's functioning, "corrective emotional experiences," assistance with reality testing, reeducation, help in disengaging from unfavorable life situations, unconscious collusive bargains of therapist and patient to bypass areas of difficulty so as to make the therapy look more effective and to avoid countertransference difficulties, and the management of external reality.

The research suggests that all the treatments had more supportive elements than were anticipated (Horwitz, 1974; Wallerstein, 1986a) and that for most patients the supportive elements contributed more to change than had been expected. However, on the basis of the same data, Kernberg and his coworkers (1972) concluded that changes depended on aggressive interpretation of the negative transference for borderline patients. Even allowing for the small sample size, these findings suggest a fruitful line of inquiry on differential effects of interventions depending on the extent of ego weakness.

Many other specific findings bear on clinical questions, related to (1) initial evaluation and the patient's suitability for psychoanalysis, (2) the analyst's technique, (3) the outcome of psychoanalytic therapies, and (4) the predictability of clinical outcomes.

INITIAL EVALUATION

During the initial evaluation patients often concealed significant pathology. This sometimes led to overoptimistic treatment recommendations. The pathology of eighteen of the forty-two patients was substantially underestimated, despite the comprehensiveness of the initial evaluation. Because Menninger at the time of the study accepted "heroic" indications for psychoanalysis, many more patients were taken into analysis than the research teams felt was appropriate. Many patients had overwhelming problems. A third were severely alcoholic, and half of these patients were also severely drug addicted; 45 percent had severe sexual disabilities; 33 percent had strong paranoid character trends; and nearly half had borderline or otherwise precarious ego organizations. Eleven of the forty-two cases (26 percent) were included in at least three of these five groups. Only two of these patients had a good outcome, and each of them required nearly three decades of therapeutic work. It made no difference whether these patients were initially selected for analysis (six cases) or for psychotherapy (five cases). Clearly, with very ill patients, the approaches available were therapeutically limited.

At the other extreme were the six hysterical patients who ordinarily would be considered suitable for analysis. Indeed, five did well. However, the analytic results with these patients were somewhat limited, often because of a failure to sufficiently analyze the maternal transference (Wallerstein, 1986a). These findings served as a basis for Wallerstein's recommendation of further studies to address these issues with such hysterical patients.

THERAPEUTIC TECHNIQUE

The rich selection of cases provided many opportunities to study varieties of transferences and their bearing on outcome. A number of cases had insoluble neurotic and psychotic transference reactions, often related to problematic countertransference. No satisfactory means were found to sharply differentiate difficulties in the patient-analyst dyad from patient characteristics in their contribution to the unfavorable results. This is not surprising, given the difficulties of such differentiation in any clinical situation. The researchers looked for and found problems in the analyst-therapist relationship, including defensive reactions to transference pressures, undue fostering of positive transferences, overinvolvement, collusion in avoiding central conflicts, rejection, and intolerance for hostility and dependency. The variables assessing therapist qualities and skill did not prove as robust in prediction as was hoped. The project showed that there were many ways for therapy and analysis to go awry.

TURNING POINTS IN TREATMENT

Wallerstein (1986b) observes that published and publicly presented accounts of analyses and therapies often involve a dramatic turning point — for example, when the analyst's first understanding and interpretation of an aspect of the patient's dynamics leads to the treatment moving ahead dramatically. Wallerstein suggests that the abundance of such descriptions in the psychoanalytic literature reflects their rhetorical power and the analysts' wish to demonstrate the importance of the "turning point" in the service of the argument of the paper. In the Menninger study such turning points were found to be rare and not necessarily desirable. Seven such events were found in the study — four for the better, three for the worse. These findings suggest that the work of analysis seldom occurs by virtue of dramatic transitions of this type.

INSIGHT AND CHANGE

A dramatic negative finding from the study calls into question a central concept of classical psychoanalysis: therapeutic change did not correlate well with the interpretive activity of the therapist/analyst or the development of insight by the patient. Psychological testing revealed that patients who achieved substantial therapeutic change often showed signs of structural change as well.

But only a limited number of patients showing such change gave evidence of insight into their core conflicts.

The meaning of this finding must be understood in terms of the study. It may be that the kind of insight traditionally associated with successful analyses rarely develops in patients as sick as these patients were initially. The finding does suggest that for some patients structural change can occur without significant insight, but the study simply does not address the question of the relation of insight to structural change in patients who are less disturbed than those studied.

Prediction of Outcome

Differential prediction of clinical outcome was poor, despite the elaborate initial evaluation. Outcomes were judged by three scales: global improvement, transference resolution, and change in ego strength. If one studies enough variables, some of them should correlate with outcome as a matter of chance. Statistical analysis shows that the factors assessed at the beginning of treatment that were significantly associated with measures of outcome were fewer than might be expected on a chance basis (Kernberg et al., 1972). Even for those factors that did correlate with outcome, the magnitude of the relationships was small (correlations in the 0.1–0.2 range). Only initial ego strength was significantly related to global improvement (but not to transference resolution and increased ego strength), and only initial level of anxiety was related to global improvement and increased ego strength (but not to transference resolution). Therapist's skill was related only to global improvement. Even this finding is open to question, as the research team was aware of the outcome when they rated "therapist's skill" in this case.

Efforts to predict treatment developments and outcomes according to a method of contingency prediction also did not do well, largely because the assumptions on which the predictions were based were often not met (Horwitz, 1974). The relation between patient qualities and outcomes assessed from the test battery (Full Wechsler-Bellevue, Babcock Story Recall, Rorschach Test, Thematic Apperception Test, Word Association Test, and Object Sorting Test), independent of any other knowledge of the patients, proved slightly better in terms of predicting outcome (Appelbaum, 1977). The magnitude of the relations (correlations were in the 0.2 range) was not statistically significant.

Conclusion

Among psychoanalytic research efforts, the Menninger Psychotherapy Research Project is in a class by itself in its methodological and clinical contributions. Among the major methodological contributions are the ingenious use of Fechner's method of paired comparisons for reducing complex clinical judgments to quantitative dimensions (Sargent, Horwitz, Wallerstein, and Appelbaum, 1968) and the development of the Health-Sickness Rating Scale (Luborsky, 1962). Using such methods, teams of experienced analysts could make sophisticated, independent, and reliable contingency predictions about the development of the cases. The predictions were reliable, that is, in the sense that the analyst predicted the same things. They were not good predictions in the sense of accurately anticipating the results. This was itself another methodological innovation (Horwitz, 1974). Other methodological merits of the study include prospective design, uncompromising clinical values and focus, scope and duration, extensive collection of rich case histories spanning decades, painstaking accumulation of follow-up information, quantitative sophistication, careful definition of terms, and systematic review of processes and outcomes from many points of view.

Clinically, the project's main contributions include its substantive findings that severely ill patients consistently do poorly in analysis with inexperienced analysts, that supportive elements are important in all psychotherapies, including psychoanalysis, and that even the most comprehensive initial evaluations do not result in good prognostication about the outcome of analyses. The study raises researchable questions about the treatment of choice for severely ill patients and about the psychoanalytic theory of therapy — that is, the relationship between insight and structural change.

The study has major limitations. The patients were severely ill and largely not suited for psychoanalysis by the current standards of the psychoanalytic community. The study used student analysts. Most, perhaps all, of the analyses involved modified analytic technique. The sample size was small in view of the number of variables the researchers addressed. Psychoanalytic processes were not studied in the detail allowed by today's methodology. The analysts' contributions to the process were studied only impressionistically.

Related methodological limitations derive from the original study design. To preserve as natural a course of treatment as possible, the research team selected cases for participation in the study without the knowledge of the analyst/therapist until termination. As a result, the data collected on the course of therapy consisted of process notes, reports from supervisors, and retrospective reports from patients and therapists at termination. Hence there were only limited studies of the *process* of psychoanalysis or psychotherapy, such as Wallerstein's (1986a) reconstruction from clinical reports. An experienced analyst and supervisor, Wallerstein was able to provide thought-provoking clinical judgments of what occurred. However, he assessed the clinical process at some remove from the actual processes. Those processes might have been better observed if, for example, the sessions had been tape-recorded.

In sum, this highly informative study suffered from significant limitations that left unanswered central questions about the effectiveness of psychoanalysis. The severe limitation of the number of cases was one price that was paid for the thoroughness with which each case was studied.

Shortly after the Menninger study was initiated, researchers at other centers attempted to study far larger groups of analytic patients. In the next two chapters we look at their investigations.

6

The Columbia Psychoanalytic Center Research

In 1959 the Columbia University Psychoanalytic Clinic launched a research effort under the chairmanship of John Weber. Extensive data were collected, coded, and stored on computer tape about the characteristics and outcomes of 700 cases of psychoanalysis and 885 cases of psychotherapy conducted from 1945 to 1971. This was the first systematic study of an extensive sample of psychoanalytic patients.

Methods

Approximately 10 percent of the 9,000 patients who applied for low-fee analysis during the study period were accepted. They were treated by candidate-analysts under supervision. Most cases came by direct application to the clinic, but 326 patients were referred for psychotherapy from the Medical Center's Psychosomatic Service. Each patient provided a history to a psychiatric social worker and had a single screening interview with an experienced analyst. On the basis of these data, the clinic chief assigned the patient to psychoanalysis or psychotherapy. This method of selection, though not identical to the decision process in ordinary psychoanalytic practice, is sufficiently similar that conclusions about it may be extended reasonably to ordinary practice.

Data were collected from case records, from patients, analysts, and supervisors, and from institute records about the student-analysts. The clinic record was evaluated by nine graduate analyst-judges according to thirty-eight demographic variables (including family, marital, occupational, educational, medical, and psychiatric history), thirty-six clinical variables (including diagnosis, social relations, work, nature, and extent of symptomatic impairment), and nine ego-strength scales (Karush, Easser, Cooper, and Swerdloff, 1964). Evaluations reflected the records at the beginning of treatment and at termination or the analyst's graduation (when the clinic record was closed), whichever came first. The reliability of these judgments was similar to levels generally obtained in psychotherapy research (Cooper, Karush, Easser, and Swerdloff, 1966; Weber, Elinson, and Moss, 1966, 1967; Swerdloff, 1963). When treatment continued after the candidate's graduation, a twenty-eight-item questionnaire (including ego-strength and other clinical rating scales) was sent to the graduates for a retrospective assessment of the cases. Seventy-three percent returned completed questionnaires. By a wide margin, this is the largest pool of data collected about psychoanalysis.

Several reports of the outcomes of the cases and the characteristics of patients associated with these outcomes appeared in the literature over the years (Weber, Elinson, and Moss, 1966, 1967; Weber et al., 1974). These reports, however, were flawed methodologically. For example, the outcomes of terminated and unterminated cases were combined, and the statistical treatment of the data was inadequate. In an effort to correct for these limitations, the data were reanalyzed using more adequate research methods (Weber, Bachrach, and Solomon, 1985a,b; Bachrach, Weber, and Solomon, 1985). The total sample was divided into two parts: (1) cases treated between 1945 and 1961 for which data about outcomes were available from the graduate analyst–judges' review of the records, and (2) cases treated between 1962 and 1971 for whom information about outcomes was obtained directly from the treating analysts and patients. Similar measures and variables were employed in both samples, so data from the second sample could be used to partially replicate findings of the first sample. For both samples final outcomes were judged according to therapeutic benefit and analyzability.

Analyzability was assessed from a combination of three four-point scales in the questionnaire completed by analysts after termination for those cases continuing beyond graduation. The scales were:

Handling of psychological data;
Use of resources at termination;
Transference manifestations during treatment.

Therapeutic benefit was measured in three ways:

1. Circumstances of termination judged according to a four-point scale (mutual agreement that "maximum benefit" for this patient had been achieved; analyst felt that "maximum benefit" for this patient had not been achieved; patient felt improved and terminated unilaterally; patient felt unimproved and terminated unilaterally, decompensated, or analyst terminated the treatment because it seemed unsuitable — that is, the analyst believed another form of treatment to be more appropriate for whatever reason);

2. Direct clinical judgments of improvement (the graduate analyst–judges directly rated the cases that terminated before the analyst's graduation on a three-point scale of overall improvement, and the treating analysts rated their privately terminated cases on four-point scales of overall improvement and improvement in principal and secondary areas of disturbance);

3. Change scores (residual gain)[1] based on the graduate-analyst's evaluation of the clinic record at the beginning and end of the treatment on five-point scales of social relations, work gratification, principal and secondary area of disturbance, and ego strength. (This measure was available only for the first sample.)

Cases were retained for study only when there was complete and unequivocal information about circumstances of termination[2] and when analysts and clinical judges were confident about their assessments (as measured by confidence ratings).

Analyzability was assessed from a combination of three four-point scales in the questionnaire completed by analysts after termination for those cases continuing beyond graduation. Cases were considered to have developed an ana-

---

1. Simple measures of change were transformed into residual gain scores, which are statistically more reliable and were the contemporaneously recommended measure of change in psychotherapy (Fiske et al., 1970). This transformation does not alter clinical interpretation of the change score — that is, how patients compare at the end of treatment with the way they were at the beginning.

2. It might be thought that this would lead to the systematic exclusion of certain types of cases — for example, cases treated by less conscientious analysts or analysts whose countertransference responses to the patient interfered with their record keeping. Comparison of the characteristics of included and excluded cases did not show systematic differences. Cases terminating for "external reasons" were also analyzed separately, and no systematic differences were found between their characteristics and those of other cases. Nor was there a systematic difference between the cases started during various periods of time — cases begun in 1945, 1950, 1955, and so on.

lytic process when the analyst at termination simultaneously gave the analysand the highest rating on handling of psychological data (for example, dreams, fantasies, self-observations), use of resources, and transference manifestations during treatment. Thus a patient judged to have developed an analytic process would be rated as follows: (1) "The patient brought psychological data into the treatment because he recognized that it could be a source of understanding as well as relief"; (2) "The patient recognized that he had resources and learned to use them to achieve realistic adaptive growth as well as relief of personal suffering"; (3) "The patient often used insights gained in the transference to plan and execute changes in his everyday life and interpersonal relations." If a patient received a lower rating on any of these scales, he was not categorized as having developed an analytic process. For example, a patient who was given a rating of 1 on each of the first two scales but a 2 on the third ("Insights gained in the transference were often unclear and changes did not necessarily involve conscious planning by the patient") was not categorized as having developed an analytic process. The extent to which this measure captures what analysts typically mean by the concept of "analytic process" is questionable.

Using rigorous criteria about completeness and quality of data, the investigators were left with 295 analyses, 172 psychotherapies, and 114 psychosomatic cases treated by psychotherapy, all conducted between 1945 and 1961, that could be studied in the desired depth (Weber, Bachrach, and Solomon, 1985b). We now examine the findings for this smaller sample for which more comprehensive data were available. These patients were primarily middle class. They were distributed more or less equally in sex and marital status. They ranged in age from 18 to 59 at the beginning of treatment, with most between 20 and 34. Analytic patients were characterized as functioning within a neurotic range in their initial examination. Patients referred for psychotherapy were considered more impaired in motivation, psychopathology, and ability to participate in an analytic process.

The analyses were conducted by 159 candidates, with 98 treating one case, 54 treating two, and the rest three to five. Among the psychotherapy cases, 105 candidates treated one case, 35 treated two, and the rest three to five.

Findings

The highest levels of therapeutic benefit were found in analyses continuing beyond the candidates' graduation. Simply by virtue of being continued after graduation, these cases were the longest and were analyzed by the most advanced candidates. Fifty-two percent of these analyses terminated by "mutual agreement that maximum benefit had been achieved"; 91 percent were judged "improved," with equally substantial improvements in primary and secondary areas of disturbances. However, even in this best-outcome population, only 43 percent were judged to have developed an analytic process. Note, however, that the study's stringent criteria for "analytic process" probably excluded many patients whom analysts would ordinarily regard as being involved in an analytic process.

In contrast, analyses terminating before the candidates' graduation (thus the shortest analyses with the least experienced candidates) showed the least benefit. Only 26 percent terminated with maximum benefit, more than half terminated unilaterally, and 44 percent were unchanged or worse. In some ways the clinical outcomes of this group resembled those of psychosomatic patients treated by psychotherapy, about half of whom terminated unilaterally as unimproved and were judged unchanged or worse by their therapists. The findings of the study are summarized in Table 6.1. Effect sizes[3] for the clinic-terminated analytic cases were substantial (.4–.5 range), even though this was the least successful group of analysands, while effect sizes for the psychosomatic cases were more modest (.1–.3 range).

Twenty-eight patients switched treatment modality from psychoanalysis to psychotherapy following their analysts' graduation from the training program. Eighty-six percent of these patients were judged "improved"; 41 percent terminated with "maximum benefit."

Analyzability was only modestly associated with measures of therapeutic benefit (correlations were in the .3–.4 range). However, 89 percent of the analyzable patients terminated with "maximum benefit," 78 percent were judged "much improved," and 91 percent were diagnosed as functioning within a neurotic range. In contrast, only 47 percent of the patients who were not judged analyzable terminated with "maximum benefit," and only 40 percent were judged "much improved." Clearly, patients who were judged analyzable achieved greater therapeutic benefit than patients who were deemed not to have developed an analytic process, but only 40 percent of the patients who remained in analysis were characterized as analyzable at termination.

3. Effect size is a statistical method of estimating the magnitude of effects of interventions in a standardized manner. It permits comparisons between different groups or interventions (Cohen, 1988). Effect size is based on differences in measures before and after treatment. Therefore, in this sample, they were obtainable only for patients terminating while still in treatment in the clinic, where the graduate analyst–judges' initial and final assessments were available. In interpreting the effect-size numbers, the reader should know that anything less than .1 is considered negligible and anything over .4 substantial.

Table 6.1 Columbia Project: Selected Measures of Therapeutic Benefit

	Psychoanalysis			Psychotherapy	
	End private (N=77)	End clinic (N=158)	Switch (N=28)	Reparative (N=138)	Psychosomatic (N=96)
Rated improvement					
Much improved or improved	91%[a]	56%	86%[b]	61%	48%
No change	5%	42%	7%	37%	45%
Worse	4%	2%	7%	1%	6%
Circumstances of termination					
Maximum benefit	66%	26%	41%	41%	23%
Not maximum	21%	17%	23%	13%	17%
Improved	6%	16%	14%	9%	12%
Unimproved	7%	41%	23%	37%	48%
Primary area of disturbance					
Much improved	41%	n.a.	15%	n.a.	n.a.
Improved	49%	n.a.	54%	n.a.	n.a.
No change	10%	n.a.	23%	n.a.	n.a.
Worse	0%	n.a.	8%	n.a.	n.a.
Secondary area of disturbance					
Much improved	45%	n.a.	22%	n.a.	n.a.
Improved	37%	n.a.	56%	n.a.	n.a.
No change	15%	n.a.	11%	n.a.	n.a.
Worse	3%	n.a.	11%	n.a.	n.a.
Effect sizes					
X ego-strength scales	n.a.	.50	n.a.	.59	.32
Social relations	n.a.	.47	n.a.	.43	.11
Work gratification	n.a.	.45	n.a.	.50	.25
Primary area of disturbance	n.a.	.40	n.a.	.47	.27
Secondary area-disturbance	n.a.	.48	n.a.	.44	.18

Source: Weber et al., 1985a.

Note: n.a. = not available.

[a] 56% much improved; 35% improved.
[b] 36% much improved; 50% improved.

Four different senior analysts served as clinic chief during the study. None of them had expectations that were more than marginally predictive of analyzability or therapeutic benefit among the patients who were offered analysis. Nor did patients' qualities evaluated at the beginning of treatment, rudimentary characteristics of the candidate-analysts (for example, demographic, faculty ratings), or combinations of these factors predict differential outcome. This finding does not mean that clinical judgment and the various factors studied do not predict the outcome of analytic efforts in a general population of potential analytic patients. The cases in this study were all highly preselected for suitability for analysis. Prediction was thus being attempted within this narrow band. The situation is analogous to predicting the outcome of a baseball game. If the teams are reasonably matched — say, two major league teams — prediction is difficult. However, if the teams are clearly mismatched — say, a major league team and a Pony League team — the outcome is much easier to predict.

The treating analysts' ratings of patient qualities (for example, motivation, psychological-mindedness, affect tolerances) at termination were more substantially correlated with clinical outcome. Investigators found correlations in the .4–.5 range.

Treatment length was the only independently measured factor consistently correlated with therapeutic benefit and analyzability. Correlations ranged between .3 and .5.

An additional study by the same investigators examined thirty-six analyses and forty-one psychotherapies conducted by forty-three candidates between 1962 and 1971 for which there were complete and reliable data (Weber, Bachrach, and Solomon, 1985b). These cases were similar to the first sample except that they were rated initially as functioning at slightly higher levels. Detailed questionnaires, including rating scales, were distributed to candidates, patients, and supervisors. Data about the analyst were obtained from institute records and faculty ratings. Essentially the same variables were studied as with the first sample. However, the data were collected differently, using questionnaires distributed to analysts and patients without evaluations of case records by independent judges.

Although 96 percent of the analytic patients were considered improved, according to their analysts (with one-third terminating with "maximum benefit" and another quarter terminating mutually but without maximum benefit), only 50 percent of the analytic patients were judged to have developed an analytic process. Analyzability was again associated with therapeutic benefit: 78 percent of the analyzable patients were judged "much improved," in contrast to 29 percent who were judged not to have developed an analytic process.

Of the analyzable cases, 75 percent terminated with maximum benefit, as opposed to 38 percent of the unanalyzable cases. An incredible 100 percent of the analytic patients reported "satisfaction" with their treatments, according to a simple self-report questionnaire administered at termination.[4] These data reflect subjective satisfaction, not necessarily change.

The fate of these treatments was again essentially unpredictable from the perspective of initial evaluation. Neither characteristics of the individual patients nor traits of the analyst nor the predictions of supervisors meaningfully anticipated outcomes. Correlation between initial variable and outcome were in the .1 range (see Table 6.2). One exception to this general lack of correlation is that the magnitude of the relation between analyzability and therapeutic benefit appeared to be enhanced by the level of insight at termination (Bachrach, Weber, and Solomon, 1985). Again, treatment length was the only independently evaluated factor substantially related to analyzability and therapeutic benefit. Correlations were in the .4–.7 range.

Evaluation

The special merit of this study is the large number of cases studied. These cases represent the type of patients seen in psychoanalytic clinics. The study examined many clinically relevant factors from multiple perspectives. It included independent judgments of outcome measured by graduate analysts for some cases. Unfortunately, the cases that were most carefully assessed tended to be those judged to have terminated prematurely. The patients in the study were judged suitable for psychoanalysis, and the institute considered that psychoanalysis was taking place, though mostly at a novice level.

Limitations of the study included the failure to sharply define many germane terms and variables. Psychoanalytic terms continue to be the subject of enormous confusion (Reed, 1990; Klumpner, 1994), but in this study it is particularly hard to know whether various terms are used in a manner consistent with contemporary practice. It was difficult to ascertain the validity of the measures — that is, whether they captured the psychoanalytic constructs that they were intended to reflect. All of the analysts were inexperienced. The study did not provide for independent study of the treatment process, nor did it explore the analyst's personal contribution to the final result in more than a rudimentary way. The data were more descriptive than intrapsychic. The use

4. The reliability and validity of simple self-report measures have serious limitations and have recently come into serious question in systematic research (Weinhardt et al., 1998; Basco, Krebaum, and Rush, 1997; Stephane et al., 1997).

Table 6.2 Columbia Project: Selected Measures of Therapeutic Benefit

	Combined		Psychoanalysis		Psychotherapy	
	Analysis (N=36)	Psychotherapy (N=41)	End private (N=16)	End clinic (N=20)	Reparative (N=29)	Psychosomatic (N=12)
Rated improvement						
Much improved or improved	52%	29%	60%	38%	33%	22%
Improved	44%	50%	40%	50%	33%	78%
No change	0%	21%	0%	0%	33%	0%
Worse	4%	0%	0%	13%	0%	0%
Circumstances of termination						
Maximum benefit	33%	32%	56%	15%	28%	42%
Not maximum	25%	39%	38%	15%	41%	33%
Improved	19%	17%	0%	35%	17%	17%
Unimproved	22%	12%	0%	35%	14%	8%
Effect size						
X change in ego-strength scales	0.39	0.11	—	—	—	—
Patient satisfaction (end of clinic treatment)						
Very satisfied	59%	62%	—	—	—	—
Satisfied	41%	28%	—	—	—	—
Not satisfied	0%	10%	—	—	—	—
Harmful	0%	0%	—	—	—	—

Source: Weber et al., 1985b. In some cases, the data appear to be in error.

of low-fee clinic cases and of treating-analysts as final judges of the outcomes of the "better" cases introduces systematic biases. These biases were made worse because the use of large-scale, multivariate statistical methodologies tends to obscure individual differences, especially as related to individual analyst-analysand dyads.

Even though it made a major contribution, the Columbia project speaks in only the most general terms to the central question of who benefits from what kind of treatment. Its findings clearly suggest that psychoanalytic clinic patients functioning in a neurotic range receive substantial therapeutic benefit when treated by psychoanalytic candidates under supervision. More impaired patients treated in psychotherapy by the same candidates do not do as well. However, this was not a comparative study; the patients were referred for psychotherapy because they were considered unsuitable for psychoanalysis by a candidate. Hence one cannot tell from the study whether the superiority of psychoanalysis over psychotherapy was a function of the treatment modality, the limitations of the patients treated by psychotherapy, or some interaction of these factors. Because of the selection process, in general we learn more about the kinds of patients who benefit from psychoanalysis by a candidate than about the kinds of patients who do not. The indeterminate reliability of many of the scales also weakens these findings.

7

The Boston Psychoanalytic Institute
Prediction Studies

A third major group of studies of the outcome of psychoanalysis began in the 1950s and continues to this day. The project asks what factors observable during the diagnostic evaluation predict satisfactory analytic progress. In 1960 Peter Knapp and his coworkers reported a project designed to investigate the suitability for analysis of 100 supervised analytic cases. The investigation was limited because the cases were studied only through the first year of treatment. Inspired by Knapp's work, Sashin, Eldred, and Van Amerongen (1975) studied 130 low-fee control cases that were treated by 66 student-analysts between 1959 and 1966. The patients ranged in age from nineteen to forty at the beginning of treatment. They were well educated and about equally distributed between the sexes.

The cases were selected in the same way as other clinic cases at the Boston Institute. Applicants for treatment were seen first by one or two experienced analysts for screening interviews. These analysts presented their findings to an intake committee, which made the final recommendation. All of the patients in the study were seen initially as functioning within a neurotic range and judged suitable for analysis by a candidate. Thirty-nine cases were diagnosed as hysteric, 37 as obsessive-compulsive, and 17 as mixed neuroses; the remainder received other diagnoses. Outcomes were reported retrospectively by the treating analysts (sometimes years after the cases had terminated) according to overall global change, circumstances of termination, and six clinical scales. Distinctions between the development of an analytic process and therapeutic benefit were not studied.

Methods

The project sought to determine whether it was possible to predict clinical outcomes from data obtained in initial evaluation and if so, what factors are most useful in making such predictions. The methodology was as follows:

A structured questionnaire was sent to each analyst. It explored the circumstances of termination of the cases (Table 7.1), assessed overall change (Table 7.2), and evaluated aspects of the patient's state at termination, using scales developed by Knight (1941) that assess symptom restriction, symptom discomfort, work productivity, sexual adjustment, interpersonal relations, and insight (Table 7.3). Seventy-two percent of the analysts responded. Those who did not respond were telephoned. No significant differences were found in the circumstances of patient termination for the analysts who responded to the initial inquiry and those who required a telephone inquiry to get information.

Two graduate analysts and one advanced candidate–senior research fellow were trained to assess the initial evaluation data from the case records. They also made independent predictions about clinical outcomes. These assessments showed a high degree of reliability. Originally 171 patient factors were selected from the literature and clinical experience as potentially predictive of clinical outcomes, but only 46 qualities were retained that could be reliably evaluated from the case records.

Findings

The study showed that many of the patients benefited from analysis. However, it was difficult on the basis of the clinical case records to predict which patients would benefit.

Table 7.3 shows the rates of improvement according to the Knight scales (+4 represents the highest level of improvement, 0 represents no change, and −4 the greatest level of deterioration). At least two-thirds of the cases were considered to have improved, and the degree of improvement was associated with the circumstances of termination; that is, improvement rates were highest in cases terminating "by mutual consent."

Attempts to determine which factors in the initial evaluation were predictive of clinical outcomes were impeded because the reliability of the analysts' ratings was uncertain, compared with those of the trained raters at termination.

Table 7.1 Termination Status of the Boston Sample

Type of termination	% of sample
By mutual consent	69
Premature	27
Interminable	4

Table 7.2 Outcomes of the Boston Study

Outcome at termination	%
Improved	75
Unchanged	4
Worse	6
Unknown	15

Circumstances of termination were therefore used as the main criterion for therapeutic outcome. Only eight initial patient factors — each a simple characteristic of clinical history — predicted the circumstances of termination. Each of these may have been idiosyncratic to the sample. All other factors, including evaluation of anxiety tolerance, diagnosis, and the judges' predictions of clinical outcomes, failed to predict the circumstances of termination. Longer treatment length, however, was associated positively with more favorable clinical outcome for those cases that terminated satisfactorily as measured using the Knight scales, overall global change (rated by analyst), and circumstances of termination.

In further statistical analyses the investigators correlated 51 predictors with 12 outcome measures. Thus the investigators scrutinized 612 possible relations between initial patient qualities and outcomes. Only 3 percent of these correlations achieved conventional levels of statistical significance, and even these correlations were small (in the .2 range). On average they accounted for only about 5 percent of the outcome variances. Given the number of correlations studied, even these positive findings could have resulted from chance alone. The findings were reviewed in clinical terms, but the groupings "made little clinical sense" (Sashin, personal communication, 1979). Hence in this study it was not possible to effectively predict the outcomes of control analyses from the analysands' characteristics as judged in initial evaluation.

The lack of predictive capacity from initial findings observed in this study

Table 7.3 Boston Project: Distribution by Percent of Degree of Improvement on Outcome Measures

	−4	−3	−2	−1	0	+1	+2	+3	+4
Overall global change	0.0	0.0	2.3	3.9	6.9	12.3	38.5	36.2	0.0
Restriction of life functioning caused by symptoms	0.0	0.0	0.0	2.3	12.3	23.1	47.0	14.6	0.7
Subjective discomfort caused by symptoms	0.0	0.0	0.7	2.3	10.0	22.3	43.1	17.7	3.8
Work productivity	0.0	0.0	0.7	3.1	24.6	27.7	28.4	14.6	0.7
Sexual adjustment	0.0	0.0	0.0	0.7	17.7	23.1	32.3	18.5	7.7
Interpersonal relationships	0.0	0.0	0.0	1.4	20.8	36.2	34.6	6.2	0.7
Insight	0.0	0.0	0.0	2.1	21.6	29.2	31.4	14.6	0.7

Source: Sashin et al., 1975. The insight data seem to contain a small error.

has several possible meanings. The investigators suggest that the poor predictive showing may have been a function of the variability of the initial screening reports. More-thorough evaluations might have yielded more-effective prediction. Furthermore, a highly selected group of cases was studied. All the patients had been judged suitable for control analyses at a time when the clinic could be very selective in choosing cases. This limited the possibilities for discrimination within a very narrow band. At initial evaluation "almost every patient . . . seemed to have high motivation, no perversion, no history of severe depression, some awareness of not having lived up to his own capacities, no difficulty with feelings of merging or fusion, seemed to function well in some external area of his life and have some affect available" (Sashin, Eldred, and Van Amerongen, 1975, p. 352).

Evaluation

This study has the virtue of looking at a large number of cases. The investigators studied clinically germane variables. They carefully attended to interjudge and predictor reliability, sampling bias, and quality of the data. The patients were carefully selected as suitable for psychoanalysis by a student-analyst under supervision. The cases and the manner of selection are representative of psychoanalytic clinic practice. Because the analysts were all supervised by experienced analysts, it is reasonable to assume that the treatment reflected current standards of psychoanalytic practice, albeit at a novice level.

The study had significant limitations. It was retrospective. The analyses were all conducted by student-analysts. No provision was made for independent study of the treatment process, the analyst's personal contribution to the final result, or analyst bias in reporting outcome. Moreover, therapeutic benefit and the development of an analytic process were not distinguished. The data collected emphasized descriptive variables at the expense of intrapsychic factors. The use of low-fee clinic cases as study subjects introduced systematic clinical biases.

Overall, this is an interesting and thorough study. It does provide information about outcomes and points to areas for future study. Its essentially negative findings about our capacity to predict the outcome of analyses may simply reflect the fact that prediction was attempted within a narrow band of psychological difficulty. The patients studied were preselected by experienced clinicians as optimal candidates for analysis, so it is not surprising that a review of the data on which those clinicians based their judgments did not yield dramatically better predictions for the population studied. On the other hand, the negative finding could be interpreted to mean that other features of the analytic situation that had not been adequately explored previously might improve the prediction of analytic outcome. The group at the Boston Institute continued this search.

Further Boston Psychoanalytic Institute Studies

Beginning in 1972, Kantrowitz and her colleagues have conducted prospective studies of suitability for psychoanalysis, employing psychological testing as well as clinical methods of assessment (Kantrowitz, Singer, and Knapp, 1975; Kantrowitz, 1992, 1993; Kantrowitz et al., 1987a, 1989; Kantrowitz, Katz, and Paolitto, 1990a,b,c; Kantrowitz et al., 1986, 1987a,b). During the study period, eighty-four patients applied for low-fee analysis at the clinic of the Boston Psychoanalytic Institute, thirty-five were accepted as suitable for analysis by a student-analyst, and twenty-two eventually entered analysis. These twenty-two patients were given a battery of psychological tests (Rorschach, TAT, Draw-A-Person, Cole Animal Test, and selected WAIS verbal subtests) before beginning analysis. The test data were evaluated in terms of reality testing, level and quality of object relations, motivation for treatment, affect availability, and affect tolerance. These ratings were made independently by two psychologists (one psychoanalytically trained). Interrater reliabilities were high (in the .8 range). The clinic interviewers also rated each patient on the same scales. Because there were twelve different interviewers, it was impossible to determine the reliability of the ratings. All the patients were seen as functioning within a neurotic range by the intake committee (which was not privy to the psychological test findings). The patients were between twenty-one and thirty-two years old. They were well educated and approximately equally distributed between the sexes. At termination the initial test battery was repeated and a brief interview was conducted by the examiner. A year later a structured, tape-recorded interview was conducted with each treating analyst, designed to elicit data regarding the analytic process and its outcome.

Outcomes were evaluated according to the development of an analytic process and therapeutic benefit. Analyzability was judged from the follow-up interview with the treating analyst on a four-point scale: (1) analyzable with resolution of transference neurosis; (2) analyzable with partial resolution of transference neurosis; (3) analyzable with variations, partial resolution of transference neurosis; (4) unanalyzable. Therapeutic benefit was judged from the follow-up interview with the treating analyst in conjunction with changes in reality testing, object relations, and affect availability and tolerance revealed by the pre-posttermination psychological test data.

Table 7.2 shows the outcomes of these twenty-two cases. In terms of therapeutic benefit, only six cases were judged improved in affect organization. (All of these were also judged analyzable.) Testers' ratings did not correlate with those of the analyst on most of the other dimensions. Patients with initially high levels of object relations did not change more than patients with lower pretreatment levels, and neither psychological testing nor ratings of reality testing showed statistically significant change. Although these cases showed a wide range of therapeutic benefit, only 41 percent were judged to have developed an analytic process. Pretreatment assessments based upon psychological testing or clinical interview failed to predict level of analyzability or therapeutic benefit. One of the most striking findings of the study was that the patients, as a group, appeared far more impaired on the basis of the psychological test data than they seemed to the intake committee or to their analysts. For example, from the testers' perspective at initial evaluation, eight patients were seen as neurotic, three as "narcissistic characters," five "borderline," three "borderline with psychotic process," and three as "psychotic characters."

Kantrowitz and her collaborators (Kantrowitz et al., 1989; Kantrowitz, Katz, and Paolitto, 1990a,b,c) conducted semistructured interviews with seventeen of the original twenty-two cases five to ten years following termination. According to the patients' reports, three continued to improve without additional treatment, four remained stable, six had a mixed course, and four became worse despite further treatment. The patients who were originally judged to be analyzable did not maintain their gains longer than those who were judged not to have developed an analytic process. Thirteen of the seventeen cases were judged to have developed self-analytic capabilities. None of the original measures predicted level of functioning five and ten years after termination.

On the basis of these negative findings, which show a lack of correlation of patient variables with outcome, the authors stress the analyst-analysand "match" as crucial to clinical outcome.

Evaluation

The principal merit of this series of studies is its effort to explore the utility of extraclinical methods in order to assess suitability and therapeutic benefit in psychoanalysis. One might anticipate that this approach would have significant limitations. The battery of psychological tests used by the group is designed to measure a very wide range of psychological functions. Many of those functions would not be expected to predict psychoanalytic outcome. Nor do they provide appropriate measures of psychoanalytic results.

For example, it is much more pertinent for assessing psychoanalytic outcome to ask whether adequate ego resources are available to cope with daily living than to examine which defenses are evident in response to the standardized, but unusual, stimuli of the psychological test. Clinical analysis of the full Wechsler scales would provide a fuller assessment of the dimensions of intrapsychic structure and change central to psychoanalytic questions (Rapaport, Gill, and Schafer, 1945; Appelbaum, 1977). It would also allow replication of the psychological test findings of the Menninger study (Appelbaum, 1977). Assessments of reality testing based on the relatively unstructured psychological tests not only disagreed with the assessments of the screening and treating analysts but also did not correlate with the treating-analysts' assessment of outcome. The average correlation for the interviewers' predictions was twice as high as for the testers. This is precisely the reverse of findings in the Menninger study, which used the full, structured Wechsler scales for purposes of clinical evaluations. Thus some of the negative findings of the study may reflect its not using the full capacities of available psychological testing.

The follow-up data from the study are also seriously limited. Follow-up was obtained though a single semistructured two-hour interview five to ten years after termination of the analyses. There is serious question about the adequacy of such interviews to assess stability of change and self-analytic capacity. As we shall see later in reviewing the follow-up studies of Pfeffer (1959, 1961) and of Schlessinger and Robbins (1975, 1983), follow-up interviews regularly stimulate the reemergence of important aspects of the analytic situation, including intense transferences to the follow-up interviewer. This means that self reports obtained during follow-up interviews must be carefully assessed in terms of the impact of such transferences. The form of the interviews in the Boston study was less inviting of regression than were the interviews by Pfeffer and by Schlessinger and Robbins. However, given the strong evidence of regression and transferential distortion in later interviews, the reliability of the self reports obtained in the Boston study must be questioned. This issue is not addressed in the study.

The study's strengths include its prospective methodology, efforts to study the contribution of the analyst to the treatment process, emphasis on the importance of follow-up beyond termination, and consistently psychoanalytic focus. The sample studied is representative of psychoanalytic clinic practice. The emphasis on the distinction between analytic process and therapeutic benefit and the importance of the match between analysand and analyst addresses matters of importance to the practicing psychoanalyst. The study also benefits from frequent clinical discussions of interacting factors in many of the cases, which enlivens the reports in an unusual way for clinical-quantitative studies.

Limitations of the study include its small sample size, dependence on the work of student-analysts, problems of data gathering, sometimes imprecise rendering of psychoanalytic concepts, indeterminate reliability of clinical ratings, and the basing of positive conclusions on a combination of impressionistic data and negative findings. The central value of these studies lies in the beginning of systematic study of analysand-analyst interactions.

Subsequent Studies

In recent years Kantrowitz has continued these investigations, but her work has shifted away from quantitative statistics and psychological measures. Instead, she has explored case studies of supervision, her own analytic work, and interviews with twenty-six experienced analysts about shifts in their analyses resulting from their focus on self-analysis during intense transference-countertransference reactions.

Starting from the hypothesized importance of patient-analyst match suggested by the earlier studies' limitations in predicting outcome on the basis of patient variables alone, Kantrowitz has begun to elucidate aspects of the patient-analyst match described in her earlier work and to further elaborate details of the interaction of the character of the analyst and the patient. In "The Uniqueness of the Patient-Analyst Pair: Approaches for Elucidating the Analyst's Role" (1993), she describes three methods that the analyst should use in elucidating the nature of his or her impact on the patient: (1) awareness of the countertransferences, (2) awareness of the patient's perceptions of the analyst, and (3) awareness of similarities and differences of the analyst's character as contrasted with the patient's character.

Reviewing the longitudinal study of analyzability (Kantrowitz et al., 1989; Kantrowitz, Katz, and Paolitto, 1990c) Kantrowitz found three patterns of impedance of analytic work attributable to the match of analyst and patient: (1) similarities in traits and expression of conflict and/or conflict derivatives, as well as character defenses; (2) negative complementarity — the analyst and patient employ different modes of expression for conflict, as when the analyst has an unconscious defense against a particular conflict that the patient is *manifestly* struggling with; (3) facilitating (or compensatory) match — the analyst's character provides a quality for the patient to identify with or for the patient to use to modify a negative identification.

Kantrowitz discovered an additional area of facilitating match. In the earlier studies, overlapping blind spots were seen to stalemate analyses. All analysts have blind spots, and when these correspond with the patient's blind spots, enactments resulted. Studying analysts in supervision, Kantrowitz noted that these enactments could be identified. The analyst could conduct self-analysis or an inquiry with a colleague or supervisor about the source of these enactments. The analytic process could be reevaluated and the analysis continued. These situations were best understood not just in terms of countertransference but also in terms of the contrasting styles of analyst and patient. Moments of interaction are difficult to reproduce retrospectively. They can be described only in an ongoing, spontaneous manner. Uninterpreted enactments lead to an impasse.

In a subsequent work, "The Beneficial Aspects of the Patient-Analyst Match" (1995), Kantrowitz used case studies of supervision to explore the subtleties of the positive impact of the often nonverbal interactions of the patient-analyst pair. Her observations suggest that in addition to technical and empathic dimensions of the treatment, subtle aspects of character in conflict of both the patient and the analyst and their interplay constitute a central therapeutic factor in analytic work. She discovered new factors that facilitate matches. Like mothers felicitously matched to infants, an analyst with particular strengths, even if these were not verbalized, may stimulate development of similar strengths in the patient. If an analysand has a limited capacity for trust, self-observation, or affect tolerance, only an analyst with particular compensatory strengths in those areas might make the work possible. In Kantrowitz's view the match is fluid through the course of an analysis. A patient who is frightened of his or her aggression might do well at the beginning of an analysis with a gentle, accommodating analyst. When, as a result of analytic work, the patient becomes more comfortable expressing aggression, the gentle analyst might impede the development of the patient's capacity to express that aggression. This shift in the patient's capacity would have to be met by a corresponding understanding and emotional adaptation to the patient's new needs on the analyst's part. Kantrowitz describes the value of supervised work in evaluating such situations. Kantrowitz observes that Freud was likely mistaken that no analyst can succeed in analyzing what he has not resolved within himself. Analysts can grow and change in the course of their work with their patients by analyzing enactments that occur.

In "A Different View of the Therapeutic Process: The Impact of the Patient on the Analyst" (1996), Kantrowitz describes a study of an analyst's work with an aggressive man who had lost his father. The central point in the paper is that the analyst's personal conflicts were not resolved following termination of his analysis but were reawakened and brought into sharp focus in his work with this patient. The treating analyst and Kantrowitz describe the reawakening in the analyst of early childhood feelings in relation to his father. This resulted from an exploration of his countertransference reactions to the patient.

This careful study demonstrates how the psychoanalytic process is enriched by emphasizing the continued psychological work of the analyst in reaction to his patients.

In the book *The Patient's Impact on the Analyst* (1996), Kantrowitz describes the nature of the impact that the patient has on the analyst. She combines theoretical discussion with descriptions of interviews with twenty-six analysts concerning ongoing analytic work. She describes the different ways analysts go about things. Some keep their thoughts about their responses to themselves in their self-analysis. Others discuss details of their conflicted work with colleagues or other intimates. Kantrowitz noted, in the extended interviews with different analysts, that many, in conversation with her, developed new ideas about their reactions to their patients and how these reactions elucidated the nature of their patients' conflicts. The descriptions of these fully trained analysts document the idiosyncratic ways of analytic work and the contributions that their patients and colleagues make to their ongoing self-analytic work.

Thus Kantrowitz's recent studies have taken a different direction than the original longitudinal study done by her research group. Her methodology has shifted to case studies derived from supervision, her own work, and interviews of colleagues. Our sense is that these data are more useful in describing psychoanalytic process than the original study. However, many of the ideas that have evolved came from the original work, particularly ideas about patient-analyst match.

8

The New York Psychoanalytic Institute Studies

The investigations we have described so far are disappointing in that they do not provide an empirical basis for the decision of whether to recommend psychoanalysis for a particular patient. Also, they all require unsupported inferences beyond their empirical findings if they are to be applied to the work of experienced analysts with the type of patients whom this group of analysts is likely to work with. A group of researchers at the New York Psychoanalytic Institute is attempting to refine analysts' predictive abilities regarding treatment outcome. They have focused particularly on the relation between clinic findings and outcome and findings about the work of experienced practitioners.

Preliminary Studies

Erle (1979) and Erle and Goldberg (1984) conducted a series of pilot studies to refine hypotheses for a prospective study of psychoanalytic outcomes. They compared forty Treatment Center cases conducted by psychoanalytic candidates between 1967 and 1969 with forty-two cases treated by seven graduate analysts from around the United States. During the study period 870 patients applied for low-fee psychoanalysis at the Treatment Center, 50 were accepted, and 40 began analysis. Most of the patients were well educated and between twenty-one and twenty-eight years old at the time of initial intake.

*Table 8.1 Initial Diagnoses of the New York
Psychoanalytic Institute Treatment Center Sample*

Diagnosis	% of sample
Mixed character neuroses	37.5
Hysterical	27.5
Obsessional	15.0
Other	20.0

*Table 8.2 Outcomes from the New York Psychoanalytic Institute
Study*

Outcome	%
Analyzable with resolution of transference neurosis	9
Analyzable with partial resolution of transference neurosis	32
Analyzable with variations	23
Unanalyzable	36

Thirty were women. Most of the patients were diagnosed with neurotic-range psychopathology (see Table 8.1).

Each patient was interviewed first by one to three screening analysts, who assessed his or her suitability for analysis by a candidate. Questionable cases were reviewed by an intake committee composed of experienced analysts. In all cases the final recommendations were made by the medical director of the Treatment Center. Acceptance for analysis was decided finally by the treating candidate and supervisor. Thus patients who were analyzed had been through a rigorous selection process.

For each case the investigator studied the application forms, reports of intake interviews, record of the intake committee meeting, and periodic case reports; each case was discussed with the analyst and supervisor at varying intervals throughout the treatment. Each patient received a questionnaire during the study period, but too few responded to permit meaningful analysis. The quality of termination was judged by the analyst's impression of mutual satisfaction and the extent of work accomplished. The analysts and supervisors also rated each case in terms of suitability for a first or second training case. Based upon all these data, the investigator categorized the cases in terms of four classes of therapeutic benefit (Table 8.2) and suitability for a first or second supervised case (development of a classical analytic process; worth-

Table 8.3 Outcome of the New York Treatment Center Cases

Therapeutic outcome	%
Very good	7.5
Substantial benefit	52.5
Little change	17.5
No significant treatment process	22.5

Table 8.4 Analytic Outcome of New York Treatment Center Cases

Analytic outcome	%
Developed analytic process	42.5
Worthwhile but not classical	5.0
Unanalyzable	37.5
Unanalyzable in this situation	7.5
Remained in treatment but not a good case for a student	7.5

while, but not classical; unanalyzable; unanalyzable in this situation; remained in treatment, but not a good case for a student [see Table 8.4]).

Of the forty cases, twenty-five (63 percent) ended by mutual agreement, though only eleven were considered complete; the remaining cases were considered incomplete because of premature termination. Of the premature terminations, three were because of external events in the patients' lives, five were because the analyst terminated the analysis, and seven resulted from other unresolved difficulties. Three-fourths of the patients remained in analysis for more than two years. Longer treatment was associated with more favorable clinical outcome.

Consistent with other investigations, 60 percent (twenty-four) of the patients were judged at least substantially improved as a result of analysis (Table 8.3), though only seventeen (42.5 percent) were judged to have developed an analytic process (Table 8.4). Therapeutic results contrasted with the analytic results. Analytic process did correlate with therapeutic outcome. Fifteen of the seventeen cases judged to have developed an analytic process were rated as having derived substantial therapeutic benefit. Only nine of the twenty-three cases deemed unsuitable for analysis achieved substantial benefit.

In nearly half the cases the final diagnoses at termination differed from the initial impression. In every instance the new diagnoses was of more-severe pathology. When the pooled data of the intake committee were studied, it was found that only eight of the fourteen cases in which there initially were substantial questions turned out to be unsuitable for analysis.

Patient characteristics such as diagnosis and demographics did not correlate with clinical outcome. However, it should be borne in mind that this group of patients was selected carefully from a large pool of potential patients as suitable for analysis by candidates. Hence the variance was small in those characteristics that were believed to be clinically salient compared with the variance in the general population or even in the population of applicants to the Treatment Center.

The forty-two patients treated by experienced analysts differed in several ways from the forty patients in the Treatment Center group. Patients of the graduate analysts were older (eleven [26 percent] were above age twenty-nine), were more equally distributed between men and woman, and held a wider range of occupations. Their predominant diagnoses were character neuroses. Twenty-three (55 percent) were judged as having achieved substantial therapeutic benefit and twenty-five (60 percent) as having developed an analytic process. However, these figures include data from cases that were still in analysis when the data were collected. Of twenty-five terminated cases, only six were rated as having satisfactory terminations; the remaining nineteen were considered prematurely terminated. As with the Treatment Center cases, diagnosis of the underlying condition was regarded as more severe than at the start of the analyses; eighteen of the twenty-five cases were considered to have more severe pathology than was initially assessed.

Comparison of the two groups was further complicated because suitability carried   different meanings in the graduate group and the student group. For the former it referred to the patient's development of an analytic process with the analyst; for the student group suitability referred to patient's capacity to conform to the needs in the educational experience for the candidate.

The Work of Experienced Practitioners

Following these preliminary studies Erle and Goldberg (1984) investigated the work of sixteen experienced analysts, all of whom had completed analytic training more than five years before the study and had predominantly analytic practices. The researchers distributed a semistructured questionnaire, which asked for demographic information about the patients, a description of each analysis, the analytic process, and the basis for the decision to recommend analysis. During the study period (1973–77) the analysts reported seeing three to fifteen cases each, with an average of ten. Altogether, 160 cases were reported. The patients' symptomatology, though wide-ranging, was generally at a neurotic level. However, some patients were seen as ideal candidates for psychoanalysis, while others were taken into analysis for heroic reasons. The patients were well educated. There were more men (61 percent) than women. Their ages ranged from twenty to fifty-four. Nineteen began treatment with psychotherapy and were converted to analysis after periods of treatment ranging from one month to two years. The longest case was in analysis for twelve and a half years.

On the basis of the questionnaire responses the investigators categorized the cases according to analyzability and therapeutic benefit. When final data were collected, 97 of the 160 cases had terminated, and 25 of these cases were considered to have developed a classical analytic process; 27 required modifications or had a more limited result, and 34 were considered unanalyzable. All the cases judged analyzable at termination were also judged to have achieved at least moderate therapeutic benefit.

Again, in this sample, the correlation between analyzability and therapeutic benefit was unclear. Sixteen unanalyzable cases were judged to have good to excellent therapeutic benefit. All 15 cases that were rated as having no significant therapeutic benefit were also unanalyzable. Treatment length was favorably associated with positive outcomes: 76 percent of the terminated patients whose analyses lasted more than three years had good to excellent therapeutic benefit; only 37 percent of the unanalyzable cases were so rated.

Evaluation

These studies clearly probe the distinction between the development of an analytic process and therapeutic benefit. They are of particular interest because of their clear psychoanalytic perspective; their thoughtful discussions of the clinical, conceptual, and methodological issues; their recognition of the need to discriminate between the work of experienced and candidate analysts; and the effort to study the work of experienced analysts. The studies were also particularly relevant to clinical practice in that all the cases were carefully selected as suitable for analysis by the treating analysts themselves, and the graduate analysts were selected on the basis of their experience and reputation among their colleagues as skillful.

On the other hand, as the investigators acknowledge, the studies are only preliminary. The methodology was largely impressionistic and retrospective, and germane variables were specified in only rudimentary terms. Crucial terms and concepts (for example, therapeutic benefit, analytic process) were not standardized or operationalized. As the investigators wisely cautioned, the responses may reflect different types or degrees of change, comparable only to a given patient's previous level of functioning. Despite great care, these researchers found no way to ensure that they shared a common language with the analysts who responded to their questionnaires. It cannot be assumed that all terms were used in the same way, and in fact they probably were not. This raises serious questions about the reliability of judgments and the comparability of observations. In addition, the only independent evaluation of whether the treatments were actually psychoanalyses was the supervisory monitoring of student cases. In spite of the investigators' recognition of the problem of grouping terminated and unterminated cases together in assessing outcome, they often report such combined findings for the experienced analysts. Finally, while the findings were reported quantitatively, the statistical treatment of the data was limited to the simplest descriptive methods. The investigators did not use more-robust methods, such as correlational analyses, to explore their data.

9

Studies of Child and Adolescent Analysis

The study of child and adolescent analysis has always been placed somewhat apart from work with adults. Freud's (1909) pessimism that children could be analyzed in ways that approximated analytic work with adults was echoed in Anna Freud's (1927) early recommendations about child psychoanalysis. Melaine Klein (1921, 1961) consistently recommended a technique in working with children that was essentially identical to her recommendation for working with adults, except that the free association of adults was replaced by play in children. For many years Klein's ideas had little impact on the clinical work of any but her followers, but by the 1960s Anna Freud and her coworkers had come to view child and adolescent analysis as much more like the analysis of adults than her early contributions suggested. Some child analysts adopted the position that many of the variations in technique that were supposed to be necessary reflected an avoidance of the child's psychological world (Kohrman et al., 1971), while others adopted the position that the young child's internal world was so contingent on the family that attempts to do independent psychological work, at least with young children, were doomed from the start (Furman, 1957). Despite many years of controversy (Harley, 1986), there is still less consensus among analysts of children and adolescents than among analysts of adults about the central features of processes that should be called psychoanalysis, such as the centrality of the transference and the interpretive stances of the analyst. This lack of consensus means that special care is needed in interpreting the results of systematic investigations of child and adolescent analysis because the nature of the process may vary even more than for adult analysis.

A second group of problems that confronts child analysis is the interpretation of change. Systematic investigators of adult analyses have generally assumed that little change would have occurred in the patient without treatment. This is consistent with the psychoanalytic view that psychopathology represents aspects of the personality that fail to adapt to changing external reality. It is also consistent with the widespread, but probably mistaken, view that significant psychological development does not ordinarily continue in adulthood (Costa and McCrae, 1989; Galatzer-Levy and Cohler, 1993a). Describing the predictable changes, continuities, and failures of change in children, whether well or disturbed, is far more difficult than is similar description in adults (Rutter and Rutter, 1993). The widespread belief that the child may outgrow his pathology becomes a serious methodological challenge in systematically assessing child analyses.

A related issue involves the problems of assessing the outcome of psychoanalyses. With regard to adults, one may ask both to what extent they have changed as a result of analysis and to what extent their current functioning approximates some ideal of psychological well-being, usually thought of as psychological maturity. Although the latter view has been criticized by those who believe that development is lifelong, it certainly is not directly applicable to children, who would not be expected to reach psychological maturity as a result of analysis. Furthermore, except in extremely broad outline, it is impossible to establish age-appropriate levels of psychological function in childhood (Freud, 1965). Because development is the major task of childhood, Anna Freud proposed that the capacity to continue psychological development be the major measure of psychological health during this period. Although many child analysts have adopted this view, the capacity for development is even more difficult to establish than is the current developmental level. Systematic demonstration of the stable emergence of this capacity would be an enormous challenge in any systematic study. In spite, or perhaps because, of these enormous difficulties, two of the methodologically most sophisticated investigations of psychoanalysis have studied children and adolescents. Although neither of them adequately addresses all the problems of studying child analysis, they are surprisingly successful in addressing important issues.

Intensive and Weekly Work Compared

In an elegant study, Christopher Heinicke (1965) compared the thera-peutic results of intensive work with those of weekly sessions in the treatment of school-aged children with emotional disturbances of learning. Eight children were assigned to more- or less-intensive treatments. Evaluations were based on the Diagnostic Profile (see Chapter 15), as well as on standardized tests of scholastic achievement and intellectual ability. Testing was performed at the start of treatment, one year into treatment, at its termination, and a year after completion of therapy. Test results from the children's schools were used at two-year follow-up. Each child was interviewed by a psychiatrist at the beginning and end of treatment. Information about school function was also obtained through school visits initially, at one year into the treatment, at termination, and one and two years after termination. Although the therapists intended to use the same approach to work with both groups of children, the different material that emerged in the treatments as a function of their intensity inevitably caused the therapists' approaches to diverge. Detailed, structured descriptions were recorded for each session. The study was further strengthened by the author's detailed report of a sample case, which allows the reader to understand in detail both how he uses psychoanalytic terms and how inferences are made from clinical occurrences to more abstract formulations. Thus a vast amount of descriptive, psychoanalytic, and test data was collected about each subject.

FINDINGS

The findings of the study strongly support the value of more-intensive treatment. Not only do they demonstrate greater improvement at the time of termination, but these improvements were sustained and extended following termination. The findings also provide convincing evidence that the more intensively treated children consistently showed a significant advantage at termination and follow-up in the areas of libidinal-phase dominance and growth of self-esteem. After termination the children seen more intensively showed a greater capacity to form more mature object ties; were more comfortably assertive (as opposed to passively defensive); made more progress in ego integration, differentiation, and adaptation; had better balanced defenses that were less dependent on the support of others; and showed greater capacity for imaginative play, wider affectivity, more capacity for humor and self-observation, and more self-reliance. At the two-year follow-up, initially evident fixations persisted for both groups of children. But in the children who were seen intensively these fixations were less intense, produced more adaptive derivatives, and were better integrated into overall functioning. Continued conflicts were less well resolved by the less intensively treated youngsters.

In terms of academic performance, a striking difference between the two treatments was evident that strongly points to a different process in the two forms of therapy. During the first year of therapy the rate of improvement in reading ability decreased for the children in intensive treatment, while it improved significantly for youngsters in less frequent therapy. By the end of therapy the rates of improvement of the two groups were comparable. After the completion of treatment the rate of improvement of the less intensively treated patients dropped precipitously, followed by recovery to approximately end-of-treatment levels by the second-year follow-up. In contrast, for the more intensively treated youngsters the rate of improvement rose steadily after the end of treatment. Not only was the end result more satisfactory, but the process of improvement was different.

CRITIQUE

This study is valuable from many points of view. Its subjects suffered from significant neurotic-range symptoms. They were treated by well-trained therapists who carefully documented their work so that we have a fair degree of confidence that psychoanalysis on the model of Anna Freud was actually being performed. Variables were clearly defined within the then-current conceptual framework, although operational definitions were lacking. Data were systematically collected from multiple sources. Statistical methods were used where appropriate.

Problematic features of the study stem primarily from the nonquantitative nature of the variables measured so that the question of whether chance variation led to some of the qualitatively described findings remains unaddressed. Comparisons are limited to the difference between psychodynamic treatments of two intensities. Although it seems reasonable to believe that patients treated infrequently would do at least as well as untreated patients, the study provides no clear data on this comparison.

A Study of Very Disturbed Adolescents

Among the patients most evidently in need of assistance, very disturbed adolescents stand out. The long history of attempts to do psychoanalytic work with such patients not only is described in the work of such analytic pioneers as Erik Erikson (1968), August Aichorn (1935), and Kurt Eissler (1950, 1958) but also is recorded in popular books and films like *I Never Promised You a*

Rose Garden, David and Lisa, and *Ordinary People.* Moses Laufer and his coworkers in London (Laufer and Laufer, 1989) have described their analytic experience with a group of eleven severely disturbed adolescents whose pathology included life-endangering actions, suicide attempts, and substance abuse. The population was also unusual among psychoanalytic patients in that many of the youngsters were poor. This work seeks to comprehend adolescent disturbance as a breakdown in development that takes place following puberty when the actualization of fantasies that were impossible in an immature body has become possible. The focus of adolescent psychological functioning is regarded as the "central masturbation fantasy," a theme that not only runs through masturbatory fantasies themselves but also affects many aspects of the youngster's mental and concrete activity (Laufer and Laufer, 1984). The study extensively illustrates how this understanding can be applied to clinical material. Each of the cases discussed is described by the treating analyst. In some instances considerable samples of clinical process are provided.

An amazing feature of this publication, which seems to have gone unnoticed by the authors, is that none of the cases described ended well. It could be argued that the simple survival of all the patients treated is a testament to the usefulness of the analytic intervention — sustaining treatment with many of these youngsters was an unusual accomplishment. Still, none of the patients described reached an analytic or even a therapeutic termination. At the end of the treatment none was functioning within a range not characterized by significant distress and maladaptation. It is difficult to see the case material as providing evidence to support the authors' views of the understanding and technical management of adolescents, though they clearly believe that these cases provide favorable evidence for those views.

Child and Adolescent Cases

Analysts of children and adolescents are often confronted with the question of whether they are practicing real analysis or psychoanalytically informed therapy (Freud, 1965.) This long-lived issue in child analysis results partly from the institutional status of child and adolescent psychoanalysis and partly from beliefs about the need to alter standard adult psychoanalytic technique in working with children (Kohrman, Fineberg, Gelman, and Weiss, 1971). Demonstrating that psychoanalytic work is possible with children and adolescents by showing cases in which such work has been done was the goal of two collections of case reports (Harley, 1974; Geleerd, 1967). However, because the editors chose to present especially problematic and challenging cases, both volumes tend to emphasize the difficulties and limitations of work with young people. There are surprisingly few descriptions in the psychoanalytic literature of "ordinary" child and adolescent analyses (Galatzer-Levy, 1985).

The Anna Freud Center Study

No previous major study has tried to identify predictors of success in child analytic treatment or to distinguish between those disorders in children that would do better with the intensive treatment of analysis versus nonintensive treatment or some form of dynamic therapy other than analysis. Peter Fonagy and Mary Target have retrospectively studied 763 cases treated at the Anna Freud Center to answer some of these questions (Fonagy and Target, 1994, 1996; Target and Fonagy, 1994). They compared children treated intensively with children, matched by diagnosis, age, and other pertinent variables, treated less intensively. They also compared many variables in terms of their impact on the outcome and course of the treatments of some of the disorders. They found that analysis was particularly effective with seriously disturbed children under age twelve, particularly those suffering from psychiatric disorders that involve anxiety.

The Anna Freud Center has long been interested in documenting features of child analysis and has maintained extraordinarily thorough and systematic treatment and diagnostic records. Because of these extensive records, the large number of case studies, the generally advanced experience of the analysts that treated the children, and the wide array of conditions that were treated with both intensive analytic therapy and nonintensive briefer treatments, the authors have been able to produce excellent statistical evidence of what types of childhood disorders lend themselves to analysis and what types would be better treated with less-intensive treatment. This study is also unique among analytic investigations in that, although the analytic framework of the investigation is preserved, measures familiar to psychiatric investigators are used to describe the changes in the children.

They studied more than two hundred parameters in each of the 763 cases. Although they required that data be available on each variable in order to meet selection criteria for the study, there is no evidence that less-well-documented cases were a different population. The measures fell into three categories:

1. *Demographic.* This included biographical and social information on child and family, the family's cultural background and socioeconomic status, and the past and present mental health of each parent.
2. *Diagnostic.* Conclusions were based on the psychoanalytic charts, using "standard psychiatric criteria." DSM III-R diagnoses on Axis I and Axis II

were made in all cases, and the reliability of these judgments was checked by independent assignments made by three senior child psychiatrists working in the United States and Great Britain. Also, each child's level of functioning was rated on the Hampstead Child Adaptation Measure (HCAM), designed to test general adjustment. A 100-point rating scale was developed based on Luborsky's Health-Sickness Rating Scale (HSRS) and the psychometric structure derived from the C.G.A.S. (Children's Global Assessment Scale; Shaffer et al., 1983) developed by Shaffer with the DSM III-R system. A manual was compiled for rating procedures with the Hampstead Measure, and the scale has been used with a high degree of reliability.

3. *Clinical.* Among the etiological factors recorded were: loss of important figures, separation from caregivers, and significant disturbances in family relationships in early childhood. Other information concerned characteristics of the therapist (years of experience), the treatment (frequency, duration, interruption, and so on), and reasons for termination. Treatments terminated following agreement between therapist and patient and/or parent were distinguished from those ended at the request of the parent or child against the advice of the therapist.

The investigators used three measures of outcome:

1. The continued significant presence of psychiatric problems led to the designation of the child as a case. A child was considered to be a case if he or she still met criteria for any psychiatric disorder and had an HCAM rating below 70. The authors offer good rationale for bifurcating cases and noncases at termination.
2. There had to be a statistically reliable change in the adaptation level from the beginning to the end of treatment as measured by the HCAM. In these data, a difference of 8–10 points, depending on the subgroup, meant that the child showed real improvement, even though he or she might still be psychiatrically diagnosable.
3. Children with HCAM ratings of less than 68 at termination were regarded as still being clinical cases. Changes in the HCAM ratings were regarded as a continuous variable in predictions of the extent of improvement.

RESULTS

The results reported are complex. The outcomes of child analyses were shown to vary with diagnostic category, length of treatment, and age of the patient. Overall, among those children whose treatment continued for at least six months, psychoanalysis was associated with the removal of all diagnosis in at least 38 percent of the cases, psychotherapy in at least 34 percent of the cases. (These figures are conservative because the information at termination was insufficient for definite diagnoses in one-third of the cases.) Psychoanalysis moved 56 percent of the children from the dysfunctional to the functional group on the HCAM measure, compared with 44 percent of those who received psychotherapy. Clinically significant improvements were observed in 62 percent of the children treated intensively and in 49 percent of those offered nonintensive treatment. Variables related to the likelihood of improvement in the full sample were longer treatment, an emotional rather than a disruptive disorder, an intact family, and younger age. Children with atypical personalities or borderline disorders showed less improvement. Those whose mothers had been in analysis improved considerably more, as did children whose parents were receiving analytically informed guidance along with the child's treatment. Children of higher social class improved somewhat more.

In order to be clearer about the effectiveness of psychoanalytic treatment in different types of cases, the authors divided their sample according to diagnostic group and age and tried to match other important variables within the groups thus created. Children who dropped out of treatment within the first six months tended to fail to respond to psychoanalysis. Children in nonintensive therapy were more likely to drop out than those in intensive therapy,[1] and attrition was highest among adolescents and children with disruptive disorders, who were most difficult to keep in treatment. If they could be kept in treatment, the likelihood of their successful outcome was greatly increased, but the investigators were unable to predict which children within the disruptive group were most likely to terminate treatment prematurely. After excluding those children who had left within the first six months, 38 percent of the children in nonintensive treatment and 18 percent of those in intensive treatment were the same or worse in terms of general adaptation at the end of their treatment. A substantial proportion of the improvement can be accounted for by specific diagnoses. Thus 33 percent of the mentally retarded children, 28 percent of the children with pervasive developmental disorders (such as autism), 41 percent of those with attention or hyperactivity disorders, and 24 percent of conduct-disorder children improved significantly, but without losing all their diagnoses or moving into the functional range in the HCAM. If one excludes these children (70) from the sample, then 66 percent of the children

---

1. This is a particularly clinically important finding because in attempting to keep children in treatment, therapists commonly recommend less intensive therapies in the hope that they will win the cooperation of the child and family by making fewer demands for attendance.

treated intensively and 50 percent of the children treated nonintensively showed significant improvement.

Age had a significant effect on the likelihood of improvement. Of the children under six, 63 percent showed improvement on the HCAM score; comparable figures were 53 percent for latency-age children and 47 percent for adolescents. It was demonstrated that this finding did not have to be an artifact of the severity of diagnosis. Adolescents benefited as much or more from nonintensive treatment (one or two sessions a week) as from a more frequent schedule, but younger children did better in four-to-five-times-a-week treatment.

There were significant findings in the families of the children that affected outcome. For example, for children under six, a history of mental illness in the mother predicted worse outcome. Sleep disorders, phobias, and significant medical history in parents were associated with good outcome. In contrast, latency-age children did well when the mother *did* have a mental disorder. With adolescents, several parental mental health issues were significant predictors. An antisocial mother or father predicted worse outcome, but anxiety in the father was associated with improvement. Difficulties in peer relationships and disruptive behavior at school predicted poor outcome. These findings suggest that the pathological factors and their accessibility to treatment differed according to age, and that predictors of outcome of child therapy must be considered within a developmental framework.

When the children with emotional disorders were compared with those with disruptive disorders, it was found that the former group did better as a whole. The major difference in outcome between the two groups could be accounted for by their capacity to remain in treatment. When intensive treatment (treatment five times a week for three years or more) was successfully administered to disruptive children, they showed gains equivalent to those of the emotionally disordered children. Within the disruptive group, improvement was greatest for children with oppositional defiant disorder and lowest for those with conduct disorders.

Other contextual factors were important in predicting outcome. For example, children were likely to do less well if they had been in foster care, if the child's mother had a history of anxiety disorder, and if the child was underachieving at school. Consistently, children were likely to do better if the mother was also receiving treatment at the center and if the child had been in the center's nursery school.

Among the children with emotional disorders, certain subgroups did better than others. Specific anxiety disorders, a parental psychiatric history, and female gender predicted better outcome. Depressive disorders (where particularly poor outcome was associated with encopresis), conduct disorder, being an only child, and having a mother with a personality disorder all predicted poorer outcome. Intensive treatment was particularly beneficial when the disorder was severe or complicated by other disorders or pathology. The less severe group improved equally in nonintensive or intensive therapy.

Despite the limitations of this study, the results are as convincing as those of any other systematic study of long-term treatment. The findings include these major features:

1. Younger children improve during psychodynamic treatment and do even better with four-to-five-times-weekly sessions.
2. Anxiety disorders, with particular specific symptoms rather than pervasive symptoms, are associated with a good prognosis even if the primary diagnosis is a disruptive disorder.
3. Children with pervasive developmental disorders do not do well even with prolonged intensive psychodynamic treatment.
4. Children with emotional disorders with severe and pervasive symptomatology respond well to intensive treatment but much less well to nonintensive psychotherapy.

The authors propose a model of psychic change based on their understanding of how psychoanalysis has been applied at the Anna Freud Center and some of the findings of their retrospective study. They posit two mechanisms of psychic change, based respectively on mental representations and the psychological processes that create and affect them. Children with serious character pathology (borderline spectrum) sacrifice their capacity to conceive of self and other representations in their effort to adapt to emotional environments where their caregivers are either lacking or destructive. Intensive clinical work at the Anna Freud Center with such children always represents a combination of insight-oriented therapy and developmental help, which can be conceived of as rehabilitative as opposed to insight-oriented. The authors attribute improvement in the severe character pathologies and pervasive anxiety disorders as stemming from intensive rehabilitative work with those children who were able to maintain intensive treatment for periods longer than six months and, optimally, two or three years. Less-intensive treatment is less likely to tackle developmental anomalies associated with the vulnerability of children with the more severe disorders. By contrast, less severe disturbances are likely to benefit more from intensive treatment than from nonintensive treatment. Less seriously disturbed children did as well with nonintensive treatment as intensive. Also, brief treatments might correct disturbances of mental representation but would not provide the child with adequate input for the rehabilitative function of therapy. A self-reflective psychotherapeutic approach would be a source of confusion and frustration for individuals with disruptive disorders.

CRITIQUE

The monumental efforts of the Anna Freud Center investigators produced monumental results. These are clearly the best studies available of ordinary psychoanalytic cases. They carry a high degree of credibility, both because of their methodological sophistication and because their complex findings, including important results not anticipated by the investigators, indicate that the results stem from within the data rather than from the presuppositions of the researchers.

Certain limitations, however, are clear from the outset. Cases were not randomly assigned to intensive and less intensive treatment groups (although the investigators go a long way toward demonstrating the equivalence of the two groups). Although diagnostic and outcome measures were assessed by independent raters on the basis of the patients charts, the data on which they made these assessments were prepared by the children's therapists. Many of the cases were treated by student-therapists, and children of mental health professionals and VIPs were excluded from the study. Although the ideas of the Anna Freud Center's analysts and therapists have been widely disseminated (Sandler, Kennedy, and Tyson, 1980) and the close scrutiny of work at the center would favor uniform procedures, the interventions provided either in analysis or in therapy remain unspecified. Furthermore, cases were treated over an extended period; changes in concepts of technique may have resulted in the use of significantly different methods at different points in time. To the investigators' credit, they are extremely careful to point out methodological difficulties in their research and carefully restrict their conclusions on the basis of these limitations.

From a psychoanalytic perspective, a limitation of this study is that the measures of outcome were in terms of surface functioning. There was no examination of the relation between analytic process and outcome. A further study to be undertaken in the future will work on ways of coding the children's adjustment in analytic terms, using a method based on the Anna Freud Diagnostic Profile. It would be interesting to discover whether there is a relation between good analytic work and positive analytic or therapeutic outcome. So far, studies of adult psychoanalyses have generally failed to show such a relationship.

Negative findings about the analysis of adolescents may reflect the study's focus on symptomatology at the expense of a more intrapsychic focus. Clinical experience with adolescents suggests that the youngsters who benefit most are, like many adult analysands, people who function on a high level from the point of view of external descriptions. The authors do not adequately address this limitation of their study.

This excellent comprehensive study, with its many interesting findings, suggests that intensive psychoanalytic psychotherapy is useful for a variety of childhood disorders. There is strong evidence that intensive therapy is better than nonintensive therapy for a whole host of conditions. These findings now need to be tested in a prospective study. At this point, it would be useful to compare nonanalytic, nonintensive therapies with analytic therapies in the categories that have been suggested. It is encouraging for analysts to expect that emotional disorders and a variety of disruptive disorders might be better handled by intensive analytic therapy.

Summary

Taken together, these studies strongly suggest that psychoanalysis is a useful treatment for children with emotional disorders. It produces qualitatively different and more desirable outcomes than less intensive forms of therapy. Children with behavioral disorders are also likely to benefit if they continue in treatment for an adequate length of time. Systematic study fails to show the effectiveness of analysis in adolescence, but this may well be an artifact of the methods used to study adolescent analyses.

IO

Series of Patients with Specific Conditions

One classical approach to the study of pathology is to examine a series of patients who are similar in diagnosis, age, treatment approach, or other significant features of their situation in the hope of discovering commonalities among the cases. Although there have been numerous reports of very small numbers of similar cases, in only a few instances have analysts looked at larger numbers of patients in this fashion. In this chapter we review several such studies.

The Good Hysteric

A study that stimulated the hope that more-careful initial evaluations might lead to more effective prescriptions of analysis began in Boston in the 1950s. Elizabeth Zetzel had observed that patients initially diagnosed as hysterics often had turbulent, brief, and unsuccessful analyses. Clinical experience and the early results of the Boston studies of analyzability (see Chapter 7) made it clear that "neither hysterical symptomatology nor apparent hysterical character structure bears conclusive evidence of the relatively unmodified ego which can best respond to traditional psychoanalysis" (Zetzel, 1968, p. 231). Close investigation of the patients presenting with hysterical symptoms and personality traits led her to divide the population of such patients with whom analyses were attempted into four groups:

True good hysterics: prepared and ready for all aspects of traditional psychoanalysis.
Potential good hysterics: with development, symptomatology, and character
structure suggesting an analyzable hysterical disorder, but less fully prepared to commit to an analytic situation.
Women with underlying depressive character structure but manifest hysterical
symptomatology that disguises their deeper pathology.
Women with pseudo-oedipal and pseudogenital organization who seldom
meet important criteria for analyzability.

Zetzel asked whether patients could be assigned to one of these groups on the
basis of the initial information gathered about them. From retrospective study
of their clinic records, she found that the cases were quite different. Those
patients who did well in psychoanalysis demonstrated an ability to form a
positive therapeutic alliance, substantial mastery of ambivalence in the early
mother-child relationship, a genuine one-to-one relationship with both parents, and attempts to approach actually available objects with realistic ends.
The second group presented as younger, less successful academically and professionally, and more conflicted about dependency, with fewer egosyntonic
obsessional defenses. The most disturbed patients, Zetzel's fourth group, often
had major problems in their developmental history, such as serious separation
from a parent in the first four years of life, serious parental psychopathology,
prolonged childhood illness, continuing hostile-dependent relationship with
mother, and absence of current meaningful object relations.

This study presents a wealth of clinical ideas and experience that comes only
from examining the vast clinical experience that a psychoanalytic clinic can
achieve. It has had considerable impact on clinical practice in the United
States, where most practitioners are now aware that manifestly hysterical
presentation does not necessarily indicate oedipal conflict as the central issue
of the patient's psychology or analyzability along classical lines. Zetzel's decision not to present her data statistically opens questions of the reliability of
her findings.

The San Francisco Study of Homosexuality

In an unusual study of patients seen by experienced analysts in private
practice, Irving Bieber and his coworkers (Bieber et al., 1962) examined the
psychology and treatment of more than one hundred homosexual men. The
study makes interesting reading in light of current views about homosexual
men (Isay, 1989; R. Friedman, 1988; Cohler and Galatzer-Levy, in press) in

that its empirical findings are in many ways consistent with these later views. However, the authors' formulations of the causal relation among these findings are not consistent with these more contemporary views, which emphasize how intrinsic aspects of the future homosexual lead to disturbed relations with important figures in childhood. The Bieber study, in contrast, concludes that the psychogenesis of homosexuality lies in these disturbed relationships.

The Bieber study is one of the very few in the psychoanalytic literature to compare a group of patients in psychoanalysis with a control group. The 106 index patients, selected because they were overtly homosexual, were contrasted with a similar-sized group of other patients from the analysts' own practices. Data were collected though a series of questionnaires administered to the analysts. The study focused primarily on the etiology and dynamics of the homosexuality. Its conclusions suggested that a large majority of homosexual patients experienced close-binding intimate relationships with their mothers.

The study was significantly flawed by the authors' inattention to then-available data about homosexuality in men. Kinsey (Kinsey, Pomeroy, and Martin, 1948) had clearly demonstrated that homosexual activity in men existed as a continuum of behaviors, with many men engaging in both homosexual and heterosexual activities for extended periods of time; the dichotomous view that sexuality was either homoerotic or heteroerotic was not supported. Yet in their discussion, Bieber and his colleagues treat homosexuality as if it were a unitary state. Of the 27 percent of the study sample who adopted a heterosexual orientation at the end of treatment, only 19 percent had been exclusively homosexual in their behavior prior to treatment, and more than half had been actively bisexual (Haldeman, 1994). The question of whether the proportion of men changing sexual orientation differed from what would be expected by chance, given the natural history of men's sexual behavior, is not addressed.

The study does not focus primarily on efficacy. It poses the interesting retrospective problem that the goal of changing sexual orientation would not be regarded as appropriate by many contemporary analysts. The treatments were varied in frequency, from once a week to five times per week. With all this in mind, the authors report a little less than a third of the homosexual patients becoming exclusively heterosexual in the course of their treatments.

Self Psychology Demonstrated

Competing psychoanalytic views are often difficult to define precisely. Their precise clinical implications and the differential effects of their use are commonly left unspecified and remain unknown. The introduction of "self psychology" by Heinz Kohut (1966, 1968, 1971, 1977) raised questions about the validity of Kohut's conceptualization of narcissistic personality disorders (disorders of the self), the nature of the technique he proposed, and the effectiveness of his technique in treating these disorders. In an attempt to address these issues, a group of his students developed a casebook describing six analyses, each by a different analyst (Goldberg, 1978). The authors took elaborate care in preparing the material to ensure both the anonymity of the patients and the authenticity of the case descriptions. Each case was described with particular emphasis on psychoanalytic technique, the self psychology formulation of the case, and analytic process. All six patients would probably be diagnosed as suffering from narcissistic personality disorders, though several had borderline features. The book succeeds in demonstrating the current ideas about technique among Kohut's early students. In each case the authors demonstrate significant change in the patient's narcissistic pathology, including increased empathy with family members and with themselves. Situations that had previously thrown them into significant symptomatic states, such as separations and rebuffs, often became manageable with some distress and mild regression. Object relations improved. In several cases the capacity for humor and creativity (regarded by self psychologists as mature forms of narcissism [Kohut, 1971]) emerged as a result of the analysis.

Although there is reason to believe that many of these patients would not have responded well to traditional psychoanalytic interventions, the case reports do not provide clear empirical evidence that interpretations based on self psychology were the operative force in change, or that the changes would not have occurred with more-traditional treatment techniques. The authors put forward alternative hypotheses to account for aspects of the patients' clinical course, usually formulated in terms of clinical ego psychology. However, many of these formulations appear to be strawmen, designed more to show the superiority of self psychology ideas than to provide serious challenges to them.

Other Published Case Reports

The literature of psychoanalysis contains many descriptions of psychoanalytic work, which might be used as a database of cases from which conclusions could be carefully drawn about certain types of patients. Naturally, this process would have to proceed with caution because cases are published precisely because they are unusual, challenging, illustrative of a new point of view, or otherwise special and are therefore not representative of some underlying population. In addition, the reporting of cases is generally incomplete and marred by distortions intended to preserve confidentiality. These attempts commonly lead to distortion of the clinical material, with the result that the reader is misled (Klumpner and Frank, 1991). Nonetheless, a vast collection of cases is available in our literature which has not been systematically described and which might in combination serve many of the same functions as the case collections discussed here.

Conclusion

In spite of the central role that case studies and collections of case studies play in psychoanalytic discourse, their contribution to systematic psychoanalytic investigation remains small. This is partly because of the intrinsic difficulties of generalizing from case findings to populations of patients. It also partly results from the unavailability, until recently, of systematic methods for studying individual cases (a topic to which we return in the final section of this book).

Yet it is striking that case study methods have not been employed more effectively. In two of the series of cases reviewed in this book, the Laufers' study of adolescent psychoanalysis and Bieber's study of the treatment of homosexuals, the data of the case reports do not support the authors' conclusions. The data of the Laufer studies suggest that their approach works poorly in treating the population they describe. The Bieber data suggest that psychoanalysis has little impact on the sexual orientation of exclusively homosexual men. Yet in both studies the authors claim that their results illustrate the effectiveness of their methods. Similarly, individual case reports commonly fail to differentiate between the dynamic explanations they provide and therapeutic effects. Many of these studies are written as convincing narratives that leave open questions of effectiveness, address them as though adequate insight entailed therapeutic effect, or otherwise pass over the question while leaving the reader with the impression that the analysis has been therapeutically effective (Spence, 1994). The net result is that the actual limitations of case studies in psychoanalytic investigations extend well beyond the problems that intrinsically limit this methodology.

Clinical Follow-Up Studies and Case Studies

Readers of the earlier chapters in this section will be understandably disappointed that, despite the enormous efforts of investigators, systematic research seems to have addressed few questions that are germane to clinical psychoanalytic practice. Either the population studied is too different from the patients ordinarily taken into psychoanalysis, or the measures of outcome and process are too crude to answer the questions that most interest analysts. The analyst wishes for investigative methods that are closer to the methods customarily used in psychoanalysis, addressing issues that confront her in daily work. The follow-up methods first introduced by Arnold Pfeffer meet many of these requirements. (In the third section of this book we will introduce many methods that address such issues but have not yet been used to study psychoanalytic outcome.)

Follow-Up Studies

Pfeffer (1959) studied psychoanalytic outcome using a series of four to six weekly, relatively unstructured interviews with terminated cases. These interviews were conducted several years after termination by an analyst other than the treating analyst. The interviews are scrutinized for data relating to symptomatology, transference manifestations, and resolution. The follow-up analyst writes a summary that is compared to an account independently prepared by the treating analyst. In nine cases reported by Pfeffer (1959, 1961, 1963) — private and clinic cases with varying degrees of therapeutic benefit — there was one consistent finding. In every case transference phenomena appeared to emerge, microscopically representative of the analysis, from which it was possible to construct a picture of the course of the analysis that was highly similar to the treating analyst's independent account. Pfeffer (1959) concluded, "Those aspects of the transference neurosis that are unanalyzed remain organized as transference residues which are available for neurotic reactions in certain life situations. These highly organized residues are also readily available for emergence in follow up studies" (p. 437). Since Pfeffer's original report three sets of investigators have studied sixty-two cases using variants of his methods. All these studies confirm Pfeffer's major findings.

From San Francisco, Jerome Oremland and his colleagues (1975) reported two analytic cases "successfully" treated by graduate analysts. In these cases patient and analyst agreed that there had been significant alleviation of presenting and uncovered pathology by an analytic process. Both felt confident the analytic process would continue after termination. Both terminated by mutual agreement. One analysand was a twenty-six-year-old married woman who began treatment because of uncontrolled episodes of anguish and crying; the other was a thirty-two-year-old salesman referred because of marital difficulties, fighting with his parents, and severe work difficulties. Follow-up interviews demonstrated areas of incomplete analyses, especially in the area of the transference.

Haskell Norman and his coworkers (1976) reported five cases conducted successfully by graduate analysts, including three training analyses, using this follow-up method. Areas of incompleteness were found again. This led the authors to conclude that the transference neurosis is not obliterated by psychoanalysis, even when the analysis is properly regarded as successful. Instead, the analytic result is that the analysand gains mastery over prior areas of conflict. The transference neurosis becomes a structure that comes under control of the unconscious ego, and the resulting capacities result in the growth evident from successful psychoanalyses.

In Chicago, Nathan Schlessinger and Fred Robbins (1974, 1975) reported six cases with an augmented methodology. Two to five years after termination the analyst of a successfully completed control case (that is, a case treated as part of the analyst's psychoanalytic training) wrote a description and provided process notes from the beginning of the analysis, the period of the decision to terminate, and the final sessions of the analysis. This material was reviewed by a group composed of advanced candidates and the investigators, who studied the material in detail. At the same time a series of unstructured follow-up interviews was conducted by one of the investigators. In every case significant areas of incompleteness were found, despite the development of an analytic process and substantial therapeutic benefit. Schlessinger and Robbins (1975) reviewed another control case in detail, and the findings confirmed the prior report. They suggest that all the cases demonstrated a mastery of conflict and the development of a self-analytic function. They found consistently that while oedipal dynamics were thoroughly analyzed, pre-oedipal issues manifest as character structure were often not well addressed (Schlessinger and Robbins, 1983). Not only were these matters unresolved in the sense of being capable of reemerging in the follow-up interviews, they also were commonly sources of ongoing distress to the patients at follow-up. Schlessinger (1984) reported that a total of fifty-five cases had been studied since the group began its work. In all the cases studied using the method developed by Pfeffer (1959), findings regarding incompleteness in successful analyses, especially in relation to character pathology, had been confirmed.

Together these studies clearly caution against perfectionistic expectations, and, in fact, suggest that such criteria as "resolution of conflicts" or "resolution of transference neurosis" are unrealistic measures of psychoanalytic outcomes. They suggest that outcomes are better conceptualized as beneficial shifts in pathological compromise formations (Brenner, 1976), transference-resistance configurations (Weinshel, 1984), or in the rapidity with which conflict can be reengaged and worked through (Weiss, 1981).

In addition to their findings and rich clinical data, these follow-up studies have the virtue of focusing on central psychoanalytic concerns, especially psychoanalytic processes. They are unique in providing new, analytically important findings using an observational tool built on a psychoanalytic understanding of transference. However, like the other formal studies, they rely almost exclusively on candidate cases. Incomplete nonoperational definitions of clinical terms make it hard to determine the reliability of the measures employed. As with many clinical reports, unsystematic collection and reporting of data in these studies leave the reader uncertain about what was observed and found (Klumpner and Frank, 1991).

Series of Case Studies

Since its inception the case study has been the center of psychoanalytic research. This way of writing and thinking about clinical material, far from being unique to psychoanalysis, was the ordinary way to collect and record medical data until the middle of the twentieth century (Major, 1932; Hunter, 1991). With time, collections of cases were gradually replaced with statistical summaries of series of patients in formal research, although the individual case study remains central to medical teaching and thought. The *New England Journal of Medicine,* the most prestigious general medical publication in the United States, devotes many pages each week to a "Clinical-Pathological Conference," where a single case is studied in detail.

The investigative suitability of the case study may be even more deeply embedded in psychoanalysis than in other healing disciplines. Several psychoanalysts have suggested that psychoanalysis primarily addresses analysands' narratives of their own experiences (Schafer, 1981b, 1992; Spence, 1982, 1983b, 1991). It is not surprising then that central aspects of psychoanalysis seem best reported by case histories. As we shall see in the final section of this book, various refinements and extensions of the case study method may be particularly suitable to studying psychoanalysis.

In addition to the major studies of groups of patients we have discussed, analysts have gathered cases with similar features to show the value of some psychoanalytic concept by demonstrating it in several cases. If the case studies show what the authors claim, it is legitimate to conclude that the findings are demonstrable in several analyses and are not accidental, nor do they represent a highly unusual situation.

A well selected group of case studies can strengthen a hypothesis in ways that individual cases cannot. Often within a single case study, unless it is much more carefully designed than the usual psychoanalytic study, it is hard to show that an alternative hypothesis does not account for clinical findings. But several cases combined often make it possible to reduce the number of reasonable alternative explanations for the clinical findings. For example, Kohut (1979) attempted to show that the interpretations and other technical procedures of self psychology were superior to those of classical analysis in working with patients with disorders of the self. Implicitly, he used a classical cross-over experimental design. In Mr. Z.'s first analysis, Kohut interpreted impulse and resistance. The result was significant but of limited benefit to the patient. In Mr. Z.'s second analysis, Kohut made interpretations and followed technical procedures based on his new concepts of self psychology, with greatly superior therapeutic results. Kohut concluded that he had demonstrated the superiority of self psychology approach in working with patients like Mr. Z. Unfortunately, several alternative hypotheses could explain the findings. Mr. Z.'s improvement could be explained as a result of Kohut's enthusiasm for his own emerging ideas, of Kohut's having provided support of Mr. Z.'s defense, or of

Mr. Z's greater age and life experience, to mention but some of the possibilities.[1] Even if limited to the sort of naturalistic experiment described in this chapter, a series of similar case studies would be likely to differentiate among some of the alternate hypotheses that can reasonably be posed in explaining this single case.

1. Cocks (1994) suggests, on the basis of striking similarities between Mr. Z.'s personal history and that of Kohut, that Mr. Z. is Kohut. Scholars with access to additional information about Kohut are almost certain that Cocks is mistaken (Charles Strozier to R. Galatzer-Levy, personal communication, 1996.) However, Cocks's suggestion raises important issues in the use of case histories for the study of psychoanalytic outcome. In older psychoanalytic paradigms, in which insight was believed to cure, a successful self-analysis using a new model would provide evidence favoring that model. However, in Kohut's (1984) concept of the therapeutic action of psychoanalysis, self-analysis using his ideas would be impossible, and so if Mr. Z. were actually Kohut, the success of the self-analysis not only would fail to support self psychology theory but would, in fact, tend against self psychology theory. Because some case reports undoubtedly continue Freud's tradition of disguised self-reports, it is important to keep in mind that the meaning of certain findings may, as in this instance, be radically different depending on whether an ordinary or self-analysis is under discussion.

12

Summary and Commentary on Systematic Studies

We have examined seven systematic, clinical-quantitative studies of terminated psychoanalyses involving approximately seventeen hundred patients experiencing a broad range of psychopathology, treated by approximately 450 students and graduate analysts at five different psychoanalytic training centers. Two provisional clinical-quantitative studies (Erle, 1979; Erle and Goldberg, 1984) have also been reported, involving 139 completed analyses conducted by 23 experienced psychoanalysts with primarily psychoanalytic practices. Seventy-one (mostly candidate) cases have also been studied with Pfeffer's clinical methodology at three psychoanalytic centers. Here are the principal findings:

Therapeutic Benefit for Suitable Patients

The majority of patients selected as suitable for psychoanalysis derive substantial therapeutic benefit from it. The most important exceptions were patients taken on for heroic reasons. Improvement rates are typically in the 60–90 percent range, depending on how improvement is measured. Effect sizes, when they have been calculated, are significant. However, the findings of the clinical follow-up studies caution against perfectionistic expectations and remind us of Freud's (1937a) final reflections on psychoanalysis as therapy:

"Our aim will not be to rub off every peculiarity of human character for the sake of a schematic normality, nor to demand that the person who has been thoroughly analyzed shall feel no passions and develop no internal conflicts. The business of the analysis is to secure the best possible psychological conditions for the functions of the ego; with that it has discharged its task" (pp. 249–50).

An alternative way of thinking about the consistent finding of incompleteness of psychoanalysis is that the studies are consistent with a concept of mental health as an ongoing, dynamic process in which adaptations to new situations and continually evolving shifts among compromise formations characterize psychological life.

In many of the studies the treating analyst was employed as the final arbiter of clinical processes and outcomes. Although it would seem that no one is in a better position to make such judgments, the analyst is inherently subject to bias. Ideally, one would want the treatments to be independently evaluated by experienced analysts on the basis of more-verifiable data. However, the methodology developed by Pfeffer (1959) reveals a considerable correspondence between the accounts of treating and research analysts. Furthermore, systematic studies show that therapists' judgments of outcomes are surprisingly reliable and that when they err they tend toward pessimism (see, e.g., Berzins, Bednar, and Severy, 1975; Mintz, Luborsky, and Christoph, 1979). Such judgments correspond highly with statistically reliable measures of outcome obtained independently. Studies of psychoanalysts as judges of outcome also suggest that analysts are likely to be more critical of their own results than are patients or outside analytic observers. This has also been observed about psychoanalytic psychotherapy (Pfeffer, 1959; Klein, 1960; Weber, Bachrach, and Solomon, 1985b; Firestein, 1984; Luborsky et al., 1988).

With the exception of the Menninger study and the studies based on Pfeffer's methodology, the studies did not provide for a careful exploration of the individual nature of change. Indeed, most studies are built upon multivariate statistical models suited to the determination of overall trends and fail to provide significant exploration of the contribution of the analyst to the treatment process. These studies therefore speak mostly to general trends, and their findings largely confirm the accumulated clinical wisdom. Although we are guided by general trends, our interest as analysts is not in general trends but in individual cases. This is what concerned Freud (1933) about summaries of large numbers of cases: "At one time a complaint was made against psychoanalysis that it was not to be taken seriously as a treatment since it did not dare to issue any statistics of its successes. Since then, the Psycho-Analytic Institute in Berlin . . . has published a statement of its results during its first ten years. Its therapeutic successes give grounds neither for boasting nor for being ashamed. But statistics of that kind are generally uninstructive; the material worked upon is so heterogeneous that only very large numbers would show anything. It is wiser to examine one's own individual experiences" (p. 152).

Freud correctly identifies heterogeneity with regard to pertinent variables as demanding samples of very large size if we are to have enough independent of the number of like cases to systematically address Oberndorf's (1943) questions about the types of cases, analyst, and so on that are likely to contribute to therapeutic success.

The Relation of Analyzability and Therapeutic Benefit

The studies seem to show a substantial relation between the development of an analytic process and therapeutic benefit. In those studies in which efforts were made to measure the development of an analytic process as distinct from therapeutic benefit, only about half of the cases selected as suitable for analysis were judged to have developed a psychoanalytic process. This distinction is important for theoretical as well as clinical reasons. The concep tual structure of psychoanalysis is built upon observable analytic data as the empirical foundation of psychoanalytic concepts independent of therapeutic benefit (Freud, 1914a, 1937b; Eissler, 1953; Brenner, 1976). Theories and concepts derived from other sources of observation, including attempts at psychoanalysis where analytic processes do not develop, may not be pertinent to psychoanalytic models (Shevrin, 1984; Bachrach, 1989). At the same time, the data may suggest that the major impact of psychoanalysis is independent of the factors traditionally believed to be effective in psychoanalytic treatment. Despite the importance of this distinction, few studies provide a precise, clinical-operational definition of the psychoanalytic process. The definition offered in the Columbia project is an exception and may capture what many analysts mean. Moreover, while many analysts find the concept useful, others have pointed to its potential ambiguity, methodological difficulties, and bias through investments in varied paradigms (Abend, 1986; Abrams, 1987; Erle and Goldberg, 1979; Rothstein, 1982). Whatever individual analysts mean, the psychoanalytic process is hardly the all-or-none affair that the methodologies of the studies tend to imply.

The studies also suggest that it is necessary to wait until a case is terminated before a true assessment of analyzability can be made (Erle, 1979; Erle and Goldberg, 1984; Heinicke, 1965). In fact, it could be argued that important elements of the hoped-for results of analytic work, such as an effective capacity for self-analysis or enduring shifts in pathological compromise formations, cannot be determined until many years after the end of analysis, even when the patient's family and professional life has fully developed. Bachrach, Weber, and Solomon (1985), for example, compared judgments made by candidate-analysts about their cases at termination with judgments made while the case was still in progress and found only marginal correspondence. This finding raises questions about the meaning of studies of analyzability in which assessments of the development of a psychoanalytic process are made while the cases are still in progress (e.g., Knapp et al., 1960; Feldman, 1968; Huxster, Lower, and Escoll, 1975; Weber et al., 1974), or about the psychoanalytic utility of studies attempting to find signs of unanalyzability in the manifest content whose meaning is not known at the beginnings of analyses (e.g., Bradlow, 1987).

Unpredictability of Therapeutic Benefit and Analyzability

The studies show that, despite careful selection efforts, levels of therapeutic benefit and analyzability are no more than marginally predictable from the vantage point of initial evaluation.[1] Although the selection processes varied in rigor, all the studies found more-severe levels of impairment in final assessments of the cases at termination than were initially suspected. The findings of experienced practitioners do not seem substantially different from those of candidates or students (Erle and Goldberg, 1984).

It may be that there are insurmountable limits to the predictive value of the data elicited in the consultation process. For example, there are inherent transference-resistance configurations that constrict the information obtained during all consultations (Erle and Goldberg, 1979), and some crucial data — for example, the quality of trust or potential for alliances — may not be available at the beginning of analyses (Kris, 1957; Wallerstein, 1986a). In this sense, all analyses actually may be trial analyses. Consistent with later developments in chaos theory (H. Stewart, 1989; Kilert, 1993; Galatzer-Levy, 1995), Waelder (1963), coming to psychoanalysis from physics, even went so far as to argue (on the basis of the general principles of determinism and predictability) that the variability inherent in the human organism is such that dynamic forces continually remain in flux, so that there is no way of knowing beforehand how they will affect later situations. Moreover, "this state of affairs is not just due to the youth of our science, or to the alleged failure to

1. In part this results from the elimination of the seemingly less suitable cases; for example, only 6–10 percent of those applying to the New York and Columbia Institute clinics during the study periods were accepted for analysis.

adhere to rigid standards of investigation and verification, but to [quantitative] factors which appear to be inherent in the subject and which therefore are, on the whole, unalterable" (p. 40).

With the exception of cases analyzed for heroic reasons, the patients in the studies were selected for psychoanalysis (in almost all instances) on the basis of their pretreatment level of functioning. The higher the level, the more likely they were to be considered suitable for analysis. This view was confirmed in the empirical studies. The better the pretreatment functioning of the patients, the more they benefited from analysis. This should come as no surprise, as the patients in most of the studies were selected for pedagogic reasons (that is, their suitability for analysis by a candidate); evaluators made stringent efforts to eliminate more difficult or unsuitable cases. None of the investigators reported assessments of patients thought unsuitable. Nor do they track what eventually became of these patients. Studies by Berk et al. (1964), Karush (1956), Knapp et al. (1960), Feldman (1968), and Lazar (1973) indicate that unsuitable cases were generally assessed as presenting with severe character and/or ego pathology. Comprehensive reviews of the literature on characteristics of patients considered suitable for psychoanalysis (Bachrach and Leaff, 1978; Tyson and Sandler, 1971) and of those likely to drop out of the broader range of psychotherapies (Baekeland and Lundwall, 1975) are consistent with these findings. Clearly, more data from the work of experienced analysts are required.

Meeting Criteria for Effective Outcome Research

As investigations of psychoanalytic outcome the studies under consideration vary in the extent to which they meet the criteria we originally put forward.

Criterion 1: In evaluating the outcome of any treatment, the treatment must be demonstrably taking place. This criterion is met to varying extents by the studies. The fact that most of the studies are based on treatments conducted by candidate-analysts carefully supervised by highly qualified practitioners operating within the highly structured institutional framework of the American Psychoanalytic Association or of the Anna Freud Center provides monitoring of the treatment process, with some assurance that the fundamentals of the treatment procedure are being observed. It seems unlikely that gross deviations in terms of frequency, psychoanalyst's activity, instructions to the patient, and similar matters would occur frequently in such a sample. But with the proliferation of varied paradigms, just what these fundamentals are is no longer a matter of clear consensus. In addition there is much anecdotal information to suggest that the practice of psychoanalysis has always been more varied than formal statements suggest. What we can say, however, is that this particular group of studies largely reflects the work of analysts operating under the ego-psychological or structural model.

At the same time, the supervisory process does not guard against the introduction of systematic biases in evaluation. Only the Menninger project (Chapter 5) included extensive procedures for evaluation of the treatments by outside observers. The striking differences between what analysts believe they say and what is observed through tape recording underscore the importance of independent means of evaluation. Although the necessarily private and confidential nature of the psychoanalytic situation raises a methodological conundrum as to how to go about independently evaluating the treatment process beyond the level of conviction derived from sustained supervision or consultation, a growing number of analysts have come to the opinion that tape recordings provide one such avenue. We believe that whether the introduction of tape recording permits an accurate rendering of the psychoanalytic process in its essential respects for all cases has not yet been settled, but there is sufficient evidence that this method provides an avenue for the study of the psychoanalytic process, at least in analog form. That tape recording has become the current methodological standard for research about other (predominantly brief) psychotherapies does not necessarily mean that it must become the methodological standard for research on psychoanalysis. Wallerstein and Sampson (1971), for example, have strongly argued that process notes also provide an effective basis for the study of psychoanalytic processes. What methods are best employed for the study of the psychoanalytic process depends upon the nature of the questions asked. Yet even the best studies have relied upon data far removed from ordinary, day-to-day clinical observation.

Criterion 2: The treatment being studied must be conducted by practitioners of sufficient training, knowledge, and experience, according to the accepted standard of practice. This is clearly not met by the majority of studies. In most studies the treatments were conducted by students in the process of learning their craft. Until recently almost all psychotherapy research was done using student-therapists. Although in most cases the analytic treatments were probably conducted at adequate levels of expertise, we do not know how the cases would have fared in the hands of more-skilled and experienced practitioners. Clearly, rigorously obtained data about the work of experienced analysts are urgently needed. Studies of the work of candidate-analysts should also be designed to provide meaningful comparisons with the work of more-experienced analysts meeting accepted standards of practice.

Criterion 3: Treatments can be meaningfully evaluated only in relation to the clinical conditions prevailing among patients considered suitable for the treatments. This is clearly met by all the studies except for the Menninger project, which was conceived at a different time in the development of psychoanalysis. The patients in almost all of the other studies were rigorously selected on the basis of indications of their suitability for psychoanalysis at levels more exacting than for most other treatments, even for customary psychoanalytic practice. It also seems clear that we know more about what makes a patient suitable for psychoanalysis than about what the indications are in relation to other currently evolving treatments.

Criterion 4: Germane variables must be specified, operationalized, and studied systematically. In almost all of the studies key patient variables were specified as clearly as possible and studied, though not as systematically and reliably as one might wish. Key treatment and process factors, perhaps with the exception of the development of a psychoanalytic process and the analyst-analysand match, received less attention, in part because of the paucity of meaningful methods of studying them. This points to another major challenge to the field: analyst factors have been studied in only the most rudimentary ways.

Matters of definition and conceptualization limit the studies insofar as there has been no clear consensus about the meanings of terms or the method of measuring clinical concepts. Such terms as *improvement, therapeutic benefit, analytic process,* and even *circumstances of termination* exist within varied conceptual and institutional frameworks and were measured differently in all the studies.

In almost every field of science, significant technical and methodological innovation has gone hand in hand with conceptual progress. The development of more-adequate research methods for outcome studies not only will allow us to make more-rational recommendations about psychoanalysis as a therapy but also will require clarification of conceptual frameworks and improved communication among analysts. With the exception of Pfeffer's contribution, relatively little thought has been given to the development of research methods specific to psychoanalysis.

Conclusion

The findings of the systematic research studies to date are consistent with the accumulated body of clinically derived psychoanalytic knowledge and demonstrate that patients suitable for psychoanalysis derive substantial therapeutic benefits from treatment. Although the diagnostic classifications of such patients may vary, the patients who benefit most are those with the highest pretreatment level of functioning. Even among such patients, some of those expected to do well do not benefit substantially, and some more-severely ill patients do benefit. As in all treatment research, predicting the extent to which cases selected as suitable will benefit is of limited reliability. The studies all have methodological weaknesses, and they do not make it possible to compare the effectiveness of psychoanalysis with that of other forms of treatment for specific kinds of patients experiencing specific kinds of illnesses when treated by psychoanalysts of varying levels of expertise and experience. The limitations of the studies in informing clinical practice are no more substantial than the limitations of any other form of psychotherapy research. The quantitative studies, in particular, have not contributed fresh insights into psychoanalysis, nor have they demonstrated findings with substantially greater rigor than previous clinical investigations. They have not added significantly to our clinical fund of knowledge, nor have they clarified formulations that have long been a part of psychoanalytic lore. What they have contributed, however, is an adumbration of directions for new methods and questions for investigation, and the systematization and summarization of overall trends. The value of such contributions should not be underestimated.

The matters addressed in this section only begin to address the issues that the working psychoanalysts would like to have resolved through empirical investigation. Having surveyed what we want to know and what we currently know, we now turn to promising research directions that might help us learn more about what we want to know.

PART **III**

Finding Out More of What We Want to Know:
Directions for Future Investigations

In earlier sections of this book we outlined questions about the efficacy, outcomes, and processes of psychoanalysis and summarized the available research data pertinent to these questions. These data show that psychoanalysis is a helpful procedure for many patients. But they do not address a wide range of important issues that we would like to understand better — for example, how the relation of qualities of patients and analysts is reflected in outcome, the relation of psychoanalytic processes and outcome, and the deeper psychological effects of psychoanalysis. Furthermore, each of the systematic investigations we reviewed had technical difficulties. The central problem with these studies is that their basic methods are intrinsically unsuited to addressing the kinds of questions about psychoanalysis that psychoanalysts are interested in having answered.

Over the past three decades a small, dedicated group of psychoanalytic investigators, together with investigators from the broader field of psychotherapy research, have been exploring promising methods for studying psychoanalytically significant issues. Many of these methods are far from obvious. Some contradict psychoanalytically informed intuition. Others run counter to received ideas about proper scientific investigation. In this part of the book we describe these emerging methodologies and explore their strengths, limitations, and the ways they have been employed to date.

We begin by considering some important questions about research generally, such as the ethics of research in psychoanalysis, the relation of research to psychoanalytic concepts, and ways of evaluating the merits of research. We then ask how data about psychoanalysis can be collected. Investigators have used procedures ranging from analysts' retrospective summaries to audio- and videotape recordings. We describe the advantages and drawbacks of each way of collecting data. As in other controversial matters in psychoanalytic research, we evaluate collection methods not only by their conceptual adequacy but also by the usefulness of the results they produce.

We next explore several ways to investigate the data of psychoanalysis, including instruments designed to explore central themes of patients' associations, the analytic or therapeutic alliance, and linguistic factors. We describe several of these methods, emphasizing their conceptual foundations, validity and reliability, and situations to which they have been applied. We hope to provide an up-to-date overview of tools currently available for systematic research on psychoanalytic processes and outcomes but not to present an exhaustive survey of relevant methods.

The most challenging problem in evaluating psychoanalysis as therapy is the selection of overall research strategies. In the twentieth century therapeutics of all kinds have come to be investigated by examining differential effects of interventions on groups of people and analyzing the results with statistical methods. The power and prestige of these methods derive from their success in studying large, homogeneous populations subjected to brief and discreet interventions (Hacking, 1983). Efforts to extend this paradigm to smaller populations and more complex, less discrete interventions have encountered great difficulties (Milliken and Johnson, 1984, 1989). Yet the approach of comparing populations in investigating therapeutics has gained great favor in the medical community and with the public. In fact, this approach is often equated with scientific investigation. It has achieved an almost religious status in medicine and social science (Salsburg, 1985). We might follow the lead of Jacob Cohen, a statistician who has probably contributed more than anyone else to the sophisticated study of methodology. Like him, we can remain agnostic (Cohen, 1990), asking pragmatically how statistical methods can help us address psychoanalytically significant questions rather than viewing the use of statistics as a virtue in itself. As we have seen, studying populations has been of limited value in understanding psychoanalytic processes and outcomes. In this section we show not only that these limited findings are the result of methodological defects in the studies but also that the populations-comparison approach is unsuitable. This does not mean that psychoanalysis is not amenable to rigorous study; rather, it means that appropriate rigorous methods should be used. In recent years investigators have found that the single-case study is an approach that can be used successfully to study psychoanalysis. We will describe this method and its use.

Some questions that arise in the study of psychoanalysis cannot be addressed empirically. Questions of values, conceptual formulations, and worldview, for example, may be informed by empirical observation but cannot be decided empirically. Clarifying the limitations of empirical methods can help analysts to use those methods in a more rewarding way in areas where they are appropriate.

We will not address a major impediment to psychoanalytic psychotherapy investigation: the vastly inadequate financial and institutional support that it receives, especially from the federal government (Wolfe, 1993a,b). Whether realistically or not, biomedical researchers generally believe that research grants carry with them expectation of investigative outcomes favorable to the grantor (Campbell, Louis, and Blumenthal, 1998). Thus the likelihood that research funded by pharmaceutical companies and their allies will be favorable to psychoanalytic treatments seems small. Nor will we address the very challenging problems of training researchers who are sophisticated both about psychoanalysis and the methods of systematic research (Bellak, 1961; Escalona, 1952; Glover, 1952; Lustman, 1963; Panel, 1975; Wallerstein, 1988).

13

Some General Problems of Psychoanalytic Research

Before we examine specific methods for systematically investigating psychoanalysis, some general problems require comment.

Increasingly sophisticated research methods promise results from systematic investigations that are more psychoanalytically significant than those of past investigations. However, systematic investigation in psychoanalysis is unfortunately associated in many analysts' minds, and also in the minds of many friends and foes of psychoanalysis, with a long history of fault finding. This attitude is epitomized in the criticisms of Eysenck (1952, 1966), Hook (1959), Grünbaum (1984, 1994), and Crews and colleagues (1995). Each of these authors asserts a rigidly positivistic view of science and shows that psychoanalysis fails to meet that standard. They present a monolithic "philosophy of science," inconsistent with the wide range of ideas about science and its methods now widely accepted in the academic study of the philosophy of science (Hacking, 1983; Losee, 1993). Their standards are not met by many recognized scientific disciplines. It would take us far afield to address the limitations of their conceptualizations (see Robinson, 1993, for a cogent discussion of many of these issues). However, it is important to note that analysts have given them undue authority, believing that either the critics must be answered on their own terms or psychoanalysts must abandon attempts at systematic investigation.

A more important question than whether psychoanalysis can meet external standards of exactitude is how it can address important questions and refine methods, consistent with psychoanalytic thinking, to yield rigorous and accurate findings. We will show in this part of the book that questions of psychoanalytic importance can be addressed rigorously, but not necessarily with the tools emerging solely from a positivistic conception of science.

A difficulty that has plagued psychoanalysis is that analysts have often been dedicated to theoretical positions to such an extent that loyalty to specific theories has often interfered with talking with one another. Status in psychoanalytic organizations has often been contingent on the adoption of "correct" ideas. The highly theory-oriented description of psychoanalytic events makes it difficult for analysts to find a common ground for reasonable discussion (Pine, 1988; Pulver, 1993; Wallerstein, 1988). In recent years some of the problems associated with differing theoretical orientations have been diminished by using several different theories, either separately or simultaneously, to explain clinical data. This process leads to clarification of theories and clinical concepts. The exploration of clinical findings through in-depth examinations of specific instances regularly leads to more collegial discourse. Systematic investigation can provide tools for the rational resolution of at least certain disagreements within the analytic community.

The Importance of Method

A discipline's methods are central to its nature. Progress in many disciplines correlates best with the availability of adequate methods to study issues of interest. Investment in the development of research methodology plays a leading role in the progress of most sciences. In most scientific disciplines research papers that describe methodology are more widely cited than any other type of publication. The discovery of chemical composition required the development of adequate means of weighing small quantities (Gillispie, 1967; Hufbauer, 1983; Partington, 1961). Modern astrophysics depended on the development of more powerful telescopes that explored a wider range of electromagnetic frequencies (Weinberg, 1977). The revolution of molecular biology directly resulted from the introduction of *E. coli* and bacteriophage as objects for genetic research and advances in X-ray crystallography (Judson, 1979). Many analysts regard Freud's discovery of the analytic method for studying mental processes as his most important contribution. But following this development there have been no widely accepted developments of methods of psychoanalytic investigation (Schlesinger, 1974).

A variety of measures have emerged in recent years to address aspects of the psychoanalytic process that are of genuine interest. Most of the tools available for studying psychotherapy (Bergin and Garfield, 1994) derive from viewpoints alien to psychoanalysis. Designed for situations distant from psychoanalysis, they are unlikely to deal with aspects of the therapeutic encounter most interesting to psychoanalysis. Therefore they are unlikely to demonstrate its specific merits as a treatment. However, a group of measures designed to explore ideas related to transference, therapeutic alliance, and emotional language specifically developed with analytic concepts in mind is far more promising for exploring the analytic situation. These tools are rapidly evolving. The psychoanalytic reader may sometimes feel that they are unduly simplistic compared with the complexity of psychoanalytic understanding. We would encourage a tolerant appreciation of these developments. First, creating tools to systematically study psychoanalysis in a reliable and valid way is inordinately difficult. Making ideas operational that seem clear to clinical analysts is an enormous challenge. Even its partial accomplishment is significant. Second, some cherished beliefs about the complexity of the psychoanalytic situation may be wrong. Simpler explanations may illuminate many phenomena. An advantage of highly specific, operationalized concepts, studied empirically, is that their explanatory limits become apparent through the research procedure.

The Poor Fit Between Research Methods and Psychoanalytic Concepts

A major problem facing investigators of psychoanalysis as therapy is the poor fit between the measures of the effects of psychoanalysis and the conceptual bases of psychoanalysis as therapy. Strupp, Schacht, and Henry (1988) proposed a principle they call problem-treatment-outcome congruence. They echo Oberndorf's (1943) formulation of the outcome problem: "The intelligibility of psychotherapy research is a function of the similarity, isomorphism, or congruence among how we conceptualize and measure the clinical problem (P), the process of therapeutic change (T) and the clinical outcome (O). The clinical problem in the outcome measure should be formulated in a form, units and language that allow practical and theoretical links of problem intervention and outcome" (p. 7).

This is particularly true of psychoanalytic research. When studies of analysis as therapy define problems using conceptual frameworks alien to psychoanalysis and assess change in terms of these concepts, it is unreasonable to expect meaningful findings. It is as if the effectiveness of an antibiotic for treating tuberculosis were studied exclusively by investigating its effects on fever. The findings would show the medication ineffective because many conditions other than tuberculosis produce fevers. Nor would the specific merits of the antibiotic in destroying the tubercle bacillus be demonstrated. It should come as no surprise if seemingly poor results emerge when interventions are only loosely linked to the problem that they are supposed to address.

Let us see how this applies to psychoanalytic research. If we try to study whether psychoanalysis is an effective treatment for DSM-IV's "dysthymic disorder," we can predict a poor result simply because the descriptive diagnosis does not refer to many aspects of the patient's condition important from a psychoanalytic understanding of pathogenesis. The diagnosis "dysthymic disorders" applies to a wide population of people who from a psychoanalytic point of view suffer from several different psychological states. Analysts believe that some of these people should be treated with psychoanalysis. Others would not seem likely to benefit from psychoanalytic intervention. Furthermore, the intended result of the intervention would be specifically psychoanalytic in the sense that the intent of the analyst would be to achieve a variety of ends, among which the most rapid relief possible of symptoms might not be the most important.

The concept of congruence between the intentions of a treatment and the measures of its outcome is essential in doing meaningful research. However, ideas about the goals of treatment are evolving both in psychoanalysis and therapeutics generally. As a result, even if we adopt this point of view, we need to address the question of what constitutes satisfactory outcome.

Ideas About Measuring Outcome

Increasingly sophisticated ideas about therapeutic endeavors are shifting the meaning of questions of therapeutic efficacy. The idea that the goal of therapeutic intervention is the relief of target symptoms is being replaced with more-complex images of satisfactory outcome in all fields of medicine and therapeutics. Quality-of-life measures are receiving wide acceptance in medical research. These concepts are consistent with intrinsic aspects of the long-standing psychoanalytic ideas of psychological health (Hartmann, 1939b). The goals of psychoanalysis have always involved more than symptom relief. Because target symptoms provide definable, clear measures, they have tended to be the object of research (Battle et al., 1966). In the absence of objective pathological findings, such as are available in some areas of physical medicine, symptom relief has become a prime outcome marker in psychotherapy research. In contrast, psychoanalysts have long recognized that the absence of symptoms is not mental health (Gitelson, 1954; Joseph, 1982). Many researchers evaluating clinical interventions have recognized that measures of clinical outcome must reflect more than the absence of pathology (Greenfield, 1989). For many procedures of medicine generally the question has become not whether disease was eradicated but how the patient's quality of life has been improved or worsened by the intervention. In evaluating coronary care units (Elwood, 1988), health-care systems (Brooks, 1991; Nord, 1991), treatment of end-stage renal disease (Parfrey et al., 1989), and treatment of cancer (Reizensetin, 1986), investigators have developed methodologies to address the patient's overall well-being instead of his pathology (see also Stewart et al., 1989; Markowitz et al., 1989; Wells et al., 1989). Investigations of psychoanalytic outcome must reflect similar considerations. Quality of life may be assessed with several validated self-report instruments that correlate with assessments by experienced clinicians (Horowitz et al., 1988). Analysts are likely to view such data as superficial. However, if the instruments are well chosen, quality-of-life measures offer the opportunity to evaluate the varying results of analytic work in settings where systematic research, clinical evaluation, or follow-up may not be feasible. More important, the overall view of the goals of therapeutics as the general capacity for richer and better living is more consistent with what psychoanalysts hope to achieve through analysis than concentration on the relief of symptoms alone.

An important aspect of assessing any therapy is the question of its cost versus its benefits. This issue may find its loudest voice in the context of third-party payment, but its importance is not limited to this context. Patients and analysts who have limited time, funds, and energies want to know whether the long, hard task of psychoanalysis is likely to "pay off" commensurate to other investments of scarce resources. Cost-effectiveness measures are increasingly important in assessing pharmacotherapy (Fisher, 1993). They are appropriately applied to psychotherapies, including psychoanalysis, provided that suitable means are developed that measure intended benefits and costs. Means of integrating cost-effectiveness measures into psychotherapy research have been described (Woody and Kihlstrom, 1997; Yates, 1997).

The principal danger is the use of inappropriate measures of benefits that unduly emphasize behavioral change over psychological well-being, study benefits over too short a time, or fail to address other areas of change intrinsically important to psychoanalysis. For example, in considering a cost-benefit analysis of a psychoanalysis it would be appropriate to include the impact of the analysis on the lifetime earning capacity of the analysand and the effects of the analysis on improved capacity to support children's development with their attendant effects into the next generation (Fraiberg, Adelson, and Shapiro, 1975; Kris, 1981), as well as the cost and benefits of the analysis that are evident while the patient is in treatment or at termination.

Psychoanalytic concepts of health include the capacity for continued psychological growth. Anna Freud (1965) cogently argued that the prime indication for psychoanalysis in children is the child's failure to continue development, regardless of the status of development in comparison with agemates. Analysts who believe that development ordinarily continues across the course of life have suggested that this criterion can be extended to adults (Cohler and Galatzer-Levy, 1991; Galatzer-Levy and Cohler, 1993). Systematic study of psychoanalysis from this point of view has not begun. Investigations in other areas that attempt to support ongoing development could help in the design of such studies. For example, the Head Start program showed only slight effects in its target goal of improving academic performance. However, it was clearly successful in reducing adolescent delinquency among youngsters who had been in the program, even though this was not a defined goal of the intervention (Weisberg, 1992). The emerging picture of ordinary adult development begins to provide an idea of the sort of issues that should be examined in this context (Vaillant, 1977, 1987, 1992; Galatzer-Levy and Cohler, 1993a,b; Elder, 1974, 1975, 1979, 1986, 1990; Gutman, 1977, 1987; Nemiroff and Colarusso, 1990). In an intervention like psychoanalysis, where the intention is to free frozen development, we may expect that the achievement of the intended freedom will result in creative, unpredicted results. We should design studies that capture this feature of analytic outcomes.

Arrangements for Psychoanalytic Research

Major developments of psychoanalysis have come primarily from individuals or groups exploring topics of clinical interest. These researchers have used material from their practice and personal experience to describe psychological life. With few exceptions, psychoanalysts have not engaged in large-scale programmatic investigations of psychoanalysis as a therapy.

Programmatic research involves a large group of individuals collaborating to address a particular problem. It emerged largely during and after the Second World War as the product of careful thinking about how to do scientific investigation. It became popular with Fermi's finding a way to develop the atomic bomb as rapidly as possible. Earlier, the Rockefeller Foundation, in a limited way, recognized the value of programmatic research in medical science (Bliss, 1982). The approach addressed empirical problems that were intractable for individuals or small groups because of their complexity, cost, and needed range of expertise. The spectacular success of "big science" (Capshew and Rader, 1992) largely results from well-planned programmatic research. To date only the Menninger study has applied this approach to investigating psychoanalysis.

Analysts should consider its appropriateness. Individual analysts are exposed to only a small number of analyses. The problems of working with the data from an analysis are great. They often involve expertise and time not usually available to a solitary analyst-researcher. Planned collaborative endeavors could address both of these problems. Exploring how the methods of large-scale scientific research can be applied to psychoanalytic issues is part of the task of developing an overall research strategy for the field.

The merits of programmatic research should not blind us to its limitations for the major tasks of psychoanalytic investigation. Extended immersion in and exploration of the psychological world of people can be achieved only through long investment in one person at a time. The psychoanalytic researcher must constantly be on guard lest in the rush to get results, core psychoanalytic goals of depth understanding be discarded.

Ethical Issues in Research

Any research that involves people carries with it the responsibilities to meet the ethical requirements of the clinician and the researcher. These issues have been carefully explored in several contexts. Here we discuss three particular problems of psychoanalytic research: (1) informed consent, (2) confidentiality, and (3) the use of interventions that the analyst may regard as nonoptimal.

INFORMED CONSENT

The widely accepted concept of informed consent is challenged in two ways by psychoanalysis. Informed consent suggests that the consequences and risks of a situation are known, or reasonably knowable. But in many areas of psychoanalytic investigation neither patient nor analyst has a clear picture of the impact of the research on treatment. As we shall discuss later, it is clear that tape recording affects the analytic process. There is limited data about the nature of this effect, so the extent to which the patient can enter reasonably into informed agreement to tape recording is limited even if there were no other impediments to informed agreement. Given the research analyst's investment in his investigations, a patient's refusal to participate in research may stimulate countertransferences that might conflict with an analysis. If one adds these problems to a patient's generally imprecise initial idea of what analysis involves, it becomes clear that informed consent to participate in research (or even to decline to participate) is a thorny issue that can be addressed only by the fullest disclosure possible and the recognition of the inevitable limitations of that disclosure. Because of the patient's transference to the analyst, special care is necessary to guard against the analyst's exploiting the patient for research purposes. For the purposes of any research this places undue demands on analysis, compared with any other therapeutic procedure. Transference is not unique to analysis; its uniqueness is in the systematic attention to it. It can be argued that distressed people with strong irrational ties to their physicians or other therapists are never in a position to enter into rational agreements with them. This situation is no different for psychoanalysis than for general surgery. The analyst's awareness of this situation entails a special moral obligation to ensure that the patient's benefit is the primary consideration in the analysis, as it should be in any therapeutic research.

CONFIDENTIALITY

Confidentiality is a second area of difficulty. Freud (1915) claimed that psychoanalysis brooks no observers. The idea that awareness of observation would interfere with psychoanalytic process collides with the central principle of modern science, first formulated by Bacon (1620), that the bases for scientific claims must be open to public scrutiny. Freud (1905) addressed this problem, arguing that patients' privacy was guarded because they could not be identified from the psychoanalytic material in the case report. In the case of Freud's patients, this opinion did not stand the test of time. Not only were his patients identifiable, but there is much to suggest that their lives were profoundly influenced by having been the object of famous case reports (Deutsch, 1957; Decker, 1991; Mahony, 1986).

In the long tradition of case reports that followed Freud's initial case description, analysts attempted to protect their patients in a variety of ways. Material was presented in "disguised" form. Facts about the patient that were thought to be inessential were changed to protect privacy. How well this succeeded is unclear, and no standards were ever formulated for the degree of disguise. Consistent with psychoanalytic thinking we may assume that the choice of "disguise" is inevitably motivating and must introduce real distortions into the analytic material. The sparse psychoanalytic literature on the subject demonstrates how complex such a small thing as a choice of the pseudonym for a patient can be (Decker, 1982). Whatever its effects on confidentiality, the practice of disguising aspects of the patient's life, by introduction of fictional substitutes for the actual materials, systematically introduced erroneous information into the case reports. Current recommendations are that information that is not pertinent to the case report be omitted rather than replaced by disinformation (Klumpner and Frank, 1991). However, this compromise still does not solve the tension between the Baconian ideal and the need for privacy.

A partial solution, commonly adopted in practice, is to disguise or censor information about patients depending on the audience. In supervision and study groups with colleagues, analysts regularly present extensive material about patients. However, analysts usually are more circumspect about issues of confidentiality as the possibility of the information's getting back to the patient or affecting the patient becomes greater. Discussions of confidentiality are further complicated because breaches of confidentiality affect not only the patient whose analytic material is disseminated but also other patients who, fearing such breaches, may be reluctant to utilize the analytic situation fully.

One solution is to obtain permission from the patient for the use in research of material from his analysis. But it may be that the process of requesting such permission is more damaging than potential violation of confidentiality. The Committee on Scientific Activities of the American Psychoanalytic Association (Klumpner, 1984) adopted a position that explicitly avoids a rigid and formulaic stance about confidentiality by placing the responsibility on the analyst to act in a manner that does not harm the patient. Recent discussions of psychoanalytic confidentiality motivated by intrusive demands of insurers have taken an absolute position that analysis is always completely confidential. This view would make research on psychoanalysis impossible.

In some situations the problems of confidentiality become minor: (*a*) when data are reported in quantitative summaries of variables; (*b*) when microscopic fragments of analytic sessions are studied (for example, the patient speaks of common matters involving no risk of identification); (*c*) when elaborate means have been introduced to purge data of specific identifying information; and (*d*) when data is then studied only by computer, which outputs information that is not identifiable as belonging to a particular patient (for example, frequency of use of adjectives or textual proximity of words). In spite of these techniques, the problem of conflict between research openness and confidentiality remains.

Several research groups, in order to allow access to patient material, have formed agreements about further dissemination of materials that promise to allow greater access to otherwise confidential data. These include providing transcripts and recordings of analyses only to researchers geographically distant from the location where the analysis was conducted, pledges to discontinue work on the material if the analysand is recognized, and similar arrangements, making materials available only to professionally qualified investigators.

NONOPTIMAL INTERVENTIONS

A final ethical dilemma arises in research designs in which the analyst deliberately employs methods that she may not regard as optimal for the purpose of studying the effects of various approaches to the patient. Obviously, it is never acceptable knowingly to withhold better treatment from a patient for the purposes of research. It is, however, appropriate when uncertain how to proceed to choose a direction and observe its consequence. Where the analyst is genuinely uncertain whether one way of proceeding is better for the patient than another, there is no ethical dilemma in proceeding in either direction (O'Leary and Borkovec, 1978).

Observing the effects of various interventions is also clinically sound practice in that it clarifies for analyst and patient what is useful and provides opportunities for the analysis of the consequences of different psychoanalytic strategies.[1] The difference between the approach suggested here and common psychoanalytic practice lies in the analyst's consciously and intentionally confronting and acting on her uncertainty about the optimal approach to treating the patient.

Problems Not Subject to Empirical Investigation

The function of empirical research is to confirm, disconfirm, amplify, and modify theory. Theory requires definitions that, as Rapaport (1944) pointed out, are always a matter of strategy. This strategy is based upon one's conception of a subject matter. Contemporary psychoanalysts view the subject matter and goals of psychoanalytic investigations variously. Some see psychoanalysis as a general psychology, others as a general clinical psychology. Still others regard it as a psychology of conflict-generated psychopathology, while some include psychopathology that results from deficient experience or biological pathology as within its purview. Depending what point of view is adopted about psychoanalysis, an investigator will have quite different attitudes about the nature of data obtained by the psychoanalytic method and the theory required to conceptualize it (Bachrach, 1989; Rapaport, 1944). These considerations apply to all aspects of psychoanalytic investigation, including the study of transference, psychoanalytic processes, outcomes, and related factors.

Let us look at this situation with regard to transference. During a large part of psychoanalytic history, psychoanalysts were educated to think about the distinctions between transferences and transference neuroses according to the intensity, qualitative features, and specific content of the patient's experience. Such conceptions give rise to empirical questions about the validity of these

---

1. Most contemporary psychoanalysts do not regard the psychoanalytic process as so delicate that it is derailed by occasional "mistakes" on the analyst's part, whatever their motive. In fact, the analysis of such mistakes has become central to contemporary psychoanalytic technique. Thus the dangers to the patient of reasonable variation in technique are small.

constructs in relation to such specific factors as the theory of technique, psychopathology, and generalizability of findings. For example, if one conceives of transference solely as a compromise formation, empirical research strategies will be different than if one includes the possibility of the direct expression of psychological needs as aspects of transference (Brenner, 1982; Gann, 1984; Kohut, 1971). Those who see transference as compromise formation will want to delineate the components of compromise formation as they oscillate in the object of study, while those committed to the idea of unmet need will scan the material for evidence of particular sorts of need.

Other examples of matters that are seen very differently depending on one's conceptualization of the scope of psychoanalysis include the meaning of data obtained from early infant observation, the significance of the origins of instinctual representations in structural and relational paradigms, or even everyday clinical concepts like the completeness of analysis, improvement, clinical change, or the circumstances of termination. These considerations necessarily implicate definitions and strategies for investigation of psychoanalytic process (Abend, 1990) and are of particular moment in the contemporary climate of proliferating psychoanalytic paradigms. To systematically study something, one must be conceptually and operationally clear about what one is studying, how it relates to neighboring models, and the boundaries between those models.

It has been four decades since Rapaport (1960) spoke to the problems faced by empirical research because of the lack of systemization of psychoanalytic theory. Meaningful empirical research can only address a systematized theory moored in a clearly organized paradigm. As different paradigms lead to differing models and theories — for example, structural object relations, relational, and self psychology models. The findings emerging from empirical research efforts constructed according to one model (or theory) may not fully pertain to those of another. It is for this reason that systematic empirical research founded in varied paradigms cannot lead to an accumulation of knowledge in which individual research findings build upon one another.

Attempting to answer certain questions as though they are empirical when they are not leads to bafflement. This is evident in the tendentious discussion and concepts of transference neurosis (Reed, 1987a, 1990). The debate about what constitutes a psychoanalytic process continues among analysts (Weinshel, 1984; Abend, 1986b; Boesky, 1990). In both instances the central issue is how words are to be used. The use of these words carries particular weight because of the administrative and credentialing functions attached to them. But questions of the correct use of words cannot be addressed by empirical research. Empirical investigation might determine how the words are commonly used and even whether the phenomena addressed by the various usages occur in psychoanalytic practice. But it cannot address the question of how words should be used.

We know that many analysts who believe themselves to be engaged in similar work behave quite differently with patients. Even self-descriptive studies of analytic efforts revealed remarkable diversity among the relatively small analytic group in England in the early fifties (Glover, 1955). Studies of therapists of all types indicate that they systematically fail to note aspects of their behavior with patients that is inconsistent with their beliefs about therapy (Rubovitz-Seitz, 1992). In effect, the analysts say they do what they think they should do.

Just as questions of definition are nonempirical, so, too, the choice of paradigm (Kuhn, 1970) is only indirectly empirical and is far too broad for empirical investigation in any field.

Psychoanalytic understanding will be moved forward by clearly recognizing that some questions are not subject to empirical investigation and by not addressing them as though they were. With this we return to some general problems of psychoanalytic research.

14

Collecting Data About Psychoanalysis

Systematic psychoanalytic research requires a body of data to investigate. Unfortunately, data about analyses adequate for research purposes are difficult to obtain, and much of the data that are available have been so transformed in the process of reduction that investigators cannot be sure of their meaning. The very fact that the data were collected may so affect the analytic process that the data do not adequately represent ordinary psychoanalytic work. Analysts who are willing to collect detailed data about their work may be highly atypical in other ways. Data that appear in published reports are usually chosen because they represent an unusual psychological configuration; therefore they are inevitably atypical. Depending on the way it is obtained and communicated, the description of the work provided to the researcher may inadequately reflect the analytic situation and process (Klumpner and Frank, 1991).

Obtaining Clear Data

A recurrent problem in psychotherapy research is determining what, in fact, happened in the treatment. Idiosyncratic and local terminology may make it impossible to determine what actually occurred in the analyses. For example, when an analyst reports that he analyzed the resistance, does he mean that he made a statement that comprehensively described how the patient barred some aspect of her psychological life from awareness, or that he observed to the patient that she was resisting, or that he did any of a number of other things that might be called analysis of resistance? The problem of accurately construing the event behind the description exists for both published clinical and investigative reports. Even in interactive meetings with colleagues it may take considerable persistence to discover the referents of terms that the participants may believe they use in common.

In psychotherapy research, treatment manuals have become a standard way to specify therapeutic procedures. They provide baseline descriptions against which it is possible to describe what has been done and to specify the extent to which the therapist has followed a specified method (Lambert, Shapiro, and Bergen, 1986; Luborsky and DeRubeis, 1984; Yeaton and Seachrest, 1981). The longer and more complex the treatment, the harder it is to maintain its integrity (that is, its having proceeded according to the specification laid out in advance of treatment), and this may make it appear ineffective in a study. Treatment manuals have been written for many forms of therapy, including psychodynamic psychotherapy (Luborsky, 1984), treatment of borderline conditions (Kernberg et al., 1989), interpersonal therapy of depression (Klerman et al., 1984), the cognitive therapy of depression (Beck et al., 1979), and anxiety disorders (Milrod et al., 1997), among others (Luborsky and Barber, 1993).

While psychoanalytic clinicians often claim that the complexity of psychoanalysis cannot be encompassed in a treatment manual, no attempts have been made to test this idea. Whether such a manual can be developed depends upon the degree to which psychoanalytic technique continues to represent a core procedural entity. Currently we know little about the analytic procedures actually employed in various analytic communities. Glover's (1955) study of British psychoanalysts revealed a wide range of views about core technical issues. It would be no surprise to discover an even broader range among contemporary American psychoanalysis.

It is difficult to know the meaning of clinical judgments unless the means by which they were reached are explicit. Even analysts trained at the same psychoanalytic institute often fail to come to similar conclusions about analytic material when simply asked to describe it (Seitz, 1966). Operationalizing a clinical judgment requires careful description of the quality to be judged, paradigmatic examples to guide the clinicians who make the judgments, and a satisfactory format for recording the judgments. Analysts have succeeded in reaching such judgments under these circumstances (Rubovitz-Seitz, 1992).

Commonly therapists do not recognize aspects of their interventions that are not explicitly called to their attention as important to clinical reporting.

For example, in clinical reports analysts seldom specify the words and affects of their greeting to the patient at the beginning of sessions. Yet this interchange may profoundly affect the session's course. It is still rarer to find reports of the clinical setting, fee arrangements, and similar matters. One solution is the multisite study, which tends to highlight the effects of unacknowledged local practice. Such studies, however, are difficult to coordinate. And even in the rigorously designed multisite study of the pharmacotherapy of depression conducted by the National Institute of Mental Health, the groups at various locations failed to comply to the drug protocols, which significantly reduced the value of the study (Klein et al., 1990).

It is extremely important to be as explicit as possible about how data are collected. The researcher must carefully track the relation between the original collection of the data and their transformation. When a researcher develops a protocol describing the goal of a study, the background of previous researchers, the auspices of the study, the procedures to be used, the data to be collected, the logic connecting those data to the research questions, and the way findings will be communicated, she is forced to critically examine each of these issues and their meanings for research findings. Throughout the investigation the written protocol remains a baseline against which the researcher can judge how much she has deviated from her initial intentions.

It is particularly important to safeguard against bias in collecting data. A major problem in non-tape-recorded psychoanalytic data is variability.[1] Social scientists have found that data collection can be made more reliable by following three cardinal rules: (1) create a systematic case study database; (2) use multiple sources of evidence; and (3) carefully note the relation between the original data, their processing, and their subsequent transformations.

Case study research is traditionally differentiated from less systematic investigation in the way data are collected and recorded. We discuss the case study method in detail in Chapter 20; here we address the data collection aspects. Because case studies are usually written as suasive narratives (Spence, 1982), the reader is seldom confident that he knows how the data were collected and reported and is aware of the limitations of the data. The Committee on Scientific Activities of the American Psychoanalytic Association has made efforts to develop procedures for specifying the nature of the data collection and to give recommendations for data presentation (Klumpner and Frank, 1991; Panel, 1991).

---

1. Tape recording does not fully guard against this problem. In a study of tape-recorded supervision, several of the supervising analysts commonly made remarks off the record after turning the recorder off.

Systematic collection of data helps safeguard against bias and may also reveal irregularities in the collected data, such as variation among sessions in the amount of information recorded. Such variation itself can be treated as important data about fluctuations in the analyst's interest or other aspects of countertransference (see Weiss, Sampson, and Mount Zion Group, 1987). When clearly defined methods of investigation are available, deviation from these methods becomes readily apparent, and systematic study of failures to follow those methods leads to deeper understanding just as deviations from analytic technique point to deeper aspects of that situation (Chused, 1990, 1991).

It is not necessarily the case that more extensive or detailed data are better. In comparison with verbatim transcripts, process notes compress data by an order of up to fifty to one. They also implicitly or explicitly include the therapist's point of view (Wallerstein and Sampson, 1971). Chevron and Rounsaville (1983) found that supervisors' appraisal of the supervisee's work, based upon the supervisee's report of sessions, accurately predicted which patients would benefit from psychotherapy. The same supervisors appraised the supervisee's work again months later on the basis of videotapes of the same sessions. Surprisingly, the videotape appraisal did not significantly correlate with benefits. Perhaps data were captured through the reporting process in supervision that did not emerge from the videotapes alone. The apparently more ample data of the videotape were less rich than the seemingly less complete oral report.

Where possible, more than one source of information should be used about a case to provide corrections for unreliability and different perspectives on the same phenomenon. Tape recordings, process notes, and psychological testing can improve the credibility of observations. Processing data through more than one means — for example, the systematic rating of recorded material by experienced analysts and the application of specific research methodology (for example, Bucci's referential activity measure or Luborsky's CCRT) to the same material — enlarges and confirms the researchers' understanding of particular findings (Dahl, Kächele, and Thomä, 1988).

The traditional method of gathering and conceptualizing psychoanalytic data largely follows Freud's (1912) technical recommendation and is built upon the clinical-historical method (Rapaport, 1954). Technical neutrality, free association, and other aspects of the analytic setup give rise to a situation in which transferences and resistances are brought into sharp focus, subject to influence by interpretation in an actual analytic relationship. As in any observational method, the data are influenced by the method and by the nature of the theory required to conceptualize them. Far from being an unsystematic methodology, psychoanalytic methods are rooted in specific clinical procedures governed by theoretical models with defined rules of inference and evidence.[2] Data obtained by application of this method give rise to empirical data specific to individual cases and provide a basis of generalization and comparison to other cases and eventually for the generation of numerous hypotheses, which are subject to test against thousands of observations in a single analysis (Edelson, 1983). Over the years the traditional methods of psychoanalytic observations have yielded revolutionary theories of mental function, including the importance of unconscious mental processes in models of the mind, developmental and group psychologies, theories of pathogenesis, psychopathology processes, and a range of therapeutic techniques. This is an impressive yield. Our focus on additional methods of investigation should be taken as supplementary to the data and findings derived from application of traditional psychoanalytic methods, not as alternatives.

There are, however, limitations to clinical psychoanalytic observation and the data it produces. Analytic data are more subjective than the data of most disciplines involved in systematic studies; it is difficult to apply psychoanalytic findings to psychological processes generally; there are problems of addressing the relation between data derived from traditional and from modified methodologies; and of course there are problems inherent in studying complex interrelations generally. Systematic, formal research helps demarcate the boundaries of conceptualizations derived from different forms of observation (Bachrach, 1989).

One traditional method of psychoanalytic investigation that has proved fruitful is the study group, in which several investigators meet regularly to discuss specific questions or problems. The method's yield depends on how frequently, regularly, systematically, and rigorously the group meets and works. Psychoanalysts have long used the study group to explore the clinical or theoretical implications of clinical data. Conscientiously conducted, the work produced by such groups has proven reliable and scientifically productive (Seitz, 1966). The contribution of the Kris Study Group on borderline disorders (Abend, Porder, and Willick, 1983) is an example of what can be accomplished by the study group method.

Concepts for Evaluating Research

Investigators in the social sciences have developed an extended conceptual framework to explore methods of research and assess their findings.

---

2. We have referred here to psychoanalytic methods because there are several different techniques, theories, and rules of inference that have been called psychoanalytic. Our point is that systematic thought and exploration of data are not alien to any psychoanalytic point of view.

These conceptualizations can save the time and energy of the psychoanalyst-researcher. At the same time he should not be cowed by the use of scientific methodology and statistics. They can serve as a helpful guide in planning and evaluating psychoanalytic investigation.

VALIDITY

A first question in assessing a completed or proposed study is its validity: whether it actually addresses the issues it purports to address. This is especially important in psychoanalysis, where concepts are often ill defined. No matter how sophisticated the methods used, the results are meaningless unless they answer the investigator's questions.

An investigator first asks whether the method has face validity — that is, whether, on the face of it, the method measures what it claims. Face validity is not necessarily a property of useful methods. Seemingly obvious methods often turn out, on closer examination, not to address the questions they are intended to address. For example, beginning candidates' reports of the status of the transference have face validity as measures of the transference but are often most closely related to the teaching to which the candidate has recently been exposed. On the other hand, some satisfactory methods lack face validity in that it is not immediately apparent that they measure the intended aspect of the situation. For example, Bucci's (1988) computerized methods for studying the emotional vigor of language through the frequency of the appearance of words in the text (see Chapter 17) uses a vocabulary that is very different from what most analysts would think of as appropriate words for measuring affectivity.

Content validity refers to whether, on detailed analysis, a method actually measures what it purports to measure. If the method measures something that is conceptually similar but in fact different from the important variable, confusion can result. For example, a measure of attitude toward the analyst that taps only the patient's conscious views of the analyst would lack content validity for psychoanalytic questions.

Construct validity demands that the concept makes scientific and conceptual sense. It is usually achieved by demonstrating both the reasoning behind the measure and its relation to other measures that purport to address related concepts.

Internal validity refers to whether other sources of variation might account for the observed changes (Cook and Campbell, 1979; Kazdin, 1980). The question of internal validity is particularly important in studies of the efficacy of treatments that take place over a long time during which external influences may significantly affect the patient. Common threats to internal validity include the occurrence of influential external events, the patient's personal maturation, repeated exposure to assessments (which may result in the patient's improvement at managing the assessment, therapeutic effects from the assessment procedure itself, or untoward effects of the assessment), changes in scoring procedures, statistical regression (that is, reversion of scores toward the mean), and subject selection so that comparison groups are not comparable. Failure to address internal validity is commonplace in psychoanalytic studies, especially in narrative case studies. Often clinical reports refer to changes in the patient's external life that common sense suggests have a profound influence. Patients are often seen at times when personal maturation would be expected. Patients initially seek help at times of greatest difficulty in their lives, so that an expectable return to an average level of function for the patient might be mistaken for therapeutic effect. The first step in the management of these challenging issues is to identify them. When the analyst's impressions are the sole measure of change, these measures are particularly vulnerable because the analyst comes to think differently about the patient across the course of analysis, in part as a result of changes in the analyst.

Finally, it is important to consider ecological validity. Research findings may not be applicable to the practical situations that they were intended to clarify. For example, many laboratory studies of children's suggestibility were undertaken to find out whether children's testimony in legal matters was so subject to suggestion as to be unreliable, but these studies seldom corresponded sufficiently to the actual situations that researchers could legitimately claim that their findings applied to those situations (Ceci and Bruck, 1995; Yuille and Wells, 1991). Similarly, documented effects of antidepressant medication from systematic studies are seldom observed in studies performed in the setting where the medications are ordinarily used (Brugha et al., 1992). In psychotherapy research outcome studies frequently fail to address such relevant issues (Bachrach, 1984; Persons, 1991) as the theoretical position on which the treatment is based. They tend to focus on descriptive diagnosis, whereas practicing analysts variously focus on change as understood from their theoretical point of view or the patient's general functioning. As we have noted, the disappearance of a target symptom means little in clinical practice unless the patient's overall functioning is improved. Furthermore, the standardized prescription of therapies does not correspond to the ordinary clinical practice of adjusting therapy to patient response; therefore studies based on this apparently rigorous approach say little about how the patient is likely to fare in actual treatment situations. Studies that take the context of the intervention into clear account have appeared only recently (Safran, Greenberg, and Rice, 1988; Shoham-Salomon, 1990; Messer, Tishby, and Spillman, 1992). In the study of the psychotherapy of children, a recurrent finding is that out-comes measured in the context of ongoing systematic research show superior results to studies of similar therapies conducted in the community (Weisz and Weiss, 1993).

There are important expectable threats to the empirical validity of studies of psychoanalysis.[3] For example, it is clear that analysts vary greatly in the technique of the treatments that they call psychoanalysis. Another threat to the validity of studies of psychoanalysis as therapy is that the value of any assessment of psychotherapy and psychoanalysis is limited if the analyst's technical skill is unknown or not established. Yet there are few means to as-sess the adequacy of psychoanalytic (or even psychotherapeutic) technique (Schafer, 1982, 1983; Beutler and Crago, 1991). A comparative study (Lubor-sky et al., 1988) of several types of therapy found that outcomes correlated with how closely the therapist adhered to whatever technique was used. This finding may have reflected the adaptive powers of the healthier patients or the fact that the therapist was not thrown off his accustomed path by disruptive defenses (cf. Clarkin et al., 1992), or that the psychologically healthier, more intelligent, or more committed therapists found it easier to follow the pre-scribed procedures.

A dramatic instance of how misleading findings can result from a failure to appreciate context emerged in a study by Piper and his colleagues (1991). Their work seemed to show that transference interpretations were correlated with worse psychotherapy outcomes. In studying brief psychotherapy con-ducted by inexperienced therapists, the researchers found that the more trans-ference interpretations the therapists made, the less well patients did. A care-ful review of the cases that did not do well reveals that there were many transference interpretations at the beginning of treatment in every session. Apparently a number of the inexperienced therapists had understood the es-sence of therapy to be transference interpretation, which they approached with unrestrained vigor. The finding that increased attention to transference results in poorer outcome could not properly be generalized to the work of experienced therapists.

One strategy for studying contexts is events analysis (Rice and Greenberg, 1984), a method related to Luborsky's (1967) symptom-context method. Mo-ments at which the patient is experiencing a conflict are systematically identi-fied, and the subsequent course of work is examined. A related approach is

---

3. The inevitability of such threats should not be taken as indicating that empirical research is impossible. It is the investigator's job to address them, reduce them as far as possible, and explicitly indicate the limitations of findings they cause.

discovery-oriented research (Elliott, 1991a,b). Because the specific events that serve as markers for study may be separated by some time from the moments being examined microanalytically, contexts may be difficult to define or to relate convincingly to clinical events. As we shall see, this problem poses a considerable challenge. However, these methods remain a good beginning at addressing the issue of context systematically.

Not only the analyst but also the patient may introduce variations that threaten the internal validity of studies of psychoanalysis. It would be an error to try to ensure that the patient conforms to analytic technique. Patients for whom the technique requires substantial alteration may be unsuitable for analysis (Eissler, 1953), but clinical experience and systematic findings (Erle, 1979; Erle and Goldberg, 1979, 1984) do not confirm that this is necessarily true. Through technical modifications respectful of the patient's resistances, analytic work has been shown to be possible with some patients who insisted on coming to only one session weekly, for example (Rothstein, 1990). Clinical experiences like these suggest solutions to the problems of the internal validity of studies of psychoanalysis.

Studies of internal validity must also address the problem of which procedures to include in studies of psychoanalysis. Skolnikoff (1990) describes analytic process in settings other than patients on the couch and four-to-five-times-per-week sessions. He asserts that one must look at the function of the process rather than its form. Stolorow (1990) argues that the use of the couch is not a sine qua non for analytic therapy and in fact often inhibits it.

Convergence of various measures that purport to study the same concept supports the validity of a particular measure (Meehl, 1996). Yet such convergence can also arise from shared prejudices. Caston and Martin (1993) developed an ingenious method to explore agreement of analysts about formulations of a recorded psychoanalysis (the case of Mrs. C.)[4] in an attempt to discover whether convergent findings reflected shared preconception or derived from the textual details of the case. They distinguished domains of a formulation — for example, wish, impulse, transference, resistance, defensive patterns, and conscious or unconscious fantasy. Events (statements by the patient) were provided to two groups of judges, who rated the material in each

---

4. Mrs. C. was a twenty-eight-year-old, married professional woman who was treated by "classical" psychoanalysis for neurotic range disturbances. The analysis was conducted by a graduate analyst, supervised by a senior analyst, lasted approximately one thousand sessions, was considered quite successful, and was fully tape-recorded for future research purposes. This analysis and its record have become a "specimen case" for psychoanalytic research and have been widely studied over the past twenty years.

domain, using scales of conflictedness, defense-impulse configurations, and historical linkage between early situations and current compromise formations. Both groups of judges were provided with a short summary of the case. One group was also given a transcript of the first five hours. The other judges were not given this context and so could rate the text only on the basis of general psychoanalytic preconceptions. Caston and Martin found that a portion of the good agreement between judges resulted from shared stereotypes requiring no knowledge of the case. However, most of the agreement was between the textwise judges and resulted from specific knowledge about the case.

RELIABILITY

The reliability of a finding is the extent to which it can be replicated — that is, the extent to which repetition of the procedure will yield the same result. To have meaning in systematic study, findings must be reasonably reliable. At the same time, it should be recognized that reliability and validity are often in conflict. Greater reliability can be achieved by limiting the possible responses of raters, but this usually requires the constriction of meaning of the concepts being rated.

A central obstacle to studying psychoanalysis has been the difficulty of establishing the reliability of clinical evaluations. Seitz (1966) found that interrater reliability could not be achieved in the unstructured assessment of psychoanalytic process material even among a group of analysts trained at the same psychoanalytic institute (see Rubovitz-Seitz, 1992). We believe that these disappointing findings reflect Seitz's methodology and are not intrinsic to the undertaking. For example, Seitz asked analysts to make global judgments without careful definition of the terms and variables. More satisfactory reliability has been obtained when careful definitions were employed (e.g., Luborsky et al., 1971). Still, some subsequent studies have had similar difficulty achieving interrater reliability (DeWitt et al., 1983) despite careful attention to method.

Attendees at clinical conferences have often observed that different psychoanalysts at times use the same words for very different clinical phenomena and at other times use different words to describe similar clinical happenings. Klumpner (1994) describes the complicated thicket of psychoanalytic language and emphasizes how psychoanalytic terms change in meaning over time. In spite of rigorous efforts to clarify psychoanalytic terminology (Moore and Pine, 1995), analytic authors continue to use technical terms in idiosyncratic and confusing ways, with obscure referents.

Generally, reliability is achieved by narrowing the judgments required by clinicians to a more specific focus than is typical of psychoanalytic work. The Core Conflictual Relationship Themes method (CCRT, discussed in detail in Chapter 17), provides a way to reliably operationalize and evaluate central aspects of the transference (Luborsky, 1984, 1988; Luborsky and Crits-Christoph, 1990). Yet the features that make systematic means of exploring psychoanalytic processes most useful may interfere with their value to psychoanalysts because of the inevitable loss of richness of the coding scheme. Thus, for instance, although the CCRT taps clinically plausible patterns of a specific type, it does not encompass the full range of phenomena currently described as transference (e.g., Kohut, 1971, 1977, 1984; Modell, 1976, 1988, 1990, 1991; Bollas, 1982, 1987). In particular, it does not capture the psychological states not encompassed by the conflict model inherent in its structure. Similarly, the measure of psychoanalytic process developed by Gill and Hoffman (see Chapter 17) does not address the role of nontransferential elements in psychoanalysis.

An effective way to achieve reliability is to provide detailed protocols for making decisions. Implementing these protocols on computers, if possible, not only allows rapid data processing but forces the investigator to specify the procedure. Computer processing is extremely reliable because it eliminates implicit judgments, with the ever-present potential for unrecognized bias. The obvious disadvantage of computer methods is a lack of subtlety of judgment and a limited capacity of current computer technology to deal with central aspects of psychoanalytic data — intent and meaning. Currently computer measures are being used in the study of the lexical properties of psychoanalytic transcripts (Bucci, 1985, 1988, 1997; Spence, 1990).

CONTROL SUBJECTS

Probably the most touted means of demonstrating the efficacy of a procedure is to compare the outcomes for otherwise comparable populations systematically treated in different ways. The first reproaches of psychoanalytic efficacy (Eysenck, 1952) charged that controlled studies were lacking. That reproach has continued (Torrey, 1992; Grünbaum, 1994). The demonstration that effects at first thought irrelevant to outcome could profoundly affect treatments led to the introduction of ever more elaborate means to keep the comparison groups as similar as possible. For example, placebo treatments designed to resemble the therapeutic agenda except in the active ingredient were introduced to limit the effects of patient beliefs on outcome. Double-blind designs attempted to keep clinicians and evaluators in the dark about the presence or absence of the "active ingredient," both so that they would not subtly communicate this information to patients and so that they would not introduce bias by treating or evaluating the patients differently based on the knowledge that they were giving active treatment or placebo.

From considerable investigation into their effects (Peck and Coleman, 1991), it seems clear that placebo controls are not possible for a treatment like psychoanalysis. Various attempts have been made in psychotherapy research to provide no-treatment control groups — for example, by comparing patients in treatment with those who are on a waiting list — but no such arrangements can control for all relevant variables. More important, as we will see, the number of subjects that can be studied in this fashion is likely to be too small for the groups to be comparable because random variations in the selection of the two groups are likely to produce noncomparable groups.

Another solution is to compare patients treated by different methods (Gehan and Freireich, 1974). Such arrangements present two sorts of difficulties. First, it is exceedingly difficult to define all the ways in which any two therapies differ in practice. Secondly, such a design almost inevitably violates the principle that the problem, treatment, and outcome measures must be congruent. Outcome measures have theoretical orientations, so that at least one of the therapies is likely to be measured by criteria inconsistent with its intended goals.

Another approach to the problem of controls is to use a knowledge of the natural history of the patients' disorders (Ryle, 1948) as a basis for comparison to the outcome of analyses. This approach is particularly promising for conditions in which one can be reasonably certain that little change would occur without intervention — for example, character disorders. However, caution is in order. Until recently most psychoanalytic theories held that the development of personality ceased or at least decreased substantially with the end of adolescence. There is now substantial evidence to the contrary (Nemiroff and Colarusso, 1990; Stevens-Long, 1990; Galatzer-Levy and Cohler, 1993a). In any case, the results of systematic studies of the stability of personality and adult development depend strongly on the methods (Costa and McCrae, 1989; Rutter and Rutter, 1993). For example, repeated phenomenological interviews of a homogeneous sample of upper-middle-class males between the ages fourteen and twenty-two revealed striking continuity of development from adolescence to adulthood (Offer and Offer, 1975). In contrast, Block and Haan (1971) found discontinuities in character organization between adolescence and young adulthood in middle-class subjects, particularly among females and certain subgroups of male subjects. Vaillant (1977, 1993), on the basis of longitudinal studies that attended particularly to mechanisms of defense, suggests that personality organization normatively shifts from reliance on less mature to more mature defenses over the course of late adolescence and adult life. These examples, which could be multiplied, suggest that it is unwarranted to assume that personalities are ordinarily stable and that significant observed change among analysands must be a result of the analysis.[5]

A major task for psychoanalytic process and outcome research is to differentiate specific therapeutic effects from ordinary development. In the Menninger Psychotherapy Research Project (Wallerstein, 1986a; see Chapter 5) a large proportion of the patients showed favorable changes in Health-Sickness Scale ratings. But the clinicians carrying out these treatments were generally convinced that the changes were heavily influenced by the therapeutic relationship. On the other hand, it is difficult to determine what improvements people make on their own or with the help of other institutions such as Alcoholics Anonymous, similar self-help groups, or organized religion. Longitudinal studies have shown that changes during the life cycle sometimes occur as a result of an individual's reflection about her own characteristic behaviors, without the intervention of psychotherapy (Jaques, 1965; Vaillant, 1976). Thus refinement is needed for the strategy of using implicit controls based on the assumption that patients would not change without intervention.

Research on the efficacy of psychoanalysis can be facilitated by careful attention to well-developed concepts of systematic investigation that have emerged in the social sciences and medicine during the past century. These concepts should be regarded as useful tools, not prescriptions. Their applicability and appropriateness must be assessed with regard to specifically psychoanalytic questions and concepts.

Situations in Which Data Are Collected

Data about psychoanalytic processes and their outcomes may be collected in the analysis itself or outside of it. Extraclinical studies produce data that can address questions that might not emerge from examination of the analytic process itself. Data from within the analysis generally provide greater

---

5. However, the idea of using predictable stability need not be abandoned entirely. Psychopathology can be conceptualized as a rigid incapacity to change and develop. The therapeutic action of psychoanalysis results in reducing impediments to development so that it may resume (Hartmann, 1939a,b; Freud, 1965; Galatzer-Levy, 1988b). Therefore we would expect patient populations to be more stable with regard to psychoanalytically pertinent qualities than normal individuals. An increased rate of change of personality variables would be a reasonable measure of psychoanalytic process.

depth of information. Such data may be collected at various times in the analysis, and inferences drawn from these data depend on the significance attributed to the findings at that time.

DATA FROM OUTSIDE THE ANALYSIS

Extra-analytically collected data range from surveys of analysts' views of their practices to psychological testing and follow-up interviews. Collecting data outside of analyses permits the researcher to look at a wide range of variables without impinging directly on the analytic process or requiring the sustained cooperation of analysts and analysands. The disadvantages include indirect impingement on the analytic process, the unavailability of direct information about the analytic process, and the relatively less rich quality of the data.

SURVEYS

Surveys of analytic practice and practitioners can tell us a great deal about the nature of a psychoanalytic practice, the kinds of patients seen, and their difficulties. In his survey of British psychoanalysts, Glover (1955) demonstrated the wide range of techniques that qualified analysts called psychoanalysis. If nothing else, he showed the need for clear descriptive language; technical terms were used in such varied ways that they lost their specificity. He also showed that many analysts routinely used analysis to treat nonneurotic patients.

Doidge and colleagues (1993), through a survey of analysts in Ontario, found that analysands, far from being the worried well who sought treatment for minor distress, suffered from severe psychopathology that significantly interfered with their functioning. Doidge and colleagues also examined the impact of psychoanalysis beyond its effects on particular patients; for example, many of the analysands were actively parenting children at the time of their treatment. Fraiberg, Adelson, and Shapiro (1975) posited on the basis of clinical experience that parenting is profoundly affected by the parent's continuing unconscious image of her own parents. The presence of these ghosts in the nursery has recently been convincingly demonstrated by the empirical work of Peter Fonagy and his coworkers (1993). One of their findings is that individuals with a history of mistreatment during childhood are far less likely to function poorly as parents and their children are less likely to show the negative impact of this parental dysfunction if the parent had psychologically worked though the impact of past mistreatment.

An ongoing survey of members of the Association for Child Psychoanalysis, intended to yield a picture of the course of child psychoanalysis over a wide geographical area, shows that many children in analysis suffer from such conditions as gender-identity disorder, arrested development, and disabling neurosis. Many are children of divorce; others have been adopted or traumatized.

Survey results allow a broader picture of psychoanalytic activities than could be achieved in any other way. They are, however, subject to a range of difficulties. Nonresponders are not a random subset of the population studied. In surveys of analytic practice, nonresponders may include analysts who are disaffected with psychoanalysis or its institutions, analysts embarrassed by their small practices, and analysts who are extraordinarily scrupulous about confidentiality. This last group may include particularly analysts who treat famous individuals and their families or other analysts and their families, so that some of the most widely respected analysts may be reluctant to participate in surveys.

Even when they have been constructed with great care, surveys entail problems with validity and reliability. For example, in Doidge's study analysts were asked to make DSM-III-R diagnoses of their patients. A subset of DSM-III-R diagnoses has been shown to be reliable in the hands of trained raters using systematic psychiatric interviews. But most psychoanalysts are not well-trained as raters. Furthermore, it is rare for psychoanalysts to use structured diagnostic interviews. Hence the meaning of the DSM-III-R diagnoses reported by the surveyed analysts is unclear. They do not have the reliability and validity of such diagnoses in other systematic studies.

Nonetheless, survey findings can be important. They may point to areas that require systematic investigation. They suggest, once again, that special care must be taken to operationalize terms in psychoanalytic investigations.

PUBLISHED DESCRIPTIONS OF ANALYSES

Many descriptions of analyses are available in the psychoanalytic literature. They are a potential source of data for the study of the effects of analysis. Their value as evidence is limited because the material presented is usually carefully chosen for the purpose of convincing the reader of the author's point; because of the inadequate detail in most of the descriptions; because the reporting analyst's selection of the material puts him in a privileged position of being alone in having the data from which conclusions may be drawn; because the data provided tend to be selected in a way that conforms to preexisting theory; and because of erratic practices of "disguise" of analytic material intended to protect confidentiality (Spence, 1994). Actively addressing these problems — for example, by employing formats to present analytic material that make sources of information clear, providing extended, detailed descriptions of psychoanalytic process differentiating events within the session from the analyst's conclusions regarding them, and allowing published commentary by other analysts — could make published case histories a more valuable source of data for psychoanalytic research (Klumpner and Frank, 1991; Spence, 1993). However, even with their current faults, these reports are useful for systematic investigation in providing a collection of possible courses for analyses that extends beyond the experience of individual analysts and thus may enrich the possibilities explored in systematic investigations. Correlations discovered or extractable in already published cases may be particularly valuable to explore in more-systematic investigations.[6] In recent years increasingly sophisticated methods have emerged for systematically exploring previously published data and reports as a source for empirical investigation.

Published descriptions of analyses by analysands, though not a source of systematic data and though often reflecting unusual circumstances, such as the analyst's fame, can nonetheless be a rich source of descriptions of the analytic situation as experienced by the patient and of the long-term effects of analysis. Reports like those of Grinker (1940), Kardiner (1977), Wortis (1954), and the Wolfman's (Gardiner, 1971) of analyses with Freud provide descriptions of Freud's technique and its impact on several patients. Similarly, accounts like Little's (1987) and Guntrip's (1975) provide analysands' views of particular methods of analytic work. Fictionalized autobiographical accounts like Hannah Greenberg's *I Never Promised You a Rose Garden* give unusually rich descriptions of the patient's experience of the analyst. Peter Heller (1990) describes the extraordinarily complex impact of an analysis in late latency and early adolescence on its author's life course through early old age. Guntrip (1975) describes his analyses with Fairbairn and Winnicott, providing a useful comparison of their techniques as experienced by an analysand.

Studying Analyses at Various Times in Their Course

The question of the points in time at which psychoanalyses should be studied is complex. Analysands usually begin treatment in some acute difficulty. But the analysis attempts to relieve chronic sources of distress. Therefore the patient's status at the beginning of treatment is not a satisfactory baseline for comparison in assessing analytic results. Similarly, because the intent of

---

6. It is important to distinguish the assertions of authors from the data they present. Thus the Laufers (1989) described the analyses of a series of severely disturbed adolescents to demonstrate the value of their approach in working with such youngsters. They conclude that their recommendations are supported by their data. Yet none of the cases has a satisfactory analytic or even therapeutic outcome (see Chapter 9).

analysis is to have a long-term impact on patients and the process of terminating analysis may itself have acute psychological effects, the patient's status at termination is not a satisfactory measure of outcome. Ideally, one would like to know the patient's status for extended periods before and after the analysis; however, there are great problems in gathering this information.

As a practical matter, the earlier that systematic investigation of analytic outcome is done, the larger the population available for study. If it were shown, for example, that patient status after a year of analysis was highly correlated with status ten years after termination, it would be possible to come to strong conclusions about the efficacy of psychoanalysis much more quickly than if it were necessary to follow the subjects for ten years after termination.

STUDIES AT TERMINATION AND FOLLOW-UP

The patient's overall functioning during termination as compared with the initial evaluation has traditionally been used as a measure of analytic outcome, with the problems we have enumerated. Termination status has been studied systematically by Firestein (1978), Pfeffer (1959, 1961, 1963), Schachter (1990; Panel, 1989), and Wallerstein (1986a).

Psychoanalysis is intended to address and alter the causes of manifest psychopathology. At one time it was thought that recontacting patients after termination of psychoanalysis might revive old conflicts or interfere with the idea that the analysis has terminated. The first idea is probably correct but generally not disadvantageous to the patient. Other concerns about the effects of follow-up interviews and evaluation have not been borne out (Schachter, 1990; Panel, 1990). Follow-up interviews not only provide an opportunity to learn how the patient is doing but give more information about the analytic process itself than was available during the analysis. Follow-up studies using various methodologies include the Menninger Psychotherapy Research Project (Wallerstein, 1986a), Pfeffer (1959, 1961, 1963), Schlessinger and Robbins (1974, 1983), Oremland, Blacker, and Norman (1975), Norman et al. (1976), Knapp et al. (1960), Klein (1960), Kantrowitz et al. (1987a,b), and Kantrowitz, Katz, and Paolitto (1990a,b,c).

Follow-up studies of analysis can also illuminate the mechanisms of therapeutic action. The data of Schlessinger and Robbins (1974, 1983; Schlessinger, 1987) bear on the relation of patient's presenting problems, the course of treatment, the patient's retrospective report of what was beneficial, and the analyst's view. Retrospective reconstruction of the pathways to change, as understood by patient and analyst (Appelbaum, 1978), is a particularly helpful way of understanding how analysis works and how analyses can be stalemated (Coen, 1992).

Follow-up interviews provide information about the postanalytic course of the patient's life, including the fate of symptoms, relations with others, capacity to work, and responses to psychologically challenging events. The patient's conscious ideas about the analysis and indications of ideas that are outside of awareness can be gathered in these interviews. The patient's psychological capacities and insight can also be evaluated and transference manifestation and their management assessed.

Pfeffer (1959, 1961, 1963) found that relatively unstructured follow-up interviews provide a rich opportunity to understand the original analysis because patients commonly repeat, in miniature and much faster, the emergence, experience, and resolution of the transference neurosis. This finding, which has been independently confirmed by other investigators (Schlessinger and Robbins, 1974, 1975, 1984; Oremland, Blacker, and Norman 1975), provides an extraordinary window into the psychoanalytic process, consistent with the psychoanalytic view that the exploration of the transference is the most powerful means for understanding psychology in depth.

Unfortunately, many follow-up investigations have been technically less than satisfactory. The data on which Schlessinger and Robbins base their findings is methodologically messy. Most of the analysands they studied were treated by analytic candidates. In all instances their analysts had volunteered the cases for study. The analyses were reconstructed from available process notes and reports several years after termination. The extent, manner of production, and content of these records varied markedly. These data were processed by means of classroom discussions involving the researchers and advanced candidates, without benefit of guiding principles and so subject to the many difficulties discussed by Seitz (1966) in regard to such unstructured discussions. The analysand is interviewed by a follow-up analyst familiar with the case material, and the process notes of these interviews are further discussed by the class. Thus the findings of this study are severely compromised. In spite (or perhaps because) of these difficulties, this study repeatedly demonstrates the recapitulation of the analytic transference in the relationship with the follow-up interviewer.

The findings of follow-up research have led to reconsideration of the meaning of satisfactory psychoanalytic outcome. Rather than resolving conflicts, psychoanalysis appears to make the analysand capable of more rapid and less maladaptive resolution of conflicts as they emerge (Weiss, 1981).

SECOND ANALYSES

Re-analyses provide opportunities for systematic study of the patient's previous psychoanalytic experience (Waldhorn, 1968; Horowitz, 1987, 1990) and provide thereby an unusual opportunity to clarify clinical theory about the contributions of patient and analyst to the analytic process.

Second analyses commonly address areas of difficulty inadequately analyzed or not even addressed in the first analysis. Two famous examples are the Wolfman's re-analysis with Ruth Mack-Brunswick (1928) and Kohut's (1979) two analyses of Mr. Z.[7] The need for further analysis to address issues not approached during the first analysis does not necessarily suggest analytic failure. As Freud (1937a) observed, conflicts that are not currently active in the patient cannot be analyzed. On the other hand, it may be that the issues were not addressed for some other reason, and understanding why this is so can provide considerable insight into the earlier analytic process. Some investigators (Baudry, 1991; Kantrowitz, 1992) suggest that particular characteristics of the analyst do much to determine the focus of the analytic process and may lead to insufficient analysis of matters that are available for analytic work.

Problems with Studying Analyses in Their Entirety

The major problem with data about whole analyses, and even more with studying whole lives of which analysis are part, is that the complexity of any analysis or life makes it difficult to determine causal relations. However, it is extremely difficult to summarize the entirety of an analysis in a reasonably condensed fashion and to identify overall effects if we require ordinary levels of evidence for such assertions. For this reason many researchers have turned to the smaller, more tractable, but still challenging problem of identifying effective elements in the psychoanalytic process. In the following chapters we explore some of these approaches.

7. Recent evidence (Cocks, 1994) that Mr. Z. was, in fact, Kohut himself and that the second analysis was a self-analysis threw this case into a state of evidential confusion. This illustrates the importance of attention to issues of disguise in writing about psychoanalytic occurrences. For purposes of describing and exploring important psychological configurations it makes little difference whether or not Mr. Z. was Kohut. But as a study of the efficacy of a therapeutic intervention and of the superiority of self psychology to traditional psychoanalytic technique, it makes a significant difference. Self psychology technique depends on specific interactions between analyst and patient to which the analyst contributes in a way that the patient cannot. This is different from analytic techniques that regard the analyst's major contribution as interpretation, which conceivably could be contributed by the patient herself. Self psychological self-analysis is not equivalent to analysis with another person in the same way that traditional self-analysis is. Thus, if Mr. Z. is Kohut, the case history fails to present direct evidence of the superiority of a self psychology approach to the patient's analysis.

15

Information About Patients

Traditionally medical treatments have been organized around the idea that certain qualities of the patient predict the efficacy of treatment. Diagnosis should determine intervention, at least after consideration of other patient attributes, such as overall health, age, and capacity to cooperate in treatment. As we have seen in earlier chapters, this model has not worked well for psychoanalysis. In this chapter we look more closely at ways of describing patients, some of which may prove fruitful in predicting response to treatment.

Psychological Testing

Psychological tests consist of a standardized series of tasks aimed at the reliable and valid assessment of particular psychological qualities. Psychological testing in the United States has important roots in psychoanalytic theory. The construction, organization, and interpretation of the tasks are dependent upon this frame of reference. In the early 1940s Rapaport, Gill, and Schafer (1945) constructed a test battery (Wechsler-Bellevue, Rorschach, Thematic Apperception Test, Babcock Story Recall, and BRL Object Sorting test) according to psychoanalytic principles. Over the years this battery became the operational right arm of psychoanalytic ego psychology. Although the particular tests have changed, the basic concept of a battery of tests that explore a range of capacities and function remains the foundation of diagnostic psychological testing (Groth-Marnat, 1997).

Testing provides information about patient functioning comparatively free of contamination by the motivations of either patient or therapist-analyst. In the hands of psychoanalytically trained examiners, it can provide a penetrating portrait of intrapsychic functioning, as is demonstrated in the Menninger project (Appelbaum, 1977). Because it addresses a wide range of psychological functions, not only those identified as problematic by patient or analyst, it is likely to pick up a wide range of difficulties. It provides comparable data about psychological functions in a way that rarely occurs in even the most careful clinical report.

Psychological testing, however, is labor intensive, and the results, especially of projective testing, are greatly dependent on the knowledge, skill, and experience of the examiner. Psychological tests that address issues of particular interest to analysts, such as unconscious fantasy, are among the least reliable of these procedures.

Several psychoanalytic and psychoanalytically oriented investigators have developed systematic means of assessing personality characteristics of patients (Wallerstein, 1988; DeWitt, Hartley, and Rosenberg, 1991; Zilberg et al., 1991; Horowitz et al., 1984; Perry and Cooper, 1986, 1987; Vaillant, 1975, 1976, 1986). Scales that measure the quality of the therapeutic alliance, including the Penn Helping Alliance Scale (Luborsky et al., 1983), the California Psychotherapy Alliance Scales (Marmor, Weiss, and Gaston, 1989; Marmor et al., 1986), and the Vanderbilt Therapeutic Alliance scale (Hartley and Strupp, 1983), are particularly valuable in investigating psychoanalysis as therapy (Horvath, Gaston, and Luborsky, 1993). Scales designed to measure insight and experience (Morgan et al., 1982; Crits-Christoph et al., 1993) and self-reports of symptoms (Battle et al., 1966), as well as many scales designed to measure and describe psychopathology and personal adjustment, can be used in psychoanalytic research. However, the meaningful use of any scale depends on its ability to address the congruence of problem, therapy, and outcome measure.

In traditional psychological testing, the examiner is expected to retain a detailed record of the subject's responses, as well as to reduce those data to standardized reporting modes. As a result it is possible to reexamine the data from points of view different from those of the original examiner. As we have noted, the elaborate psychological test battery performed as part of the Menninger study was a disappointing predictor of change. Projective tests, such as the Rorschach, were especially poor at differentiating patients who did well from those who did poorly in analysis. Blatt and his coworkers (Blatt, 1990,

1992; Blatt and Berman, 1984) reexamined transcripts of Rorschach test protocols (available because the retention of such information is standard procedure in psychological testing), reinterpreted test findings on the basis of an
object-relations perspective, and found that broad object-relations characteristics correlated with treatment outcomes (Blatt, 1996).

Psychiatric Diagnosis

In the medical model a diagnosis refers to a disease entity whose current
manifestations (signs, symptoms, history, and laboratory findings) are linked
to a specific etiology and mode of pathogenesis (pathophysiology), as well as
a prognosis without treatment (natural history) and expectations of the effects of various treatments (Ryle, 1948). Diseases are regarded as progres-
sively well understood as various aspects of these descriptions are filled in
more completely.

This enormously effective way of thinking about disease in general was first
systematically applied to psychiatric conditions by Kraeplin. It became popular in the United States following the demonstration of its value in the management of and research about psychotic disorder and certain forms of panic
disorder (Goodwin and Guze, 1984). Early psychoanalytic authors assumed
that the symptom complexes of descriptive psychiatry correlated with specific
psychodynamics and described the dynamics of many psychiatric conditions
(Fenichel, 1945). However, increasingly sophisticated study repeatedly indicated that the correlation between clinical findings and psychodynamics was
not as strong as had once been believed. Some analysts approached this problem by attempting to develop a nosology that correlated better with psychodynamics. A few psychoanalysts attempted to classify patients in this way
(Zetzel and Meissner, 1973) and found the approach particularly helpful in
differentiating seemingly similar patients whose conditions differed dramatically in psychogenesis and response to psychoanalysis. Zetzel (1968), for
example, showed that a group of patients who had been diagnosed as hysteric
but who responded very differently to attempts at psychoanalysis could be
differentiated on the basis of history, symptoms, and response to treatment.
Promising attempts to update a psychoanalytic diagnostic framework (Mc-
Williams, 1994) have not yet received the attention they deserve.

The current dominant implementation of the medical model in the mental
health professions is the fourth edition of the Diagnostic and Statistical Manual of the American Psychiatric Association, DSM-IV (Task Force on DSM-IV,
1994). Its authors attempted to design a classificatory system that avoided
inadequately proven presumptions about pathogenesis, such as the idea that

certain symptoms result from unconscious conflict. They eliminated the term *neurosis* from the diagnostic vocabulary because psychoanalytic usage had so permeated psychiatric thought that the term carried a clear etiological implication. The resulting volume is far from its avowed atheoretical stance. In its selection of data and organization of syndromes, it reflects the position that psychiatric syndromes should be organized primarily by manifest symptoms (Michaels in Panel, 1987; Millon, 1991; Millon and Davis, 1996; Carson, 1991; Morey, 1991; Skinner, 1981; Benjamin, 1993). By choosing this organization the authors of DSM-IV strongly suggest that each symptom complex is associated with a common etiology and mechanisms of pathogenesis. In fact, insofar as DSM-IV is attempting to follow modern medical nosology, its use of diagnoses implies that its authors strongly believe that they are describing more than symptom complexes. The classifications in DSM-IV are not comparable to the classificatory systems current in medicine today. The systems in medicine are based first on common pathogenesis, second on histologic features of affected tissue, and third on anatomical location of the lesion. DSM-IV is like older classifications of disease that categorized disease entities by their manifestation — for example, listing fevers as a category of ailments.

The overall strategy of diagnostic classification has proven a powerful practical and research tool. By studying groups of people who share a carefully delineated diagnosis, researchers have been able to advance far more rapidly in finding specific causes, mechanisms, and treatments of disease than if they were studying heterogeneous but similar-seeming groups of patients. If we possessed reliable psychodynamic diagnoses, a full description of conditions in terms of such diagnosis could be carried out and related to the psychoanalytic process with patients with the diagnosis. Psychodynamic diagnosis could be carefully correlated with descriptive diagnosis. Where meaningful correlations exist, information derived from descriptive studies could be employed in psychoanalytic investigations.[1]

1. Enormous confusion about diagnosis arises because of the use of identical terms to refer to distinct entities. In many instances, similar terms are used when entirely different conceptual frameworks are employed. For example, the ancient term *hysteria* (Veith, 1965), which was widely used in the end of the nineteenth century, came to refer to a specific psychodynamic configuration in the work of psychoanalysts (Fenichel, 1945). Subsequently it was adopted by descriptive psychiatrists (Goodwin and Guze, 1984) to refer to a condition (previously called Briquet's syndrome) on the basis of descriptive findings. The population described as hysterics by descriptive psychiatrists overlaps minimally with the population described by analysts using the same term. Furthermore, the conceptual framework in which the diagnosis is made is entirely different. Similar issues arise for a variety of terms used in common but having quite different meanings.

A clear advantage of descriptive diagnosis over psychodynamic diagnosis is that the information needed to make descriptive diagnoses is generally more readily available and requires less inference on the part of the diagnostician. However, this advantage is important only insofar as descriptive diagnoses meaningfully classify psychological disturbances. Another apparent advantage of descriptive diagnosis is their greater reliability. However, this reliability has not been demonstrated for many DSM-IV categories, especially personality disorders (Millon and Davis, 1996). Finally, because descriptive diagnoses are widely used in psychiatric research generally, including psychotherapy outcome research (Roth and Fonagy, 1996), the use of such classification in psychoanalytic investigations would facilitate comparisons between psychoanalysis and other treatments.

Michaels (Panel, 1987) claims that a reliable and valid psychodynamically based diagnostic system is possible, although studies supporting this claim are not yet available. Recent studies have begun to address the issue of validity and reliability of psychodynamic formulations (Hoglend, Guldberg, and Perry, 1992; Horowitz et al., 1989; Messer, 1991; Perry, Luborsky, et al., 1989; Perry, Augusto, and Cooper, 1989). Descriptions have been developed of a systematic psychodynamic formulation for adults (Perry, Cooper, and Michaels, 1987, 1988) and children and adolescents (Shapiro, 1989c). Several psychodynamic perspectives have been explored in this manner (Collins and Messer, 1991; Perry, 1989; Sabelli and Carlson, 1991; McWilliams, 1994). Psychodynamic formulations have been used in prescribing and assessing therapies (Hinshelwood, 1991).

Although they are not yet available as a research tool for the study of psychoanalytic outcomes, psychodynamic formulations and diagnoses hold the promise of providing a means by which the medical model of correlating specific therapeutics with specific diagnoses can be applied to psychoanalysis using psychoanalytically meaningful diagnostic categories. This would permit the correlations of diagnosis, therapy, and outcome typical of medical investigation in a context where diagnostic categories are meaningfully related to the therapeutic process — as they are not with purely descriptive diagnoses.

The Diagnostic Profile

Extending earlier psychoanalytic concepts, Anna Freud (1965) developed the concept of developmental lines — regularly expectable sequences of capacities that emerge in children (and possibly adults) with maturation. An individual can be described by her status with regard to each of several developmental lines. Psychopathology can often be understood as a failure to continue along one or more of these lines or as the result of strains when developmental lines become discoordinated. Anna Freud and her coworkers created the diagnostic profile to assess developmental lines in patients systematically.

The profile, based on interviews with patients (and sometimes family and teachers), assesses drive, ego function, and superego development and the relations among them. It describes the reaction of the total personality to specific life-situation demands, tasks, or opportunities.

Initially, this ambitious undertaking did not take into consideration the complexities of translating clinical observation into psychodynamic formulations. For example, it was difficult to construct from clinical material the sequence of steps by which one achieves overall developmental solutions such as adult sexuality and love, an ability to work, and the capacity for peer relationships. The mere observation of a symptom or conflict does not speak to the individual's overall developmental stage or functioning, nor does it make clear the history and status of these compromise formations. Studies of the concept of developmental line and the diagnostic profile led to many attempts to clarify the common psychoanalytic concepts used in the profile (Freud, 1968; Nagera, 1966, 1967, 1969; Sandler, Kennedy, and Tyson, 1975; Sandler and Freud, 1985). However, the diagnostic profile has found only limited application in published investigations of particular cases and clinical situations (see, e.g., Bolland and Sandler, 1965; Brinich, 1981; Burlingham, 1975; Freud, 1971; Meers, 1966; Thomas, 1966; Wills, 1981). In its current form, it does not appear to provide an adequate tool for assessing psychoanalytic outcome in developmental terms. The long attempt to develop it into such a tool demonstrates many of the difficulties that face attempts to capture the wide range of psychoanalytically important issues in patients' personalities and analyses.

Other Classification Schemes

Among the other means used to systematically describe patients in terms of psychoanalytic concepts, classification according to characteristic defense style (A. Freud, 1936; Kernberg, 1976; Panel, 1954; Pumpian-Mindlin, 1967) is closely tied to the technique of psychoanalysis. Psychological difficulties may be classified as predominantly interpersonal or as experienced internally. This classification correlates in some ways with the outcome of brief psychodynamic psychotherapy.

Short-term insight-oriented therapy has been found to be more effective for patients with interpersonal problems and especially for those with problems in assertion than for patients who are less interpersonally focused or who have problems with intimacy (Horowitz et al., 1988). However, there is good evidence of the difficulty in relating patient characteristics to treatment course in psychotherapy, particularly when patient characteristics are evaluated before the beginning of treatment (Horwitz, 1974; Bachrach, Weber, and Solomon, 1985; Luborsky et al., 1988; Garfield, 1994; Crits-Christoph and Connolly, 1993). The early interaction of patient and analyst may have a greater prognostic value (Luborsky et al., 1988). Freud's (1913) contention that a trial of analysis is the best prognostic tool may be confirmed in systematic studies. It is consistent with the idea that the outcome of analysis may be best understood in terms of the match of analyst and patient rather than the qualities of one of these alone.

Global Measures of Psychological Health

One of the more surprising findings from investigations of the efficacy of dynamic therapies generally is that much of what can be predicted about the outcome of dynamic psychotherapies can be predicted on the basis of general measures of psychological health (Luborsky et al., 1993). Obviously, then, studies of psychoanalysis as therapy should include careful assessments of overall psychological health.

Several global measures of mental health have been developed in the last quarter-century and have proved to be powerful predictors of the outcome of dynamic psychotherapy, as well as other forms of psychotherapy (Luborsky et al., 1988, 1993). The Health-Sickness Rating Scale (HSRS), developed at the Menninger Foundation, consists of seven 100-point graphic scales measuring: (1) the need to be protected or supported versus the ability to function autonomously; (2) seriousness of symptoms; (3) subjective discomfort and distress; (4) effects of the environment; (5) utilization of abilities; (6) interpersonal relationships; and (7) breadth and depth of interests. The rater compares the case to thirty sample cases and ranks it both with respect to each of these criteria and globally (Luborsky, 1975). The Global Assessment Scale, or GAS, is a simplified reworking of the HSRS. Incorporated as axis 5 of DSM-III-R, it has wide currency in systematic psychiatric studies of all kinds.

Global measures of psychological health have been shown to be valid and reliable. They are highly intercorrelated. However, global measures of mental health are only moderately correlated with diagnosis. This means that they provide information that is different from that available from diagnosis alone. The correlation between overall psychological health and therapeutic benefit was first noted by Freud in 1937 (1937a), but the reasons for this correlation remain unclear. Delineation of the ways in which global psychological health affects psychoanalytic processes is an important research issue. In addition, the finding is of great importance for researchers who try to investigate more-specific patient-based determinants of psychoanalytic outcome. A positive finding should not be taken at face value because it may simply replicate the finding of the impact of global psychological health on outcome by way of showing that the particular marker studied also predicts outcome. For example, a positive finding that the capacity of mature object relations predicts good psychoanalytic outcome would need to be reevaluated to determine whether the finding was specific to object relations or resulted because the finding was strongly associated with many other indications of good psychological health.

Conclusion

The tools used in the past to study patient characteristics have not proved to be strongly effective predictors of psychoanalytic outcome. This suggests that characteristics of the patient are significant only insofar as these characteristics are part of the psychoanalytic dyad. Therefore, within the range of patients likely to benefit from psychoanalysis, one would expect patient characteristics alone to be weak predictors of outcome. Alternatively, the finding may reflect the inadequacy of the tools used to study patient characteristics. Some tools, such as descriptive diagnosis, are not designed to measure matters of psychoanalytic significance. Others, like some forms of psychological testing, may not be helpful because of inherent psychometric weakness or because the interpretive strategies do not address features of the personality salient to psychoanalytic effect.

Several attempts are being made to provide more psychoanalytically meaningful descriptions of patients. These include diagnostic classifications and formulations that tap psychoanalytically pertinent features (McWilliams, 1994) and new ways of interpreting projective tests that address issues more relevant to psychoanalytic outcome (Blatt, 1990, 1992).

Any investigation of patient characteristics needs to be informed by the robust finding of a strong correlation between the effects of psychotherapies generally and the global psychological health of the patient.

16

Data About Psychoanalytic Processes

In studying psychoanalytic processes or any other complex phenomenon, enough data must be collected to be meaningful, the data must be reduced to a tractable form without undue loss of significance, and the extent to which particular findings can be generalized must be described. Not only is the analytic process complex, but it varies from one analysis to another. It is therefore important that many detailed instances of psychoanalytic practice be available for close study. During the eighteenth and nineteenth centuries, the painstaking collection of information in chemistry, descriptive biology, geology, and many other fields led to the generalizations that are the foundations of these sciences. For example, Mendeleyev's creation of the periodic table depended on the collection and classification of thousands of chemical compounds by his predecessors. In the twentieth century the study of the language of children leaped forward as large numbers of tape-recorded specimens of children's speech became available for systematic study (MacWhinney, 1991). In each instance the discipline has been well rewarded for the enormous effort involved in collecting data and making them available for study.

Psychoanalysts are just beginning this process. Their principal source of information consists of empirical data generated by the application of psychoanalytic methods and reported by analysts, patients, supervisors, and participants in classes and study groups. But this source is problematic from the point of view of systematic research because of the unsystematic way in which most of the data are collected, their lack of public availability, and their limited scope — all of which increase the likelihood that the analyst's conclusions are idiosyncratic. Because the data to which they refer are unavailable for critical perusal, these conclusions often cannot be corrected through exposure to critical discussion. And because the sample on which the conclusions are based is not specified, the generalizability of the conclusions remains unknown. Most publicly available clinical material appears in published case histories, usually intended to convince the reader of the author's viewpoint. As a result, little attention is given to providing data that do not support the author's contention. Whatever the merits of such reports as education, persuasion, or communication, they seldom provide adequate information for any other purpose. And those data collected with systematic research in mind tend to be based on a very small number of analyses, representing the work of an even smaller number of analysts. The result is that these collections may provide distorted and noncomparable pictures of other analyses.

Methods of Data Collection

Analysts have used many means to collect and present data about psychoanalytic process, from writing case summaries to videotaping analytic sessions. Each of these methods has both advantages and disadvantages.

CASE HISTORIES

Starting with Freud, case histories have been a major means of describing psychoanalytic process and findings. They are usually organized as narratives and designed to be persuasive. Case histories usually omit the obscure, boring, or contradictory.[1] Their value as scientific evidence about psychoanalytic process is therefore usually limited, although they may convincingly demonstrate the possibility of psychoanalysis in special circumstances (for

---

1. Very skillful writers, like Freud, commonly obscure the extent to which their case histories are designed as suasive narratives by presenting material as if it were unfolding and as if contradictions and inconsistencies were included. Thus Freud's cases read very much like detective stories in which the reader is repeatedly confronted by obscure clues and contradictions. However, unlike real-life situations in which such matters often go unresolved and remain obscure, in Freud's case histories we ultimately return to these apparently obscure matters, discovering how they can be psychoanalytically explained. Genuinely obscure matters, in the sense that the author does not understand and cannot significantly elaborate on their meaning, are almost never referred to in Freud's (and other analysts') case reports.

example, with certain types of borderline patients) or paint a picture of a mode of psychoanalytic work from which a systematic description can be derived, or even provide convincing evidence against the author's contention. Because a description of a case history is concrete, it often communicates its author's ideas more effectively than abstract statements.

Case histories inevitably convey much more than the authors intend. As numerous studies demonstrate, Freud's case histories commonly contain a rich, indirect discourse on psychoanalytically important matters and reward careful study with wide-ranging understandings of the process between analyst and patient (e.g., Glenn, 1986; Decker, 1992; Mahony, 1984, 1986, 1987, 1996). Studied in this way, published case histories can provide much information about analytically important matters. They also have the virtue of presenting materials that are subject to psychoanalytic interpretation by the reader, who may refer back to the text to see whether and how it supports particular interpretations of the analyst-author and evaluate the adequacy of the interpretation offered.

For all their methodological problems, psychoanalytic case histories have proved enormously useful in showing what analysis can do, clarifying analytic concepts, and encouraging psychoanalytic exploration.

PROCESS SUMMARIES

Many analysts routinely keep notes about analytic occurrences and the progress of treatments. These notes typically include summary statements of analytic process, along with detailed descriptions of matters that the analyst believes to be important, such as the patient's dreams, important analytic interventions, and particularly clear, interesting, or enigmatic statements by the patient.

As tools for research, process summaries have the advantage of being minimally disruptive to the analysis. They are generally written near the time of the occurrences they report and therefore are less likely to reflect lapses in the analyst's memory than are case histories, which are commonly written long after the events they describe. However, as we shall see, even very brief hiatuses between analytic events and their recording can introduce major distortions into the clinical record.

The principal disadvantage of process summaries is that analysts are very selective in the material they record. This problem could be addressed by systematizing the writing of process summaries, as has been done with medical records and process notes (Gravenstein, 1989; Hengeveld et al., 1988; Crouch and Thiedke, 1986; Starfield et al., 1979; Switz, 1976). Systematic recording artificially brings to prominence the topics that have been chosen for systematic commentary. However, it ensures that the temporal unfolding of these matters will be recorded.

Viewed psychoanalytically, the failure to record information is itself informative. As we shall discuss later, the systematic exploration of data distortions and omissions can reveal elements of the psychoanalytic process outside the analyst's awareness.

PROCESS NOTES

Process notes are attempts by the analyst to record the details of analytic sessions. They may be made during or shortly after a session. They range in detail from brief descriptions of a dialogue to stenographic records. They may or may not include the analyst's associations and speculations.

Process notes can be valuable sources of information about analytic processes. They are usually far briefer than verbatim transcripts, so they are easier to study. They can provide an overview of an extended series of hours and a guide to critical incidents, and they can reveal recurrent patterns and significant changes that are difficult to detect in transcripts or tape recordings. Verbatim transcripts combined with process notes have proved valuable in some studies (Sampson and Weiss, 1986). For certain types of studies, process notes are sufficiently accurate, as Wolfson and Sampson (1976) have demonstrated by comparing process notes to verbatim transcripts in process studies.

When they include the analyst's point of view, process notes provide data unavailable from transcripts alone (Wallerstein and Sampson, 1971; Wolfson and Sampson, 1976). The increasing emphasis on the analyst's responses has highlighted new types of data as valuable in studying psychoanalytic processes including the analyst's unspoken thoughts, feelings, associations, visual imagery, and bodily sensations (Blum, 1986; Chused, 1990, 1991; Gardner, 1983; Jacobs, 1973, 1983, 1986; Jaffe, 1986; Kohrman et al., 1971; McLaughlin, 1981; Racker, 1968; Schwaber, 1992; Tower, 1956; Tyson, 1986).

Short of audio- or videotaping, the notes taken by the analyst during the session provide the most detailed and accurate access to the analytic process. Analysts develop ways of note taking consonant with their personal and professional styles, from briefly focused note taking during sessions, to automatic note taking, to reconstructions of the central themes or events immediately after an analytic hour or at the end of the day. In Freud's (1912) early view, supported by several later writers (Isakower, 1974; Glover, 1955; Lewin, 1959), taking notes during an analytic session interfered with the evenly suspended attention that he believed facilitates the communication of unconscious forms, contents, and processes. He therefore recommended that events be recorded after a session or at the end of the day. This recommendation made particular sense for Freud, who enjoyed a superb memory (Jones, 1953). With the evolution of psychoanalytic technique, especially the analysis of defense and the close monitoring of the immediate impact of interventions, many analysts today conceive of the optimal clinical data-gathering attitude as an oscillation between evenly suspended attention and close process monitoring (see Wyman and Rittenberg, 1992), which may or may not be disrupted by taking notes. Greenacre (1966), for example, recommended taking notes during sessions in an automatic manner that, in her view, did not interfere with listening or have disruptive effects on the analytic process. The effects of note taking on the analytic process and analytic data gathering have not been the subject of systematic empirical research, although Miller (1964) has discussed the meanings of note taking during sessions.

The major disadvantage of process notes for research, as of process summaries, is the analyst's selectivity in what is recorded. Again, studies of omissions and distortions can in themselves be informative about the psychoanalytic process. Meyer (1988) has reported the results of a comparison of recorded hours and the analyst's dictated commentary immediately following the hour in a small but useful study.

Process notes have been used successfully in psychoanalytic process research. Sampson and Weiss (1986), for example, have studied changes in the materials produced by an analysand on the interpretation of a defense. They showed that the patient's use of the defense of undoing was changed in the direction of a more adaptive pattern of coping following interpretations of this defense. A study of warded-off mental contents using process notes (Horowitz et al., 1975) was replicated and extended using recorded analyses (Gassner et al., 1982).

TAPE RECORDINGS

The study of tape-recorded psychoanalyses rapidly brings into focus the complex details of the analytic situation and demonstrates the many aspects of the psychoanalytic interaction of which the analyst may have been unaware. It can help psychoanalytic conceptualization by providing clear examples of various types of analytic phenomena. It is uniquely valuable for studies of prosody, the music of speech.

Those who first used tape recordings of analyses and therapies were immediately struck by the unreliability of process notes and recollections of analytic happenings.

> When for the first time a student psychiatrist or an experienced analyst hears himself participate in an interview or a psychotherapeutic session, it

is always a surprisingly illuminating experience. He hears himself echo the patient. Or he hears himself outshouting or outwhispering the patient, always louder and always softer. Or he hears himself playing seesaw with his patient — loud when the patient is soft, and soft when the patient is loud. Or with surprise and dismay he hears in his own voice the edge of unintended scorn or sarcasm, or impatience or warmth. Or he hears for the first time his own unnoted tic-like noises punctuating and interrupting the patient's stream. From such data . . . he and the group as a whole learn a great deal about themselves and about the process of interchange with patients and what this process evokes in them in the form of automatic and therefore indescribable patterns of vocal interplay.

They learn also to watch for and to respect the subtle tricks of forgetting and false recall to which the human mind is prone. In one session a young psychiatrist reported that in a previous interview at one point his patient had asked that the recording machine be turned off while he divulged some material which was particularly painful to him. The group discussed the possible reasons for this, basing our discussion on our knowledge of the patient from previous seminars. Then to check the accuracy of our speculative reconstruction, the psychiatrist was asked to play to the group about five minutes of the recorded interview which had preceded the interruption, and then about five of the minutes which followed when the recording had been resumed. To the amazement of the young psychiatrist and of the group as a whole, as we listened to the recording we discovered that it had been the psychiatrist and not the patient who had suggested that the recording should be interrupted. Of his role in this, the young psychiatrist had not the slightest memory. Furthermore, as we heard the patient's halting speech, his change of pace and volume, the later affecting pitch and placing of his voice, it became clear to the whole group that the young psychiatrist's intuitive move had been sound: that he had correctly evaluated the patient's mounting tension and had perceived the need for the gesture of special consideration and privacy. The result was that the patient's rapport was more firmly established than before, to such an extent that the psychiatrist could now recall that it had been [the patient] who had suggested that the recording be resumed after a relatively brief interruption, and who then, with the machine turned on, had continued to discuss frankly and without embarrassment the material about which he had been so touchy before. The illuminating implication of this episode for the data itself and for the transference and countertransference furnished the group with material for reflection and discussion throughout the remaining course of the seminars. These could not have been studied without the recording machine. (Kubie, 1958, quoted in Kächele, Luborsky, and Thomä, 1988, pp. 233–34)

But the use of tape recordings also has disadvantages in psychoanalytic investigation. The sheer bulk of data obtained makes investigation difficult. It tends to focus researchers on short time intervals so as to diminish the amount of data the researcher must process. But this focus may interfere with research on longer-term trends and effects. The prestige of objective data may lead the researcher and others to believe that the researcher has hold of data that have particular merit or unusual validity and may inappropriately elevate the importance of findings that include this method as part of the investigation.

Many analysts are concerned that tape recording will interfere in the analytic process. But other forms of systematic retention of information about psychoanalytic processes may also be interfering. For example, in anticipation of the attempt to recall a session after its completion, the analyst may make mental notes of events in the session, and this may divert his attention during the session. Evidence has accumulated that tape recording may be carried out without adversely affecting the psychoanalytic process in some kinds of patients (Gill et al., 1968; Dahl, 1974; Klumpner, 1984; Tobin and Offenkrantz, 1973). However, recording of analyses can strain a particular analyst. Protestations that recording would negatively affect the patient may rationalize the analyst's distress. Often inadequately analyzed overidealization of analysis and analysts leads many analysts to fear being shamed in revealing their technique, which fails to live up to unrealistic ideals (Greenacre, 1966; Goldberg, 1991).

Some investigators have found that recording and being a research subject have specific, analyzable transference significance. Offenkrantz and Tobin (1973) repeatedly found references to primal-scene fantasies of being observed and the interaction of the analyst with his research group in the material of patients whose analyses had been recorded. Skolnikoff (1988) described the analyst's fantasy of being observed in the research setting as influencing his interpretations. It seems very likely that the impact of recording is specific to the patient and analyst and will affect various analytic couples differently. We know of no investigation that actually tries to demonstrate when audio recording is detrimental or when it is neutral or even helpful to the analytic process.

The tape recording of analyses for research purposes presents thorny ethical problems. Truly informed consent is difficult to obtain because any analysand will have problems refusing a highly motivated request from the analyst, and the patient and analyst cannot know in advance how recording (or not recording) will affect the analytic processes. A program of making primary data available for scrutiny by researchers challenges attempts to maintain analytic confidentiality.

Several methods have been developed to protect the privacy of recorded analysands. Recordings and transcripts can be sanitized to remove identifying information. They can be distributed only to qualified investigators, geographically distant from the place of origin, who agree to guard the patient's confidentiality by ceasing to work with the material if they recognize the patient and by agreeing to publish only highly abstracted information about the material in research reports.

Storing and distributing tape recordings and transcripts of psychoanalyses themselves constitute a challenge. Often recorded on unstable media, tape-recorded analyses are subject to deterioration, physical damage, or simply being lost. In the United States the Psychoanalytic Research Consortium (Waldron, 1989, 1991) has undertaken to collect, preserve, and disseminate tape-recorded analysis for research purposes. The Ulm Textbank serves a similar function in Germany (Mergenthaler and Kächele, 1993, 1994). At this time the holdings of the Psychoanalytic Research Consortium consist of approximately twenty-six analyses, fourteen of which are complete analyses in various states of completeness and transcription. Currently, the Ulm Textbank holds many psychotherapies but only six complete analyses and samples of an additional one (in German). Protecting these holdings and adequately cataloguing them so that pertinent data can be retrieved involves numerous technical problems (Mergenthaler and Kächele, 1988, 1993). Some analysts personally retain the only copy of tape recordings, thus depriving the wider analytic community of opportunities for systematic research and risking the permanent loss of these irreplaceable assets.

Transcripts of tape-recorded analyses are currently the most widely used data in the detailed study of psychoanalytic processes. In spite of the loss of data about prosody and timing, they have been found adequate for many purposes and are much less time-consuming to deal with than tapes (Luborsky, 1990a). Standardized transcription methods have been developed to facilitate their use in computer-aided text analysis (Mergenthaler and Stinson, 1992).

As we shall see in Chapter 17, tape-recorded analyses have been used successfully to study psychoanalytic processes by Dahl, Gill, Luborsky, and others. Waldron (1992) showed how tape recording could be used to address the clinically important topic of the analyst's slips of the tongue.

The paucity of tape-recorded analyses available for study threatens to raise to undue importance idiosyncratic features of the work of particular analysts and even particular analysands in the systematic study of analytic process. It is worth a major investment of the energies of the analytic community to enlarge the archive of tape-recorded analyses.

SUPERVISORY REPORTS

A very different kind of data is available from supervisors' and consultants' reports. Fleming and Benedek (1966) were among the first to use tape recordings to collect data about supervision. Unfortunately, the report of their findings, while conceptually rich, involved little systematic use of the data they collected. Other thoughtful contributions about the supervisory situation have followed (Arlow, 1963; Wallerstein, 1981), but there has been no systematic attempt to collect detailed material about a series of patient hours and to correlate it with similarly detailed material about related supervisory hours.

Ekstein and Wallerstein's (1972) concept of a parallel process is a promising tool for studying psychoanalysis in depth. In this process interactions of the treating analyst and the supervisor repeat crucial issues between the patient and the treating analyst (Arlow, 1963; Ekstein and Wallerstein, 1958, 1972; Gediman and Wokenfel, 1980). These repetitions are then used as a source of information about the analytic process.

Supervisory reports are particularly useful in focusing on issues outside the analyst's awareness, such as countertransferences. The analyst's difficulty in reporting clinical material can be particularly informative. His management of process notes, how he records them, their thoroughness or lack of thoroughness, how they are presented to the supervisor, and the extent to which the supervisee attempts to go beyond the notes to refer to other sources of information about the patient — all are revealing of the analytic processes themselves (Wallerstein, 1981).

The problem of using the supervisory situation as a source of information about a psychoanalysis is that the analyst is frequently inexperienced and usually wants to please the supervisor (if only to facilitate progression through analytic training). Other complex transferential relationships, including displacements from the training analysis and the supervisee's characterological difficulties in learning, may profoundly affect the analyst's descriptions. The same parallel process that may make supervision valuable for gaining information about psychoanalysis also interferes with the use of supervisory data to explore simpler aspects of the analytic situation, like the ongoing interaction of patient and analyst.[2]

ADDITIONAL TECHNIQUES FOR STUDYING PSYCHOANALYSES

Skolnikoff (1985) described a research method called consensual analysis, in which the analyst records his observation of the previous week of an

---

2. Historians (Charles Strozier, personal communication, 1990) point out that analytic data include the most detailed and intimate reports of personal life in the culture of the analysand and thus provide unique sources of historical data. Although not part of the psychoanalytic research venture per se, this constitutes an additional reason for the careful archiving of tape-recorded analyses.

analysis in the presence of a listening analyst who does not comment. These memories of the previous week are compared with process notes dictated immediately following each analytic hour. In some weeks, the discrepancies between the process notes and the verbal recollection were more significant than in other weeks. These discrepancies made it possible to study the countertransference in detail. Outside observers noted that those weeks when there were large discrepancies and countertransference reactions abounded appeared to correspond to a period of change in the patient.

Cohler and Galatzer-Levy (1992) proposed a systematic method of studying transcripts of psychoanalyses derived from the methods of countertransference analysis and contemporary literary criticism. In this approach the researcher carefully tracks his responses to the material, including enactments such as choosing to put it aside, losing the transcript, and so on. These responses and enactments can be used as data about the analysis under study.

In another vein, a useful measure of a reader's understanding of a text is the ability to restore its prosody. Educational studies show that when children understand a written text, they can supply the appropriate prosody while reading aloud (Gurney, 1982; see also Brazil, Coulthard, and Johns, 1980; Chapman, 1983). Psychoanalytic comprehension could be studied in a similar way, comparing the prosody constructed by the analytic reader to tape recordings of analyses to test the rating or treating analyst's affective comprehension of the material. This could be used as a specific measure related to empathy and/or the fit between patient and analyst (Kantrowitz et al., 1989; Kantrowitz, Katz, and Paolitto, 1990c; Kantrowitz, 1996).

WHAT TO STUDY ABOUT PSYCHOANALYTIC PROCESSES

Systematic study of psychoanalyses and analytic therapies is in its infancy. Such simple classifications as the relative amount of speech of analyst and analysand and the frequencies of confrontations, clarifications, interpretations, and references to the relationship between analyst and patient have scarcely been studied. There have been virtually no studies of how such frequencies change in the course of treatment or are related to analytic outcome. To what degree does the analyst confine herself to interpretive remarks? Does focus on interpretation change in the course of treatment? How supportive is the analyst? In what ways? How active is she?

An important impediment to such investigation is the tendency for analysts to attempt to define a psychoanalysis negatively — that is, by characterizing events or behaviors as unanalytic — probably a result of the wide discrepancy between metapsychological theory and clinical practice. Consequently, many analysts are hesitant to describe fully what they actually do with their patients lest it be labeled unanalytic (Reed, 1987a, 1994). This state of affairs could be substantially improved by systematic study of the range of phenomena found in a series of cases called analyses by experienced colleagues.

Appelbaum (1977, 1978) has discussed the variety of therapeutic influences observed in the Menninger Psychotherapy Research Project and other systematic studies, including the effects of insight, corrective emotional experience, and the interpersonal relationship. However, the Menninger patient population was considerably sicker than most outpatient analysands, so it is open to question whether the range of interventions used with that population is appropriate to more typical psychoanalytic patients.

Classifying Interventions

Several investigators have provided classifications of interventions, and some of these are reaching a stage of reasonable reliability (Gill and Hoffman, 1982; Suh et al., 1986; Horowitz et al., 1984; Cooper, 1991). These classification systems generally differentiate interpretations, including transference interpretations, from confrontations, clarifications, questions, and comments that have to do with facilitating the treatment. Some of these systems have proved unreliable. First, interventions tend to be of mixed character; an analytic intervention might begin with a confrontation (pointing out some action of the patient), continue with an interpretation of the motives for that action, and finish with an exhortation to further associate to the material in question. One solution to the problem of classifying complex interventions is to rate the interventions in terms of the extent to which they fit in each of several categories rather than assigning them to a single category. Another factor leading to difficulty in these classifications is the failure to define terms carefully, along with adequate descriptions and examples.

HOW MUCH DATA TO COLLECT

Generally, analysts agree that long segments of analysis are necessary to understand psychoanalytic happenings and that meaningful study of analytic cases usually cannot be achieved through the study of brief segments of analysis. Even the study of single whole hours by experienced analysts has proved inadequate. Jones, Ghannam, and Nigg (1993) clearly show that interesting psychological features of a psychotherapy would have been missed had only short segments been studied.

During the first four decades of formal psychotherapy research, brief segments of treatment hours — as brief as five minutes — were employed as the unit of study. In 1971 Mintz and Luborsky compared judgments of central process factors obtained from studying brief tape-recorded segments with those obtained from complete tape-recorded sessions and found a correspondence among many variables, with the exception of quality of the therapeutic relationship. Subsequently, Bachrach et al. (1981) conducted a similar study and found that judgments based on whole sessions were more reliable than those based on segments, and that they more fully captured the major dimensions of treatment processes and the therapeutic relationship. These studies clearly recommend entire sessions over brief segments for the measurement of psychoanalytic process. However, the minimum number and sequence of sessions required to study psychoanalytic processes are not yet known. It is not clear that we need long sequences of hours to study psychoanalytic process. Like all human communication, free association is intensely redundant. Dahl (1974, 1988; Dahl et al., 1978; Teller and Dahl, 1986) has demonstrated the enormous richness of psychoanalytic transcripts when they are subjected to sufficiently close scrutiny.

In recent years mathematicians have explored the properties of a group of structures called fractals, which are characterized by the property of self-similarity — that is, a magnified image of a small part of the original structure contains a structure markedly similar to the original. Self-similarity turns out not only to be a powerful mathematical concept but to have many other potential uses. Quite realistic-looking images of landscapes, trees, plants, and so on can be computer generated by using concepts of self-similarity (Barnsley, 1988). Self-similar structures are empirically important because one can study their essential qualities by examining small portions of them microscopically.

Applying these ideas to psychoanalytic research is consistent with the clinical impression that psychoanalytic data are highly self-similar and that careful attention to the material of single hours or even fragments of hours commonly reveals the way in which a patient typically approaches and works out difficulties inside and outside analysis. The patient's interests, concerns, and style are detectable in very small fragments of material because of the self-similarity of the personality and speech about emotionally important matters. It is a common clinical impression that certain points in the analysis — such as the hours in which the first dream is reported or termination date is set — seem to be particularly revelatory of the patient's underlying approach to issues. From this model, we can interpret this as reflecting times when we have chosen the right framework, revealing a major chunk of a self-similar structure at once (see Galatzer-Levy, 1995).[3]

---

3. Those familiar with fractal structures like the Mandelbrot set will recognize the situation as similar to when we explore a region of the Mandelbrot set that includes many images of Mandelbrot-like sets rather than one of those areas that are not rich in these self-similar structures.

COMPUTER ANALYSIS OF PSYCHOANALYTIC DATA

Second only to the difficulties of finding an adequate conceptual framework for studying psychoanalytic process is the problem of dealing with the sheer mass of data produced in a psychoanalysis. Even stripped of prosody and nonverbal elements, transcripts of single psychoanalytic sessions are long—commonly, twenty double-spaced pages. The application of the methods described above to individual analytic sessions requires many hours, sometimes even years, of work by trained professionals.

Studying the course of an analysis in depth is greatly facilitated when methods are found that require much less time for performance. For example, Sanger's Nobel prize–winning discovery of the sequence of amino acids in insulin in 1955 was the result of an enormous effort lasting over several years. Today this sequencing would be achieved in approximately a week of laboratory work if the gene that coded the protein was not known, and much less if it was. The comparative study of primary structures of proteins, which is now central to research in evolution, would have been an unthinkable undertaking only three decades ago. Similarly, much of the advance in the theories of chaos and fractals has resulted from computer technology that makes it possible to explore matters graphically in a matter of seconds that could only be conceived with the greatest difficulty seventy years ago when the subject first entered mathematical awareness. The ability to meaningfully study psychoanalytic materials without the enormous demands of time made by current methods would dramatically move the field forward.

Investigations in other fields clearly demonstrate how systematic computer study of human verbal discourse can lead to psychologically meaningful insights. For instance, studies of the conversations of friends, using computer analysis of discourse, yielded psychologically rich and empirically convincing descriptions (Gottman and Parker, 1986). Oxman and colleagues (1982) studied the language of paranoia in a systematic way with interesting results. Where meaningful aspects of analytic process can be studied using computers, otherwise intractably large quantities of data can be usefully processed.

There are secondary benefits to computer-aided study of analytic material. The explicit description of the measures being used—and the elimination of nonexplicit elements in assessing clinical material required by the computer—greatly reduce threats to validity and reliability, as well as sources of bias. Furthermore, computer analysis makes privacy easier to ensure. For example, Spence's (1990) method of looking for co-occurrences can be applied without a human's ever looking at the material of the analysis itself.

Various methods of systematic study of psychoanalysis have already been computerized and developed to a point where clinically trained raters are no longer required. Bucci (1985, 1988, 1996) developed a method for transforming her referential-activity measure to a dictionary-based computer scoring of transcribed texts. Dahl and his coworkers (Dahl, 1991; Dahl, Holzer, and Berry, 1992) have systematized the mapping of emotions so that clinician-raters are not required.

Donald Spence (1990) has reported another method of studying the language of psychoanalysis that is not dependent on a person as rater. He has designed a program that assesses the co-occurrences of thematically related words in transcripts of an analysis by exploring the text immediately surrounding a given emotionally significant word. It is hypothesized that the program will find meaningful co-occurrences of unconsciously connected words and that these co-occurrences will increase as the patient becomes more tolerant of conflicts and develops more associative freedom. Note that in terms of confidentiality this method can be applied to transcripts without the researcher's having any knowledge of their content.

Herbert Schlesinger is developing computer protocols to study the prosody of speech in audio-recorded psychoanalyses. The dynamics, pitch, and metrical aspects of speech carry much information about the meaning of the communication though the degree of their redundancy with words and syntax. Formal studies of prosodic elements have shown correlations between prosodic patterns and affective states (Couper-Kuhlen, 1991; John-Lewis, 1986). Changing correlations between prosody and lexical content may demonstrate the changing role of affects, defenses, and conflict as an analysis proceeds. Computer-based analysis of the sound patterns of speech may serve a variety of research strategies. For instance, the patient's depressive response to separation could be demonstrated by characteristic alterations in prosody in the sessions preceding interruptions in the analysis. Current analytic thinking would predict increasing convergence between the patient's prosody and the content of his speech when the analysis is going well.

17

Strategies for Exploring Psychoanalytic Processes

In this chapter we discuss several strategies for systematically exploring psychoanalytic concepts related to transference and ideas of alliance. In each instance we describe the conceptual basis of the method, how it is used, its validity and reliability, its advantages and drawbacks, and situations where it has found application. We pay particular attention to Luborsky's Core Conflictual Relationship Theme method because it is the most thoroughly explored and developed of these methodologies.

The Core Conflictual Relationship Theme Method (CCRT)

The Core Conflictual Relationship Theme method was developed by Lester Luborsky, based on repeated examples that he found in psychotherapies that could be characterized in terms of what the patient wanted from another, how the other reacted, and how the patient, in turn, responded to that reaction. Luborsky's ideas paralleled and arose from Freud's (1912) concept of transference as "a stereotyped template (or several such), which is constantly repeated—constantly reprinted afresh—in the course of a person's life" (pp. 99–100), and from later contributions of Blos (1941), French and Wheeler (1963), and Arlow (1961, 1969a,b), emphasizing patients' unconscious preoccupation with a central theme. He also drew on the work of personality researchers like Henry Murray (1938) in an attempt to find a valid and systematic means to describe the transference in psychotherapy and psychoanalysis. It has been used to support the underlying concept (Fried, Crits-Christoph, and Luborsky, 1992).

The CCRT is designed to identify patterns of narratives about relations with people as these narratives appear in therapeutic sessions. The unit of study is a relationship episode. The identification of relationship episodes is facilitated by their narrative structure — having a beginning, middle, and end. Generally, raters work on transcripts of sessions because they are easier and faster to score than tape recordings. Transcripts are adequate despite the loss of additional information conveyed by prosody (Luborsky and Crits-Christoph, 1990). Relationship episodes may be stories about relationships involving another person, stories about the relationship with a therapist, or stories about a relationship to oneself. They may also be enactments in which patient and therapist put the narrative into action. The episode is also described as referring to a past or current event. Finally, the completeness of each narrative is assessed. Those narratives that are relatively incomplete are dropped from further consideration.

Having been located in this way, each episode is scored by a process of two passes through the material. In the first pass, the judge identifies components of the episode — that is, the wishes, needs, or intentions of the patient, the responses from others, and the responses of the patient. Wishes are generally the most difficult elements to judge. They are described either as virtually direct expressions or as clear inferences from what the patient has said. The response from others and the responses of the self are designated as positive or negative, depending on whether they promote or interfere with the fulfillment of the wish. They are also differentiated depending on whether they are expected by the patient or are put into action by the other. In a second step, the judge searches for themes that apply to the most relationship episodes. This may be difficult. The method assumes the existence of at least one core conflictual relationship theme. Luborsky underlines the human interpretive element: "This step, with its necessity for a moderate level of inference, especially requires wet, gray software — the cortex of the human judge — a tool not likely soon to be supplanted by dry, any color hardware, the computer" (Luborsky, 1990a, p. 23).

In the second pass the scores are reviewed to make sure that the components of the general formulation arrived at during the first pass have been scored. The judge then lists each component on a summary sheet in order of frequency, grouping together components that refer to very similar feelings and ideas. She then tabulates the frequency of components, the intensity of the theme components, and the patient's experience of the components. The result is a set of tailor-made categories for the material analyzed which usefully capture the individuality of the patient.

The application of such categories is limited in situations where findings for a group of students are to be compared or where the researcher wishes to calculate standard reliability coefficients. Such undertakings require predefined rating categories. Luborsky and his coworkers have developed two sets of categories designed to be used in place of tailor-made categories when intersubject comparison is a goal (Barber, Crits-Christoph, and Luborsky, 1990). One is based on the categories most frequently found in a normative sample of sixteen psychotherapy cases studied using the CCRT (Luborsky, 1986). The other is an expanded version that includes other major category sets described in the psychological literature (Crits-Christoph and Demorest, 1988).

VALIDITY

Luborsky (1990c, 1994) argues for the validity of the CCRT method because of its association with meaningfully related phenomena. He and his coworkers demonstrate this correlation in several studies. The CCRT can be shown to correspond well to many of Freud's ideas about transference (Luborsky, 1990b). It is pervasive in patients' narratives and continues to be pervasive (with changes in successful cases) throughout treatment (Crits-Christoph, Luborsky, et al., 1990). Its pattern appears in relation to the therapist (Fried, Crits-Christoph, and Luborsky, 1990) and in dreams (Popp, Luborsky, and Crits-Christoph, 1990). The argument of Crits-Christoph, Cooper, and Luborsky (1990) that the finding that patients receive more benefit from interpretations focused on the CCRT than those that are not supports the validity of the measure. However, this is a questionable conclusion because generally, therapists who follow whatever methodology they believe to be correct do better than those who deviate from it.

There are limitations to the extent to which the CCRT measure corresponds to similar concepts from psychoanalysis. One is that wish and response from the other, and response of the self are simply the most frequently appearing element of that type in the relationship episodes. This is different from the usual psychoanalytic approach, in which sequences of material and associative connections are used to derive meaning (Ricoeur, 1970, 1977). The CCRT assumes that the patient has expressed a certain wish in the narratives rated and that there has been an expression of an attitude from the other and an attitude toward the self. However, actual clinical material often does not confirm that these are responses to the wish, as implied by the CCRT description (Luborsky and Crits-Christoph, 1990, chapter 4). In other words, the CCRT represents a kind of rough outline of issues that the patient is expressing in narrative and has the limitations intrinsic to any simplification. By its very structure, it is poorly suited to exploring transference situations in which the autonomy of self and object is unclear. Because these transferences are currently the focus of much psychoanalytic investigation (Kohut, 1971; Bollas, 1987; Kernberg, 1975), this is an unfortunate limitation.

RELIABILITY

Luborsky and his coworkers have extensively documented their procedures with detailed descriptions of their methods and extended illustrations of its use (Luborsky and Crits-Christoph, 1990; Luborsky, Popp, and Barber, 1994). Still, the reliability of the CCRT method has been demonstrated only with difficulty (Luborsky, 1977; Levin and Luborsky, 1981; Luborsky, Crits-Christoph, and Mellon, 1986; Crits-Christoph, Luborsky, et al., 1990). Much of the unreliability observed in this task resulted from judges' failure to identify incomplete episodes or what constituted the relationship episode. Judges commonly disagreed about where the episode began and, to a greater extent, about where it ended. As expected, reliability decreased as episodes were less complete. When this happened, judges were able to achieve only moderate levels of reliability. The reliability was not improved by using videotapes of sessions, although the coding time increased dramatically. However, the study of videotape has significant methodological problems (Luborsky, 1995).

Judging the reliability of tailor-made categories is a challenge because, by definition, each judge creates her own categories. The assessment of reliability for these categories was achieved using the method of mismatched cases (cases that are different) in which an additional set of judges compares the coding of relationship episodes in the same and mismatched cases. The difference between these cases was found to be highly statistically significant. Using Cohen's (1968; Landis and Coch, 1977) method of comparing agreement on scale ratings and interrater reliabilities, the wish, negative-response, and negative-response-from-other ratings were all found to fall at the upper end of the fair-to-good range of this measure. These levels of reliability, which are higher than those achieved in any other clinicians' judgment of complex concepts in psychotherapy research, are achieved because of the use of guided clinical judgment of a limited number of standard categories. They may also reflect a limited clinical sample of investigation and particularly the extensive training of judges, which focuses strongly on the appropriate level of inference and the structuring of their formulation in terms of the CCRT components.

APPLICATIONS

Use of the CCRT has led to several clinically significant findings. For example, successful psychoanalytic psychotherapy is associated with mobilization of a greater variety of conflictual relationship themes than in successful therapies. And interpretations of core conflictual relationship themes are often accompanied by clinical improvement.

The Patient's Experience of the Relationship with the Therapist (PERT)

The PERT coding scheme for audio-recorded sessions of psychoanalysis and psychotherapy was developed by Gill and Hoffman (1982; Hoffman and Gill, 1988). It originates in Gill's assertion of the centrality of transference and its analysis to psychoanalytic process (Gill, 1979, 1982, 1995). The scheme rests on several basic assumptions:

1. Analysis of the transference is an important aspect of analytic process.
2. In comparable situations, analytic process and outcome are enhanced by good work on the transference, particularly the analyst's accurate transference interpretations.
3. Collaborative exploration of the patient's experience of the here-and-now relationship is a very important aspect of the analysis of transference. Genetic interpretations are, at most, of secondary significance.
4. In the ambiguous situation with the analyst, the patient constructs a plausible perspective on the interaction. The plausibility of this perspective arises in part because of the patient's active repetition of patterns of interaction with the analyst that are consistent with transference-driven expectations (Hoffman, 1983).
5. The patient is in conflict between revealing and hiding aspects of his experience of the relationship with the analyst. He solves this conflict in part by communicating his experience of the relationship in disguised form.
6. The analyst's task is to identify the meaning of these disguised communications and to encourage the patient, through interpretation or other means, to elaborate the underlying idea. This is a mutual task in which the analyst's interpretation not only communicates its content but also indicates that the analyst has overcome his own resistance to articulating what the patient has said. Thus it invites the patient to communicate directly about sensitive matters in the relationship.

Gill and Hoffman (1982) developed measures of transference-related phenomena that operationalize Gill's concepts about the importance of being aware of and working with transference. The PERT tracks the patient's experience of the relationship with the therapist by reading between the lines of the patient's associations to discern those resisted aspects of the experience which the patient is simultaneously wanting to conceal and wanting to reveal. The heart of the coding scheme is this tracking process and the provision of certain guidelines for deciding what may or may not qualify as disguised allusion to the transference (Hoffman and Gill, 1988, p. 69).

Allusions to relationships are of three types: r allusions are communications that are manifestly about the relationship with the therapist; x allusions are manifestly about other experience not overtly related to the therapist; and xr allusions are connections that the patient himself makes between extratransference and transference experiences.

Patient's allusions to the relationship with the therapist are central to the coding system. Those that are not manifestly associated with the therapist are coded Jxr (the J standing for judged). They are recognized as related to the therapist because they are similar to either previous or subsequent references to material that is directly related to the therapist. (Remember that the rating is done retrospectively, not during the session, so that subsequent material can be included in the analysis.) Disguised allusions that are manifestly about the relationship to the therapist but are believed to have additional latent meanings having to do with the interaction are coded as Jrr.

In addition to explicit references to the therapist, Jxrs and Jrrs may also be based on some significant event (SE) observed by the judge but not spoken of by the analyst or the patient. If the judge notices an event or quality of interaction that he thinks may have an impact on the patient's experience before it can be demonstrated that it in fact does, it is coded as a Potentially Significant Event (PSE). An example of a PSE would be the analyst's announcement of an imminent vacation. Retrospectively Significant Events (RSE) are coded when the judge notes something that can be seen as a response to an event after its occurrence. Judging the presence of Jxrs or Jrrs depends to a large extent upon the patient's conscious response to interpretation that the analyst actually offers (Hoffman and Gill, 1988, p. 72). The requirement for the responsive evidence avoids the assumption that every association that might refer to the analyst is coded as though it were actually an unconscious reference to the analyst.

The analyst's interventions are also coded. X refers to interventions about matters other than the patient-therapist relationship. Those addressed to associations already manifestly about the relationship are coded R. Analyst statements about the patient's behavior toward the analyst are coded A. Interpretations by the analyst of latent transference issues in associations not manifestly about the relationship are coded XR. Where extratransference situations are clarified by reference to known features of the transference, they are coded RX. When the analyst encourages but does not interpret further exploration of the meaning of the relationship, this is coded as ER.

VALIDITY

The PERT is an attempt to make a central aspect of the analytic situation — the transference — explicit. Gill's equation of transference with the patient's conscious and unconscious experience of the analyst is at variance with many views of transference. And the exclusive focus of the PERT on transference and its interpretation is also at variance with many contemporary views of what is centrally important to analysis (Meissner, 1991). While this is not in itself a fault, Gill's repeated valorization of transference and its interpretation implicitly diminishes the value placed on other conceptualizations without actually demonstrating that they are less useful.

RELIABILITY

The reliability of the PERT has not been systematically studied.

APPLICATIONS

Gill and Hoffman have applied their methods to the study of transcripts of single sessions from nine tape-recorded analyses (Gill and Hoffman, 1988), as well as materials from the analysis of Mrs. C. (Hoffman and Gill, 1988). This approach produced published detailed annotated transcripts of sessions. Of the cases that Gill and Hoffman studied, four were conducted from a point of view not informed by Gill's conceptualization of transference. The remainder reflected Gill's thinking about technique. The PERT shows that the first group of analysts did not interpret many transference references. Sometimes these references were quite numerous. In the second group of analyses there was much more direct talk about transference. The skeptical reader is left uncertain about the meaning of these findings. The analysts' very active style in the second group of analyses, while clearly superior for identifying transference derivatives, is not clearly of greater therapeutic effect, nor does one feel confident that the analysand is better understood.

Paul Gedo (Gedo, 1988; Gedo and Schaffler, 1989) has used the PERT method to trace changes in this measure across the course of an analysis. Transcriptions of audiotapes of a 324-session analysis were scored and analyzed, using Markov models and comparative probability tests. Throughout the analysis interpretations facilitated transference insight to a greater extent than other interventions in the same hours. Furthermore, the patient was more likely to follow one insight with a second during later hours. Gedo asserts that the combination of Markov methods with the PERT holds promise for differentiating the value of various theoretical ideas about the interpretation of transference.

Frames

Hartvig Dahl (1988; Teller and Dahl, 1981) defines FRAMES (Fundamental Repetitive and Maladaptive Emotions Structures) as emotion-related structures that may be discovered in the stories that patients tell. In recent years Dahl has gradually increased the systematic aspects of frame analysis so that it can be used as a research tool. Clinicians generally observe repetitive structures in the free associations of patients in psychoanalysis. These structures may be equated with what the cognitive scientist Marvin Minsky has termed frames for stereotyped knowledge structures. A frame, Minsky says, is a sort of skeleton, somewhat like an application form with many blanks or slots to be filled (1986, p. 245). More precisely, frames are data structures for representing a stereotyped situation. A frame is characterized by sequentially ordered events that are predicates summarizing instances of specific acts (including psychological acts). A prototype is the most complete example of a particular frame. An instantiation of a frame is a repetition of an identified frame with the association evidence for each event. The default is the value of an event in the prototype frame, which is the expected or presumed value in any instantiation when evidence to the contrary is lacking. A frame system is a network of frames that interact or have overlapping elements. A frame provides the person with an expected sequence of actions. Thus the frame going to the store describes an expectable set of events, the details of which will be specifiable by the insertion of appropriate variables (which store, for what goods, and so on) and many of whose elements will be assumed to have default values (for example, goods will be paid for with money) unless explicitly specified (for example, it is a swap store). Many of these variables will be filled by defaults. Note that frames can, and often do, contain other frames and that very elaborate structures can be built up from frames (see Minsky, 1986). Dahl states that the advantages of frame structures over clinical themes as units of analysis are the requirement that evidence be specified explicitly and precisely, that the sequence of events itself be repeated, and that specific, confirmable or disconfirmable clinical predictions be created.

The method of frame analysis treats as primary data the psychoanalytic text as manifest in transcripts of tape-recorded psychoanalytic sessions. Following Ricoeur's (1977) emphasis on the centrality of the analysand's speech, Teller and Dahl assert, "If one takes these words, the patient's words, seriously, if one records them and transcribes them, if one then searches and re-searches them, one is rewarded with the discovery of patterns and structures that are embedded there to be found, that are not merely invented or arbitrarily imposed on unwilling data" (1986, p. 765). Their analyses depend heavily on the details of these texts, particularly the ubiquitous dysfluency of speech that is full of meaning but is processed out of awareness by the casual listener and can be captured only by careful transcription of recorded sessions. Such investigation is made possible by the enormous redundancy of speech. Teller and Dahl claim that certain structures lie embedded in these texts and propose a three-step procedure for revealing them.

1. The first step is the generation of the text from tape recordings. The patient's words are transcribed, carefully preserving dysfluent speech (for example, "I uh went to the [pause] the store"). The authors believe that not transcribing the prosody of the speech does not result in the loss of centrally important information for purposes of their studies.

2. The text so created is then transformed into category maps, using categories based not only on syntax and semantics but also on parenthetic comments of similar types (for example, "Oh, by the way"). How these categories are found is not rigidly specified. In fact, the method is sensitive to the categorizers' views of what is meaningful and important. However, Teller and Dahl identify such clues to characterization as grammatical elements like tense, or words that refer back to previous instances of the topic or related topics. The content of the text also suggests bases for categories.

   These maps maintain the contiguity of the patient's associations, consistent with the central psychoanalytic contention that the associativ process is itself meaningful. In category maps sequential elements of the text are put into columns so that each column represents a category of information. These classifications represent an attempt to cut at the joints, to dissect along natural boundaries, to uncover some of the hidden structure in the discourse. Representing analytic data in category maps clearly shows not only themes intrinsic to the material but also the preoccupations of the person who constructed the map.

3. Frame systems can be constructed from category maps. Prototypes of frames are identified in the text by identifying the narrative episodes in the text; selecting as prototype the narrative episode within a group of narratives that contains the most complete description of the event sequence; deconstructing the patient's story into its main components, a series of single statements in the manifest content of the text; and abstracting from the primary statements a sequence of summary predicates, which become the event sequence of the frame.

This classificatory process depends on the categorizer's knowledge of normative human thought and actions and of narrative structure. Dahl's several publications on frames (Dahl, Kächele, and Thomä, 1988; Teller and Dahl, 1992; Dahl, 1992; Dahl and Teller, 1992) vary in details of how frames are to be identified.

As the means of frames have been operationalized, the procedure has become more reliable and has been shown to be useful in a variety of contexts (Dahl and Teller, 1994). Recently, the method has been further specified by breaking it down into a five-step procedure.

VALIDITY

Other measures of central themes in analysis may be viewed as studying specialized types of frames. Thus CCRTs can be understood as frames whose structure is partly imposed by the assumed structure of the interaction. The PERT focuses on transference frames exclusively. Frames differ from them in being composed of categories of events that are explicitly represented in the discrete narrative of the patient's associations. They reflect the unique internal structure of a particular patient's memories.

The frame method is conceptually so wide that it is difficult to assess how satisfactorily it relates to other psychoanalytic concepts. Indeed, Minsky (1986) has used the frame idea in his general theory of higher psychological function. Although Teller and Dahl limit their study to verbally expressed matters of psychoanalytic interest, their method should pick up all verbalized structures of thought. Dahl's frame concept's foundation in the cognitive science concept of frames suggests that it validly identifies Minsky's frames in psychoanalytic associations. Whether it identifies all such frames is less clear. In particular, this method would probably overlook frames that are not evident in the microstructure of association. Though Teller and Dahl (see also Galatzer-Levy, 1996) plausibly argue that the high redundancy of material in the analytic text ensures that major themes will be represented in the talk of the patient, many psychoanalytic configurations have been documented only in the larger structure of analytic material. For example, a common form of difficulty in psychoanalysis arises when a patient who wishes unconsciously to demonstrate the ineffectiveness of the analyst compliantly provides seemingly rich and meaningful associations without changing (Malcolm, 1981). This frame may or may not be manifest in the microstructure of associations.

RELIABILITY

The reliability of frame analysis and its various components has not been explored. However, the redundancy of material anticipated in the frame concept suggests that reliability is not a significant problem for this method. Because many issues in the construction of the analysis are poorly specified — for example, the clues to central features of the analysis — it is hard to see how the method otherwise could achieve high degrees of reliability. Consistent with much contemporary thinking about interpretive activity (Hiley, Bohman, and Schusterman, 1991), the frame method explicitly recognizes the role of the categorizer in interpreting the text. Interrater reliability is thus not an appropriate goal. Leeds (1989) has described a systematic method for objectively identifying repetitive frame structures, and Davies (1989) has used this method to explore interpersonal and emotional structures in the talk of three-year-olds.

APPLICATIONS

Application of the frame method demands an enormous amount of time and effort. The richness of the picture it produces must be evaluated against the difficulties of using it. To date the frame method has been employed most extensively in examinations of the case of Mrs. C. (Dahl, 1988). The findings show that rich, highly plausible understandings can be achieved when the method is applied even to very brief segments of text. However, it is unclear whether the method would produce equally interesting results in the study of a wider range of patients.

Dual Coding and Referential Activity (RA)

Wilma Bucci (1985, 1988, 1996) has studied referential activity — the nonverbal, emotion- and image-laden aspects of speech, such as the imagery, concreteness, clarity, and specificity of the language. Referential activity points to aspects of verbal output that refer to the nonverbal realm of experience. Winston Churchill, in his first speech as prime minister, said, "I have nothing to offer but blood, toil, tears, and sweat." Had he said, "I will work hard in these sad times using my military knowledge," one doubts that he would have led the British to victory in World War II. The difference between the two statements is in their referential activity. Churchill evoked strong vision, olfactory, and emotional experiences in his listeners. Scores for RA can be derived from small segments of text, so it is possible to chart the degree of activation of the nonverbal realm as it changes over an analytic hour, over the course of treatment, and in response to interventions, and as it co-varies between patient and therapist and from patient to patient. Computerized forms of the scales are now available.

The referential activity measure is based on a well-developed theoretical linguistic framework (Bucci, 1984, 1985, 1988, 1993, 1996; Bucci and Freedman, 1978). It has been applied in many contexts; the reliability of its various scales is well established and is easily achieved with little training and no requirement for clinical sophistication on the part of the judges. A manual on this procedure is available (Bucci, Kabasakalian-McKay, and the RA Research Group, 1985).

The relation of RA to central psychoanalytic concepts is unclear. Certainly an expectable result of successful analytic work is the greater availability of emotional speech about important matters. Empirically, RA was found to increase when plan-compatible interventions were made. Similarly, a comparison of RA levels of analytic hours previously differentiated according to the level of resistance versus manifest work found higher RA in the work hours (Dahl, 1972, 1974). In the study of Mrs. C., high RA correlated with the emergence of emotional patterns in the material (Bucci, 1988). These findings, taken together with the clear rationale of the procedure, strongly suggest that it taps the issues that it is intended to measure. It has already been used by several investigators as an independent measure of the psychoanalytic process (Luborsky, 1988). Referential activity would then seem to be a valid, reliable, and relatively easy way to examine the extent to which nonverbal, emotional issues are available for verbal expression. It does not measure any particular psychological configuration but makes explicit and measurable a centrally important indicator of the analytic process.

Control Mastery Theory and the Patient's Plan

A research group at Mount Zion Hospital in San Francisco has developed a distinctive view of psychoanalysis based on control-mastery theory (CMT), an extension and elaboration of ego psychology. Early Freudian theory held that the unconscious is controlled by the automatic functioning hypothesis. This theory, among other things, predicts the patient's resistance to therapy: the patient is, in this view, highly motivated to resist treatment so as to retain the infantile gratifications that he obtains from symptoms. Ego psychology, by contrast, holds that the unconscious portion of the ego regulates the patient's unconscious through higher mental functions, so that one can hypothesize a process of higher mental functioning. This theory appears in Freud's later work and was further developed by Hartmann (1950), Rangell (1979, 1987), and others. From this point of view, the patient has an unconscious wish to master the difficulties that are represented in his symptoms (Sampson and Weiss, 1986).

The hypothesis of higher mental functioning assumes that previously repressed mental contents emerge because the patient unconsciously decides that they may be safely experienced for the purpose of working out the difficulties they pose. The hypothesis of automatic functioning, by contrast, assumes that repressed mental contents are pushed through by the drives to consciousness. Gassner and colleagues (1982; Gassner et al., 1986) showed that previously repressed mental contents came forth without interpretation and under conditions of safety, with reduced anxiety.

Pathogenic beliefs are fantasies that have negatively altered the patient's adult behavior. Under the hypothesis of higher mental functioning, the task of analysis is to provide an opportunity for the patient to test his pathogenic beliefs, correct them, and thus alter his neurotic behavior. According to the older hypothesis of automatic functioning, the patient makes demands of the therapist in an attempt to gratify unconscious impulses. In higher mental functioning, the patient unconsciously hopes to demonstrate that the therapist will not behave as his pathogenic beliefs predict. He therefore gives the therapist a transference test, which, if passed (if the therapist is neutral), will help the patient give up his pathogenic beliefs.

Thus the patient has an unconscious plan for the therapy. Any effort to disprove his pathogenic beliefs and to pursue the goals that they forbid is understood as part of the patient's unconscious plan. This plan can be discerned in the first several hours of an analysis. (This was carried out using the first ten hours of Mrs. C.'s analysis.)

The plan can be broken down into four components (Caston, 1986): (1) the patient's goals, (2) the obstructions (pathogenic beliefs) that impede the patient in pursuit of those goals, (3) the test that the patient might perform in an effort to disprove the pathogenic beliefs, and (4) the insights that the patient might use in efforts to disprove pathogenic beliefs.

For example, a patient wished to feel free to be admired for her intelligence in a professional context (the patient's goals). She unconsciously believed that other people, of whom her mother was the first, would be angrily envious of any success that she might have and, like her mother, obscure that success by acting confused and uncomprehending of it (the pathogenic beliefs). In analysis, the patient described many work situations in an ambiguous way that contained both information suggesting that she was very bright and information that invited the analyst to notice her limitations and failings. She thus repeatedly tested her belief that the analyst would respond with envious destructiveness to her intellectual success. Insights that showed the patient the origins of her pathogenic beliefs in her experiences with her mother and that demonstrated how she arranged tests in such a way that the analysts and others were often hard-pressed to pass them helped her to reexamine these beliefs and subject them to more effective tests.

The Mount Zion researchers developed a systematic and reliable method of formulating the patient's unconscious plan in undertaking treatment (Weiss, Sampson, and Mount Zion Psychotherapy Research Group, 1986; Silberschatz, Fretter, and Curtis, 1986). It posits a universal category of underlying fantasies that result in the psychological distress for which the patient seeks treatment and for which the discovery of the therapist's neutrality will provide satisfying relief. Using this formulation they study the degree to which the analyst's responses are compatible with that plan. They found evidence to suggest that plan-compatible interventions are associated with better outcomes — a finding that has been questioned as perhaps applying only to Mrs. C. (Lazar, 1989).

Many analysts regard the Mount Zion group's conceptualization of the therapeutic action of analysis as too narrow. Although fantasies of the type the researchers specify were very much the focus of past psychoanalytic investigations, mounting clinical evidence suggests that many patients suffer from other types of difficulty and are in search of positive experiences with another person, not simply confirmation that their fears are unfounded. Further, the unconscious-plan model assumes that patients unconsciously know what will help them. It is assumed not merely that the ego determines the fantasy but that the ego's formulation is essentially correct. This implies a static state in the ego in which a plan, once in place, is satisfied or there is a return to older modes of functioning.

Although the Mount Zion methods can usefully be applied to therapies that are not based on the researchers' theoretical framework, the limited conceptual base of the group's hypothesis does not allow it to be tested against competing possibilities.

RELIABILITY

If judges are limited to a predetermined selection of plans, high levels of reliability can be achieved using this method. Caston (1993a,b; Caston and Martin, 1993) gave extensive list of possible goals, pathogenic beliefs, tests, and insights to independent judges, asking them to rate material from the sessions on each of these categories for their pertinence to the patient's plan. He found a high level of reliability. Reliability has not been explored for situations in which judges were not asked to choose among preset options.

APPLICATIONS

In a series of studies of psychotherapy, the Mount Zion group showed that plan-compatible interventions were associated with better outcome. Silberschatz, Fretter, and Curtis (1986) studied brief therapy (sixteen sessions) and found that proplan interpretations convey insight and led to more, and more lasting, changes than antiplan interventions. This applied to both immediate and long-term change. Patients were less bold and less insightful after antiplan interventions. Weiss (1971), who studied fifteen-session therapies, found that proplan interpretations conveyed more insight to the patient in the initial and final phases of treatment but that in the middle phase, there was a diminution of insight. Weiss hypothesized that this diminution in insight was intended to test the pathogenic beliefs in a transference to the therapist. Insight increased in the termination phase because of the threat of termination, as well as the success of the previous tests.

The Mount Zion methods have been used in exploring a group of therapies in which the interventions were conceptually based on Fairbairn's (1952) object relations theory, which stresses dependency and separation anxiety as central dynamic issues, rather than Mount Zion's cognitive-psychoanalytic theory, which emphasizes guilt over leaving or surpassing others (Collins and Messer, 1990, 1991). As predicted, there were highly significant differences in the dynamic content of the plans, corresponding to the different orientations of the therapists. More important than the specific findings is the demonstration that the plan-formulation method is adaptable to an object relations perspective with high interjudge reliability and was very stable over a three-month period (Collins and Messer, 1991). Silberschatz and Curtis (1991, in press) continue to apply the method to forms of therapy other than control mastery, demonstrating that they can measure the impact of therapist behaviors on the process and outcome of treatment.

The Vanderbilt Clinical Qualities Research

As part of a large project in psychotherapy research (Henry and Strupp, 1991), a group of researchers at Vanderbilt University has developed a time-limited dynamic psychotherapy based on a concept of patterns of repetitive interpersonal transaction experiences organized as vicious circles (Strupp and Binder, 1984). Therapeutic work centers on these patterns of interaction particularly as they are manifest between the patient and therapist. The Vanderbilt group developed the cyclical maladaptive pattern (CMP) or dynamic focus measure to identify the patient's problem, evaluate the therapist's interventions, and facilitate study of the process. This measure may be appropriately applied to psychoanalysis but was not developed in that context (Suh, 1986).

The approach is based on two central assumptions. First, the interpersonal world is the primary arena for construing life experience. This will reveal itself in interactions with significant others, most immediately the therapist. Second, the best way to explore this process is through the patient's stories about himself and others.

The CMP characterizes actions in four categories:

1. Acts of self, including affects and motives, perceiving situations, cognition, and overt behaviors; these may be either private or externally manifest, in or out of awareness.
2. Expectations of others, which may be conscious, preconscious, or unconscious and can be understood in a transactional context — that is, in relation to some act of the self.
3. Acts of others that are viewed as occurring in specific relationship to acts of the self; these also may be internal or manifest.
4. Acts of self toward self — that is, how one treats oneself — articulated in terms of reactions to acts of the self.

The validity of the CMP is subject to essentially the same criticisms and has essentially the same merits as that of the CCRT and PERT.

The reliability of this method is unclear. Using Benjamin's (1974) Structural Analysis of Social Behavior (SASB) methods, Schacht and Henry (1992) have developed a method intended to reliably describe the interpersonal aspects of cyclical maladaptive patterns. However, although the codings of the elements of cyclical maladaptive patterns using SASB have been shown to be reliable (Benjamin, 1982; Henry, Schacht, and Strupp, 1986), the formulation of the cyclical maladaptive patterns themselves has not been shown to be reliable (Barber and Crits-Christoph, 1993).

Comparing Transference Measures

In the study of a psychological phenomenon, the convergence of several measures of that quality suggests that each measure taps some significant aspect of the underlying situation and that each measure validly reflects that underlying phenomenon. Such comparative studies of measures also highlight which aspects of the phenomenon the measures tap. The resulting nomothetic net has long been used as a means of exploring the validity of psychological measures (Meehl, 1973). Among the several measures of transference we have discussed, some would be expected to give more adequate pictures than others of particular forms of transference. Collaborative comparative studies of the various transference measures are producing such a network of measures and exploring the relation between those measures (Luborsky and Barber, 1994;

Luborsky, Popp, and Barber, 1994). These comparisons included methods not described here, such as role relationship models developed by Horowitz and his coworkers (Horowitz, 1994).

Studying Resistance

Since the 1920s (e.g., Busch, 1995; Reich, 1933, 1975), analysts have increasingly recognized the importance of resistance to the psychoanalytic process. Anna Freud's (1936) formulations of the ego's function of defense led to increasing sophistication about the key role of defensive operations in psychology and the importance of their manifestation as resistance in psychoanalysis. Later contributions (e.g., Weinshel, 1983; Gray, 1990) emphasize the centrality of resistance analysis to psychoanalytic work. Recently, a reliable scale has been published that characterizes analytic material in terms of the phenomenology of the manifest resistance (Schuller, Crits-Christoph, and Connolly, 1991). It categorizes four components of resistance: abrupt-shifting, oppositional, flat-halting, and vague-doubting. Building on his studies of life-course development of defense and adaptation, Vaillant (1992) has also provided a systematic means of studying defense mechanisms and their flexibility and has developed reliable scales for this purpose.

Idiopathic Conflict Formulation

The difficulty in the analyst's achieving reliable descriptions of patients conflicts arises largely because of the wide range of choices open to the analyst in free discussion. Perry and his colleagues (Perry, Augusto, and Cooper, 1989; Perry and Cooper, 1986) developed a method of reliably describing particular conflicts in relation to four factors: (1) conscious and unconscious wishes and fears, (2) symptomatic and avoidant outcomes resulting from conflicting wishes and fears, (3) stressors to which the patient is vulnerable, and (4) the patient's best level of adaptation to the conflict. Judges are required to provide specific evidence for their ratings on each of these dimensions. The rating system was developed for psychiatric interviews and is not directly applicable to psychoanalytic sessions. The wishes and fears, as well as symptomatic outcomes, are selected from a standardized list based on Erikson's (1963) description of development and hence reflect that theory with its strengths and weaknesses. Formulations arrived at by this method are not related to standard psychiatric diagnostic categories. The method's reliability for case formulations has been rigorously demonstrated (Perry, Augusto, and Cooper, 1989).

The Psychotherapy Q-Set

The specific measures discussed to this point have the common disadvantage of looking at only one aspect of the analytic process at a time. This is contrary to accepted psychoanalytic practice, in which the analyst is expected to attend to the process from several points of view. The psychotherapy Q-set offers a systematic way of exploring ideas commonly used in clinical work by providing a highly reliable assessment of multiple clinical concepts. Enrico Jones and his colleagues (Jones, Hall, and Parke, 1991) adapted Block's (1971) version of the Q-sort procedure in personality research to psychoanalytic process research. Q-sort methods were developed to systematically explore subjective impressions of raters (Stephenson, 1974) and have been applied to a wide range of studies of personal experience, from sibling relations to politics (Parloff, Stephenson, and Perlin, 1965; Brown, 1981; Baas and Brown, 1973). On the basis of a thorough literature review, Jones and his coworkers constructed a 100-item deck of Q-cards, which included statements about the functioning of the patient, the analyst, and the patient-analyst dyad during the treatment hour. The items assess aspects of such central clinical psychoanalytic concepts as resistance, transference, interpretations, and therapeutic alliance. Experienced raters then sort the statements into nine categories, from most characteristic to least characteristic of what happened in that hour. The number of statements to be classified in each category is fixed, so that the rater is permitted to place only a few statements at the extremes. Essentially a normal distribution is forced. The method permits a comprehensive portrayal of each hour in contemporary analytic language in a form suitable for quantitative comparison across hours, judges, and patients.

The Q-sort method has been used effectively in single-case research (Jones, Cumming, and Pulos, 1993). But it cannot determine causal relationships between treatment procedures and outcomes. It is always possible that an undetected variable has a confounding influence. The Q-set, however, covers a broad range of variables in the therapy process, so it is unlikely to overlook the influence of any treatment variables.

The primary goal in applying the Q-sort technique to the single case is descriptive. It allows for confidence that the research has assessed factors thought to be of psychoanalytic importance in the case under study and avoids the pitfalls of nonsalient constructs, vague and impressionistic clinical description, and rater bias.

Unlike much previous psychoanalytic process research, the Jones study addresses centrally important psychoanalytic issues and studies a psychoanalysis over a significant period of time. Also, it does not rely on the judgment of inexperienced raters about global characteristics like the nature of transference, therapeutic alliance, or the analyst's empathy.

RELIABILITY

The Q-sort method has been demonstrated to be highly reliable in the evaluation of psychoanalytic hours (Jones and Windholz, 1990).

APPLICATIONS

To date, this method has been applied to only one analytic case, that of the ubiquitous Mrs. C. In this case it reliably captures important aspects of the treatment as they evolved across the course of the analysis (Jones, 1990). Application of the Q-sort method to the comparative study of cognitive-behavioral therapy and the psychodynamic psychotherapy of depression demonstrated that the two treatments were indeed distinct in practice. In cognitive-behavioral therapy, negative affects were controlled by using intellect and rationality in the context of therapist encouragement, support, and reassurance. Psychodynamic psychotherapies emphasized evoking affect, bringing troublesome feelings into awareness, and relating current difficulties to earlier experience, using the relationship of the therapist and patient as change agent. The precepts of psychodynamic psychotherapy were supported by the data (Jones and Pulos, 1993). Another study using the Q-sort method demonstrated the effectiveness of brief psychodynamic psychotherapies in private practice. It showed how the patients shifted the locus of difficulty from external situations to their inner lives and captured other clinical realities of the treatments (Jones, Parke, and Pulos, 1992). Yet another study using the Q-sort technique demonstrated the effectiveness of specific therapist interventions (as opposed to a generic model of therapy) in brief treatments of bereavement (Jones, Cumming, and Horowitz, 1988). Thus the method seems particularly suitable to capturing issues of importance in studying psychoanalysis.

Consensual Response

Another important development aimed at capturing the richness of clinical judgments is the consensual response method of identifying areas of spontaneous agreement among clinicians (Horowitz et al., 1989; Horowitz and Rosenberg, 1992). The method also addresses the problem of the unreliability of single-judge ratings of psychodynamic issues. The method uses videotapes of psychiatric interviews. After viewing the tape, eight clinicians first briefly formulate the material within certain broad preset themes. They then discuss the material for a half-hour and rewrite their formulations without referring to the original. A group of four students divide the latter formulations into thought units on the basis of detailed instructions. Finally, five judges assess the similarity of the resulting thought units across the raters. If three or more of the eight clinicians include a thought unit, that unit is incorporated in the consensual formulation.

VALIDITY

The use of several clinicians free to address matters of importance with relatively little structure suggests that there was an opportunity to include clinically important issues in the formulation. When the patients assessed in this way were actually seen in treatment, it was found that the issues noted in the formulation were important matters in the therapies (Horowitz et al., 1989). The method has not been used in psychoanalytic or psychotherapeutic sessions.

RELIABILITY

Although good reliability can be achieved using this method, the thought units eventually incorporated in the consensual formulation were usually present in only three or four of the formulations of the eight individual judges, so that reducing the number of judges can be expected to drastically reduce the reliability of the method. Studies determining the overlap between the consensual formulations of two groups of judges and the students' capacities to recognize the consensual formulation endorse the reliability of the method.

Psychological Capacities

A recurrent problem in psychoanalytic research is translating psychoanalysts' rich understanding of the clinical situation into concepts that can be operationalized and systematically investigated. The complexity and ambiguity of the technical language of psychoanalysis have greatly impeded the design of systematic operational measures in the field as have the inordinate energies devoted to disputes between adherents of different psychoanalytic schools. These disputes often obscure broad areas of conceptual agreement and even broader areas of agreement about clinical practice (Wallerstein, 1990, 1992). Using data from analysts of various backgrounds to create a common ground for discourse about analytically important matters is a major step toward resolving this problem. This method has been used to develop an understanding of the ego capacities that could be derived from direct clinical observation and that would transcend differences among ego psychology, self psychology, object relations, and Kleinian theories (Zilberg et al., 1991;

DeWitt, Hartley, and Rosenberg, 1991). The methodology of these studies is to attempt to develop so-called scales of psychological capacities, which match psychological resources to particular purposes, using everyday language. The capacities include both the psychopathological and the normal. Scales were developed on a variety of factors. For example, a trust scale includes items ranging from openness to extreme suspiciousness. Other scales include descriptions of self-esteem, zest for life, and self-organization. As these examples suggest, optimal function is not necessarily at the endpoint of the scale; to be either too trusting or too suspicious is problematic. This approach holds much promise for psychoanalytically meaningful techniques. Sundin, Armelius, and Nilsson (1994), studying the reliability of this scale for severely disturbed patients, found that it needed refinement. Its reliability for subtler disturbances, like those commonly treated through analysis, is not known.

Measures of Alliance

Along with global psychological health, the alliance of therapist and patient is the most robust predictor of good psychotherapy outcome as measured in systematic research on psychotherapy (Luborsky et al., 1988; Horvath, Gaston, and Luborsky, 1993). Freud (1912, 1913) described the patient's willingness to collaborate in analysis as the result of positive transference to the analyst. With the widening scope of psychoanalysis, Zetzel (1956) and Greenson (1965) developed concepts of a working or therapeutic alliance — a reality-based collaboration of analyst and patient toward the therapeutic goal. The concept has since developed in several directions (Meissner, 1992, 1996). An important distinction has been drawn between the concept of therapeutic alliance (the realistic agreement of patient and therapist to work toward therapeutic improvement) and analytic alliance (the agreement to work toward insight and resolution of transferences). These are not identical goals. Luborsky's (1976) studies suggest that the alliance changes in the course of therapy as the patient moves from a position of accepting help to one of collaborating with the therapist against the disturbance. Bordin (1976, 1980, 1989) has further described the dimension of the alliance in terms of its tasks during treatment, the goals of treatment, and the bond of therapist and patient.

There are approximately eleven available measures of alliance currently in use in psychotherapy research (Horvath and Luborsky, 1993). All are psychometrically satisfactory, although they measure different aspects of alliance, including therapists' and clients' contributions to the treatment (both positive and negative), the extent to which therapist and patient share therapeutic goals, capacity for relationship, acceptance of therapeutic tasks, and active participation in therapy. The scales also vary in the relative importance they give to these matters (Hansell, 1990; Hartley, 1985). The scales appear to overlap in their measurements. The low correlation of subscales in the instruments suggests that they are indeed measuring distinct aspects of alliance (Gaston and Ring, 1992).

Conclusion

As is evident, a wide range of well-studied tools is available to the researcher who wants to explore psychoanalytically significant aspects of treatment systematically. Some of these tools can be applied to psychoanalysis with little modification of either the instrument or the analysis; others require modification. The tools also vary markedly in the amount of time and work required to apply them to psychoanalytic material. However, the major difficulty concerns the validity with which these tools tap specifically psychoanalytic concepts as opposed to ostensibly similar concepts that are part of psychotherapy or that are ambiguous in psychoanalysis itself.

In applying these tools to actual analyses, we face the problem of the sheer bulk of information that is typical of the data of psychoanalysis. This raises the question of what tools are available to analyze and reduce this huge quantity of data. In the next chapter we address this problem.

18

Methods of Data Analysis

Effective and appropriate data analytic methods have been enormously powerful tools in moving forward many disciplines that deal with complex and difficult to manipulate situations. Typically in such situations it is hard to differentiate specific meaningful effects from other sources of variation in observations (Tanur et al., 1985). Detecting effects within a morass of data, determining most likely values for variables and like variation in those values, studying the likelihood that an apparent effect really depends upon a particular intervention, and estimating the magnitude of the effect are all jobs that have been remarkably well performed statistically. Unfortunately, the very effectiveness of statistics sometimes promotes a "religion of statistics" (Salsburg, 1985), in which the prestige of statistical and quantitative findings becomes more important than their value as a means to clarify matters of importance to the investigator. At times this attitude can so distort research that less meaningful but statistically and methodologically tractable questions substitute for investigation of centrally important issues. Many analysts have been "turned off" to statistical investigation because it so often has been used to give false authority and apparent substance to trivial findings in the social sciences. Worse, misrepresentations of statistical findings and attacks on analysis based on the paucity of quantitative studies in psychoanalysis have led many analysts to equate such attacks with the methods on which they (often improperly) are claimed to be based.

Data analytic tools, properly used, can be of help in the study of psychoanalytic processes and outcomes. They can reveal unseen regularities in the welter of data. They can provide a way to assess the degree to which data support or fail to support a hypothesis. Psychoanalysts, more than any other group, should be aware of the capacity for self-delusion. Because human intuition about probablistic phenomena and the evolution of complex systems is poor, and because of the strong motives that invite misperceptions about psychoanalytic processes, analysts should welcome any means that clarify the status of belief about psychoanalytic matters.

Data analytic methods must, however, be appropriate to the subject studied. Both the chain saw and the microtome are excellent tools for their intended uses. It would be nonsensical to ask which is better for cutting. Each is inadequate to the other's function. Data analytic methods are a group of tools carefully designed to do certain jobs. They should be used for those jobs for which they are effective. Unfortunately, the situations in which particular data analytic tools are ineffective are not so obvious as our analogy suggests. For example, in a subsequent chapter we will see why many of the methods used to compare groups of individuals — which would seem so promising in studying the efficacy of psychoanalysis — are not useful in the study of psychoanalytic process and outcome. In this chapter we explore some data analytic methods that are particularly appropriate to the study of psychoanalysis.

Time Series

Investigation of psychoanalytic processes entails understanding the temporal relationship between analytic events. Learning to listen for meaningful sequences of association is a central and difficult aspect of analytic training. A recent group of studies aimed at systematically characterizing such sequences of material in analytic session (Paniagua, 1985; Levy and Inderbitzen, 1990). This approach has been used in seeking evidence that interpretations are mutative (Davison, Pray, and Bristol, 1990). This work continues several earlier efforts to clarify analytic process through the systematic study of the temporal sequence of analytic events (Garduk and Haggart, 1972; Luborsky et al., 1979; Sampson et al., 1972; Silberschatz, Fretter, and Curtis, 1986; Windholz and Silberschatz, 1988; Jones and Windholz, 1990). Although the study of associative sequences has a long history in academic psychology (Rapaport, 1971), despite its importance to clinical work, there have been few studies of it in psychoanalysis proper. This paucity of study reflects the great difficulty in studying sequences of events within a complex system. When we speak of psychoanalytic process, it is precisely such temporal sequences to which we generally refer.

The group of methods known as time series analysis is designed to address such situations. Time series analysis has developed into a well-defined and sophisticated discipline with wide-ranging applications, including applications to the social sciences (Gottman, 1982). The demonstration of meaningful correlations between a series of events requires statistical methods because, just as in the study of populations, unaided human observers tend to do a poor job of differentiating chance variation from significant differences. Furthermore, it is difficult to distinguish the various sources of the change in the course of a process over time. For example, determining whether a change in average temperature over time reflects seasonal variation or has another basis would be a question for time series analysis. Unfortunately, correlations of the type we study in psychoanalysis (for example, the effects of interpretation on the emergence of subsequent material) require many data points to achieve statistical significance even when sophisticated statistical analytic methods are used (Chatfield, 1989). The requirements of time series analysis point to the need for more extensive and more detailed data from which to draw conclusions that observed temporally related changes are in fact meaningful. These demands are not artifacts of the technical difficulties of time series analysis. Rather, attempts at time series analysis expose and make explicit inherent difficulties in making valid inferences from data. With this in mind we explore some of the issues that arise in studying psychoanalyses using time series analysis.

The findings of time series analyses depend heavily on how events are divided into time frames. In the study of analytic material, this takes the form of questions about appropriate blocks of material to study—the problem of segmentation. Some intuitive answers to the problem of segmentation have merit. One can divide an analysis into hours, for instance, and let each hour constitute a discrete unit for purposes of analysis. This is the strategy used by Jones and Windholz (1990) in applying the Q-sort to analytic material. They examined the characteristics of hours sequentially. Causal relations are suggested but not proven, based upon which changes came in earlier hours and which changes followed. For instance, if the analyst interprets unconscious sexual wishes in relation to transferences, and these interpretations are followed in subsequent hours by a significant alteration in the analytic atmosphere, a causal inference can be proposed.

While segmentation of analysis into session hours may be useful in addressing some questions, it would not be appropriate for the study of questions like the immediate response of patients to specific interventions. If, for example, one wished to explore the effects of defense interpretation on the patient's association for the purpose of validating ideas of the centrality of such interpretation to analytic progress (Weinshel, 1984; Gray, 1990), division of the material into session-long segments would be far less likely to reveal significant patterns than shorter intervals or segments based on change of speaker would be. Segmentation should be chosen in a way that is consistent with the phenomena under study.

Several approaches to segmentation have actually been used in studying psychoanalytic and psychotherapeutic sessions. In some studies, segmentation process involves an arbitrary unit (for example, fifty lines of typescript [Horwitz et al., 1989]). Segmentation may be based on natural changes in the process, ranging in complexity from change of speaker to moments in the hour when specific alterations of psychological state occur. A common segmentation of material for time series analysis is based on arbitrary units of time. Even verbatim typescripts of psychoanalytic sessions usually do not record the passage of clock time, which is the commonest means of ordering material in time series analyses in other fields. Audiotaped materials retain information about the actual passage of time and so may be particularly useful for certain types of time series analysis. Change-of-speaker segmentation may be complicated by the varying level of activity of analysts, the degree to which they make incidental remarks ("Go on;" "uh-huh"), and simultaneous speech of patient and analyst. Luborsky's (1977) method of identifying relationship episodes is one reliable approach to the problem of segmentation. However, in his system much of the spoken material remains unclassified. Furthermore, story fragments are not reliably coded in duration. Another way of segmenting text is into major thematic units (Bucci, Kabasakalian-McKay, and RA Research Groups, 1985; Stinson et al., 1992). This division of text is based on obvious shifts of subject matter, which are commonly demarcated by setting a new scene or introduction of new characters (Dodd and Bucci, 1987) or linguistic markers of subject change. Idea units are less evident. They are defined by changes in the mood or feeling of the passage, the introduction of new imagery, or shifts in experiential quality, as well as changes in the major theme unit.

Many of the findings described in the previous chapter depend on segmenting procedures. Here we mention two additional ones. Gassner and coworkers (1982) showed, in the first one hundred hours of Mrs. C.'s analysis, warded-off mental contents emerged without the analyst's specifically interpreting them (with one exception). Similarly, in a study of psychotherapy, Elliott (1991a) used discourse analysis to show that the client's response of developing an important insight did not follow specific interpretations.

Segmentation procedures should not be used naively or indiscriminately. Consistent with the work of Mintz and Luborsky (1971), Bachrach et al. (1981) found that clinical and quantitative judgments about treatment-related variables based on twenty-four five-minute segments excerpted from psychoanalytic sessions did not correlate with assessment of the same variables based on the twelve complete sessions from which segments were taken. In other words, judgments based upon segments were less reliable.

Some Applications of Time Series

Time series analyses have been widely used and highly developed in numerous contexts. A picture of some of these nonpsychoanalytic applications will give an idea of why the method is appropriate to the study of psychoanalyses.

Time series have been used extensively by social scientists to analyze discourse (Gottman, 1981; Gottman and Parker, 1986). Time series analysis of discourse methods have been used to study psychoanalytic process itself by Gedo and Schaffler (1989). The basic idea is to compare scores on a process variable in segments of analytic material. The temporal change in the variable is examined with regard to other variables or the original variable. For example, in tracking referential activity one would expect, if analytic thinking is correct, to find increased referential activity following accurate transference interpretations.

In order for time series analyses to be meaningful, the investigator not only must examine the response of a variable to interventions but also must establish a baseline of its course without intervention. This is because the analytic material may change and evolve without the analyst's overt intervention. For example, a patient who has been speaking with high referential activity may become anxious because dangerous material is coming too close to awareness. This would lead to increased defense. At that point we would expect a spontaneous drop in referential activity. The effects of interpretations could be properly studied only in relation to this and other expectable fluctuation in referential activity that are independent of the interpretation. In real analytic situations we expect that the time evolution variables will be multiply determined (Waelder, 1936). The problem of separating multiple determinants in the evolution of a time series is highly challenging. Such analyses can lead to very surprising results. For example, the study of daily fluctuation of stock prices has demonstrated that most of their variation is best modeled as a "random walk" — that is, the outcome of a process in which each given point is determined by the addition or subtraction of a randomly distributed quantity (Malkiel, 1990).

This finding, achieved by time series analysis, clearly goes against our intuition that prices respond predominantly to changes in economic conditions and the extensive analyses of the supposed determinants of stock market prices.[1]

Treatment of data in which not time but sequential change is used to describe a process requires different statistical methods from time series analysis. Much of the data and discourse about psychoanalysis concerns sequences of events. Methods for analyzing event sequences have been developed for systems that involve complex interactions (Gottman and Roy, 1990).

Time series analysis has been used to study psychoanalysis. Gedo and Schaffler (1989) developed methods of assessing alteration in interplay between analyst and patient, based upon ten randomly chosen sessions from early in a 324-hour analysis, and ten from late hours. They coded analyst statements as interpretations or not interpretations, and analysand statements as to whether they demonstrated insight with reference to the transference as measured by the PERT coding scheme. Ratings of insight were not as reliable as desired. Even so, the authors were able to characterize the degree to which the patient changed during the analysis in achieving more insight and more sequences of insights later in the analysis. They also showed that the patient's insights were responsive, starting early in the analysis, to transference interpretations. They used a Markov chain approach to analyzing sequential material. This consists of studying the probability that any given remark is an insight, on the one hand, compared with the probability that the remark is an insight following an interpretation immediately before it, on the other.

Following Freud's (1905) concept of the central importance of cohesive personal narratives in psychological health, several analysts have proposed that a central mode of action of psychoanalysis is the transformation of important personal narratives into more coherent, useful and adaptive stories (Schafer, 1992; Novey, 1968). Nye (1988) developed a way to systematically assess whether both patient and analyst were telling stories unchanged or transforming them in the process of retelling. She used transformation to operationalize the concept of activities leading toward insight. Her conclusions illustrate the kinds of findings possible using time series analysis: "Changes in narrative process over the three phases of treatment corresponded to predictions made based on the psychoanalytic literature on the acquisition of the self analytic function. Early in treatment, the analyst provided the function of questioning and exploring narrative meaning; during the middle phase, the

1. This example is of particular interest to psychoanalysis because the clinically useful stance of always looking for meaning and significance may prove a hindrance in scientific endeavors that should include the possibility of true randomness.

function was performed jointly, and during the end phase the analyst was less active and the patient assumed the function" (p. 28).

The overlap between the studies of Gedo and Schaffler (1989) and Nye (1991) can be expressed as follows: using totally different methodology, they were both able to show evidence for the impact of interpretation in changing the patient's self-understanding in the course of an analysis.

We will not try here to give a summary of the methods of time series analysis. (For a recent overview that particularly addresses issues in the social sciences and the single-case study, see McCleary and Welsh [1992] and the work cited earlier.) What the reader should take away from this discussion is the knowledge that there are powerful systematic methods for exploring the temporal relation of variables in complex systems. These methods can demonstrate relations that are not evident from more casual inspection of data and they can also show that apparently meaningful temporal associations do not stand up to closer scrutiny. Because psychoanalysis is a discipline largely based on the study of the temporal unfolding of psychoanalytic process, the methods of time series analysis hold particular promise as useful tools in its systematic study.

Meta-Analysis

Thus far we have discussed specific methodologies that help us look at clinical material in greater depth and with more precision. A very different strategy is to gather many instances to provide more convincing evidence than can be provided by smaller studies. This approach is familiar to psychoanalysts in the form of surveys of published reports that summarize their findings, critically review them, characterize the present state of research in the field, and reach conclusions by comparing and integrating the findings of the original studies. Recently this process has been made more rigorous through a group of methods called meta-analysis, a term coined by Glass in 1976.

Investigators studying the same or similar phenomena commonly do so in ways that differ in the populations sampled, the methods of studying the sample, and the means used to reduce the data. It is therefore impossible in most instances to simply lump together the published data from various studies to construct a single larger study. Some systematic means must be found for integrating the data of independent studies. This group of means is called meta-analysis.

Bangert-Drowns (1986) describes five types of meta-analysis. In Glassian meta-analysis, all studies relevant to a question are collected and their findings are transformed into a combined metric that allows comparison across the different scales and different dependent measures, thus allowing description of a combined outcome and variance for all the studies together and the exploration of additional relations between dependent and independent variables. Parametric tests are used to identify relations between study outcomes and coded study features. The drawbacks of this approach are its inclusion of methodologically poor or even inappropriate studies, overly broad categories in averaging effects, and problems in the way data are managed that may suggest that there are more independent findings than there are in fact.

Study effect meta-analysis (Mansfield and Busse, 1977) uses studies, not subjects, as the unit of analysis. An effect size[2] is calculated for each study. This yields a quantitative picture of what the literature has to say about a matter. Such analysis can pick up difficulties in Glassian meta-analysis. For example, Landman and Dawes (1982) used this method to show that Smith and Glass's (1977) meta-analysis of psychotherapy outcomes produced lower effect sizes than would have been found otherwise because the researchers included methodologically poorer studies and lumped together studies that measured dissimilar situations, thereby obscuring potentially important findings. Combined probability methods (Cooper, 1979; Rosenthal, 1976, 1978, 1983; Rosenthal and Rubin, 1982a,b) involve collecting all studies relevant to a question of interest and estimating treatment effects on the basis of a combination of measures of the statistical significance of the findings and the observed effect sizes.

Approximate data pooling with tests of homogeneity attempts to bring together the data of many studies while specifically addressing the question of the comparability of findings. Approximate data pooling with sampling error correction tests similarly pools data but attempts to correct for variations resulting from sampling error and similar limitations in the data.

Meta-analytic studies are of particular interests to psychoanalysts because of the difficulty of finding sufficiently large samples for many types of psychoanalytic research, the hope of pooling data from uncoordinated studies, and the wish to clearly state and evaluate the findings of the analytic literature with regard to some matter. Meta-analysis has been satisfactorily applied in disciplines where many studies were available. The small number of quantitative studies in psychoanalysis process and outcome currently makes its direct

---

2. Effect size refers to the size of the effect observed — that is, how much difference was observed in the dependent variable as a result of a change in the independent variable. It is a wholly different concept from statistical significance, which is a measure of the improbability that the observed difference occurred as a result of chance.

application inappropriate.[3] Refinements of meta-analytic methods could allow more systematic use of the vast clinical experience already incorporated in the psychoanalytic literature. Meta-analytic methods have been developed for single-case studies (Busk and Serlin, 1992). But the extremely unsystematic nature of the descriptions of psychoanalytic experience and the nonrandom way in which they have been selected for publication make meta-analysis far less promising in psychoanalysis than it is in other fields.

Modeling Psychoanalytic Processes

Thus far we have discussed methods of study in which observations are used to discover underlying features of analytic processes. Our approach has been analytic in the sense that it breaks down the topic of study for the purpose of discovering its underlying qualities. An alternative approach is synthetic. Believing that we understand some phenomenon, we should be able to reproduce the phenomenon (no matter what the source of our knowledge). Our theories, if good enough, should allow construction of what they claim to understand.

Freud's theories and subsequent developments can be usefully divided into clinical theory and metapsychology. In recent years many authors have shown that metapsychology is less adequate as theory and may be an impediment to clinical theory (Klein, 1976; Gill, 1976; Cohler and Galatzer-Levy, 1990). However, this leaves psychoanalysis without general abstract theory that generates testable hypotheses. Several workers have proposed that ideas borrowed from cognitive science may appropriately replace metapsychology as a general psychoanalytic theory (Erdelyi, 1985; Peterfreund and Schwartz, 1971; Colby et al., 1972; Colby, 1975; Colby and Stoller, 1989). These theories could be tested using computer models designed to emulate some aspect of the psychoanalytic situation (Colby, 1981; Colby et al., 1972; Galatzer-Levy, 1991).[4] As in organic chemistry, the test of the validity of a hypothesized

3. In the preparation of this book we deliberately chose not to use meta-analytic methods in reviewing systematic studies of psychoanalysis outcome because we believe that to do so would give a false impression of statistical rigor to both the studies and our summary of them. In addition, the data from these studies were not expressed in a form that was easily emendable to such analysis.

4. In the 1950s Thomas French (1952, 1954, 1958) proposed a rigorous model of psychological function that modeled behavior as the resultant of psychological forces and which could be modeled in the same way discussed here. In his teaching French tested his method by having students synthesize dreams on the basis of posited conflicts of the patient.

structure would be synthesis based on that structure. At this point in time, however, both the models and the theory are in their early stages and there are no actual programs running.[5]

Teller and Dahl (1986) have borrowed concepts from cognitive science in formulating the idea of frames. Other psychoanalytic investigators have become increasingly convinced that narrative structures are at the center of psychoanalytically interesting psychological function (Schafer, 1992; Spence, 1982). The rich description of narratives available from literary studies, in particular the various genre of narrative (Bakhtin, 1981; Smith and Morris, 1992), might provide already highly developed methods for investigating narrative structures (see, e.g., Britton and Pellegrini, 1990). Cognitive scientists have studied the structures of narratives in a manner that is readily transferable to psychoanalytic discussions (Shank, 1990). Buchsbaum and Emde (1990) have described and operationalized models of narrative of psychoanalytic interest. This line of investigation is highly promising for abstract models of psychoanalytic process. Such models, instantiated as computer programs, could then be judged by raters for the adequacy with which they approximate genuine psychoanalytic process.[6]

Conclusion

The study of psychoanalysis poses extraordinary challenges to data analysis, partly because it is inherently complex and partly because much of data analysis was developed to address very different problems than those posed by psychoanalysis. What is important to psychoanalytic investigation involves change and transformation. Psychoanalytic investigations also entail close attention to the idiosyncratic aspects of people. Statistics was developed principally to study static, homogeneous populations. The problem of how to study change statistically is the subject of active research (see, e.g., Collins and Horn, 1991). While time series and sequential analysis are important, it is clear that much more sophisticated tools will emerge in the coming decades.

5. Models of psychological phenomena have been designed for computers, however. The striking recurrent finding is that the core model (putting aside the complexities of getting information in and out of the computer and related issues) tends to be much simpler than psychoanalytic ideas or our intuition would suggest.

6. This is essentially a variation of Turing's (1950) test of whether a machine could be said to be intelligent. Because of the conceptual difficulty of specifying the concept of intelligence (Winograd and Flores, 1987), Turing's test may be less than satisfactory for the purpose for which it was devised. But it does seem to be a highly useful tool for examining the adequacy of models of psychological process (Colby, 1975).

The individuality of patients seriously calls into question whether psycho-analysis can be usefully studied from the point of view of comparing populations of patients. In the next chapter we describe issues that arise in attempts to study analytic patients as members of populations. In the subsequent chapter we explore the major alternative to this approach.

19

Studies of Populations of Patients

Many of the questions we would like to have answered about psychoanalysis involve comparing groups of people. Do introspective people do better in analysis than action-oriented people? Do patients seen five times weekly develop more analyzable transferences than those seen less frequently? Are people who have been analyzed better off than unanalyzed people? Do analysts with character structures similar to the patient's analyze those defenses that patient and analyst share less well than analysts whose defenses are dissimilar to the patient's (Baudry, 1991)?

These questions share a similar logical structure. It is assumed that two (or more) groups can be meaningfully distinguished, and an attempt is made to correlate variance in some quality with variance in another. Methods based on this logical structure have been central to social science and other systematic studies and have been the subject of very thorough mathematical analysis (Cramer, 1946; Hoel, 1984). Generally, these questions are approached by studying a comparatively small group of people (a sample) to reach conclusions about an overall population.

The Logic of Sampling Populations

If one selects members of a population at random and studies that sample, it can be shown that for qualities that occur frequently in the larger population, the sample will increasingly show a similar distribution of that quality as sample size increases (Feller, 1950). Thus if we have a million balls, 400,000 of which are red and 600,000 white, we expect that the proportion of red to white balls would increasingly approach 2:3 as sample size increases. It is not difficult to calculate the probability of a particular deviation from that ratio given the size of the sample. Similarly, given the actual results of a sampling of this type, one can calculate the likelihood that the ratio will be 2:3. Such calculations show that one gets excellent approximations of the ratio in the population from samples that are very small compared with the size of the population.

If some quality is very rare — say, there is one green ball in the entire population — such sampling methods will not give a true picture of the population with regard to the instance of such balls (that is, there is a green ball, but there is only one of them) unless a very large sample is taken. Further, in order to be meaningful for these purposes, the sample studied must be random; it must not favor the selection of a particular type within the population. If balls of one type are more likely to be picked, the method is unsound unless one introduces some way to compensate for the differential probability of choice. Finally, the method assumes that the attribute studied has some meaning that can be reliably judged. Generally, sampling methods assume a meaningful underlying population and the meaningful distribution of qualities studied in that population.

The study of sampling statistics is well developed. Typically, one investigates a sample of a population to discover some feature of the population (for example, the average length of analyses) or the relation of one set of variables (for example, initial diagnosis) to another set (for example, analytic outcome). Investigators implicitly or explicitly generalize from the sample studied to the larger population from which the study subjects were drawn.[1]

---

1. Note that one of the weaknesses of much psychoanalytic investigation is the lack of care with which this step is taken. Unlike Freud, who addressed this question carefully (Freud, 1905) in discussing normal development, many analytic writers have generalized from samples of populations to the populations as a whole without demonstrating the logic of the generalizations. Much of the psychoanalytic description of adolescents, for example, is based on the study of disturbed youngsters in treatment and assumes, without demonstration, that findings from these youngsters may be properly generalized to all adolescents (Offer, 1969). Similarly, analytic writers commonly generalize from a small

This is a classical method of population sampling for which statistical methods have been developed. During the nineteenth and twentieth centuries, ever more sophisticated procedures have been elaborated by which investigators draw reliable and valid conclusions about the larger population from studying a sample and provide quantitative estimates of the probability that a given conclusion is valid (Stigler, 1986).

The prestige of population statistics associated with quantitative investigations in sampling methodology should not blind the psychoanalytic investigator to the availability of other methodologies. Nor should statistical sampling methods necessarily be equated with rigorous research methodology.

Problems in Sampling Studies

Comparative studies of populations provide information only about composite, average patients in each population, whereas case studies can provide insights into the mechanism of change (Barlow, 1980). Population studies lose information about the idiosyncratic features of patients that may be central to their psychopathology (Kazdin, 1981) or about details of treatments. Just as the green ball discussed earlier cannot be meaningfully studied using sampling techniques, so, too, unusual aspects of any analytic population cannot be studied with sampling techniques. In the case of an occasional unique situation, the loss of information is not great. If the population in question has many importantly different and rare members, and individual rare types together make up an important part of the population, sampling studies will give a false picture of the population.

Population studies assume unitary processes when, in fact, we may be looking at several different processes in studying the effects of psychoanalysis. Averaging across subjects prematurely may be highly misleading when the basic form of the relation is different across subjects (Hilliard, 1993). For example, the question of how long a trial of psychoanalysis is adequate to predict psychoanalytic outcome probably cannot be satisfactorily answered as posed because clinical experience strongly suggests that the answer differs for various subpopulations of analysands. Some people who ultimately have good analytic results may require an extended period in which the analyst does little

---

population of people bearing some diagnosis to the entire population of individuals who are so diagnosed, without establishing the validity of this generalization. Freud's (1911b) less careful generalization about the relationship of paranoia to homosexuality based on the study of a single case became a mainstay of psychoanalytic thinking about paranoia despite the failure of further study to support this theory.

interpretive work (Modell, 1968, 1976); some obsessional individuals have very good analyses, although the pace of change near the beginning of treatment may be so glacial as to suggest intractability. On the other hand, people with manifestly hysterical characters quite rapidly form distinct subpopulations with very different prognoses (Zetzel, 1965). If there are large significant subpopulations, it is possible to aggregate across the subpopulation with respect to pertinent variables without losing information.[2]

Certain types of questions — typically those involving who, what, where, how many, or how much — are particularly likely to yield to the sampling methods. Questions of causal relationships are less likely to yield to such methods. Because the method can only demonstrate correlation of two variables, researchers should be cautious in inferring causation. For example, as discussed above, psychotherapy research has shown that greater therapist compliance with all standard methods of treatment correlates with better results than instances where the therapist deviates from her avowed technique (Luborsky et al., 1988). The causal relationship in this correlation might operate in several ways: more-disturbed patients may force greater deviation from any particular technique; less talented therapists or therapists with less integrity may deviate more from their avowed technique. In any case, the observed correlation does not entail a causal relationship.

Technical Problems in Population Studies
GETTING AND MANAGING DATA

Especially for a treatment as elaborate as psychoanalysis, the problems of data collection and reduction can be enormous, if not intractable. Any study of analysis that begins to address the type of questions raised in the first part of this book involves massive amounts of data collected from many analysts. In the recent National Institute of Mental Health Collaborative Study of Depression (Elkin et al., 1989; Klein et al., 1990), it was found impossible to achieve reliable compliance of the staff on inpatient units at university research hospitals in providing medication according to the protocols of the study. The difficulties of gaining the collaboration of analysts even in collecting data in an agreed fashion can only be imagined.

2. It should be noted that aggregation within subjects may also be misleading. For example, at different phases of analysis the meaning of seemingly similar situations may be different. The global question of whether interpretation of transference is an optimal intervention may have different answers at different phases of the same patient's analysis.

RANDOM ASSIGNMENT OF PATIENT

A traditional way of studying the effects of treatment is to randomly assign subjects to groups that are treated differently (Cook and Campbell, 1979; O'Fallon et al., 1978). A major advantage of this procedure, if correctly carried out, is that the researcher need not attend to nuisance variables — variables that may affect outcome but are not the focus of the current study. For example, if one wishes to study the influence of the patient's diagnosis on the analytic process, the patient's socioeconomic status becomes a nuisance variable. It probably affects analytic process but may produce misleading results in studies of the influence of diagnosis. Random assignment is commonly adopted as a solution to this problem, on the assumption that these variables will effectively be canceled out.[3]

The logic of random assignment does not properly apply when the number of subjects is small, as is the case in most psychotherapy research studies. Randomization will not result in the equivalence of small samples with regard to nuisance variables (Hsu, 1989). For example, Shapiro's (1983) meta-analysis of controlled psychotherapy researches found that the mean number of patients treated and the mean number of subjects in control groups in the studies was approximately twelve. This would be a very large number for a study of psychoanalysis. If there are just five nuisance variables (for example, analyst's gender, patient's gender, socioeconomic status, patient's age, and patient's marital status) and the twenty-four subjects are randomly assigned, there is a 50 percent likelihood that the groups will be significantly non-equivalent with regard to at least one of the nuisance variables. This non-equivalence of groups will result in overestimation or underestimation of the outcome measure.

The difficulties of finding subjects and of adequate control designs often combine in actual efforts. One might hope to take advantage of situations in which for reasons having nothing to do with experimental design essentially comparable groups of patients receive different treatments or treatment and

---

3. Another strategy is to identify all "nuisance" variables and assign subjects to different categories to provide comparable groups with regard to these variables. This has the advantage that specific information about the effects of each of the nuisance variables becomes available. But unless the population is very large and the capacity to assign people to categories is great, either such a design will be impossible or the number of subjects in each category will be so small as to make valid statistical inferences impossible. Furthermore, this design can address only nuisance variables that are identified in advance of the research.

no treatment. With extraordinary good humor, Swedish investigators described their efforts to take advantage of the extended waiting list for subsidized long-term psychotherapy and psychoanalysis to compare those patients who were forced to wait to those who received treatment (Sandell, Blomberg, and Lazar, 1997). The idea was that the waiting-list group would essentially form a no-treatment control group to be compared to those who received intensive treatment. After the arduous work of collecting the data was complete, these investigators discovered that the extent to which their waiting-list "controls" had actually engaged in treatment "surpassed our most pessimistic expectations." By the time of the first follow-up interviews, 90 percent of the waiting-list group had privately sought treatment, which disqualified them as controls for the study.

COHORT AND HISTORICAL EFFECTS

Sampling a population to elicit meaningfully generalizable data while dealing adequately with nuisance variables is not possible unless the variables are statistically distributed in the underlying population from which the sample can be taken. When the object of study is a unique or historical event, no such population exists. Psychoanalytic discussion often proceeds as though the course of time and history does not change the population from which patients are drawn; yet there is ample evidence that this is not the case. The hysterics whom Freud initially treated were the product of a highly sexually repressive society. They are seen rarely today, at least by psychoanalysts. There is considerable evidence that disturbances in the sense of self are more common now than in Freud's time (Lasch, 1979; Kohut, 1976). Numerous studies have demonstrated that the psychological impact of historical events like the Great Depression depend on the sex and age of patients when the event occurred (Elder, 1974). Such factors challenge the generalizability of any findings of the effects of psychoanalysis on a population unless they are given explicit attention and must result in narrower findings in the long run than researchers might hope for.

THE IMPOSSIBILITY OF PLACEBOS

The idea of comparing treated and untreated patients to discover the effect of treatment is problematic because factors other than the presence or absence of the supposed effective agent might well be therapeutic. In pharmacological research, nontreatment controls were replaced with placebo-treated controls who received every aspect of treatment received by actively treated patients except for the presumptive efficacious element of the treatment. Eventually, investigators realized that physicians' attitudes differed depending on whether active or placebo treatment was given. This could be subtly communicated to the patient and so could directly affect the efficacy of treatment. Recognition of this problem led to the introduction of double-blind studies, in which an attempt is made to ensure that not only the patient but also those treating and evaluating him are unaware of which patients received the active agent and which the placebo. In the course of such studies the efficacy of placebos in the treatment of even clearly organic disease was demonstrated, as was the need for placebo controls and the difficulty of maintaining true double-blind conditions (Benson and McCallie, 1979; Boissel et al., 1986; Haegerstam et al., 1982).

A placebo control of psychoanalysis is impossible for both practical and ethical reasons (see Michels, 1994). Yet one would certainly expect large placebo effects among those treated through analysis. As Glover (1931) noted long ago in discussing the therapeutic effects of inexact interpretations, interventions that are known to be inaccurate may result in symptom relief. In the context of the concept of placebo controls, the logic of comparison of treated to nontreated groups seems again to break down for the study of psychoanalysis.

THE INADEQUACY OF SAMPLING METHODS
FOR STUDYING PSYCHOANALYSIS

Studies of populations of subjects may also be misleading because differences among members of the population may result in differential effects that are lost or distorted by the aggregation of data. This type of error is particularly likely to occur in the study of psychoanalysis. For example, on clinical grounds we can predict that transference interpretations will lead some patients to greater insight, will lead some to greater resistance, and will not affect other patients (Hilliard, 1993). The same patient may be affected in each of these ways at various points in the analysis. Aggregating the effects of transference interpretation across several patients or even in the same patient at various times in the analysis produces a distorted picture.

Important information can be lost even if attempts are made to produce homogenous groups of subjects. Sidman (1952), for example, showed how combining data from two studies, each of which demonstrated a significant relation between two variables, could result in a combined finding without statistical significance. Generally, the aggregation of data loses the fine structure of those data (Hilliard, 1993; Mook, 1982; Henry, Schacht, and Strupp, 1986).

The supposed homogeneity of groups reflects the underlying assumption that the processes studied have fixed meanings independent of context and that they discretely and uniquely contribute to outcomes (Shoham-Salomon, 1990). But in psychoanalysis it is clear that meaning and effect are dependent on context. This makes it difficult to identify simple direct associations between analysts' actions or analysands' behaviors and treatment outcomes in grouped data (Jones, Cumming, and Horowitz, 1988; Stiles, 1988). Any study of a sample that claims to be based on a homogeneous population thus requires careful evaluation of this claim (Hilliard, 1993). Psychoanalytic researchers can learn from the experience of psychotherapy researchers in this regard. Even for much more easily studied forms of psychotherapy, conventional group comparison designs and controlled clinical trials have been relatively ineffective in identifying associations between the therapy process and outcome (Garfield, 1990).

The adequacy of population-sample research can be improved by studying variables that are precisely defined so that measurements sharply differentiate possibilities. Even in general psychiatry research, the failure to clearly define variables has resulted in the need for very large samples (Leon, Marcak, and Portera, 1995).

Conclusion

The limitations of population studies strongly suggest that investigating psychoanalysis by studying populations through sampling is bound to be unsatisfactory. By whatever method it is accomplished, satisfactory understanding of psychoanalytic outcomes cannot be achieved through the study of global outcomes alone but must break down these outcomes into a series of smaller interrelated changes and discover how the therapeutic process affects these changes (Kiesler, 1982; Greenberg, 1986). Clearly, these processes cannot be satisfactorily studied using measures that compare different subjects but can be approached only through designs that study change in a single subject. As Strupp, Schacht, and Henry (1988) suggest about the merits of intensive design in studying psychotherapy generally: "We remain firmly convinced that scientific understanding of the variables instrumental in therapeutic change will be best advanced through intensive study of individual dyads. Traditional group comparisons, in our view, can be invaluable because they help to define and demarcate a controlled context; however, to bring greater magnification to bear on the patient-therapist transaction which is, after all, the place where therapeutic change ultimately is located, we must turn to process research" (pp. 1–2). Insofar as analysts wish to proceed using population study methods, they need to invest in techniques that will define variables sufficiently sharply that very large numbers of subjects will not be needed for studies (Leon, Marcak, and Portera, 1995).

Does this mean that the systematic study of psychoanalytic efficacy is impossible? Not at all. It means only that methods of study developed to explore very different sorts of therapeutic interventions cannot be applied to psychoanalysis. Thus it appears that the methods of statistical investigation will not be useful in answering centrally important questions about psychoanalysis as therapy. This does not mean that the effectiveness of psychoanalysis cannot be rigorously demonstrated. Fortunately, over the past several decades a group of effective methods for studying psychoanalytic processes has emerged.

20

The Single-Case Method

All that we have considered in this volume now brings us to our penulti-mate point — namely, that single-case methods are the most promising line of approach to exploring the efficacy of psychoanalysis. Case studies differ from case reports in that they employ rigorous and systematic means of collecting, analyzing, and reporting data, with the goal of making the epistemological status of the investigation clear. Case studies explore a single situation in depth and attempt to reach valid conclusions on the basis of such exploration. Be-cause this method is most commonly used to describe complex phenomena, and because many case studies have suffered from limited methodologies, they are often seen as being less rigorous than other empirical methods. However, this shortcoming is not inherent in the method.

Many terms have been used to refer to single-case methods, including N=1 or *single-case strategies* (Hersen and Barlow, 1976); *intrasubject replication* (Kazdin, 1980); *intensive* (as opposed to extensive) *research* (Chassan, 1967, 1979); and *own-control* (Millon and Diesenhaus, 1972), as well as *time series analysis* (Campbell and Stanley, 1963; Glass, Wilson, and Gottman, 1978). The methodology of case studies has been refined and clarified over the past three decades (Kratochwill, 1992; Yin, 1994). The single-case study focuses on changes in the subject over time. The potential rigor of the case study method is often unappreciated because the method is misunderstood as a variation on survey or quasi-experimental designs (Cook and Campbell, 1979) with a very small sample. In fact, the analysis of single-case studies does not use aggregate data from more than one subject.

The choice of the case study method in part reflects the expected depth of study. If subjects must be studied intensively to yield the level of information pertinent to the investigation, it becomes impractical to use many subjects (Chassan, 1979).

The single-case study has a long history of denigration. Campbell and Stanley (1963) described the one-shot case study, a design that had no control group, assessed the dependent variable only once, and was not replicated. In their words, "Such studies have such a total absence of control as to be of almost no scientific value" (p. 6). Although Campbell has since changed his mind (Hilliard, 1993), the negative attitude toward such studies persists to this day. Hayes (1981) describes several reasons for this. The method is undertaught: most clinical research training continues to emphasize group-comparison methods. Studies using single-case methods tend defensively to emphasize their methodological sophistication at the expense of their clinical significance, such that the actual value of the method may be obscured. The method was highly developed by behaviorists and bears the burden of this association, though it is not actually attached to any particular theory of treatment. Clinicians who are dissatisfied with group-comparison researches are likely to discard all methodologically sophisticated research. Because the method is inadequately appreciated, it is underrepresented in published research. For all these reasons single-case research generally has less prestige than it deserves.

Case Study Design and Method

Useful case studies are characterized by careful design that lays out what the study is attempting to do, its methods, the situation to be studied, the logic linking observations with conclusions, and the criteria for determining to what extent the link is satisfactory (Nachmias and Nachmias, 1976; Philiber, Schwab, and Samsloss, 1980). Statistical methods do not make a case a population study. For example, in the study of the economic development of a single community, statistical sampling technique may be employed to investigate an aspect of the community, but the object of the study remains a single entity, the community's economic development. Variations in the frequency of interpretations or the use of effectively charged words across an analysis could be described quantitatively while retaining focus on but one case.

Internal Validity

Single-case designs are particularly vulnerable to threats to internal validity (Kazdin, 1981), especially when studying a process like psychoanalysis, which occurs over an extended period of time, because — depending on the number and timing of evaluations — much else besides treatment may have occurred between assessments. Hence, rigorously concluding that effects are the result of treatment is difficult. The narrower the interval between assessments and the more closely that change in the analysand is associated with change in treatment, the less plausible it is that the observed effects had sources outside the treatment. Similarly, the question of whether the effect results from maturation can be addressed by the availability of an extended history or knowledge of the natural history of the condition in question (Ryle, 1948). Thus if an adult with a character trait in evidence from childhood changes that trait during treatment, it seems likely that the change resulted from treatment. A close temporal association of a supposed effect and its cause, and a reasonable relation between the intensity of the change and the supposed cause, suggest a causal relationship. A larger number of cases and a more heterogeneous group of cases responding to treatment also suggest a treatment effect. Thus if patients with different demographic characteristics and different life circumstances respond to a treatment, their response suggests the success of the treatment intervention. Similarly, if the treatment offered is itself diverse and heterogeneous, it becomes increasingly implausible that the study demonstrates a causal relationship between change and treatment.

In designing and evaluating single-case studies, rival hypotheses should be explicitly formulated and tested against the available data. Experimental designs should rule out threats to internal validity by performing experiments that explicitly test alternative hypotheses. Case study designs often do not allow such explicit protections, but they can be arranged to address many important issues of internal validity (Kazdin, 1981). The first step in this process is to make alternative hypotheses explicit and to describe their expected impact on the data. Repeated measurements of the patient's situation across time increase validity. This should start early and involve several measures if possible. It is highly desirable that these measures be systematic.

Estimates of the degree of variability in the patient's behavior are critical to single-case methodology. Data must be sufficiently stable to be meaningful in the context of the study — that is, they must not simply reflect an accident at the moment of sampling. Excessive variation may be handled in several ways. One can wait for the pattern of behavior to become clearer; one can try to investigate the sources of changing behavior; one can change the temporal unit of analysis to more accurately reflect the natural rhythm of the situation. For instance, it may be that sampling affects at intervals that are too long or too short will result in a loss of the structure of the evolution of emotions in a session, just as it is impossible to see the content of a painting from too far away or too near.

Studying single cases involves careful attention to the implications of various ways of introducing changes into the situation. Trying to change only one thing at a time improves the likelihood of clarifying the sources of the observed effects. If a patient changes after the analyst simultaneously becomes more self-revealing and comments more on the patient's affects, it is difficult to judge which of these factors caused the change.

Where possible, a baseline should be established. This does not necessarily mean that some manifest aspect of the process is stable. It may be that the rate of change in the process or its variability is the more pertinent issue and constitutes the stable baseline. For example, in studying the degree of confrontation useful in analyzing character defenses, the pertinent stable baseline may be the rate of change in these defenses with the analyst's ordinary analytic technique.

Generally, if a change is introduced gradually, it is more difficult to see its effect than if it is introduced full force. However, introducing some technical variation at full strength may lead to artifacts in the study of psychoanalysis because abrupt changes in the analyst's behavior may be more influential simply by virtue of their abruptness. In addition, the analyst as a responsible clinician may wish to evaluate the impact of a change in a relatively low dosage to be confident that it will not harm the patient. In this instance, there would seem to be significant tension between optimal clarity for the research finding and ordinary clinical practice.

A particular problem in assessing the impact of interventions is that delayed effects are always possible. Clearer findings result when an effect is observed and then disappears or is diminished at the withdrawal of the intervention. At least for long periods of time during analysis, the patient's use of an interpretation is thought to be contingent on its repetition and application to a variety of situations. Most analysts would regard it as unethical to withhold interpretations or other interventions for experimental purposes, and their absence at otherwise appropriate times is likely to result from other important concurrent factors, especially the analyst's countertransference. However inevitable, interruptions in the analytic work because of weekends and vacations often function as periods of withdrawal and have been studied extensively. The reappearance of the effect when the intervention is again implemented argues in favor of its specific effectiveness. Although analysts expect some regression in response to the cessation of the intervention, they generally do not expect a return to the original level, and this is not required to demonstrate specific effects.

Selecting Cases for Study

Should cases for intensive case study be chosen from a group? When properly done, such selection allows statements about the relationship of group findings to the case studies. This strategy has been employed by several investigators (Strupp, 1980a,b,c,d, 1990; Grawe, 1992). The combination of group and case research is a promising direction for investigations (Elkin et al., 1988).

Common sense suggests that cases for intensive study be carefully selected because of the large investment of time that research requires. It is usually the goal of the investigator to make statements that can be generalized beyond the particular case. If the particular case is extremely unusual — for example, if the analyst uses a technique that is widely different from that used in the analytic community generally — such generalization is likely not to be possible. Similarly, it would seem prudent to undertake single-case studies only with subjects who are likely to be available and willing to participate to the completion of the study. Other things being equal, patients who seem likely to complete their analyses, to be geographically available for follow-up, and to cooperate in research procedures are preferred for single-case investigation. However, such patients may form an atypical subset of individuals seeking analysis, so findings based on such studies should not be generalized.

Time Series in Single-Case Studies

The reduction and statistical treatment of data from single-case studies has been studied from several viewpoints (Parsonson and Baer, 1992; Wampold, 1992; Edgington, 1992; Busk and Marascuilo, 1992). A brief overview of time series approaches to the analysis of single-case studies will suggest the type of issues involved (Hayes, 1981; McCleary and Welsh, 1992).

Within-series strategies involve simple or complex phase changes. In studying simple phase changes, one establishes a baseline, introduces a change, and observes fluctuations in the stability, level, or trend at a series of data points. The clearer the data change and the closer it is to the intervention, the greater the confidence in the effect observed. One can also study complex phase changes by introducing various sequences of elements of change to reveal the relation between them. For example, if one wanted to study the interacting effects of two treatment components known to be effective, one could study a series of interventions in which they were used separately, in combination, and in sequence, in order to discover how they interacted in effecting change.

A *between-series strategy* studies the effects of altering two or more conditions in rapid and random relation to one another, collecting each group of effects into a separate series. If there is a clear separation between such series, differences among conditions are inferred. This design is particularly useful (and ethical) when it is clinically appropriate to intervene in several ways at once, but at the same time the investigator wishes to separate out the effects of the various forms of intervention.

Combined-series designs use coordinated sets of comparisons between and within series measures. For example, a multiple-baseline design randomly varies the duration of the baseline and postintervention interval to detect coincidental events that affect change. Multiple baselines often arise naturally in clinical practice because analysts tend to treat problems sequentially rather than all at once. As Hayes (1981) observes, multiple baselines can be found easily in clinical work where simply recording work on similar problems approached through the same treatment is likely to result in a collection of instances of intervention with baselines of different duration.

Advantages of Case Study Designs

Many experienced analysts doubt that systematic research can reveal very much of psychoanalytic interest. Because each case is unique, generalization beyond the most simple level is not possible. Single-case study provides a bridge between the idiosyncrasies of individuals and generalizations about them. When one specifies dimensions of the personality that are relevant to a particular individual, whether in regard to symptoms (Battle et al., 1966), defenses or character traits (Perry and Cooper, 1986; Perry, Cooper, and Michels, 1987; Vaillant, 1986), more generally conceived ego capacities of all sorts (Wallerstein, 1988; DeWitt, Hartley, and Rosenberg, 1991; Zilberg et al., 1991), or personality styles (Horowitz et al., 1984), there are many opportunities for studying how these characteristics are engaged in the analytic process and what changes are observable in these specific dimensions of the individual. Thus the single-case study provides a way to understand particular features of personality as they interact with therapy, and this can be generalized across cases.

Another advantage of single-case designs is that they are very close in spirit to the way clinicians think and work (Hayes, 1981). They may therefore bridge the gap between research and clinical practice, which plagues psychotherapy research. The fit between clinical decision making and single time series methods is outstanding. In fact, good clinical practice often implicitly follows a single subject experimental design. The clinician intervenes, notes the effect of the intervention, and, depending on the observed outcome, decides upon the next intervention. Clinicians' increasing sophistication about time series methods for analyzing the effects of interventions could improve clinical skills based on assessment of the impact of interventions. At the same time, time series research methods that extend the ordinary logic of clinical work should be particularly easy for clinicians to appreciate.

Applications

Whatever their other merits or disadvantages, Freud's case studies have had an enormous impact on psychotherapy. Series of case studies in other fields of psychotherapy have also had substantial impact or psychotherapeutic thinking (Wolpe, 1958; Masters and Johnson, 1970). In physical medicine, case studies constituted the primary mode of investigation of diagnosis, pathology, and therapeutics until the middle of the twentieth century (Major, 1932). We need to underline that multiple-case studies are distinct from population sampling methods. The report of twenty cases in which a pathological finding is associated with a disease entity is the report of twenty cases, not a statistical sample. The accumulation of case histories over the centuries led to generalizations of their findings that constitute the major basis for classification of physical illness. Similarly, biology owes a great deal to case study methods. Darwin's researches, for example, largely focused on the case study of creatures living in a variety of environments. From these case studies, he generalized principles in a manner that illustrates the power of nonexperimental methods to reveal underlying mechanisms. Case study methods have proved highly effective in disciplines ranging from the history of science (Conant, 1957) to the study of business enterprises (Cheape, 1985; Dalzell, 1987; Smith, 1966; Tolliday, 1987) to anthropology (Geertz, 1983) and sociology (Yin, 1994). The direct application of single-case designs to systematic research in psychoanalysis promises to produce important results (Fonagy and Moran, 1993).

What Case Studies Tell Us

Single-case design allows a sharper assessment of whether the observed change resulted from treatment. The flexibility of the single-case study permits quasi-experimentation that provides a clearer picture of causal links than population studies generally can. Particular phenomena of interest can be isolated for detailed study as they occur in this particular case, and further instances can be sought from the same patient.

Case study designs are particularly well suited for studying the mechanism of change (Barlow, 1980), for assessing observed change, and for capturing the idiosyncratic features of patients and therapies (Kazdin, 1982). They are most useful for answering questions of how and why. Although causal relations are generally not clearly demonstrable in case studies, occasionally a slam-bang effect reveals evidence of massive change following an intervention so that it is entirely clear that the intervention caused the effect (Gilbert, Light, and Mosteller, 1975).

Single-case designs allow the exploration of situations where the significance of each of a set of events can be well understood only by relating it to the other events (Shoham-Salomon, 1990; Pinsof, 1989). This is particularly important in studying such matters as the patient's influence on the analyst and the resulting emerging patterns in the analyst. Psychoanalytic observations from a wide range of points of view clearly show the influence of the analysand on the analyst (Racker, 1953, 1957; Money-Kyrle, 1956; Reich, 1951; Little, 1951; Stolorow and Lachmann, 1992; Fleiss, 1942; Tower, 1956; Grinberg, 1962; Winnicott, 1965; Jacobs, 1973, 1983, 1986; Kernberg, 1965; Sandler, 1976; Dahl et al., 1978; McLaughlin, 1981; Tyson, 1986; Blum, 1986; Panel, 1986; Abend, 1989; Kantrowitz, 1996). Systematic research on psychotherapy supports these psychoanalytic observations. One of the few robust findings of psychotherapy research is the importance of such patient characteristics as capacity for relationship (Garfield, 1986), though this has not yet been demonstrated for psychoanalysis. The exploration of such phenomena is particularly well suited to single-case study methods.

Data for Case Studies

Authentically quantitative data are sometimes especially useful, because time series analytic methods are more fully developed for such data. However, the introduction of meaningless quantities for qualitative or only slightly quantitative data (for example, ordinal scales) may obscure findings.

The data of single-case studies may be experimental, in the sense that the investigator directly manipulates independent variables, or passive-observational, in the sense that she simply observes occurrences (Cook and Campbell, 1979). Direct manipulation of independent variables is generally regarded as necessary to demonstrate rigorous causal connections between independent and dependent variables, but passive observation is often adequate to address the concomitant variations that are highly relevant to causal classes.

Case study methods can be used to falsify hypotheses. In ethnography, Campbell (1979) and Rosenblatt (1981), both of whom were seeking data to confirm prior beliefs, found those beliefs to be wrong through single-case studies. Similarly, investigators studying a generalized interpretative strategy by means of a single-case study method found evidence that their original hypothesis was false (Galatzer-Levy and Gruber, 1992).

Data may be collected to test hypotheses (justification) or to generate them (discovery). Many of the same problems exist with regard to the aggregation of data within a single-case study as were discussed in Chapter 19 regarding the aggregation of data across cases (Hilliard, 1993). Aggregating data from different phases of the analysis, for example, is often conceptually unsound because the meaning of a situation depends on the context in which it occurs and often on its details. Whether an interpretation of resistance leads to richer material will depend on the history of previous work, the phrasing of the interpretation, and other factors. Aggregating defense interpretations (or even interpretations of a particular defense) within an analysis is likely to lead to errors in which quite different clinical happenings are mistakenly lumped together.

Multiple-Case Design

The study of multiple cases allows the replication of results and also the comparative study of cases. Breuer and Freud's *Studies in Hysteria* (1893) illustrates how a series of cases taken together can sharpen the meaning of the findings of each case.

The collection of single cases should be carefully differentiated from investigations based on sampling methods. In order to make the claim that a group of cases represents some larger population, issues of sampling must be addressed. As questions are answered by multiple-case studies, the findings become applicable to some population of cases, if only those treated by the particular researchers. The issue of how representative is a given series of cases also needs to be addressed. Nevertheless, it is clear that there is no absolute differentiation between case studies and population studies. Psychoanalytic writers have often failed to address the relation between the case reported and the population of potential cases.

Generalizations from Single-Case Studies

What can be said on the basis of a single case, and how can the findings be generalized? The question of what is possible rather than what is common can be answered clearly from single-case studies (Mook, 1982). Only case studies can detect the possible patterns of behavior that may then be explored with regard to their frequency and their relation to other patterns (Thorngate, 1986). Single-case methodology is not exclusively idiographic, for the investigators are attempting to address questions that will ultimately be generalizable beyond the subject.

Sometimes the logic of the single-case study is compelling in its generalizability because the features of the situation are such that the investigator may reliably assume that the findings can be generalized without much further investigation. B. F. Skinner's (1961) single-case researches in operant conditioning were properly regarded as generalizable because it was clear that within a wide range there was no reason to believe that subjects would differ in regard to the findings.[1]

The logic of psychoanalytic investigations often allows reasonable generalization from a single case or a few cases because, once demonstrated, the theory provides sufficient reason to believe a finding. Freud's seminal clinical investigations of dreams, jokes, and slips of the tongue all rely in their logic on multiple-case instances joined to a plausible clinical theory.

Replication of a single case provides a reason to be confident of their generalizability. Replications may be direct or systematic (Sidman, 1960). In direct replication an attempt is made to repeat the study in another case that is thought to match the first with regard to pertinent variables. In systematic replication one attempts to show that findings differ in predictable ways when cases are selected that differ along critical individual variables. In fact, however, very few single-case studies have been replicated in psychotherapy research (Hilliard, 1993).

Problems and Difficulties with Case Studies

Single-case methods are limited to exploring variations within a subject. Any variable that does not vary within an individual requires a replication design for its exploration. For example, leading proponents of therapies for borderline-range pathology disagree about the importance of confronting and

1. Note that this logic of clinical interventions is closer to generally recognized good clinical practice than the style of intervention suggested by a treatment manual approach (see pp. 173, 195, 196). Although a treatment manual could be designed that includes the clinician's memory of past experiences with various types of interventions and that prescribes appropriate branching in the choice of technique based on those past and current experience, no manual has in fact been written in this way.

analyzing negative transference. Kernberg (1984) regards these activities as central to the work with such patients, while Kohut (1984) asserts that such activity (beyond noticing that the patient's rage reflects threatened fragmentation of the self) interferes with the analytic process. This is a question that probably cannot be answered by a single-case study, because the analyst could not vary his interpretive stance between these two poles while maintaining analytic credibility. Only comparison of two analyses could address this question.

Single-case studies are particularly subject to researcher bias because of the inevitable engagement of the researcher in the material studied (Becker, 1958, 1967). Psychoanalysts have become sophisticated about the management and use of countertransference in the treatment situation. However, the research situation commonly involves problems that have not been addressed even by analysts who are regularly attentive to countertransference in clinical work. In analysis, we expect distortions, resistances, and other defensive operations. These issues also exist in the research arena. Although a sophisticated appreciation of our irrational attachment to psychoanalytic ideas and a working knowledge of how to protect ourselves from contradictions (Greenacre, 1966) are partial insurance against distortions arising from our own needs, our understanding is inevitably incomplete. In addition, because psychoanalysis involves a dialogue between analyst and analysand, there are numerous opportunities in the clinical situation for the analyst to test her understanding against the patient's statements and to correct misunderstandings. In contrast, the feedback that analysts receive in doing research is sparse. The analyst who employs case study methodology needs to work hard to avoid bias.

Social scientists have identified several means to reduce observer bias in case studies, such as training in case study methodology, the development of adequate protocols — including a description of the work to be done — and systematic peer review (Yin, 1994).

Examples of Rigorous Case Studies

A two-and-a-half-year-long psychotherapy of a patient with major depression, treated by an experienced therapist using the control-mastery theory of Weiss and Sampson (1986), was studied in depth (Jones, Ghannam, et al., 1993). The investigators used a time series method to model fluctuations in the therapy process with time, preserving the context-determined meaning of therapist and patient actions. They clearly showed reciprocal effects and convincingly demonstrated a causal function. By subjecting the Q-sort ratings to exploratory factor analysis, they found four conceptually interpretable clusters in the time series analysis: therapist's acceptance and neutrality; interactivity of therapist and patient; psychodynamic technique; patient dysphoria. The first gradually declined, the second gradually increased. An increase in the third factor was associated with a diminution in the fourth, but a causal relation could not be demonstrated.

Causality can be shown by demonstrating that the predictability of the patient's behavior is improved by knowledge of the therapist's past behavior. This permits tests of bidirectionality of effects, and indeed, the authors found bidirectional effects. They regarded this mutual influence as central to understanding the therapy process; for example, the patient's depressive affect seems to have gradually moved the therapist from a nonjudgmental, facilitative, empathic, neutral stance to a more authoritative and emotionally reactive and involved posture. This in turn seemed to lead to gradual reduction in the patient's symptom level. This empirical finding is consistent with contemporary conceptions of interactive analytic processes (Boesky, 1990; Chused, 1990, 1991). Although the therapist had a control-mastery framework, toward the middle and end phases of therapy, the work more resembled a corrective emotional experience, with the therapist consciously and deliberately trying to react to the patient differently from the patient's mother. The therapeutic process that emerged corresponded more to Oremland's (1976, 1985) concept of an interactive psychotherapy, in which important features of the therapist-patient interaction were not discussed and interpreted or their meaning explicated.

The impact of interpretation on associative freedom was studied in the analysis of Mrs. C. Spence, Dahl, and Jones (1993) found that freedom in association significantly increased over the course of treatment and was related to the rate of analyst interventions per hour. The correlation was particularly strong in the later stages of treatment. Three types of therapist interventions — pointing out the patient's use of defensive maneuvers such as undoing or denial, identifying a recurrent theme in the patient's experience or conduct, and discussing dreams and fantasies — were found to increase associative freedom in the later stages of treatment. They influenced the session containing the interpretation and the next three sessions as well. These findings suggested that the effect of an intervention during the latter phase of treatment, when transference resistances have diminished, may run beyond the limits of the hour in question. However, it was not clear whether the therapist was constantly gauging the analytic surface and refraining from speaking until the associative freedom of the patient had exceeded a certain minimum value.

It is rarely possible to link the impact of psychoanalytic interventions to an externally verifiable, quantitative variable. In an extraordinary investigation, Fonagy and Moran (1990) did exactly this. Using time series, they studied the relation of psychoanalytic process variables to the insulin requirements of juvenile diabetics who were analytic patients. They demonstrated clear quantitative correlations.

Conclusion

Single-case methods are conceptually consistent with ideas of how psychoanalysis might best be studied. The fear that they may be unrigorous is misplaced. Careful case studies can be highly rigorous and highly informative. Interesting, clinically significant findings are beginning to emerge from single-case studies. We regard them as the most promising direction for future research into psychoanalytic process and outcome.

21

Summary and Overview

In its first century, psychoanalysis has been widely recognized as providing the richest understanding of the most interesting aspects of human psychology. At the same time, its claims to validity as an empirical science have remained open to question. These questions have been particularly marked with regard to therapeutics.

From its founding until the middle of the twentieth century psychoanalysis was unique as a rational system of therapeutics for psychological distress in which intervention was based on a specific understanding of the genesis of the disturbance. The emergence of alternative rational therapeutics in combination with the promise of treatments requiring less of both therapist and patient has placed psychoanalysis in competition with many other forms of intervention. Although these developments understandably have caused considerable distress among analysts, they have also had the salutary effect of encouraging analysts to be more rigorous about their claims for the efficacy of our treatment.

In this book we have repeatedly tried to emphasize the importance of asking appropriate questions as a first step to finding meaningful answers. An activity can be efficacious only with respect to some particular end. In all discussions of therapeutic efficacy, the goal must be specified as clearly as possible. It was for this reason that we began our study by asking what we as analysts hope to learn from empirical investigations.

Popular descriptions to the contrary, psychoanalysis is by no means lacking in empirical studies. As our review shows, in addition to the far-reaching clinical experience of the analytic community, there is ample systematic evidence for the efficacy of psychoanalysis in aiding many patients for whom it is an appropriate treatment. These systematic findings carry with them the characteristic stamp of good empirical investigations — negative findings that run contrary to the wishes and beliefs with which investigators started their study. These negative findings include that systematic investigation does not support the effectiveness of psychoanalysis when it is used to help otherwise untreatable patients and that within the range of ordinarily analyzable disturbances it is currently impossible to predict at the beginning of treatment which patients will do well in analysis and which poorly. The available empirical findings about the efficacy of psychoanalysis all have substantial methodological limitations. In addition, many of them reflect clinical practice of years ago, although many analysts believe that analytic practice has changed dramatically.

For these reasons it would seem appropriate that the analytic community should be interested in answering questions about the efficacy of psychoanalysis using recently developed empirical methods. A rich group of ideas and methods is now available, many of which are close in spirit to psychoanalysis itself.

At this writing there is much concern in the analytic community about the future of psychoanalysis. The enormous — and largely irrational — prestige that it enjoyed in the quarter-century following World War II has been greatly diminished. Analysis has been attacked, sometimes unfairly, from many sides. Financial support for analysis as therapy and as an intellectual discipline has dwindled. All of this puts considerable pressure on the researcher into psychoanalytic efficacy to produce convincing results. We think that this aim will best be achieved through continued rigorous investigations of this deepest source of information about human psychological functioning.

References

Abend, S. (1982a). Serious illness in the analyst: Countertransference considerations. *Journal of the American Psychoanalytic Association* 30: 365–79.

———. (1982b). Some observations on reality testing as a clinical concept. *Psychoanalytic Quarterly* 51: 218–38.

———. (1986a). Countertransference, empathy, and the analytic ideal: The impact of life stresses on analytic capability. *Psychoanalytic Quarterly* 55: 563–75.

———. (1986b). Some problems in the evaluation of the psychoanalytic process. In A. Richards and M. Willick (eds.), *Psychoanalysis, the Science of Mental Conflict: Essays in Honor of Charles Brenner,* 102–37. Hillsdale, N.J.: Analytic Press.

———. (1989). Countertransference and psychoanalytic technique. *Psychoanalytic Quarterly* 58: 374–95.

———. (1990). The psychoanalytic process: Motives and obstacles in the search for clarification. *Psychoanalytic Quarterly* 59:532–49.

Abend, S., Porder, M., and Willick M. (1983). *Borderline Patients: Psychoanalytic Perspectives.* New York: International Universities Press.

Abrams, S. (1987). The psychoanalytic process: A schematic model. *International Journal of Psychoanalysis* 68: 441–52.

Abrams, S., and Shengold, L. (1978). Some reflections on the topic of the 30th Congress: "Affects and the psychoanalytic situation." *International Journal of Psychoanalysis* 59: 395–407.

Aichorn, A. (1935). *Wayward Youth.* New York: Wiley.

Alexander, F. (1925). A metapsychological description of the process of cure. *International Journal of Psychoanalysis* 6: 13–34.

——. (1930). *The Psychoanalysis of the Total Personality*. New York: Nervous and Mental Disease Publishing.

——. (1937). *Five-Year Report of the Chicago Institute for Psychoanalysis, 1932–1937*. Chicago: Chicago Psychoanalytic Institute.

Allen, A. (1971). The fee as a therapeutic tool. *Psychoanalytic Quarterly* 40: 132–40.

Altman, L. (1975a). *The Dream in Psychoanalysis*. Rev. ed. New York: International Universities Press.

——. (1975b). A case of narcissistic personality disorder: The problem of treatment. *International Journal of Psychoanalysis* 56: 187–95.

Anthony, E. (1986). The contribution of child psychoanalysis to psychoanalysis. *Psychoanalytic Study of the Child* 41: 61–87.

Appelbaum, S. (1977). *The Anatomy of Change*. New York: Plenum.

——. (1978). Pathways to change in psychoanalytic therapy. *Bulletin of the Menninger Clinic* 4: 239–51.

Appy, G. (1989). Where does the common ground among psychoanalysts end? *International Journal of Psychoanalysis* 70: 7–11.

Arlow, J. (1961). Egopsychology and the study of mythology. *Journal of the American Psychoanalytic Association* 9: 371–93.

——. (1963). The supervisory situation. *Journal of the American Psychoanalytic Association* 11: 576–94.

——. (1969a). Fantasy, memory, and reality testing. *Psychoanalytic Quarterly* 38: 28–51.

——. (1969b). Unconscious fantasy and disturbances of conscious experience. *Psychoanalytic Quarterly* 38: 1–27.

——. (1972). Some dilemmas in psychoanalytic education. *Journal of the American Psychoanalytic Association* 20: 556–66.

——. (1979). The genesis of interpretation. *Journal of the American Psychoanalytic Association* 27 (suppl.): 193–206

——. (1985). The concept of psychic reality and related problems. *Journal of the American Psychoanalytic Association* 33:521–35.

Arlow, J., and Brenner, C. (1964). *Psychoanalytic Concepts and the Structural Theory*. New York: International Universities Press.

——. (1988). The future of psychoanalysis. *Psychoanalytic Quarterly* 57: 1–14.

——. (1990). The psychoanalytic process. *Psychoanalytic Quarterly* 59: 678–92.

Atwood, G., and Stolorow, R. (1984). *Structures of Subjectivity: Explorations of Psychoanalytic Phenomenology*. Hillsdale, N.J.: Analytic Press.

Baas, L., and Brown, S. (1973). Generating rules for intensive analysis: The study of transformations. *Psychiatry* 36: 172–83.

Bacal, H. (1985). Optimal responsiveness and the therapeutic process. In A. Goldberg (ed.), *Progress in Psychology* 1: 202–26. Hillsdale, N.J.: Analytic Press.

Bachrach, H. (1983). On the concept of analyzability. *Psychoanalytic Quarterly* 52: 180–204.

——. (1989). On specifying the scientific methodology of psychoanalysis. *Psychoanalytic Inquiry* 9: 282–304.

Bachrach, H., Curtis, H., Escoll, P., Graff, H., Huxster, H., Ottenberg, P., and Pulver, S.

(1981). Units of observation and perspectives on the psychoanalytic process. *British Journal of Medical Psychology* 54: 25–33.

Bachrach, H., Galatzer-Levy, R., Skolnikoff, A., and Waldron, S. (1991). On the efficacy of psychoanalysis. *Journal of the American Psychoanalytic Association* 39: 871–916.

Bachrach, H., and Leaff, L. (1978). "Analyzability": A systematic review of the clinical and quantitative literature. *Journal of the American Psychoanalytic Association* 26: 881–920.

Bachrach, H., Weber, J., and Solomon, M. (1985). Factors associated with the outcome of psychoanalysis (clinical and methodological considerations) of the Columbia Psychoanalytic Center research project (IV). *International Review of Psychoanalysis* 43: 161–74.

Bacon, F. (1620). *Novum organum*. T. Fowler (ed.), 2d. ed. Oxford: Oxford University Press.

Baekeland, R., and Lundwall, L. (1975). Dropping out of treatment: A critical review. *Psychological Bulletin* 82: 738–83.

Bakhtin, M. M. (1981). *The Dialogic Imagination*. C. Emerson and M. Holquist (trans.). Austin: University of Texas Press.

Balint, M. (1936). The final goal of psychoanalytic treatment. *International Journal of Psychoanalysis* 17: 206–16.

———. (1949). Changing therapeutic aims and techniques in psycho-analysis. In *Primary Love Psycho-Analytic Technique*, 209–22. London: Tavistock.

———. (1968). *The Basic Fault*. London: Tavistock.

Bangert-Drowns, R. (1986). Review of developments in meta-analytic methods. *Psychological Bulletin* 99: 388–99.

Barber, J., and Crits-Christoph, P. (1993). Advances in measures of dynamic formulation. *Journal of Consulting and Clinical Psychology* 61: 574–85.

Barber, J., Crits-Christoph, P., and Luborsky, L. (1990). A guide to the CCRT standard categories and their classifications. In L. Luborsky and P. Crits-Christoph (eds.), *Understanding Transference: The Core Conflictual Relationship Theme Method*, 37–50. New York: Basic.

Barlow, D. (1980). Behavioral therapy: The next decade. *Behavior Therapy* 11: 315–28.

Barnsley, M. (1988). *Fractals Everywhere*. Boston: Academic Press.

Basch, M. (1989). The teacher, the transference, and development. In K. Field, B. Cohler, and G. Wood (eds.), *Learning and Education: Psychoanalytic Perspectives*, 771–88. Madison, Conn: International Universities Press.

———. (1991). Psychic change: Developments in the theory of technique. *International Journal of Psychoanalysis* 72: 3–5.

Basco, M., Krebaum, S., and Rush, A. Outcome measures of depression. In H. Strupp at al. (eds.), *Measuring Patient Changes in Mood, Anxiety, and Personality Disorders: Toward a Core Battery*, 191–245. Washington, D.C.: American Psychological Association.

Battle, C., Imber, S., Hoehn-Saric, R., Stohe, A., Nash, C., and Frank, J. (1966). Target complaints as criteria of improvement. *American Journal of Psychotherapy* 20: 184–92.

Baudry, F. (1983). The evolution of the concept of character in Freud's writings. *Journal of the American Psychoanalytic Association* 31: 3–31.

——. (1984). Character: A concept in search of an identity. *Journal of the American Psychoanalytic Association* 32: 455–77.

——. (1989). Character, character type, and character organization. *Journal of the American Psychoanalytic Association* 37: 655–86.

——. (1991). The relevance of the analyst's character and attitudes to his work. *Journal of the American Psychoanalytic Association* 39: 917–38.

Bayer, R., and Spitzer, R. (1985). Neurosis, psychodynamics, and DSM-III: A history of the controversy. *Archives of General Psychiatry* 42: 187–96.

Becal, H., and Newman, K. (1990). *Theories of Object Relations: Bridges to Self Psychology.* New York: Columbia University Press.

Beck, A., Rush, J., Shaw, B., and Emery, G. (1979). *Cognitive Therapy of Depression.* New York: Guilford.

Becker, H. (1958). Problems of inference and proof in participant observation. *American Sociological Review* 23: 652–60.

——. (1967). Whose side are we on? *Social Problems* 14: 239–47.

Bellak, L. (1961). Research in psychoanalysis. *Psychoanalytic Quarterly* 30: 519–48.

Bellak, L., and Smith, W. (1956). An experimental exploration of the psychoanalytic process. *Psychoanalytic Quarterly* 25: 385–414.

Benedek, T. (1950). Climacterium: A developmental phase. In T. Benedek, *Psychoanalytic Investigations,* 323–49. New York: Quadrangle.

——. (1959). Parenthood as a developmental phase. In T. Benedek, *Psychoanalytic Investigations,* 378–401. New York: Quadrangle.

Benjamin, L. (1974). Structural analysis of social behavior. *Psychological Review* 81: 392–425.

——. (1982). Use of structural analysis of social behavior (SASB) to guide intervention in psychotherapy. In J. Anchin and D. Kiesler (eds.), *Handbook of Interpersonal Psychotherapy,* 120–42. New York: Pergamon.

——. (1993). Every psychopathology is a gift of love. *Psychotherapy Research* 3: 1–24.

Benson, H., and McCallie, D. (1979). Angina pectoris and the placebo effect. *New England Journal of Medicine* 300: 1424–28.

Bergin, A., and Garfield, S. (eds.). (1994). *Handbook of Psychotherapy and Behavior Change.* 4th ed. New York: Wiley.

Berk, R., Ouker, R., Goldart, N., Swerdloff, B., and Wolf, L. (1964). A profile study of the applicant not accepted for treatment at analytic clinics. *Psychiatric Quarterly* 30: 1–17.

Bernfeld, S. (1941). The facts of observation in psychoanalysis. *International Review of Psychoanalysis* 12: 342–51.

——. (1949). Freud's scientific beginnings. *American Imago* 6: 163–96.

——. (1951). Sigmund Freud, M.D., 1882–1885. *International Journal of Psychoanalysis* 32: 204–17.

Berzins, J., Bednar, R., and Severy, L. (1975). The problem of intersource consensus for measuring therapeutic outcome: New data and multivariate perspectives. *Journal of Abnormal Social Psychology* 84: 10–19.

Beutler, L., and Crago, M. (eds.). (1991). *Psychotherapy Research: An International Review of Programmatic Studies*. Washington: American Psychological Association.

Beutler, L., Crago, M., and Arizmendi, T. (1986). Research on therapist variables in psychotherapy. In A. Bergin and S. Garfield (eds.), *Handbook of Psychotherapy and Behavior Change*, 257–310. 3d ed. New York: Wiley.

Beutler, L., Machado, P., and Neufeldt, S. (1994). Therapist variables. In A. Bergin and S. Garfield (eds.), *Handbook of Psychotherapy and Behavior Change*, 229–69. 4th ed. New York: Wiley.

Bibring, E. (1954). Psychoanalysis and the dynamic psychotherapies. *Journal of the American Psychoanalytic Association* 2: 745–70.

Bieber, I., Dain, H., Dince, P., Drellich, M., Grand, H., Gundlach, R., Kremer, M., Rifkin, A., Wilbur, C., and Bieber, T. (1962). *Homosexuality: A Psychoanalytic Study of Male Homosexuals*. New York: Basic.

Bird, B. (1972). Notes on transference: Universal phenomenon and hardest part of analysis. *Journal of the American Psychoanalytic Association* 20: 267–301.

Blanck G., and Blanck, R. (1988). The contribution of ego psychology to understanding the process of termination in psychoanalysis and psychotherapy. *Journal of the American Psychoanalytic Association* 36: 961–84.

Blatt, S. (1990). Interpersonal relatedness and self-definition: Two personality configurations and their implications for psychopathology and psychotherapy. In J. Singer (ed.), *Repression and Dissociation: Implications for Personality Theory, Psychopathology and Health*, 299–335. Chicago: University of Chicago Press.

———. (1992). Comparison of therapeutic outcome in psychoanalysis and psychotherapy: The Menninger Psychotherapy Project revisited. *Journal of the American Psychoanalytic Association* 40: 691–724.

Blatt, S., and Behrends, R. (1987). Internalization, separation-individuation, and the nature of therapeutic action. *International Journal of Psychoanalysis* 68: 279–97.

Blatt, S., Stayner, D., Auerbach, J., and Behrends, R. (1996). Change in object and self-representations in long-term, intensive, inpatient treatment of seriously disturbed adolescents and young adults. *Psychiatry: Interpersonal and Biological Processes* 59: 82–107.

Blatt, S., Wiseman, H., Prince-Gibson, E., and Gatt, C. (1991). Object representations and change in clinical functioning. *Psychotherapy* 28: 273–83.

Bliss, M. (1982). *The Discovery of Insulin*. Chicago: University of Chicago Press.

Block, J., and Haan, N. (1971). *Lives Through Time*. Berkeley, Calif.: Bancroft.

Blos, P. (1941). *The Adolescent Personality: A Study of Individual Behavior for the Commission on Secondary School Curriculum*. New York: Appleton-Century-Crofts.

———. (1967). The second individuation process of adolescence. *Psychoanalytic Study of the Child* 22: 162–86.

Blum, H. (1971). On the conception and development of the transference neurosis. *Journal of the American Psychoanalytic Association* 19: 41–53.

———. (1986). Countertransference and the theory of technique: Discussion. *Journal of the American Psychoanalytic Association* 34:309–28.

———. (1989). The concept of termination and the evolution of psychoanalytic thought. *Journal of the American Psychoanalytic Association* 37:275–95.

Boesky, D. (1989). The questions and curiosity of the psychoanalyst. *Journal of the American Psychoanalytic Association* 37: 579–603.

——. (1990). The psychoanalytic process and its components. *Psychoanalytic Quarterly* 59: 550–84.

Boissel, J., Philippon, A., Gauthier, E., Schbath, J., and Destors, J. (1986). Time course of long-term placebo therapy effects in angina pectoris. *European Heart Journal* 7: 1030–36.

Bolland, J., and Sandler, J. (1965). *The Hampstead Psychoanalytic Index: A Study of the Psychoanalytic Case Material of a Two-Year-Old Child*. New York: International Universities Press.

Bollas, C. (1982). On the relation to the self as an object. *International Journal of Psychoanalysis* 63: 347–59.

——. (1987). *The Shadow of the Object*. New York: Columbia University Press.

Bordin, E. (1976). The generalizability of the psychoanalytic concept of the working alliance. *Psychotherapy: Theory, Research, and Practice* 16: 252–60.

——. (1980). Of human bonds that bind and free. Paper presented at the annual meeting of the Society for Psychotherapy Research, Pacific Grove, Calif.

——. (1989). Building therapeutic alliances: The base for integration. Paper presented at the annual meeting of the Society for Psychotherapy Research, Berkeley, Calif.

Bradlow, P. (1987). On prediction and the manifest content of the initial dream reported in psychoanalysis. In A. Rothstein (ed.), *The Interpretations of Dreams in Clinical Work*, 155–78. Madison, Conn.: International Universities Press.

Bradlow, P., and Coen, S. (1975). The analyst undisguised in the initial dream in psychoanalysis. *International Journal of Psychoanalysis* 56: 415–25.

Brazil, D., Coulthard, M., and Johns, C. (1980). *Discourse Intonation and Language Teaching*. London: Longman.

Brenner, C. (1976). *Psychoanalytic Technique and Psychic Conflict*. New York: International Universities Press.

——. (1982). The concept of the superego: A reformulation. *Psychoanalytic Quarterly* 51: 501–25.

——. (1987) How theory shapes technique: A structural theory perspective. *Psychoanalytic Inquiry* 7: 167–72.

Breuer, J., and Freud, S. (1893). Studies in hysteria. In J. Strachey (ed. and trans.), *Standard Edition of the Complete Psychological Works of Sigmund Freud*. Vol. 2. London: Hogarth.

Brinich, P. (1981). Application of the metapsychological profile to the assessment of deaf children. *Psychoanalytic Study of the Child* 36: 3–32.

Britton, B., and Pellegrini, A. (1990). *Narrative Thought and Narrative Language*. Hillsdale, N.J.: Lawrence Erlbaum.

Brooks, R. (1991). EuroQol — health-related quality of life measurement: Results of the Swedish questionnaire exercise. *Health Policy* 18: 1–24.

Brown, S. (1981). Intensive analysis. In D. Nimmo and K. Sanders (eds.), *Handbook of Political Communication*, 627–49. Beverly Hills, Calif.: Sage.

Brugha, T., Bebbington, P., MacCarthy, B., Sturt, E., and Wykes, T. (1992). Antidepressants may not assist recovery in practice: A naturalistic prospective survey. *Acta Psychiatrica Scandinavica* 86: 5–11.

Bucci, W. (1984). Linking words and things: Basic processes and individual variation. *Cognition* 17: 137–53.

———. (1985). Dual coding: A cognitive model for psychoanalytic research. *Journal of the American Psychoanalytic Association* 33: 571–607.

———. (1988). Converging evidence for emotional structures: Theory and method. In H. Dahl, H. Kächele, and H. Thomä (eds.), *Psychoanalytic Process Research Strategies,* 29–50. New York: Springer-Verlag.

———. (1993). The development of emotional meaning in free association. In A. Wilson and J. Gedo (eds.), *Hierarchical Concepts in Psychoanalysis: Theory, Research, and Clinical Practice,* 3–47. New York: Guilford.

———. (1997). *Psychoanalysis and Cognitive Science.* New York: Guilford.

Bucci, W., and Freedman, N. (1978). Language and hand: The dimensions of referential competence. *Journal of Personality* 46: 594–622.

Bucci, W., Kabasakalian-McKay, and RA Research Groups. (1985). Instructions for scoring referential activity (R.A.) in transcripts of spoken narrative text. Garden City, N.Y.: Adelphi University.

Buchsbaum, H., and Emde, R. (1990). Play narratives in 36-month-old children: Early moral development and family relationships. *Psychoanalytic Study of the Child* 45: 129–65.

Burgner, M. (1988). Analytic work with adolescents: Terminable and interminable. *International Journal of Psychoanalysis* 69: 179–87.

Burlingham, D. (1975). Special problems of blind infants: Blind baby profile. *Psychoanalytic Study of the Child* 30: 3–13.

Busk, P., and Marascuilo, L. (1992). Statistical analysis in single-case research: Issues, procedures, and recommendations, with applications to multiple behaviors. In T. Kratochwill and J. Levin (eds.), *Single-Case Research Design and Analysis: New Directions for Psychology and Education,* 159–85. Hillsdale, N.J.: Erlbaum.

Busk, P., and Serlin, R. (1992). Meta-analysis for single-case research. In T. Kratochwill and J. Levin (eds.), *Single-Case Research Design and Analysis: New Directions of Psychology and Education,* 187–212. Hillsdale, N.J.: Erlbaum.

Calef, V. (1971a). On the current concept of the transference neurosis: Introduction. *Journal of the American Psychoanalytic Association* 19: 22–25.

———. (1971b). Transference neurosis: Concluding remarks. *Journal of the American Psychoanalytic Association* 19: 89–97.

———. (1972). A report of the 4th Pre-Congress on Training (Vienna, 1971) to the 27th International Psycho-analytical Congress. *International Journal of Psychoanalysis* 53: 37–45.

Calef, V., and Weinshel, E. (1973). Reporting, nonreporting, and assessment in the training analysis. *Journal of the American Psychoanalytic Association* 21: 714–26.

Campbell, D., and Stanley, J. (1963). *Experimental and Quasi-Experimental Designs for Research.* Boston: Houghton Mifflin.

Campbell, E., Louis, K., and Blumenthal, D. (1998). Looking a gift horse in the mouth: Corporate gifts supporting life sciences research. *Journal of the American Medical Association* 279: 995–99.

Carson, R. (1991). Dilemmas in the pathway of the DSM-IV. *Journal of Abnormal Psychology* 100: 302–7.

Caspi, A., Elder, G., Jr., and Herbener, E. (1990). Childhood personality and the prediction of life-course patterns. In L. Robins and M. Rutter (eds.), *Straight and Devious Pathways from Childhood to Adulthood,* 13–35. Cambridge, England: Cambridge University Press.

Caston, J. (1986). The reliability of the diagnosis of the patient's unconscious plan. In J. Weiss and H. Sampson (eds.), *The Psychoanalytic Process,* 241–55. New York: Guilford.

———. (1993). Can analysts agree? The problems of consensus and the psychoanalytic mannequin: I. A proposed solution. *Journal of the American Psychoanalytic Association* 41: 493–511.

Caston, J., and Martin, E. (1993). Can analysts agree? The problems of consensus and the psychoanalytic mannequin: II. Empirical tests. *Journal of the American Psychoanalytic Association* 41: 513–48.

Cavenar, J., and Nash, J. (1976). The dream as a signal for termination. *Journal of the American Psychoanalytic Association* 24: 425–36.

Ceci, S., and Bruck, M. (1995). *Jeopardy in the Courtroom: A Scientific Analysis of Children's Testimony.* Washington, D.C.: American Psychological Association.

Chapman, J. (1983). *Reading Development and Cohesion.* London: Heinemann Educational.

Chase, G. (1982). Assessing the emotional fit between parent and child: Developmental needs, temperament, and parental empathy: Criteria for evaluations in child custody and visitation disputes. *Conciliation Courts Review* 20: 25–29.

Chassan, J. (1967). *Research Design in Clinical Psychology and Psychiatry.* New York: Appleton-Century-Crofts.

———. (1979). *Research Design in Clinical Psychology and Psychiatry.* 2d ed. New York: Irvington.

Chatfield, C. (1989). *The Analysis of Time Series: An Introduction.* 4th ed. London: Chapman and Hall.

Cheape, C. (1985). Family firm to modern multinational: Norton Company, a New England enterprise. *Harvard Studies in Business History* 36. Cambridge: Harvard University Press.

Chevron, E. S., and Rounsaville, B. (1983). Evaluating the clinical skills of psychotherapists: A comparison of techniques. *Archives of General Psychiatry* 40: 1129–32.

Chused, J. (1988). The transference neurosis in child analysis. *Psychoanalytic Study of the Child* 43: 51–81.

———. (1990). Neutrality in the analysis of action-prone adolescents. *Journal of the American Psychoanalytic Association* 38: 679–704.

———. (1991). The evocative power of enactments. *Journal of the American Psychoanalytic Association* 32: 615–29.

Clarkin, J., Koenigsberg, H., Yeomans, F., Selzer, M., Kernberg, P., and Kernberg, O. (1992). Psychodynamic psychotherapy of the borderline patient. In J. Clarkin et al. (eds.), *Borderline Personality Disorder: Clinical and Empirical Perspectives,* 268–87. New York: Guilford.

Cocks, G. (1994) Introduction. In G. Cocks (ed.), *The Curve of Life: Correspondence of Heinz Kohut, 1923–1981.* Chicago: University of Chicago Press.

Coen, S. (1992). *The Misuse of Persons: Analyzing Pathological Dependency*. Hillsdale, N.J.: Analytic Press.

Cohen, J. (1968). Weighted kappa: Nominal scale agreement with provision for scale disagreement on partial credit. *Psychological Bulletin* 70: 213–20.

———. (1990). Things I have learned (so far). *American Psychologist* 45: 1304–14.

Cohler, B., and Galatzer-Levy, R. (1992). Psychoanalysis and the classroom: Intent and meaning in learning and teaching. In N. Szajnberg (ed.), *Educating the Emotions: Bruno Bettelheim and Psychoanalytic Development*, 41–91. New York: Plenum.

———. (In press). *Gay and Lesbian Lives: Psychoanalytic Perspectives on Development*. Chicago: University of Chicago Press.

Cohler, B., and Grunbaum, H. (1981). *Mothers, Grandmothers, and Daughters: Personality and Child Care in Three Generations of Families*. New York: Wiley-Interscience.

Colby, K. (1975). *Artificial Paranoia: A Computer Simulation of Paranoid Processes*. New York: Pergamon.

———. (1981). Modeling a paranoid mind. *Behavioral Brain Sciences* 4: 515–60.

Colby, K., Hilf, F., Weber, S., and Kraemer, H. (1972). Turing-like indistinguishability test for the validation of a computer simulation of paranoid processes. *Artificial Intelligence* 3: 199–221.

Colby, K., and Stoller, R. (1989). *Cognitive Science and Psychoanalysis*. Hillsdale, N.J.: Analytic Press.

Collins, L., and Horn, J. (eds.). (1991). *Best Methods for the Analysis of Change: Recent Advances, Unanswered Questions, Future Directions*. Washington, D.C.: American Psychological Association.

Collins, W., and Messer, S. (1990). *Extending the Plan Formulation Method to an Object Relations Perspective: Reliability, Stability, and Adaptability*. Wintergreen, Va.: Society for Psychotherapy Research.

———. (1991). Extending the plan formulation method to an object relations perspective: Reliability, stability, and adaptability. *Journal of Consulting and Clinical Psychology* 3: 75–81.

Conant, J. (1957). *Harvard Case Studies in the History of Science*. J. Dunner (ed.). Cambridge: Harvard University Press.

Cook, T., and Campbell, D. (1979). *Quasi-Experimentation: Design in Analysis Issues for Field Settings*. Chicago: Rand McNally.

Cooper, A. (1984). Psychoanalysis at one hundred: Beginnings of maturity. *Journal of the American Psychoanalytic Association* 32: 245–67.

———. (1986). Some limitations on therapeutic effectiveness: The "burnout syndrome" in psychoanalysts. *Psychoanalytic Quarterly* 55: 576–98.

———. (1987). Changes in psychoanalytic ideas: Transference interpretation. *Journal of the American Psychoanalytic Association* 35: 77–98.

———. (1989). No longer invisible: Gay and lesbian Jews build a movement. *Journal of Homosexuality* 18: 83–94.

Cooper, A., Karush, A., Easser, R., and Swerdloff, B. (1966). The adaptive balance profile and the prediction of early treatment behavior. In G. Goldman and D. Shapiro (eds.), *Developments in Psychoanalysis at Columbia University*, 212–32. New York: Haffner.

Cooper, H. (1979). Statistically combining independent studies: A meta-analysis of sex differences in conformity research. *Journal of Personality and Social Psychology* 37: 131–46.

Cooper, S. (1991). The psychodynamic intervention scale. Unpublished.

Coriat, T. (1917). Some statistical results of the psychoanalytic treatment of the psychoneuroses. *Psychoanalytic Review* 4: 209–16.

Costa, P., and McCrae, R. (1989). Personality continuity and the changes of adult life. In M. Storandt and G. VandenBos (eds.), *The Adult Years: Continuity and Change*, 41–77. Washington, D.C.: American Psychological Association.

Couper-Kuhlen, C. (1991). *An Introduction to English Prosody.* Maryland: Edward Arnold.

Cramer, B., and Flournoy, O. (1976). Panel on "the changing expectations of patients and psychoanalysts today." *International Journal of Psychoanalysis* 57: 419–27.

Cramer, H. (1946). *Mathematical Methods of Statistics.* Princeton: Princeton University Press.

Crews, F. (ed.), Blum, H., Cavell, M., Eagle, M., and Crews, F. (1995). *The Memory Wars: Freud's Legacy in Dispute.* New York: New York Review of Books Press.

Crits-Christoph, P., Barber, J., Miller, N., and Beebe, K. (1993). Evaluating insight. In N. Miller, L. Luborsky, J. Barber, and J. Docherty (eds.), *Psychodynamic Psychotherapy Research: A Handbook for Clinicians*, 407–22. New York: Basic.

Crits-Christoph, P., and Connolly, M. (1993). Patient pretreatment predictors of outcome. In N. Miller, L. Luborsky, et al. (eds.), *Psychodynamic Treatment Research: A Handbook for Clinical Practice*, 177–88. New York: Basic.

Crits-Christoph, P., Cooper, A., and Luborsky, L. (1990). The measurement of accuracy of interpretations. In L. Luborsky and P. Crits-Christoph (eds.), *Understanding Transference: The Core Conflictual Relationship Theme Method*, 173–88. New York: Basic.

Crits-Christoph, P., Luborsky, L., Popp, C., Mellon, J., and Mark, D. (1990). The reliability of choice of narratives and of the CCRT measure. In L. Luborsky and P. Crits-Christoph (eds.), *Understanding Transference: The Core Conflictual Relationship Theme Method*, 93–101. New York: Basic.

Curtis, H. (1979). The concept of therapeutic alliance: Implications for the "widening scope." *Journal of the American Psychoanalytic Association* 27 (suppl.): 159–92.

Dahl, H. (1972). A quantitative study of psychoanalysis. In R. Holt and E. Peterfreund (eds.), *Psychoanalysis and Contemporary Science*, 237–57. New York: Macmillan.

———. (1974). The measurement of meaning in psychoanalysis by computer analysis of verbal contexts. *Journal of the American Psychoanalytic Association* 22: 37–57.

———. (1988). Frames of mind. In H. Dahl, H. Kächele, and H. Thomä (eds.), *Psychoanalytic Process Research Strategies*, 51–66. New York: Springer-Verlag.

———. (1991). The key to understanding change: Emotions as appetitive wishes and beliefs about their fulfillment. In J. Safran and L. Greenberg (eds.), *Emotion, Psychotherapy, and Change*, 130–65. New York: Guilford.

Dahl, H., Holzer, M., and Berry, J. (1992). *How to Classify Emotions for Psychotherapy Research.* Ulm, Germany: University of Ulm Press.

Dahl, H., Kächele, H., and Thomä, H. (eds.). (1988). *Psychoanalytic Process Research Strategies.* Berlin: Springer-Verlag.

Dahl, H., and Teller, V. (1994). The characteristics, identification, and applications of FRAMES. *Psychotherapy Research* 4: 253–76.

Dahl, H., Teller, V., Moss, D., and Trujillo, M. (1978). Countertransference examples of the syntactic expression of warded-off contents. *Psychoanalytic Quarterly* 47: 339–63.

Dalzell, R (1987). Enterprising elite: The Boston associates and the world they made. *Harvard Studies in Business History* 40. Cambridge: Harvard University Press.

Davies, J. (1989). The development of emotional and interpersonal structures in three-year-old children. *Dissertation Abstracts International* 50 (5-A): 1249–50.

Davison, W., Pray, M., and Bristol, C. (1990). Mutative interpretation and close process monitoring in a study of psychoanalytic process. *Psychoanalytic Quarterly* 59: 599–628.

Decker, H. (1982). The choice of a name: "Dora" and Freud's relationship with Breuer. *Journal of the American Psychoanalytic Association* 30: 113–36.

Deutsch, F. (1957). A footnote to Freud's "Fragment of an analysis of a case of hysteria." *Psychoanalytic Quarterly* 26: 159–67.

Deutsch, H. (1944). *The Psychology of Women*. Vol. 1, *Psychoanalytic Interpretation*. New York: Grune and Stratton.

——. (1945). *The Psychology of Women*. Vol. 2, *Motherhood*. New York: Grune and Stratton.

DeWitt, K., Hartley, D., and Rosenberg, S. (1991). Scales of psychological capacities: Development of an assessment approach. *Psychoanalysis and Contemporary Thought* 14: 343–61.

DeWitt, K., Kaltreider, N., Weiss, D., and Horowitz, M. (1983). Judging change in psychotherapy: Reliability of clinical formulations. *Archives of General Psychiatry* 40: 1121–28.

Diatkine, R. (1968). Indications and contraindications for psychoanalytical treatment. *International Journal of Psychoanalysis* 49: 266–70.

Dodd, M., and Bucci, W. (1987). The relationship of cognition and affect in the orientation process. *Cognition* 27: 53–71.

Doidge, N., Simon, B., Gillies, L., and Ruskin, R. (1993). Characteristics of psychoanalytic practice under a nationalized health plan: DSM-III-R diagnoses, previous treatment, and childhood trauma. *American Journal of Psychiatry* 51: 586–90.

Eagle, M. (1984). Psychoanalysis and "narrative truth": A reply to Spence. *Psychoanalysis and Contemporary Thought* 7: 629–40.

Edelson, M. (1983). Is testing psychoanalytic hypotheses in the psychoanalytic situation really impossible? *Psychoanalytic Study of the Child* 38: 61–112.

——. (1992). Can psychotherapy research answer this psychotherapist's questions? *Contemporary Psychoanalysis* 28: 118–51.

Edgington, E. (1992). Nonparametric tests of single-case experiments. In T. Kratochwill and J. Levin (eds.), *Single-Case Research Design and Analysis: New Directions in Psychology and Education*, 133–57. Hillsdale, N.J.: Erlbaum.

Eissler, K. (1950). Ego psychological implications of the analytic treatment of delinquents. *Psychoanalytic Study of the Child* 5: 97–121.

——. (1953). Effect of the structure of the ego on psychoanalytic technique. *Journal of the American Psychoanalytic Association* 1: 104–43.

——. (1958). Notes on problems of technique in the psychoanalytic treatment of adolescents. *Psychoanalytic Study of the Child* 13: 223–54.

———. (1974). On some theoretical and technical problems regarding the payment of fees for psychoanalytic treatment. *International Review of Psycho-Analysis* 1: 73–101.

Ekstein, R., and Wallerstein, R. (1972). *The Teaching and Learning of Psychotherapy.* 2d ed. New York: International Universities Press.

Elder, G. (1974). *Children of the Great Depression.* Chicago: University of Chicago Press.

———. (1975). Age differentiation and the life course. *Annual Review of Sociology* 1: 165–90.

———. (1979). Historical change in life patterns and personality. In P. Baltes and O. Brim (eds.), *Life-span Development and Behavior,* 117–59. New York: Academic Press.

———. (1986). Military times and turning points in men's lives. *Developmental Psychology* 22: 233–45.

———. (1992). The life course. In E. Borgatta and M. Borgatta (eds.), *The Encyclopedia of Sociology,* 482–510. New York: Macmillan.

Elkin, I., Pilkonis, P., Docherty, J., and Sotsky, S. (1988). Conceptual and methodological issues in comparative studies of psychotherapy and pharmacotherapy. Part 1, Active ingredients and mechanisms of change. *American Journal of Psychiatry* 145: 909–17.

Elkin, I., Shea, M., Watkins, J., Imber, S., et al. (1989). NIMH treatment of depression collaborative research program: General effectiveness of treatments. *Archives General Psychiatry* 46: 971–82.

Elliott, R. (1991a). Five dimensions of therapy process. *Psychotherapy Research* 1: 92–103.

———. (1991b). University of Toledo: Investigating significant therapy events. In L. Beutler and M. Crago (eds.), *Psychotherapy Research: An International Review of Programmatic Studies,* 317–21. Washington, D.C.: American Psychological Association.

Epstein, R. (1990). Assessment of suitability for low-fee control psychoanalysis: Some theoretical and technical considerations. *Journal of the American Psychoanalytic Association* 38: 951–83.

Erdelyi, M. (1985). *Psychoanalysis: Freud's Cognitive Psychology.* New York: Leaman.

Erikson, E. (1962). Reality and actuality: An address. *Journal of the American Psychoanalytic Association* 10: 451–74.

———. (1963). *Childhood and Society.* 2d ed. New York: Norton.

———. (1968). *Identity, Youth, and Crisis.* New York: Norton.

Erle, J. (1979). An approach to the study of analyzability and analyses: The course of forty consecutive cases selected for supervised analysis. *Psychoanalytic Quarterly* 48: 198–228.

Erle, J., and Goldberg, D. (1979). Problems in the assessment of analyzability. *Psychoanalytic Quarterly* 48: 48–84.

———. (1984). Observations on assessment of analyzability by experienced analysts. *Journal of the American Psychoanalytic Association* 32: 715–37.

Escalona, S. (1952). Problems in psychoanalytic research. *International Journal of Psychoanalysis* 33: 11–21.

Eysenck, H. (1952). The effects of psychotherapy: An evaluation. *Journal of Consulting Psychology* 16: 319–24.

———. (1966). *The Effects of Psychotherapy.* New York: International Science Press.

Fairbairn, W. (1952a). *Psychoanalytic Studies of the Personality*. London: Routledge and Kegan Paul.

———. (1952b). *An Object Relations Theory of Personality*. New York: Basic.

———. (1963). Synopsis of an object relations theory of personality. *International Journal of Psychoanalysis* 44: 224–25.

Farrington, D., Loeber, R., and Van Kammen, W. (1990). Long-term criminal outcomes of hyperactivity-impulsivity-attention deficit and conduct problems in childhood. In L. Robins, M. Rutter, et al. (eds.), *Straight and Devious Pathways from Childhood to Adulthood*, 62–81. Cambridge: Cambridge University Press.

Feldman, D. (1986). How development works. In I. Levin (ed.), *Stage and Structure: Reopening the Debate*, 284–306. Norwood, N.J.: Ablex.

Feldman, F. (1968). Results of psychoanalytic case assignments. *Journal of the American Psychoanalytic Association* 16:274–300.

Feller, W. (1950). *An Introduction to Probability Theories and Its Applications*. New York: Wiley.

Fenichel, O. (1930). Statistisher Bericht uber die therapeutische Tatigkeit, 1920–1930. In *Zehn Jahre Berliner Psychoanalytishes Institut*, 13–19. Vienna: International Psychoanaltyishes Verlag.

———. (1945). *The Psychoanalytic Theory of Neurosis*. New York: Norton.

Firestein, S. (1969). Problems of termination in the analysis of adults. *Journal of the American Psychoanalytic Association* 17: 222–37.

———. (1974). Termination of psychoanalysis of adults: A review of the literature. *Journal of the American Psychoanalytic Association* 22: 873–94.

———. (1978). *Termination in Psychoanalysis*. New York: International Universities Press.

———. (1984). The dilemma of analyzability. In G. Pollock and J. Gedo (eds.), *Psychoanalysis: The Vital Issues*, 227–48. New York: International Universities Press.

Fisher, L. (1993). New standard for drug makers: Proving the cure is worth the cost. *New York Times*, Jan. 18.

Fisher, S., and Greenberg, R. (1977). *The Scientific Credibility of Freud's Theories and Therapy*. New York: Basic.

Fiske, D., Hunt, H., Luborsky, L., Orne, M., et al. (1970). Planning of research on effectiveness of psychotherapy. *American Psychologist* 25: 727–37.

Fleiss, R. (1942). The metapsychology of the analyst. *Psychoanalytic Quarterly* 11: 211–27.

Fleming, J. (1961). What psychoanalytic work requires of the analyst. *Journal of the American Psychoanalytic Association* 9: 719–29.

Fleming, J., and Benedek, T. (1966). *Psychoanalytic Supervision: A Method of Clinical Teaching*. New York: Grune and Stratton.

Fonagy, P., and Moran, G. (1990). Studies of the efficacy of child psychoanalysis. *Journal of Consulting and Clinical Psychology* 58: 684–95.

———. (1993). Selecting single case research designs for clinicians. In N. Miller, L. Luborsky, J. Barber, and J. Docherty (eds.), *Psychodynamic Treatment Research: A Handbook for Clinical Practice*, 63–96. New York: Basic.

Fonagy, P., and Target, M. (1994). The efficacy of psychoanalysis for children with disruptive disorders. *Journal of the American Academy of Child and Adolescent Psychiatry* 33: 45–55.

———. (1996). Prediction of the outcome of child psychoanalysis: A retrospective study of 763 cases at the Anna Freud Center. *Journal of the American Psychoanalytic Association* 44: 27–77.

Fraiberg, S., Adelson, E., and Shapiro, V. (1975). Ghosts in the nursery. *Journal of the American Academy of Child Psychiatry* 14: 387–421.

Frank, J., and Frank, J. (1991). *Persuasion and Healing*. 3d ed. Baltimore: Johns Hopkins University Press.

Freeman, M. (1985a). Paul Ricoeur on interpretation: The model of the text and the idea of development. *Human Development* 28: 295–312.

———. (1985b). Psychoanalytic narration and the problem of historical knowledge. *Psychoanalysis and Contemporary Thought* 8: 133–82.

French, T. (1952). *The Integration of Behavior*. Vol. 1, *Basic Postulates*. Chicago: University of Chicago Press.

———. (1954). *The Integration of Behavior*. Vol. 2, *The Integrative Process of Dreams*. Chicago: University of Chicago Press.

———. (1958). *The Integration of Behavior*. Vol. 3, *The Reintegrative Process in Psychoanalytic Treatment*. Chicago: University of Chicago Press.

French, T., and Wheeler, D. (1963). Hope and repudiation of hope in psychoanalytic therapy. *International Journal of Psychoanalysis* 44: 304–16.

Freud, A. (1927). Four lectures on child analysis. In *The Writings of Anna Freud*, 1: 3–69. New York: International Universities Press.

———. (1936). *The Ego and the Mechanisms of Defense*. New York: International Universities Press.

———. (1954). The widening scope of indications for psychoanalysis: Discussion. *Journal of the American Psychoanalytic Association* 2: 607–20.

———. (1965). *Normality and Pathology in Childhood: Assessments of Development*. New York: International Universities Press.

———. (1968). Acting out. *International Journal of Psychoanalysis* 49: 165–70.

———. (1971). The infantile neurosis: Genetic and dynamic considerations. *Psychoanalytic Study of the Child* 26: 79–90.

———. (1979). The role of insight in psychoanalysis and psychotherapy: Introduction. *Journal of the American Psychoanalytic Association* 27: 3–8.

Freud, A., Nagera, H., and Freud, E. (1965). Metapsychological assessment of the adult personality: The adult profile. *Psychoanalytic Study of the Child* 20: 9–41.

Freud, S. (1892). A case of successful treatment by hypnotism. *Standard Edition* 1: 115–28. London: Hogarth.

———. (1895). Project for a scientific psychology. *Standard Edition* 1: 295–387. London: Hogarth.

———. (1896). The aetiology of hysteria. *Standard Edition* 3: 191–221. London: Hogarth.

———. (1904). Freud's psychoanalytic procedure. *Standard Edition* 7: 249–54. London: Hogarth.

———. (1905). Fragment of an analysis of a case of hysteria. *Standard Edition* 7: 3–122. London: Hogarth.

———. (1909). Analysis of a phobia in a five-year-old boy. *Standard Edition* 10: 5–147. London: Hogarth.

———. (1911a). Formulations on the two principles of mental functioning. *Standard Edition* 12: 215–26. London: Hogarth.

———. (1911b). Psycho-analytic notes on an autobiographical account of a case of paranoia *(dementia paranoides)*. *Standard Edition* 12: 3–82. London: Hogarth.

———. (1912). The dynamics of transference. *Standard Edition* 12: 97–108. London: Hogarth.

———. (1913). On the beginning of the treatment. *Standard Edition* 12: 123–44. London: Hogarth.

———. (1914a). On narcissism: An introduction. *Standard Edition* 14: 73–102. London: Hogarth.

———. (1914b). Remembering, repeating, and working through: Further recommendations on the technique of psychoanalysis II. *Standard Edition* 12:146–56. London: Hogarth.

———. (1915). Introductory lectures on psychoanalysis. *Standard Edition* Vols. 15–16. London: Hogarth.

———. (1917). A childhood recollection. *Standard Edition* 17: 147–56. London: Hogarth.

———. (1918). From the history of an infantile neurosis. *Standard Edition* 17: 7–122. London: Hogarth.

———. (1920a). A note on the prehistory of the technique of analysis. *Standard Edition* 18: 263–65. London: Hogarth.

———. (1920b). Beyond the pleasure principle. *Standard Edition* 18: 1–64 London: Hogarth.

———. (1924). A short account of psycho-analysis. *Standard Edition* 19: 189–209. London: Hogarth.

———. (1925). An autobiographical study. *Standard Edition* 20: 7–74. London: Hogarth.

———. (1926). The question of lay analysis. *Standard Edition* 20: 183–250. London: Hogarth.

———. (1933). New introductory lectures on psycho-analysis. *Standard Edition* 22: 5–182. London: Hogarth.

———. (1937a). Analysis terminable and interminable. *Standard Edition* 23: 216–53. London: Hogarth.

———. (1937b). Constructions in analysis. *Standard Edition* 23: 255–70. London: Hogarth.

———. (1938). Constructions in analysis. *International Journal of Psycho-Analysis* 19: 377–87.

———. (1940). An outline of psychoanalysis. *Standard Edition* 23: 139–207. London: Hogarth.

Freud, W. (1967). Assessment of early infancy: Problems and considerations. *Psychoanalytic Study of the Child* 22: 216–38.

———. (1968). Some general reflections on the metapsychological profile. *International Journal of Psychoanalysis* 49: 498–501.

———. (1971). The baby profile, part 2. *Psychoanalytic Study of the Child* 26: 172–94.

Fried, D., Crits-Christoph, P., and Luborsky, L. (1992). The first empirical demonstration of transference in psychotherapy. *Journal of Nervous and Mental Disease* 180: 326–31.

Friedman, R. (1988). *Male Homosexuality: The Contemporary Psychoanalytic Perspective*. New Haven: Yale University Press.

Furman, E. (1957). Treatment of under fives by way of the parent. *Psychoanalytic Study of the Child* 12: 250–62.

Galatzer-Levy, R. (1976). Psychic energy: A historical perspective. *Annual of Psychoanalysis* 4: 41–64. New York: International Universities Press.

———. (1984a). Adolescent crisis and mid-life crisis. In D. Brockman (ed.), *Psychoanalytic Perspectives on the Older Adolescent*, 29–51. New York: International Universities Press.

———. (1984b). Perspectives on the regulatory principles of mental functioning. *Psychoanalysis and Contemporary Thought* 6: 255–89.

———. (1988a). Manic-depressive illness: Analytic experience and a hypothesis. In A. Goldberg (ed.), *Frontiers in Self Psychology, Progress in Self Psychology,* 87–102. Hillsdale, N.J.: Analytic Press.

———. (1988b). On working through: A model from artificial intelligence. *Journal of the American Psychoanalytic Association* 36: 125–51.

———. (1991). Computer models and psychoanalytic ideas. *Society for Psychoanalysis and Psychotherapy Bulletin* 6: 23–33.

———. (1995). Psychoanalysis and dynamical systems theory: Prediction and self similarity. *Journal of the American Psychoanalytic Association* 43: 1085–1114.

Galatzer-Levy, R., and Cohler, B. (1990). The developmental psychology of the self: A new worldview in psychoanalysis. *Annual of Psychoanalysis* 18: 1–43.

———. (1993a). *The Essential Other: A Developmental Psychology of the Self*. New York: Basic.

———. (1993b). The psychological significance of others in adolescence: Issues for study and intervention. In B. Cohler and P. Tolan (eds.), *Handbook of Clinical Research Practice with Adolescents*, 63–94. New York: Wiley.

Galatzer-Levy, R., and Gruber, M. (1992). What an affect means: A quasi-experiment about disgust. *Annual of Psychoanalysis* 20: 69–92.

Gann, E. (1984). Some theoretical and technical considerations concerning the emergence of a symptom of the transference neurosis: An empirical study. *Journal of the American Psychoanalytic Association* 32: 797–829.

Gardiner, M. (1971). *The Wolfman by the Wolfman*. New York: Basic.

Gardner, R. (1983). *Self-Inquiry*. Boston: Little, Brown and Atlantic Monthly Press.

Garduk E., and Haggard, E. (1972). *Immediate Effects on Patients of Psychoanalytic Interpretations*. New York: International Universities Press.

Garfield, S. (1990). Issues and methods in psychotherapy process research. *Journal of Consulting and Clinical Psychology* 58: 273–80.

———. (1994). Research on client variables in psychotherapy. In A. Bergin and S. Garfield (eds.), *Handbook of Psychotherapy and Behavior Change* (4th ed.), 190–228. New York: Wiley.

Garfield, S., and Bergin, A. (eds.). (1986a). *Handbook of Psychotherapy and Behavior Change*. 3d ed. New York: Wiley.

Garfield, S., and Bergin, A. (1986b). Introduction and historical overview. In Garfield and Bergin (eds.), *Handbook of Psychotherapy and Behavior Change*, 3–22. New York: Wiley.

————. (1994). Introduction and historical overview. In Bergin and Garfield (eds.), *Handbook of Psychotherapy and Behavior Change* (4th ed.), 3–18. New York: Wiley.

Gassner, S., Sampson, H., Brumer, S., and Weiss, J. (1986). The emergence of warded-off contents. In J. Weiss, H. Sampson, and Mount Zion Psychotherapy Research Group, *The Psychoanalytic Process: Theory, Clinical Observation, and Empirical Research,* 55–77. New York: Guilford.

Gassner, S., Sampson, H., Weiss, J., and Brumer, S. (1982). The emergence of warded-off contents. *Psychoanalysis and Contemporary Thought* 5: 55–75.

Gaston, L., and Ring, J. (1992). Preliminary results on the inventory of therapeutic strategies. *Journal of Psychotherapy Practice and Research* 1: 135–46.

Gay, P. (1989). *A Godless Jew: Freud, Atheism, and the Making of Psychoanalysis.* New Haven: Yale University Press.

Gediman, H. (1985). Imposture, inauthenticity, and feeling fraudulent. *Journal of the American Psychoanalytic Association* 33: 911–35.

Gediman, H., and Wokenfel, K. (1980). Parallelism in supervision: A triadic system. *Psychoanalytic Quarterly* 49: 234–45.

Gedo, J. (1979). *Beyond Interpretation.* New York: International Universities Press.

————. (1989). Self psychology: A post-Kohutian view. In D. Detrick and S. Detrick (eds.), *Self Psychology: Comparisons and Contrasts,* 415–28. Hillsdale, N.J.: Analytic Press.

Gedo, P. (1988). The significant hour in psychoanalysis: Insight and facilitative therapist interventions. Ph.D. diss., University of Chicago.

Gedo, P., and Schaffler, N. (1989). An empirical approach to studying psychoanalytic process. *Psychoanalytic Psychology* 6: 277–92.

Geertz, C. (1983). Local knowledge: Fact and law in comparative perspective. In *Local Knowledge: Further Essays in Interpretive Anthropology, 167–234.* New York: Basic.

Geleerd, E. (1967). *The Child Analyst at Work.* New York: International Universities Press.

Gill, M. (1951). Ego psychology and psychotherapy. *Psychoanalytic Quarterly* 20: 62–71.

————. (1976). Metapsychology is not psychology. *Psychological Issues* 9 (monograph 26): M. Gill and P. Holzman (eds.), *Psychology Versus Metapsychology.* New York: International Universities Press.

————. (1979). The analysis of the transference. *Journal of the American Psychoanalytic Association* 27 (suppl.): 263–88.

————. (1982). *Analysis of Transference.* Vol. 1, *Theory and Technique.* New York: International Universities Press.

————. (1984). Psychoanalysis and psychotherapy: A revision. *International Review of Psychoanalysis* 11: 161–80.

————. (1988). Converting psychotherapy to psychoanalysis. *Contemporary Psychoanalysis* 24: 262–74.

Gill, M., and Hoffman, I. (1982). A method for studying the analysis of aspects of the patient's experience of the relationship in psychoanalysis and psychotherapy. *Journal of the American Psychoanalytic Association* 30: 137–67.

Gill, M., and Muslin, H. (1976). Early interpretation of transference. *Journal of the American Psychoanalytic Association* 24: 779–94.

Gill, M., Simon, J., Fink, G., Endicott, N., and Paul, I. (1968). Studies in audio-recorded psychoanalysis. Part 1, General considerations. *Journal of the American Psychoanalytic Association* 16: 230–44.

Gillispie, C. (1967). *The Edge of Objectivity*. Princeton: Princeton University Press.

Gillman, R. (1982). Termination phase, analytic practice: A survey of 42 completed cases. *Psychoanalytic Inquiry* 2: 463–72.

Gitelson, M. (1954). Therapeutic problems in the analysis of the "normal" candidate. *International Journal of Psychoanalysis* 35: 174–83.

——. (1962). On the curative factors in the first phase of analysis. In *Psychoanalysis: Science and Profession*, 311–41. New York: International Universities Press.

Glass, G., Wilson, V., and Gottman, J. (1978). *Design and Analysis of Time-Series Experiments*. Boulder: University of Colorado Press.

Glenn, J. (1986). Freud, Dora, and the maid: A study of countertransference. *Journal of the American Psychoanalytic Association* 34: 591–606.

Glover, E. (1931). On the therapeutic effect of inexact interpretation. *International Journal of Psychoanalysis* 12: 379–411.

——. (1952). Research methods in psychoanalysis. *International Journal of Psychoanalysis* 33: 403–9.

——. (1955). *The Technique of Psycho-Analysis*. New York: International Universities Press.

Goldberg, A. (ed.). (1978). *The Psychology of the Self: A Casebook*. New York: International Universities Press.

——. (1984). The tension between realism and relativism in psychoanalysis. *Psychoanalysis and Contemporary Thought* 7: 367–89.

——. (1988). *A Fresh Look at Psychoanalysis: The View from Self Psychology*. Hillsdale, N.J.: Analytic Press.

Goldberg, S. (1991). Patients' theories of pathogenesis. *Psychoanalytic Quarterly* 60: 245–75.

Goodwin, D., and Guze, S. (1984). *Psychiatric Diagnosis*. 3d ed. New York: Oxford University Press.

Gottman, J. (1982). *Time Series Analysis: A Comprehensive Introduction for Social Scientists*. New York: Cambridge University Press.

Gottman, J., and Parker, J. (eds.). (1986). *Conversations of Friends: Speculations on Affective Development*. Cambridge: Cambridge University Press.

Gottman, J., and Roy, A. (1990). *Sequential Analysis: A Guide for Behavioral Researchers*. New York: Cambridge University Press.

Gould, S. (1981). *The Mismeasure of Man*. New York: Norton.

Gray, P. (1973). Psychoanalytic technique and the ego's capacity for viewing intrapsychic activity. *Journal of the American Psychoanalytic Association* 21: 474–94.

——. (1982). "Developmental lag" in the evolution of technique for psychoanalysis of neurotic conflict. *Journal of the American Psychoanalytic Association* 30: 621–55.

——. (1990). The nature of therapeutic action in psychoanalysis. *Journal of the Psychoanalytic Association* 38: 1083–97.

Greenacre, P. (1966). Problems of overidealization of the analyst and of analysis: Their manifestations in the transference and countertransference relationship. *Psychoanalytic Study of the Child* 21: 193–212.

Greenberg, J., and Mitchell, S. (1983). *Object Relations and Psychoanalytic Theory.* Cambridge: Harvard University Press.

Greenberg, L. (1986). Change, process, research. *Journal of Consulting and Clinical Psychology* 54: 4–9.

Greenfield, S. (1989). The state of outcome research: Are we on target? *New England Journal of Medicine* 320: 1142–43.

Greenson, R. (1965). The working alliance and the transference neurosis. *Psychoanalytic Quarterly* 34: 155–81.

———. (1967). *The Technique and Practice of Psychoanalysis.* New York: International Universities Press.

Greenspan, S. (1989). The development of the ego: Biological and environmental specificity in the psychopathological developmental process and the selection and construction of ego defenses. *Journal of the American Psychoanalytic Association* 37: 605–38.

Greenspan, S., and Cullander, C. (1975). A systematic metapsychological assessment of the course of an analysis. *Journal of the American Psychoanalytic Association* 23: 107–38.

Grinberg, I. (1962). Countertransference due to the patient's projective identification. *International Journal of Psychoanalysis* 43: 436–40.

Grinker, R. (1940). Reminiscences of a personal contact with Freud. *American Journal of Orthopsychiatry* 10: 850–55.

Groth-Marnat, G. (1997). *Handbook of Psychological Assessment.* 3d ed. New York: Wiley.

Grünbaum, A. (1984). *The Foundations of Psychoanalysis: A Philosophical Critique.* Berkeley: University of California Press.

———. (1994). *Validation in the Clinical Theory of Psychoanalysis: A Study in the Philosophy of Psychoanalysis.* Madison, Conn.: International Universities Press.

Guntrip, H. (1968). *Schizoid Phenomena, Object Relations, and the Self.* London: Hogarth.

———. (1975). My experience with Fairbairn and Winnicott. *International Review of Psychoanalysis* 2: 145–56.

Gutman, D. (1977). Parenthood: A key to the comparative psychology of the life-cycle. In N. Datan and L. Ginsberg (eds.), *Life-span Developmental Psychology: Normative Life Crises,* 167–84. New York: Academic Press.

———. (1987). *Reclaimed Powers: Towards a Psychology of Men and Women in Later Life.* New York: Basic.

Guttman, S. (1968). Indications and contraindications for psychoanalytic treatment: Introduction to the symposium. *International Journal of Psychoanalysis* 49: 254–55.

Hacking, I. (1983). *Representing and Intervening.* New York: Cambridge University Press.

Haegerstam, G., Huitfeldt, B., Nilsson, B., Sjovall, J., and Syvalahti, E. W. (1982). Placebo in clinical drug trials: A multidisciplinary review. *Methods and Findings of Experimental Clinical Pharmacology* 4: 261–78.

Haldeman, D. (1994). The practice and ethics of sexual orientation conversion. *Journal of Consulting and Clinical Psychology* 62: 221–27.

Hale, J., and LaSalle, J. (1963). Differential equations: Linearity vs. nonlinearity. In C. Abbott (ed.), *The Chauvenet Papers* 2: 366–90. Washington, D.C.: Mathematical Association of America, 1978.

Halpert, E. (1972). The effect of insurance on psychoanalytic treatment. *Journal of the American Psychoanalytic Association* 20: 122–33.

———. (1985). Insurance. *Journal of the American Psychoanalytic Association* 33: 937–49.

Hamburg, D., et al. (1967). Report of the ad hoc committee on central fact-gathering data of the American Psychoanalytic Association. *Journal of the American Psychoanalytic Association* 15: 841–61.

Hansell, J. (1990). The relationship of the California Psychotherapy Alliance Scales to other measures of alliance. Paper presented at the annual meeting of the Society for Psychotherapy Research, Wintergreen, Va.

Harley, M. (1971). The current status of transference neurosis in children. *Journal of the American Psychoanalytic Association* 19: 26–40.

———. (1986). Child analysis, 1947–1984: A retrospective. *Psychoanalytic Study of the Child* 41: 129–53.

Hartlaub, G., Martin, G., and Rhine, M. (1986). Recontact with the analyst following termination: A survey of seventy-one cases. *Journal of the American Psychoanalytic Association* 34: 895–910.

Hartley, D. (1985). Research on the therapeutic alliance in psychotherapy. In R. Hales and A. Frances (eds.), *Psychiatry Update Annual Review,* 532–49. Washington, D.C.: American Psychiatric Press.

Hartley, D., and Strupp, H. (1983). The therapeutic alliance: Its relationship to outcome in brief psychotherapy. In J. Masling (ed.), *Empirical Studies in Analytic Theories,* 1–37. Hillsdale, N.J.: Erlbaum.

Hartmann, H. (1927). Understanding and explanation. In *Essays in Ego Psychology,* 369–404. New York: International Universities Press.

———. (1939a). *Ego Psychology and the Problem of Adaptation.* New York: International Universities Press.

———. (1939b). Psychoanalysis and the concept of health. In *Essays in Ego Psychology,* 3–18. New York: International Universities Press.

———. (1950). Comments on the psychoanalytic theory of the ego. In *Essays in Ego Psychology,* 113–41. New York: International Universities Press.

———. (1959). Psychoanalysis as scientific theory. In *Essays in Ego Psychology,* 318–50. New York: International Universities Press.

Hartmann, H., Kris, E., and Loewenstein, R. (1946). Comments on the formation of psychic structure. In Hartmann, Kris, and Loewenstein, Papers on Psychoanalytic Psychology, *Psychological Issues* 14: 27–55. New York: International Universities Press.

Hartmann, H., and Loewenstein, R. (1962). Notes on the superego. In Hartmann, E. Kris, and Loewenstein, Papers on Psychoanalytic Psychology, *Psychological Issues* 14: 144–82. New York: International Universities Press.

Hatch, T., and Gardner, H. (1986). From testing intelligence to assessing competencies: A pluralistic view of intellect. *Roeper Review* 8: 147–50.

Hayes, S. (1981). Single case experimental design and the empirical clinical practice. *Journal of Consulting and Clinical Psychology* 49: 193–211.

Heinicke, C. (1965). Frequency of psychotherapeutic session as a factor affecting the child's developmental status. *Psychoanalytic Study of the Child* 20: 42–98.

Heller, P. (1990). *A Child Analysis with Anna Freud*. Madison, Conn.: International Universities Press.

Hengeveld, M., Huyse, F., van-der-Mast, R., and Tuinstra, C. (1988). A proposal for standardization of psychiatric consultation-liaison data. *General Hospital Psychiatry* 10 (6): 410–22.

Henry, W., Schacht, T., and Strupp, H. (1986). Structural analysis of social behavior: Applications to the study of interpersonal process in differential psychotherapeutic outcome. *Journal of Consulting and Clinical Psychology* 54: 27–31.

Henry, W., and Strupp, H. (1991). Vanderbilt University: The Vanderbilt Center for Psychotherapy Research. In L. Beutler and M. Crago (eds.), *Psychotherapy Research: An International Review of Programmatic Studies*, 166–74. Washington, D.C.: American Psychological Association.

Hersen, M., and Barlow, D. (1976). *Single Case Experimental Designs: Strategies for Studying Behavior Change*. New York: Pergamon.

Hiley, D., Bohman, J., and Shusterman, R. (eds.). (1991). *The Interpretive Turn*. Ithaca: Cornell University Press.

Hilliard, R. (1993). Single-case methodology in psychotherapy process and outcome research. *Journal of Consulting and Clinical Psychology* 61: 373–80.

Hinshelwood, R. (1991). Psychodynamic formulation in assessment of psychotherapy. *British Journal of Psychotherapy* 8: 166–74.

Hoel, P. (1984). *Introduction to Mathematical Statistics*. New York: Wiley.

Hoffman, I., and Gill, M. (1988). A scheme for coding the Patient's Experience of the Relationship with the Therapist (PERT): Some applications, extensions, and comparisons. In H. Dahl, H. Kächele, and H. Thomä (eds.), *Psychoanalytic Process Research Strategies*, 67–98. Berlin: Springer-Verlag.

Hoffman, M. (1983). Empathy: Its limitations and its role in a comprehensive moral theory. In W. Kurtines and J. Gewirtz (eds.), *Morality, Moral Behavior, and Moral Development*, 181–205. New York: Wiley.

Hoffs, J. (1972). After the analysis: A note on the post-termination phase. *Psychoanalytic Review* 59: 89–94.

Hoglend, P., Guldberg, C., and Perry, J. (1992). Scientific approaches to making psychodynamic formulations. *Nordic Journal of Psychiatry* 46: 41–48.

Hook, S. (ed.). (1959). *Psychoanalysis, Scientific Method, and Philosophy*. New York: New York University Press.

Horowitz, M. (1987). Some notes on insight and its failures. *Psychoanalytic Quarterly* 56: 177–96.

———. (1990). A model of mourning: Change in schemes of self and other. *Journal of the American Psychoanalytic Association* 38: 297–324.

Horowitz, M., Marmor, C., Krupniuk, J., Wilner, N., and Wallerstein, R. (1984). *Personality Styles and Brief Psychotherapy*. New York: Basic.

Horvath, A., Gaston, L., and Luborsky, L. (1993). The therapeutic alliance and its measure. In N. Miller, L. Luborsky, J. Barber, and J. Docherty (eds.), *Psychodynamic Treatment Research: A Handbook for Clinical Practice,* 247–73. New York: Basic.

Horvath, A., and Luborsky, L. (1993). The role of the therapeutic alliance in psychotherapy. *Journal of Consulting and Clinical Psychology* 61: 561–73.

Horwitz, L. (1974). *Clinical Prediction in Psychotherapy.* New York: Jason Aronson.

Horwitz, L., and Rosenberg, S. (1994). The consensual response: I. Method and research results. *Psychotherapy Research* 4: 222–33.

Horwitz, L., Rosenberg, S., Bauer, B., Ureno, G., and Villasenor, V. (1988). Inventory of interpersonal problems: Psychometric properties and clinical applications. *Journal of Consulting and Clinical Psychology* 56: 885–92.

Horwitz, L., Rosenberg, S., Ureno, G., Kalehzan, B., and O'Halloran, P. (1989). Psychodynamic formulation, consensual response method, and interpersonal problems. *Journal of Consulting and Clinical Psychology* 57: 599–606.

Horwitz, L., Sampson, H., Siegelman, E., Wofson, A., and Weiss, J. (1975). On the identification of warded off mental contents: An empirical and methodological contribution. *Journal of Abnormal Psychology* 84: 545–58.

Hsu, L. (1989). Random sampling, randomization, and equivalence of contrasted groups in psychotherapy outcome research. *Journal of Consulting and Clinical Psychology* 57: 131–37.

Hunter, K. (1991). *Doctors' Stories: The Narrative Structure of Medical Knowledge.* Princeton: Princeton University Press.

Huxster, H., Lower, R., and Escoll, P. (1975). Some pitfalls in the assessment of analyzability in a psychoanalytic clinic. *Journal of the American Psychoanalytic Association* 23: 90–106.

Isakower, O. (1974). Self-observation, self-experimentation, and creative vision. *Psychoanalytic Study of the Child* 29: 451–72.

Isay, R. (1989). *Being Homosexual: Gay Men and Their Development.* New York: Farrar, Straus, and Giroux.

Jacobs, T. (1973). Posture, gesture, and movement in the analyst: Cues to interpretation and countertransference. *Journal of the American Psychoanalytic Association* 21: 77–92.

———. (1983). The analyst and the patient's object world: Notes on an aspect of countertransference. *Journal of the American Psychoanalytic Association* 31: 619–42.

———. (1986). On countertransference enactments. *Journal of the American Psychoanalytic Association* 34: 289–307.

Jaffe, D. (1986). Empathy, counteridentification, countertransference: A review, with some personal perspectives on the "analytic instrument." *Psychoanalytic Quarterly* 55: 215–43.

Jaques, E. (1965). Death and the mid-life crisis. *International Journal of Psychoanalysis* 46: 502–14.

Jones, E. (1936). *Decannual Report of the London Clinic of Psychoanalysis.* 1926–36.

———. (1953). *The Life and Work of Sigmund Freud.* New York: Basic.

Jones, E., Cumming, J., and Horowitz, M. (1988). Another look at the nonspecific hypothesis of therapeutic effectiveness. *Journal of Consulting and Clinical Psychology* 56: 48–55.

Jones, E., Cumming, J., and Pulos, S. (1993). The psychotherapy process Q-set: Applications in single case research. In N. Miller, L. Luborsky, J. Barber, and J. Docherty (eds.), *Psychodynamic Treatment: A Handbook for Clinical Practice*, 14–36. New York: Basic.

Jones, E., Ghannam, J., Nigg, J., and Dyer, J. (1993). A paradigm for single-case research: The time series study of a long-term psychotherapy for depression. *Journal of Consulting and Clinical Psychology* 61: 381–94.

Jones, E., Hall, S., and Parke, L. (1991). The process of change: The Berkeley Psychotherapy Research Group. In L. Beutler and M. Crago (eds.), *Psychotherapy Research: An International Review of Programmatic Studies*, 98–106. Washington, D.C.: American Psychological Association.

Jones, E., Parke, L., and Pulos, S. (1992). How therapy is conducted in the private consulting room: A multidimensional description of brief psychodynamic treatments. *Psychotherapy Research* 2: 16–30.

Jones, E., and Pulos, S. (1993). Comparing the process in psychodynamic and cognitive-behavioral therapies. *Journal of Consulting and Clinical Psychology* 61: 306–16.

Jones, E., and Windholz, M. (1990). The psychoanalytic case study: Toward a method for systematic inquiry. *Journal of the American Psychoanalytic Association* 38: 985–1015.

Joseph, B. (1982). Addiction to near-death. *International Journal of Psychoanalysis* 63: 449–56.

———. (1988). Object relations in clinical practice. *Psychoanalytic Quarterly* 57: 626–42.

Judson, H. (1979). *The Eighth Day of Creation: Makers of Revolution in Biology*. New York: Simon and Schuster.

Jung, C. (1933). *Modern Man in Search of a Soul*. New York: Harcourt, Brace, and World.

———. (1954a). *The Development of Personality*. Princeton: Princeton University Press.

———. (1954b). *The Practice of Psychotherapy*. New York: Pantheon.

———. (1968). *Analytic Psychology*. New York: Vintage.

Kächele, H., Luborsky, L., and Thomä, H. (1988). Ubertragung ale Structur und Verlaufsmuster: Zwei Methoden zur Erfassung dieser Aspekte. In L. Luborsky and H. Kächele (eds.), *Der zentrale Bezichungskonflikt*, 8–21. Ulm: PSZ-Verlag.

Kagan, J. (1980). Perspectives on constancy. In O. Brim and J. Kagan (eds.), *Constance and Change in Human Development*, 1–27. Cambridge: Harvard University Press.

———. (1988). The meanings of personality predicates. *American Psychologist* 43: 614–20.

Kamm, B. (1976). Personal communication.

Kantrowitz, J. (1992). The analyst's style and its impact on the analytic process: Overcoming an analyst-patient stalemate. *Journal of the American Psychoanalytic Association* 40: 169–81.

———. (1993). The uniqueness of the patient-analyst pair: Approaches for elucidating the analyst's role. *International Journal of Psychoanalysis* 74: 893–904.

———. (1995). The beneficial aspects of the patient-analyst match. *International Journal of Psycho-Analysis* 76: 299–313.

——. (1996). *The Patient's Impact on the Analyst*. Hillsdale, N.J.: Analytic Press.

Kantrowitz, J., Katz, A., Greenman, D., Morris, H., Paolitto, F., Sashin, J., and Solomon, L. (1989). The patient-analyst match and the outcome of psychoanalysis: A study of 13 cases. *Journal of the American Psychoanalytic Association* 37: 893–920.

Kantrowitz, J., Katz, A., and Paolitto, F. (1990a). Follow up of psychoanalysis five to ten years after termination. Part 1, Stability of change. *Journal of the American Psychoanalytic Association* 38: 471–96.

——. (1990b). Follow up of psychoanalysis five to ten years after termination. Part 2, The development of the self-analytic function. *Journal of the American Psychoanalytic Association* 38: 637–54.

——. (1990c). Follow up of psychoanalysis five to ten years after termination. Part 3, The relation between the resolution of the transference and the patient-analyst match. *Journal of the American Psychoanalytic Association* 38: 655–78.

Kantrowitz, J., Katz, A., Paolitto, F., Sashin, J., and Solomon, L. (1987a). The role of reality testing in psychoanalysis: Follow up of 22 cases. *Journal of the American Psychoanalytic Association* 35: 367–85.

——. (1987b). Changes in the level and quality of object relations in psychoanalysis: Follow up of a longitudinal, prospective study. *Journal of the American Psychoanalytic Association* 35: 23–46.

Kantrowitz, J., Paolitto, F., Sashin, J., Solomon, L., and Katz, A. (1986). Affect availability, tolerance, complexity, and modulation in psychoanalysis: Follow up of a longitudinal, prospective study. *Journal American Psychoanalytic Association* 34: 529–59.

Kantrowitz, J., Singer, J., and Knapp, P. (1975). Methodology for a prospective study of suitability for psychoanalysis: The role of psychological tests. *Psychoanalytic Quarterly* 44: 371–91.

Kardiner, A. (1977). *My Analysis with Freud*. New York: Norton.

Karmiloff-Smith, A. (1986). Stage/Structure versus Phase/Process in modeling linguistic and cognitive development. In I. Levin (ed.), *Stage and Structure: Reopening the Debate,* 164–90. Norwood, N.J.: Ablex.

Karush, A. (1956). People who seek help: A diagnostic survey. In S. Rado and G. Daniels (eds.), *Changing Concepts of Psychoanalytic Medicine,* 69–84. New York: Grune and Stratton.

Karush, A., Easser, R., Cooper, A., and Swerdloff, B. (1964). The evaluation of ego-strength: I. A profile of adaptive balances. *Journal of Nervous and Mental Diseases* 130: 332–49.

Kazdin, A. (1980). *Research Design in Psychology*. New York: Harper and Row.

——. (1981). Drawing valid inferences from case studies. *Journal of Consulting and Clinical Psychology* 49: 183–92.

——. (1982). Single-case experimental designs in clinical research and practice. *New Directions for Methodology of Social and Behavioral Science* 13:33–47.

Kazdin, A., and Bass, D. (1989). Power to detect differences between alternative treatments in comparative psychotherapy outcome research. *Journal of Consulting and Clinical Psychology* 57: 138–47.

Kepecs, J. (1966). Theories of transference neurosis. *Psychoanalytic Quarterly* 35: 497–521.

Kern, J. (1987). Transference neurosis as a waking dream: Notes on a clinical enigma. *Journal of the American Psychoanalytic Association* 35: 337–66.

Kernberg, O. (1965). Notes on countertransference. *Journal of the American Psychoanalytic Association* 13: 38–56.

———. (1975). *Borderline Conditions and Pathological Narcissism*. New York: Aaronson.

———. (1976). *Object-Relations Theory and Clinical Psychoanalysis*. New York: Aaronson.

———. (1980). *Internal World and External Reality*. New York: Aaronson.

———. (1983). Object relations theory and character analysis. *Journal of the American Psychoanalytic Association* 31 (suppl.): 247–72.

———. (1988a). Clinical dimensions of masochism. *Journal of the American Psychoanalytic Association* 36: 1005–29.

———. (1988b). Object relations theory in clinical practice. *Psychoanalytic Quarterly* 57: 481–504.

Kernberg, O., Coyne, L., Horwitz, L., Appelbaum, A., and Burstein, E. (1972). Psychotherapy and psychoanalysis: Final report of the Menninger Foundation psychotherapy research project. *Bulletin of the Menninger Clinic* 36: 3–275

Kernberg, O., Seizer, M., Koenisberg, H., Carr, A., and Appelbaum, A. (1989). *The Treatment of Borderline Patients*. New York: Basic.

Kessel, L., and Hyman, H. (1933). The value of psychoanalysis as a therapeutic procedure. *Journal of the American Medical Association* 101: 1612–15.

Kestenberg, J.(1980). Psychoanalyses of children of survivors from the Holocaust: Case presentations and assessment. *Journal of the American Psychoanalytic Association* 28: 775–804.

Khan, M. (1983). *Hidden Selves: Between Theory and Practices in Psychoanalysis*. New York: International Universities Press.

Kiesler, D. (1982). Interpersonal theory for personality and psychotherapy. In J. Anchin and D. Kiesler (eds.), *Handbook of Interpersonal Psychotherapy*, 3–24. New York: Pergamon.

Kilert, S. (1993). *In the Wake of Chaos*. Chicago: University of Chicago Press.

Kinsey, A., Pomeroy, W., and Martin, C. (1948). *Sexual Behavior in the Human Male*. Philadelphia: Saunders.

Kitcher, P. (1992). *Freud's Dream: A Complete Interdisciplinary Science of Mind*. Cambridge: M.I.T. Press.

Klein, D., et al. (1990). NIMH collaborative research on treatment of depression: Commentaries. *Archives of General Psychiatry* 47: 682–88.

Klein, G. (1976). *Psychoanalytic Theory: An Exploration of Essentials*. New York: International Universities Press.

Klein, H. (1960). Changes in and after psychoanalytic treatment. In P. Hoch and J. Zubin (eds.), *Current Approaches to Psychoanalysis*, 151–75. New York: Stratton.

Klein, M. (1921). Early analysis. In *Love, Guilt, and Reparation and Other Works, 1927–1945*, 77–106. New York: Delacorte/Seymour Lawrence.

———. (1948a). *Contributions to Psychoanalysis, 1921–1945*. London: Hogarth.

———. (1948b). On the theory of anxiety and guilt. In *Envy and Gratitude and Other Works, 1946–1963*, 25–47. London: Hogarth.

———. (1961). *Narrative of a Child Analysis.* New York: Delta.

Klerman, G., Weissman, M., Rounsaville, B., and Chevron, E. (1984). *Interpersonal Psychotherapy of Depression.* New York: Basic.

Kline, M. (1972). *Mathematical Thought from Ancient to Modern Times.* Oxford: Oxford University Press.

Klumpner, G. (1994). *A Thesaurus of Psychoanalytic Terms.* Madison, Conn.: International Universities Press.

Klumpner, G., and Frank, A. (1991). On methods of reporting clinical material. *Journal of the American Psychoanalytic Association* 39: 537–51.

Knapp, P., Levin, S., McCarter, R., Wermer, H., and Zetzel, E. (1960). Suitability for psychoanalysis: A review of one hundred supervised analytic cases. *Psychoanalytic Quarterly* 29: 459–77.

Knight, R. (1941). Evaluation of the results of psychoanalytic therapy. *American Journal of Psychiatry* 98: 434–46.

Kohrman, R. (1969). Problems of termination in child analysis. *Journal of the Psychoanalytic Association* 17: 191–205.

Kohrman, R., Fineberg, H., Gelman, R., and Weiss, S. (1971). Technique of child analysis: Problems of countertransference. *International Journal of Psychoanalysis* 52: 487–98.

Kohut, H. (1959). Introspection, empathy, and psychoanalysis: An examination of the relationship between mode of observation and theory. In P. Ornstein (ed.), *The Search for the Self,* 1: 205–32. New York: International Universities Press.

———. (1966). Forms and transformations of narcissism. *Journal of the American Psychoanalytic Association* 14: 243–72.

———. (1968). The psychoanalytic treatment of narcissistic personality disorders: Outline of a systematic approach. *Psychoanalytic Study of the Child* 23: 86–113.

———. (1971). *The Analysis of the Self.* New York: International Universities Press.

———. (1976). Creativeness, charisma, and group psychology. In P. Ornstein (ed.), *The Search for the Self,* 2: 793–843. New York: International Universities Press.

———. (1977). *The Restoration of the Self.* New York: International Universities Press.

———. (1979). The two analyses of Mr. Z. *International Journal of Psychoanalysis* 60: 3–27.

———. (1982). Introspection, empathy, and the semi-circle of mental health. *International Journal of Psychoanalysis* 63: 395–407.

———. (1984). *How Psychoanalysis Cures.* Chicago: University of Chicago Press.

———. (1991). The psychoanalytic treatment of narcissistic personality disorders. In M. Kets de Vries, S. Perzow, et al. (eds.), *Handbook of Character Studies: Psychoanalytic Explorations,* 529–56. Madison, Conn.: International Universities Press.

Kolden, G., and Howard, K. (1992). An empirical test of the generic model of psychotherapy. *Journal of Psychotherapy Practice and Research* 1: 225–36.

Kramer, M. (1959). On the continuation of psychoanalysis after termination. *International Journal of Psychoanalysis* 40: 117–25.

Kratochwill, T. (1992). Single-case research design and analysis: An overview. In Kratochwill and J. Levin (eds.), *Single-Case Research Design and Analysis: New Directions for Psychology and Education,* 3–14. Hillsdale, N.J.: Erlbaum.

Kris, A. (1981). On giving advice to parents in analysis. *Psychoanalytic Study of the Child* 36: 151–62.

Kris, E. (1951). Ego psychology and interpretation in psychoanalytic therapy. *Psychoanalytic Quarterly* 20: 15–30.

———. (1952). *Psychoanalytic Explorations in Art*. New York: Schocken.

———. (1956). On the vicissitudes of insight in psychoanalysis. *International Journal of Psychoanalysis* 37: 445–55.

Kris, M. (1957). The use of prediction in a longitudinal study. *Psychoanalytic Study of the Child* 12: 175–89.

Kubie, L. (1958). *Neurotic Distortions of the Creative Process*. Kansas City: University of Kansas Press.

Kuhn, T. (1970). *The Structure of Scientific Revolutions*. 2d ed. Chicago: University of Chicago Press.

Kuiper, P. (1968). Indications and contraindications for psychoanalytic treatment. *International Journal of Psychoanalysis* 49: 261–64.

Lambert, M., and Bergin, A. (1994). The effectiveness of psychotherapy. In Bergin and S. Garfield (eds.), *Handbook of Psychotherapy and Behavior Change* (4th ed.), 143–89. New York: Wiley.

Lambert, M., Shapiro, D., and Bergin, A. (1986). The effectiveness of psychotherapy. S. Garfield and Bergin (eds.), *Handbook of Psychotherapy and Behavior Change* (3d ed.), 157–212. New York: Wiley.

Landis, J., and Coch, G. (1977). The measurement of observer agreement for categorical data. *Biometrics* 33: 159–74.

Lasch, C. (1979). *The Culture of Narcissism: American Life in an Age of Diminishing Expectations*. New York: Norton.

Laufer, M. (1965). Assessment of adolescent disturbances: The application of Anna Freud's diagnostic profile. *Psychoanalytic Study of the Child* 20: 99–123.

Laufer, M., and Laufer, M. (1984). *Adolescence and Developmental Breakdown*. New Haven: Yale University Press.

———. (1989). *Developmental Breakdown and Psychoanalytic Treatment in Adolescence*. New Haven: Yale University Press.

Lazar, N. (1973). The nature and significance of changes in patients in a psychoanalytic clinic. *Psychoanalytic Quarterly* 42: 579–600.

Leary, K. (1989). Psychoanalytic process and narrative process: A critical consideration of Schafer's "narrational project." *International Review of Psychoanalysis* 16: 179–90.

Leeds, J. (1989). Repetition, science, and psychoanalysis: Theoretical considerations and an empirical study. *Dissertation Abstracts International* 49 (12-B, part 1): 5524–25.

Leon, A., Marcak, P., and Portera, L. (1995). More reliable outcome measures can reduce sample size requirements. *Archives of General Psychiatry* 52:867–71.

Levy, S., and Inderbitzin, L. (1990). The analytic surface and the theory of technique. *Journal of the American Psychoanalytic Association* 38: 371–91.

Lewin, B. (1959). The analytic situation: Topographic considerations. *Psychoanalytic Quarterly* 28: 455–69.

Lifschutz, J. (1976). A critique of reporting and assessment in the training analysis. *Journal of the American Psychoanalytic Association* 24: 43–59.

Lipton, S. (1977a). The advantages of Freud's technique as shown in his analysis of the Rat Man. *International Journal of Psychoanalysis* 58: 255–73.

———. (1977b). Clinical observations on resistance to the transference. *International Journal of Psychoanalysis* 58: 463–72.

———. (1979). An addendum to "The advantages of Freud's technique as shown in his analysis of the Rat Man." *International Journal of Psychoanalysis* 60: 215–16.

Little, M. (1951). Countertransference and the patient's response to it. *International Journal of Psychoanalysis* 32: 32–50.

———. (1987). On the value of regression in dependence. *Free Associations* 10: 7–22.

Loewald, H. (1960). On the therapeutic action of psychoanalysis. *International Journal of Psychoanalysis* 41: 16–33.

———. (1971). The transference neurosis: Comments on the concept and the phenomenon. *Journal of the American Psychoanalytic Association* 19: 54–66.

———. (1988). Termination analyzable and unanalyzable. *Psychoanalytic Study of the Child* 43:155–70.

Loewenstein, R. (1963). Some considerations on free association. *Journal of the American Psychoanalytic Association* 11: 451–73.

Loewenstein, R., Newman, L., Schur, M., and Solnit, A. (1966). *Psychoanalysis: A General Psychology Essay in Honor of Heinz Hartmann*. New York: International Universities Press.

London, N. (1987). In defense of the transference neurosis concept in psychoanalysis. *Psychoanalytic Inquiry* 7: 587–98.

Losee, J. (1993). *A Historical Introduction to the Philosophy of Science*. 3d ed. Oxford: Oxford University Press.

Luborsky, L. (1962). Clinicians' judgments of mental health: A proposed scale. *Archives of General Psychiatry* 7: 407–17.

———. (1967). Momentary forgetting during psychotherapy and psychoanalysis: A theory and research method. In R. Holt (ed.), *Motives and Thought: Psychoanalytic Essays in Honor of David Rapaport*, 175–217. New York: International Universities Press.

———. (1976). Helping alliances in psychotherapy: The groundwork for a study of their relationship to its outcome. In J. Claghorn (ed.), *Successful Psychotherapy*, 92–116. New York: Brunner/Mazel.

———. (1977). Measuring a pervasive psychic structure and psychotherapy: The core conflictual relationship theme. In N. Freedman and S. Grand (eds.), *Communicative Structures and Psychic Exchange*, 367–95. New York: Plenum.

———. (1984). *Principles of Psychoanalytic Psychotherapy: A Manual for Supportive-Expressive Treatment*. New York: Basic.

———. (1988). A comparison of three transference related measures applied to the specimen hour. In H. Dahl, H. Kächele, and H. Thomä (eds.), *Psychoanalytic Process Research Strategies*, 109–16. Berlin: Springer-Verlag.

———. (1990a). A guide to the CCRT method. In Luborsky and P. Crits-Christoph (eds.), *Understanding Transference: The Core Conflictual Relationship Theme Method*, 15–36. New York: Basic.

———. (1990b). The convergence of Freud's observations about transference and the

CCRT evidence. In Luborsky and P. Crits-Christoph (eds.), *Understanding Transference: The Core Conflictual Relationship Theme Method*, 251–66. New York: Basic.

———. (1990c). Where we are in understanding transference. In Luborsky and P. Crits-Christoph (eds.), *Understanding Transference: The Core Conflictual Relationship Theme Method*, 267–84. New York: Basic.

Luborsky, L., and Bachrach, H. (1974). Factors influencing clinicians' judgments of mental health: Experiences with the Health-Sickness Rating Scale. *Archives of General Psychiatry* 31: 292–99.

Luborsky, L., Bachrach, H., Graff, H., Pulver, S., and Christoph, P. (1979). Preconditions and consequences of transference interpretations: A clinical-qualitative investigation. *Journal of Nervous and Mental Disease* 169: 391–401.

Luborsky, L., and Barber, J. (1993). Benefits of adherence to psychotherapy manuals, and where to get them. In N. Miller, L. Luborsky, J. Barber, and J. Docherty (eds.), *Psychodynamic Treatment Research: A Handbook for Clinical Practice*, 211–26. New York: Basic.

———. (1994). Perspectives on seven transference-related measures applied to the interview with Ms. Smithfield. *Psychotherapy Research* 4: 152–54.

Luborsky, L., Chandler, M., Auerbach, A., Cohen, J., and Bachrach, H. (1971). Factors influencing the outcome of psychotherapy: A review of quantitative research. *Psychological Bulletin* 75: 145–85.

Luborsky, L., and Crits-Christoph, P. (1988). Measures of psychoanalytic concepts: The last decade of research from "the Penn studies." *International Journal of Psychoanalysis* 69: 75–86.

——— (eds.). (1990). *Understanding Transference: The Core Conflictual Relationship Theme Method*. New York: Basic.

Luborsky, L., Crits-Christoph, P., Alexander, L., Margolis, M., and Cohen, M. (1983). Two helping alliance methods for predicting outcomes of psychotherapy. *Journal of Nervous and Mental Disease* 17: 480–91.

Luborsky, L., Crits-Christoph, P., and Mellon, J. (1986). The advent of objective measures of the transference. *Journal of Consulting and Clinical Psychology* 54: 39–47.

Luborsky, L., Crits-Christoph, P., Mintz, J., and Auerbach, A. (1988). *Who Will Benefit from Psychotherapy?* New York: Basic.

Luborsky, L., and DeRubeis, R. (1984). The use of psychotherapy treatment manuals: A small revolution in psychotherapy research style. *Clinical Psychology Review* 4: 5–14.

Luborsky, L., Diguer, L., Luborsky, E., McLellan, A., Woody, G., and Alexander, L. (1993). Psychological Health-Sickness (PHS) as a predictor of outcomes in dynamic and other psychotherapies. *Journal of Consulting and Clinical Psychology* 61: 542–48.

Luborsky, L., Popp, C., and Barber, J. (1994). Common and special factors in different transference-related measures. *Psychotherapy Research* 4: 277–86.

Luborsky, L., Singer, B., and Luborsky, E. (1975). Comparative studies of psychotherapies: Is it true that "everyone has won and all must have prizes"? *Archives of General Psychiatry* 32: 995–1008.

Lustman, S. (1963). Some issues in contemporary psychoanalytic research. *Psychoanalytic Study of the Child* 18: 51–74.

Macalpine, I. (1950). The development of transference. *Psychoanalytic Quarterly* 19: 501–39.

Mack-Brunswick, R. (1928). A supplement to Freud's "History of an infantile neurosis." *International Journal of Psychoanalysis* 9: 439–76.

MacWhinney, B. (1991). *The* CHILDES *Project: Tools for Analyzing Talk*. Hillsdale, N.J.: Lawrence Erlbaum Associates.

Mahony, P. (1984). Further reflections on Freud and his writing. *Journal of the American Psychoanalytic Association* 32: 847–64.

———. (1986). *Freud and the Ratman*. New Haven: Yale University Press.

———. (1987). *Psychoanalysis and Discourse*. London: Tavistock.

———. (1996). *Freud's Dora: A Psychoanalytic, Historical, and Textual Study*. New Haven: Yale University Press.

Major, R. (1932). *Classic Descriptions of Disease: With Biographical Sketches of the Authors*. London: Bailière, Tindall, and Cox.

Malcolm, R. (1981). Technical problems in the analysis of a pseudo-compliant patient. *International Journal of Psychoanalysis* 62: 477–84.

Malkiel, B. (1990). *A Random Walk Down Wall Street*. New York: Norton.

Mandelbrot, B. (1982). *The Fractal Geometry of Nature*. San Francisco: Freeman.

Mansfield, R., and Busse, T. (1977). Meta-analysis of research: A rejoinder to Glass. *Educational Researcher* 6: 3.

Markowitz, J., Weissman, M., Ouellete, R., Lish, J., and Klerman, G. (1989). Quality of life in panic disorder. *Archives of General Psychiatry* 46: 984–92.

Marmor, C., Horowitz, M., Weiss, D., and Marziali, E. (1986). The development of the therapeutic alliance rating system. In L. Greenberg and W. Pinsof (eds.). *The Psychotherapeutic Process: A Research Handbook,* 367–90. New York: Guilford.

Marmor, C., Weiss, D., and Gaston, L. (1989). Toward the validation of the California Therapeutic Alliance Rating System. *Psychological Assessment* 1: 46–52.

Martin, A. (1982). Learning to hide: The socialization of the gay adolescent. *Adolescent Psychiatry* 10: 52–65.

Martinez, D. (1989). Pains and gains: A study of forced terminations. *Journal of the American Psychoanalytic Association* 37: 89–115.

Masters, W., and Johnson, V. (1970). *Human Sexual Inadequacy*. Boston: Little, Brown.

May, R. (1990). The idea of history in psychoanalysis: Freud and the "Wolf-Man." *Psychoanalytic Psychology* 7: 163–83.

McCleary, R., and Welsh, W. (1992). Philosophical and statistical foundations of time-series experiments. In T. Kratochwill and J. Levin (eds.). *Single-Case Research Design and Analysis,* 41–91. Hillsdale, N.J.: Erlbaum.

McLaughlin, J. T. (1973). The non-reporting training analyst, the analysis, and the institute. *Journal of the American Psychoanalytic Association* 21: 697–712.

———. (1981). Transference, psychic reality, and countertransference. *Psychoanalytic Quarterly* 50: 639–64.

McWilliams, N. (1994). *Psychoanalytic Diagnosis: Understanding Personality Structure in the Clinical Process*. New York: Guilford.

Meehl, P. (1996). *Clinical Versus Statistical Prediction: A Theoretical Analysis and a Review of the Evidence*. New York: Aronson.

Meers, D. (1966). A diagnostic profile of psychopathology in a latency child. *Psychoanalytic Study of the Child* 21: 483–526.

Meissner, W. (1984a). *Psychoanalysis and Religious Experience*. New Haven: Yale University Press.

——. (1984b). Studies on hysteria: Dora. *International Journal of Psychoanalytic Psychotherapy* 10: 567–98.

——. (1989). A note on psychoanalytic facts. *Psychoanalytic Inquiry* 2: 191–217.

——. (1991). *What Is Effective in Psychoanalytic Therapy: The Move from Interpretation to Relation*. Northvale, N.J.: Aronson.

——. (1992). The concept of the therapeutic alliance. *Journal of the American Psychoanalytic Association* 40: 1059–88.

——. (1996). *The Therapeutic Alliance*. New Haven: Yale University Press.

Meltzoff, J., and Kornreich, M. (1970). *Research in Psychotherapy*. New York: Atherton.

Menninger, K., Mayman, M., and Pruyser, P. (1962). *A Manual for Psychiatric Case Study*. 2d ed. New York: Grune and Stratton.

Mergenthaler, E., and Kächele, H. (1988). The Ulm text bank management system: A tool for psychotherapy research. In H. Dahl, Kächele, and A. Thomä (eds.), *Psychoanlytic Process Research Strategies*, 195–212. Berlin: Springer-Verlag.

——. (1993). Locating text archives for psychotherapy research. In N. Miller, L. Luborsky, J. Barber, and J. Docherty (eds.), *Psychodynamic Treatment Research: A Handbook for Clinical Practice*, 53–61. New York: Basic.

——. (1994). The Ulm Textbank. [German]. *Psychotherapie Psychosomatik Medizinische Psychologie* 44: 29–35.

Mergenthaler, E., and Stinson, C. (1992). Psychotherapy transcription standards. *Psychotherapy Research* 2: 125–42.

Messer, S. (1991). The case formulation approach: Issues of reliability and validity. *American Psychologist* 46: 1348–50.

Messer, S., Tishby, O., and Spillman, A. (1992). Taking context seriously in psychotherapy research: Relating therapists' interventions to patient progress in brief psychodynamic psychotherapy. *Journal of Consulting and Clinical Psychology* 60: 678–88.

Meyer, J. (1988). A case of hysteria, with a note on biology. *Journal of the American Psychoanalytic Association* 36: 319–46.

Michels, R. (1994). Validation in the clinical process. *International Journal of Psycho-Analysis* 75 (5–6): 1133–40.

Mikkelsen, E., and Gutheil, T. (1979). Stages of forced termination: Uses of the death metaphor. *Psychiatric Quarterly* 51:15–27.

Miller, I. (1964). On taking notes. *International Journal of Psychoanalysis* 45: 121–22.

Milliken, G., and Johnson, D. (1984). *Analysis of Messy Data*. Vol. 1, *Designed Experiments*. New York: Van Nostrand.

——. (1989). *Analysis of Messy Data*. Vol. 2, *Nonreplicated Experiments*. New York: Van Nostrand.

Millon, T. (1991). Classification in psychopathology: Rationale, alternative, and standards. *Journal of Abnormal Psychology* 100: 289–93.

Millon, T., and Davis, R. (1996). *Disorders of Personality:* DSM-IV *and Beyond*. 2d ed. New York: Wiley.

Millon, T., and Diesenhaus, H. (1972). *Research Methods in Psychopathology*. New York: Wiley.

Milrod, B., Busch, F., Cooper, A., and Shapiro, T. (1997). *Manual of Panic-Focused Psychodynamic Psychotherapy*. Washington, D.C.: American Psychiatric Press.

Minsky, M. (1986). *The Society of Mind*. New York: Simon and Schuster.

Mintz, J., and Luborsky, L. (1971). Segments vs. whole sessions: Which is the better unit for psychotherapy research? *Journal of Abnormal Psychology* 78: 180–91.

Mintz, J., Luborsky, L., and Christoph, P. (1979). Measuring the outcomes of psychotherapy: Findings of the Penn Psychotherapy Project. *Journal of Consulting and Clinical Psychology* 47: 319–44.

Mirowski, P. (1989). *More Heat Than Light: Economics as Social Physics, Physics as Nature's Economics*. Cambridge: Cambridge University Press.

Modell, A. (1968). *Object Love and Reality*. New York: International Universities Press.

———. (1976). "The Holding Environment" and the therapeutic action of psychoanalysis. *Journal of the American Psychoanalytic Association* 24: 285–307.

———. (1978). The conceptualization of the therapeutic action of psychoanalysis. *Bulletin of the Menninger Clinic* 42: 493–504.

———. (1988). The centrality of the psychoanalytic setting and the changing aims of treatment: A perspective from a theory of object relations. *Psychoanalytic Quarterly* 57: 577–96.

———. (1990). *Other Times, Other Realities: Toward a Theory of Psychoanalytic Treatment*. Cambridge: Harvard University Press.

———. (1991). A confusion of tongues; or, Whose reality is it? *Psychoanalytic Quarterly* 60: 227–44.

Money-Kyrle, R. (1956). Normal countertransference and some of its deviations. *International Journal of Psychoanalysis* 37: 360–65.

Mook, D. (1982). *Psychological Research: Strategy and Tactics*. New York: Harper and Row.

Morey, I. (1991). Classification of mental disorder as a collection of hypothetical constructs. *Journal of Abnormal Psychology* 100: 289–93.

Morgan, R., Luborsky, L., Crits-Christoph, P., Curtis, H., and Solomon, J. (1982). Predicting the outcomes of psychotherapy using the Penn Helping Alliance rating method. *Archives of General Psychiatry* 39: 397–402.

Morley, S. (1991). Graphical analysis of single-case time series data. *British Journal of Clinical Psychology* 30: 97–115.

Murray, H. (1938). *Explorations in Personality: A Clinical Experimental Study of 15 Men of College Age*. New York: Science Editions.

Nachmias, D., and Nachmias, C. (1976). *Research Methods in the Social Sciences*. New York: St. Martin's.

Nacht, S. (1957). Technical notes on the handling of the transference neurosis. *International Journal of Psychoanalysis* 38: 196–203.

Nagera, H. (1966). *Early Childhood Disturbances: The Infantile Neurosis and the Adult Disturbances*. New York: International Universities Press.

———. (1967). The concepts of structure and structuralization: Psychoanalytic usage and implications for a theory of learning and creativity. *Psychoanalytic Study of the Child* 22: 77–102.

———. (1969). *Basic Psychoanalytic Concepts on the Libido Theory*. New York: Basic.

Nemiroff, R., and Colarusso, C. (1985). Adult development and transference. In Nemiroff and Colarusso (eds.), *The Race Against Time: Psychotherapy and Psychoanalysis in the Second Half of Life*, 59–72. New York: Plenum.

———. (1990). *New Dimensions in Adult Development*. New York: Basic.

Nicolis, G., and Prigogine, I. (1977). *Self-Organization in Nonequilibrium Systems: From Dissipative Structures to Order Through Fluctuations*. New York: Wiley.

Nord, E. (1991). EuroQol—Health-related quality of life measurement: Valuations of health states by the general public in Norway. *Health Policy* 18: 25–36.

Norman, H., Blacker, K. H., Oremland, J., and Barrett, W. (1976). The fate of the transference neurosis after termination of a satisfactory analysis. *Journal of the American Psychoanalytic Association* 24: 471–98.

Novey, S. (1966a). The sense of reality and values of the analyst as a necessary factor in psychoanalysis. *International Journal of Psychoanalysis* 47: 492–501.

———. (1966b). Why some patients conduct actual investigations of their biographies. *Journal of the American Psychoanalytic Association* 14: 376–87.

———. (1968). *The Second Look*. Baltimore: Johns Hopkins University Press.

Novick J. (1976). Termination of treatment in adolescence. *Psychoanalytic Study of the Child* 31: 389–414.

———. (1982). Termination: Themes and issues. *Psychoanalytic Inquiry* 2: 329–66.

Noy, P. (1979a). Form creation in art: An ego-psychological approach to creativity. *Psychoanalytic Quarterly* 48: 229–56.

———. (1979b). The psychoanalytic theory of cognitive development. *Psychoanalytic Study of the Child* 34: 169–216.

Nye, C. (1988). Psychoanalytic narratives: The formulation of meaning. Ph.D. diss., University of Chicago.

Oberndorf, C. (1943). Results of psychoanalytic therapy. *International Journal of Psychoanalysis* 24: 107–14.

———. (1953). *A History of Psychoanalysis in America*. New York: Harper and Row.

Oberndorf, C., Greenacre, P., and Kubie, L. (1948). Symposium on the evaluation of therapeutic results. *International Journal of Psychoanalysis* 29: 7–33.

O'Fallon, J., Dubey, S., Salsburg, D., Edmondson, J., Soffer, A., and Colton, T. (1978). Should there be statistical guidelines for medical research papers? *Biometrics* 34: 687–95.

Offenkrantz, W., and Tobin, A. (1973). Problems of the therapeutic alliance: Freud and the WolfMan. *International Journal of Psychoanalysis* 54: 75–78.

———. (1978). Problems of the therapeutic alliance: Analysis with simultaneous therapeutic and research goals. *International Review of Psychoanalysis* 5: 219–30.

Offer, D. (1969). *The Psychological World of the Teenager: A Study of Normal Adolescent Boys*. New York: Basic.

Offer, D., and Offer, J. (1975). *From Teenage to Young Manhood*. New York: Basic.

Offer, D., and Sabshin, M. (1974). *Normality*. Rev. ed. New York: Basic.

O'Leary, K., and Borkovec, T. (1978). Conceptual, methodological, and ethical problems of placebo groups in psychotherapy research. *American Psychologist* 33: 821–30.

Oremland, J. (1973). A specific dream during the termination phase of successful psycho-analyses. *Journal of the American Psychoanalytic Association* 21: 285–302.

Oremland, J., Blacker, K., and Norman, H. (1975). Incompleteness in "successful" psycho-analyses: A follow-up study. *Journal of the American Psychoanalytic Association* 23: 819–44.

Orens, M. (1955). Setting a termination date: An impetus to analysis. *Journal of the American Psychoanalytic Association* 3: 651–65.

Orlinsky, D., and Howard, K. (1986). Process and outcome in psychotherapy. In S. Garfield and A. Bergin (eds.), *Handbook of Psychotherapy and Behavior Change* (3d ed.), 311–81. New York: Wiley.

———. (1987). A generic model of psychotherapy. *Journal of Integrative and Eclectic Psychotherapy* 6: 6–27.

Orlinsky, D., and Russell, R. (1994). Tradition and change in psychotherapy research: Notes on the fourth generation. In Russell (ed.), *Reassessing Psychotherapy Research*, 185–214. New York: Guilford.

Oxman, T., Rosenberg, S., and Tucker, G. (1982). The language of paranoia. *American Journal of Psychiatry* 139: 275–82.

Panel. (1953). The traditional psychoanalytic technique and its variations. *Journal of the American Psychoanalytic Association* 1: 526–37.

———. (1958). Variations in classical psychoanalytic technique. *International Journal of Psychoanalysis* 39: 200–242.

———. (1960). Criteria for analyzability. *Journal of the American Psychoanalytic Association* 8: 141–51.

———. (1963). Analysis terminable and interminable: Twenty-five years later. *Journal of the American Psychoanalytic Association* 11: 131–42.

———. (1964). Theory of psychoanalytic therapy. *Journal of the American Psychoanalytic Association* 12: 620–31.

———. (1968). Indications and contraindications for psycho-analytic treatment. *International Journal of Psychoanalysis* 49: 254–75.

———. (1970). Psychoanalysis and psychotherapy. *International Journal of Psychoanalysis* 51: 219–32.

———. (1973a). Separation-individuation: Infancy and childhood. *Journal of the American Psychoanalytic Association* 21: 135–54.

———. (1973b). Separation-individuation: Adolescence, maturity. *Journal of the American Psychoanalytic Association* 21: 155–67.

———. (1973c). Technique and prognosis in narcissistic personality disorders. *Journal of the American Psychoanalytic Association* 21: 617–32.

———. (1975). Conference on psychoanalytic education and research. *Journal of the American Psychoanalytic Association* 23: 569–86.

———. (1976). Current concept of the psychoanalytic process. *Journal of the American Psychoanalytic Association* 24: 181–95.

———. (1977). Psychic change in psychoanalysis. *Journal of the American Psychoanalytic Association* 25: 669–78.

———. (1979). Conceptualizing the nature of the therapeutic action in psychoanalysis. *Journal of the American Psychoanalytic Association* 27: 627–42.

———. (1980). Technical consequences of object relations theory. *Journal of the American Psychoanalytic Association* 28: 623–36.

———. (1986). Countertransference in theory and practice. *Journal of the American Psychoanalytic Association* 34: 699–708.

———. (1987). Psychoanalytic contributions to psychiatric nosology. *Journal of the American Psychoanalytic Association* 35: 693–712.

———. (1989). Changing psychic structure through treatment. *Journal of the American Psychoanalytic Association* 37: 173–85.

———. (1990). Does a panel discussion on analytic technique have any effect on an audience of analysts? *Journal of the American Psychoanalytic Association* 38: 733–41.

———. (1991). Concepts and controversies about transference neurosis. *Journal of the American Psychoanalytic Association* 39: 227–40.

———. (1992a). Psychoanalysis and psychotherapy — Similarities and differences: Therapeutic technique. *Journal of the American Psychoanalytic Association* 40: 211–22.

———. (1992b). Psychoanalysis and psychotherapy — Similarities and differences: Conceptual overview. *Journal of the American Psychoanalytic Association* 40: 233–38.

———. (1993). Panel: Differences in the termination of psychotherapy and psychoanalysis. *Journal of the American Psychoanalytic Association* 41: 765– 74.

———. (1997). The relevance of frequency of sessions to the creation of an analytic experience. *Journal of the American Psychoanalytic Association* 45:1241–51.

Paniagua, C. (1985). A methodological approach to surface material. *International Review of Psychoanalysis* 12: 311–26.

Parfrey, P., Vavasour, H., Bullock, M., Henry, S., and Harnett, J. (1989). Development of a health questionnaire specific for end-stage renal disease. *Nephron* 52: 20–28.

Parloff, M., Stephenson, W., and Perlin, S. (1965). Myra's perception of self and others. In D. Rosenthal (ed.), *The Genain Quadruplets,* 212–49. New York: Basic.

Parsonson, B., and Baer, D. (1992). The visual analysis of data, and current research into stimuli controlling it. In T. Kratochwill and J. Levin (eds.), *Single-Case Research Design and Analysis: New Directions for Psychology and Education,* 15–40. Hillsdale, N.J.: Erlbaum.

Partington, J. (1961). *A History of Chemistry.* New York: Dover.

Paul, I. (1967). The concept of schema in memory theory. *Psychological Issues* 18: 218–58.

Peck C., and Coleman, G. (1991). Implications of placebo theory for clinical research and practice in pain management. *Theoretical Medicine* 12: 247–70.

Pedder, J. (1988). Termination reconsidered. *International Journal of Psychoanalysis* 69: 495–505.

Perry, J. (1989). Scientific progress in psychodynamic formulation. *Psychiatry* 53: 245–49.

Perry, J., Augusto, F., and Cooper, S. (1989). Assessing psychodynamic conflicts: I. Reliability of the idiographic conflict formulation method. *Psychiatry* 52: 289–301.

Perry, J., Cooper, A., and Michels, R. (1987). The psychodynamic formulation: Its purpose, structure, and clinical application. *American Journal of Psychiatry* 144: 543–50.

————. (1988). More on the psychodynamic formulation [letter]. *American Journal of Psychiatry* 145: 130–32.

Perry, J., and Cooper, S. (1986). A preliminary report on defenses and conflicts associated with borderline personality disorder. *Journal of the American Psychoanalytic Association* 34: 863–93.

Perry, J., Luborsky, L., Silberschatz, G., and Popp, C. (1989). An examination of three methods of psychodynamic formulation based on the same videotaped interview. Annual Meeting of the Society for Psychotherapy Research (1986, Wellesley, Massachusetts). *Psychiatry* 52: 302–23.

Persons, J. (1991). Psychotherapy outcome studies do not accurately represent current models of psychotherapy: A proposed remedy. *American Psychologist* 46: 99–106.

Peterfreund, E., and Schwarz, J. (1971). Information systems and psychoanalysis and evolutionary biological approach to psychoanalytic theory. *Psychological Issues* 24–25. New York: International Universities Press.

Pfeffer, A. (1959). A procedure for evaluating the results of psychoanalysis: A preliminary report. *Journal of the American Psychoanalytic Association* 7: 418–44.

————. (1961). Follow-up study of satisfactory analysis. *Journal of the American Psychoanalytic Association* 2: 698–718.

————. (1963). The meaning of the analyst after analysis: A contribution to the theory of therapeutic results. *Journal of the American Psychoanalytic Association* 11: 229–44.

————. (1974). The difficulties of the training analyst in the training analysis. *International Journal of Psychoanalysis* 55: 79–84.

Philiber, S., Schwab, M., and Sloss, G. (1980). *Social Research: Guides to a Decision-Making Process*. Itasca, Ill.: Peacock.

Piaget, J., and Inhelder, B. (1969). *The Psychology of the Child*. New York: Basic.

Pine, F. (1979). On the pathology of the separation-individuation process as manifested in later clinical work: An attempt at delineation. *International Journal of Psychoanalysis* 60: 225–42.

————. (1988). The four psychologies of psychoanalysis and their place in clinical work. *Journal of the American Psychoanalytic Association* 36: 571–96.

Pinsof, W. (1989). A conceptual framework and methodological criteria for family therapy process research. *Journal of Consulting and Clinical Psychology* 57: 53–59.

Piper, W., Azim, H., Joyce, A., and McCallum, M. (1991). Transference interpretations, therapeutic alliance, and outcome in short-term individual therapy. *Archives of General Psychiatry* 48: 946–53.

Popp, L., Luborsky, L., and Crits-Christoph, P. (1990). The parallel of the CCRT from therapy narratives with the CCRT from dreams. In Luborsky and Crits-Christoph, *Understanding Transference: The Core Conflictual Relationship Theme Method*, 158–72. New York: Basic.

Pulver, S. (1993). The eclectic analyst; or, The many roads to insight and change. *Journal of the American Psychoanalytic Association* 41: 339–58.

Pumpian-Mindlin, E. (1967). Defense organization of the ego and psychoanalytic technique. *Journal of the American Psychoanalytic Association* 15: 150–65.

Racker, H. (1953). A contribution to the problem of countertransference. *International Journal of Psychoanalysis* 34: 313–24.

——. (1957). The meanings and uses of countertransference. *Psychoanalytic Quarterly* 26: 303–57.

——. (1968). *Transference and Countertransference*. New York: International Universities Press.

Rangell, L. (1954). Psychoanalysis and dynamic psychotherapy. *Journal of the American Psychoanalytic Association* 2: 734–44.

——. (1969). The intrapsychic process and its analysis: A recent line of thought and its current implications. *International Journal of Psychoanalysis* 50: 65–77.

——. (1979). Contemporary issues in the theory of therapy. *Journal of the American Psychoanalytic Association* 27 (suppl.): 81–112.

——. (1981a). From insight to change. *Journal of the American Psychoanalytic Association* 29: 119–41.

——. (1981b). Psychoanalysis and dynamic psychotherapy: Similarities and differences twenty-five years later. *Psychoanalytic Quarterly* 50: 665–93.

——. (1984a). The analyst at work. The Madrid Congress: Synthesis and critique. *International Journal of Psychoanalysis* 65: 125–40.

——. (1984b). The Anna Freud experience. *Psychoanalytic Study of the Child* 39: 29–43.

——. (1987). A core process in psychoanalytic treatment. *Psychoanalytic Quarterly* 56: 222–49.

——. (1988). The future of psychoanalysis: The scientific crossroads. *Psychoanalytic Quarterly* 57: 313–40.

——. (1989). Rapprochement and other crises: The specific and nonspecific in analytic reconstruction. *Psychoanalytic Study of the Child* 44: 19–39.

Rapaport, D. (1951a). *Organization and Pathology of Thought: Selected Sources*. New York: Columbia University Press.

——. (1951b). The conceptual model of psychoanalysis. In M. Gill (ed.), *The Collected Papers of David Rapaport*, 405–31. New York: Basic.

——. (1954). Clinical implications of ego psychology. In M. Gill (ed.), *The Collected Papers of David Rapaport*, 574–85. New York: Basic.

——. (1960). *The Structure of Psychoanalytic Theory: A Systematizing Attempt*. New York: International Universities Press.

——. (1971). *Emotions and Memory*. 5th ed. New York: International Universities Press.

Rapaport, D., and Gill, M. (1958). The points of view and assumptions of metapsychology. *International Journal of Psychoanalysis* 50: 153–62.

Rapaport, D., Gill, M., and Schafer, R. (1945). *Diagnostic Psychological Testing*. New York: International Universities Press.

Reed, G. (1987a). Scientific and polemical aspects of the term transference neurosis in psychoanalysis. *Psychoanalytic Inquiry* 7: 465–83.

——. (1987b). Rules of clinical understanding in classical psychoanalysis and in self psychology: A comparison. *Journal of the American Psychoanalytic Association* 35: 421–46.

——. (1990). A reconsideration of the concept of transference neurosis. *International Journal of Psychoanalysis* 71: 205–17.

――. (1994). *Transference Neurosis and Psychoanalytic Experience*. New Haven: Yale University Press.

Reich, A. (1951). On countertransference. *International Journal of Psychoanalysis* 32: 25–31.

Reich, W. (1933). *Character Analysis*. T. Wolfe (trans.). New York: Orgone Institute Press.

――. (1975). *Early Writings*. New York: Farrar, Straus, and Giroux.

Reizenstein, P. (1986). Quality of life in cancer patients. *Medical Oncology and Tumor Pharmacotherapy* 3: 51–54.

Rice, L., and Greenberg, L. (1984). *Change Episodes in Psychotherapy: Intensive Analysis of Patterns*. New York: Guilford.

Ricoeur, P. (1970). *Freud and Philosophy*. New Haven: Yale University Press.

――. (1977). The question of proof in Freud's psychoanalytic writings. *Journal of the American Psychoanalytic Association* 25: 835–72.

Ritvo, S. (1966). Correlation of a childhood and adult neurosis: Based on the adult analysis of a reported childhood case. *International Journal of Psychoanalysis* 47: 130–31.

Robins, L., and McEvoy, L. (1990). Conduct problems as predictors of substance abuse. In Robins and M. Rutter (eds.), *Straight and Devious Pathways from Childhood to Adulthood,* 182–204. Cambridge: Cambridge University Press.

Robinson, P. (1993). *Freud and His Critics*. Berkeley: University of California Press.

Rosenblatt, P. (1981). Ethnographic case studies. In M. Brewer and B. Collins (eds.), *Scientific Inquiry and the Social Sciences: A Volume in Honor of Donald T. Campbell,* 194–225. San Francisco: Jossey-Bass.

Rosenthal, G. (1988). "Analysis terminable and interminable" 50 years afterwards: Analysis of adolescents. *International Journal of Psychoanalysis* 69: 327–34.

Rosenthal, R. (1976). Interpersonal expectancy effects: A follow-up. In *Experimental Effects in Behavioral Research,* 440–71. New York: Irvington.

――. (1978). Combining results of independent studies. *Psychological Bulletin* 86: 638–41.

――. (1983). Assessing the statistical and social importance of effects of psychotherapy. *Journal of Consulting and Clinical Psychology* 51: 4–13.

Rosenthal, R., and Rubin, D. (1982a). Comparing effect sizes of independent studies. *Psychological Bulletin* 92: 500–504.

――. (1982b). Further meta-analytic procedures for assessing cognitive gender differences. *Journal of Educational Psychology* 74: 708–12.

Rosenzwieg, S. (1936). Some implicit common factors in diverse methods of psychotherapy. *American Journal of Orthopsychiatry* 6: 422–25.

Roth, A., and Fonagy, P. (eds.). (1996). *What Works for Whom? A Critical Review of Psychotherapy Research*. New York: Guilford.

Rothstein, A. (1982). The implications of early psychopathology for the analyzability of narcissistic personality disorders. *International Journal of Psychoanalysis* 63: 177–88.

――. (1990). On beginning with a reluctant patient. In T. Jacobs, A. Rothstein, et al. (eds.), *On Beginning an Analysis,* 153–62. Madison, Conn.: International Universities Press.

Roustang, F. (1976). *Dire Mastery*. N. Lukacher (trans.). Baltimore: Johns Hopkins University Press.

Rubovitz-Seitz, P. (1992). Interpretive methodologies: Problems, limitations, strategies. *Journal of the American Psychoanalytic Association* 40: 139–68.

Rudominer, H. (1984). Peer review, third-party payment, and the analytic situation: A case report. *Journal of the American Psychoanalytic Association* 32: 773–95.

Rutter, M., and Rutter, M. (1993). *Developing Minds: Challenge and Continuity Across the Lifespan*. New York: Basic.

Ryle, J. (1948). *The Natural History of Disease*. 2d ed. London: Geoffrey Cumberlege, Oxford University Press.

Sabelli, H., and Carlson-Sabelli, L. (1991). Process theory as a framework for comprehensive psychodynamic formulations. *Genetic Social and General Psychology Monographs* 117: 5–27.

Sachs, II. (1939). The prospects of psychoanalysis. *International Journal of Psychoanalysis* 20: 460–64.

Safran, J., Greenberg, L., and Rice, L. (1988). Integrating psychotherapy research and practice: Modeling the change process. *Psychotherapy* 25: 1–17.

Salsburg, D. (1985). The religion of statistics as practiced in medical journals. *American Statistician* 39: 220–23.

Sampson, H., and Weiss, J. (1986). Testing hypotheses: The approach of the Mount Zion Psychotherapy Research Group. In L. Greenberg and W. Pinsof (eds.), *The Psychotherapeutic Process: A Research Handbook*, 591–613. New York: Guilford.

Sampson, H., Weiss, J., Mlodnosky, L., and Hause, E. (1972). Defense analysis and the emergence of warded-off mental contents: An empirical study. *Archives of General Psychiatry* 26: 524–32.

Sandell, R., Blomberg, J., and Lazar, A. (1997). When reality doesn't fit the blueprint: Doing research on psychoanalysis and long-term psychotherapy in a public health service program. *Psychotherapy Research* 7: 333–44.

Sandler, J. (1976). Countertransference and role responsiveness. *International Review of Psychoanalysis* 3: 43–48.

———. (1988). Psychoanalytic technique and "analysis terminable and interminable." *International Journal of Psychoanalysis* 69: 335–45.

Sandler, J., and Freud, A. (1985). *The Analysis of Defense: The Ego and the Mechanism of Defense Revisited*. New York: International Universities Press.

Sandler, J., Kennedy, H., and Tyson, R. (1975). Discussions on transference: The treatment situation and technique in child psychoanalysis. *Psychoanalytic Study of the Child* 30: 409–41.

———. (1980). *The Technique of Child Psychoanalysis*. London: Hogarth.

Sargent, H., Horwitz, L., Wallerstein, R., and Appelbaum, A. (1968). Prediction in psychotherapy research: Methods and the transformation of clinical judgements and testable hypotheses. *Psychological Issues* 6. New York: International Universities Press.

Sashin, J. (1979). Personal communication.

Sashin, J., Eldred, S., and Van Amerowgen, A. (1975). A search for predictive factors in institute supervised cases: A retrospective study of 183 cases from 1959–1966 at the

Boston Psychoanalytic Society and Institute. *International Journal of Psychoanalysis*
56: 343–59.

Sass, L., and Woolfolk, R. (1988). Psychoanalysis and the hermeneutic turn: A critique of
narrative truth and historical truth. *Journal of the American Psychoanalytic Association* 36: 429–54.

Savitt, R. A. (1977). Conflict and somatization: Psychoanalytic treatment of the psycho-
physiologic response in the digestive tract. *Psychoanalytic Quarterly* 46: 605–22.

Schachter, J. (1990). Post-termination patient-analyst contact. Part 1, Analysts' attitudes
and experience; part 2, Impact on patients. *International Journal of Psychoanalysis* 71:
475–86.

Schachter, J., and Butts, H. (1968). Transference and countertransference in interracial
analyses. *Journal of the American Psychoanalytic Association* 16: 792–808.

Schafer, R. (1970a). An overview of Heinz Hartmann's contributions to psychoanalysis.
International Journal of Psychoanalysis 51: 425–46.

———. (1970b). The psychoanalytic vision of reality. *International Journal of Psychoanalysis* 51: 279–97.

———. (1981a). La relevancia de la interpretación transferencial en el "aquí y ahora" para
la reconstrucción del desarrollo temprano. [The relevance of the "here and now"
transference interpretation to the reconstruction of early development.] *Revista de
Psicoanálisis* 38: 1167–76.

———. (1981b). *Narrative actions in psychoanalysis.* Vol. 14 of the Heinz Werner Lecture
Series. Worcester, Mass.: Clark University Press.

———. (1982). The relevance of the "here and now" transference interpretation to the reconstruction of early development. *International Journal of Psychoanalysis* 63: 77–82.

———. (1983). *The Analytic Attitude.* New York: Basic.

———. (1985). The interpretation of psychic reality, developmental influences, and unconscious communication. *Journal of the American Psychoanalytic Association* 33:
537–54.

———. (1987). Self-deception, defense, and narration. *Psychoanalysis and Contemporary
Thought* 10: 319–46.

———. (1992). *Retelling a Life: Narration and Dialogue in Psychoanalysis.* New York:
Basic.

Schlesinger, H. (1974). Problems of doing research on the therapeutic process in psychoanalysis. *Journal of the American Psychoanalytic Association* 22: 3–13.

Schlessinger, N. (1984). On analyzability in psychoanalysis. In J. Gedo and G. Pollock
(eds.), *Psychoanalysis: The Vital Issues,* 249–74. New York: International Universities
Press.

Schlessinger, N., and Robbins, F. (1974). Assessment and follow-up in psychoanalysis.
Journal of the American Psychoanalytic Association 22: 542–67.

———. (1975). The psychoanalytic process: Recurrent patterns of conflict and change in
ego functions. *Journal of the American Psychoanalytic Association* 23: 761–82.

———. (1983). *A Developmental View of the Psychoanalytic Process: Follow-Up Studies
and Their Consequences.* New York: International Universities Press.

Schuller, R., Crits-Christoph, P., and Connolly, M. (1991). The resistance scale: Background and psychometric properties. *Psychoanalytic Psychology* 8: 195–211.

Schwaber, E. (1983). A particular perspective on analytic listening. *Psychoanalytic Study of the Child* 38: 519–46.

———. (1992). Countertransferences: The analyst's retreat from the patient's vantage point. *International Journal of Psychoanalysis* 73: 349–62.

Seitz, P. (1966). The consensus problem in psychoanalytic research. In L. Gott and A. Auerbach (eds.), *Methods of Research in Psychotherapy*, 209–25. New York: Appleton-Century-Crofts.

Settlage, C. (1989). Therapeutic and developmental process. *Psychoanalytic Inquiry* 2: 375–96.

Shadish, W., and Sweeney, R. (1991). Mediators and moderators in meta-analysis: There's a reason we don't let dodo birds tell us which psychotherapies should have prizes. *Journal of Consulting and Clinical Psychology* 59: 883–93.

Shaffer, D., Gould, M., Brasic, J., Ambrosine, P., Fisher, P., Bird, H., and Aluwahlia, S. (1983). A children's global assessment scale (CGAS). *Archives of General Psychiatry* 40: 1228–31.

Shane, M., and Shane, E. (1984). The end phase of analysis: Indicators, functions, and tasks of termination. *Journal of the American Psychoanalytic Association* 32: 739–72.

Shank, R. (1990). *Tell Me a Story: A New Look at Real and Artificial Memory*. New York: Scribner.

Shapiro, D. (1976). The analyst's own analysis. *Journal of the American Psychoanalytic Association* 24: 5–42.

Shapiro, E., Shapiro, R., Zinner, J., and Berkowitz, D. (1977). The borderline ego and the working alliance: Indications for family and individual treatment in adolescence. *International Journal of Psychoanalysis* 58: 77–87.

Shapiro, T. (1983). The unconscious still occupies us. *Psychoanalytic Study of the Child* 38: 547–67.

———. (1989a). Our changing science. *Journal of the American Psychoanalytic Association* 37: 3–6.

———. (1989b). Psychoanalytic classification and empiricism with borderline personality disorder as a model. *Journal of Consulting and Clinical Psychology* 57: 187–94.

———. (1989c). The psychodynamic formulation in child and adolescent psychiatry. *Journal of the American Academy of Child and Adolescent Psychiatry* 28: 675–80.

Sharpe, R. (1987). Psychoanalysis and narrative: A structuralist approach. *International Review of Psychoanalysis* 14: 335–42.

Shevrin, H. (1984). The fate of the five metapsychological principles. *Psychoanalytic Inquiry* 4: 33–58.

Shoham-Salomon, V. (1990). Interrelating research processes of process research. *Journal of Consulting and Clinical Psychology* 58: 295–303.

Sidman, M. (1952). A note on the functional relations obtained from group data. *Psychological Bulletin* 49: 263–69.

———. (1960). *Tactics of Scientific Research*. New York: Basic.

Silberschatz, G., and Curtis, J. (1993). Measuring the therapist's impact on the patient's therapeutic progress. *Journal of Consulting and Clinical Psychology* 61: 403–11.

Silberschatz, G., Fretter, P., and Curtis, J. (1986). How do interpretations influence the process of psychotherapy? *Journal of Consulting and Clinical Psychology* 54: 646–52.

Silverman, M. (1985a). Countertransference and the myth of the perfectly analyzed analyst. *Psychoanalytic Quarterly* 54: 175–99.

——. (1985b). Sudden onset of anti-Chinese prejudice in a four-year-old girl. *Psychoanalytic Quarterly* 54: 615–19.

Skinner, B. (1961). *Cumulative Records.* Enlarged ed. New York: Appleton-Century-Crofts.

Skinner, H. (1981). Toward the integration of classification theory and methods: Perspectives from psychology. *Journal of Abnormal Psychology* 90: 68–87.

Sklansky, M. (1972). Panel report: Indications and contraindications for the psychoanalysis of the adolescent. *Journal of the American Psychoanalytic Association* 20: 134–44.

Skolnikoff, A. (1985). Consensual analysis: A case study. In C. Settlage and K. Brockban (eds.), *New Ideas in Psychoanalysis,* 235–44. Hillsdale, N.J.: Analytic Press.

——. (1988). The silent observer. Paper presented at the meeting of the American Psychoanalytic Association, New York.

——. (1990). The emotional position of the analyst in the shift from psychotherapy to psychoanalysis. *Psychoanalytic Inquiry* 10: 107–18.

Smith, J., and Morris, H. (eds.). (1992). *Telling Facts: History and Narration in Psychoanalysis.* Baltimore: Johns Hopkins University Press.

Smith, M., and Glass, G. (1977). Meta-analysis of psychotherapy outcome studies. *American Psychologist* 32: 752–60.

Smith, M., Glass, G., and Miller, T. (1980). *The Benefits of Psychotherapy.* Baltimore: Johns Hopkins University Press.

Spence, D. (1982). Narrative truth and theoretical truth. *Psychoanalytic Quarterly* 51: 43–69.

——. (1983a). Ambiguity in everyday life. *Psychoanalytic Inquiry* 3: 255–78.

——. (1983b). Narrative persuasion. *Psychoanalysis and Contemporary Thought* 6: 457–81.

——. (1986). When interpretation masquerades as explanation. *Journal of the American Psychoanalytic Association* 34: 3–22.

——. (1989a). Narrative appeal vs. historical validity. Scientific Symposium: Clinical controversies and the interpersonal tradition. *Contemporary Psychoanalysis* 25: 517–24.

——. (1989b). Psychoanalysis and the hermeneutic turn: A critique of "Narrative truth and historical truth": Reply to Louis A. Sass and Robert L. Woolfolk. *Journal of the American Psychoanalytic Association* 37: 1128–30.

——. (1990). The rhetorical voice of psychoanalysis. *Journal of the American Psychoanalytic Association* 38: 579–603.

——. (1991). Saying good-bye to historical truth. *Philosophy of the Social Sciences* 21: 121–38.

——. (1993). Traditional case studies and prescriptions for improving them. In N. Miller, L. Luborsky, et al. (eds.), *Psychodynamic Treatment Research: A Handbook for Clinical Practice,* 37–52. New York: Basic.

——. (1994). The rhetorical voice of psychoanalysis: Displacement of evidence by *theory.* Cambridge: Harvard University Press.

Spence, D., Dahl, H., and Jones, E. (1993). Impact of interpretation on associative freedom. *Journal of Consulting and Clinical Psychology* 61: 395– 402.

Spruiell, V. (1979a). Freud's concepts of idealization. *Journal of the American Psychoanalytic Association* 27: 777–95.

———. (1979b). Object relations theory: Clinical perspectives. *Journal of the American Psychoanalytic Association* 27: 387–98.

Starfield, B., Steinwachs, D., Morris, I., Bause, G., Siebert, S., and Westin, C. (1979). Concordance between medical records and observations regarding information on coordination of care. *Medical Care* 17: 758–66.

Stephane, B., Pelletier, M., Gauthier, J., Cote, G., and Laberge, B. (1997). The assessment of panic using self-report: A comprehensive survey of validated instruments. *Journal of Anxiety Disorders* 11: 89–111.

Stephenson, W. (1974). Methodology of single case studies. *Journal of Operational Psychiatry* 5: 3–16.

Stern, D. (1985). *The Interpersonal World of the Infant*. New York: Basic.

Stevens-Long, J. (1990). Adult development: Theories past and future. In R. Nemiroff and C. Colarusso (eds.), *New Dimensions in Adult Development*, 125–65. New York: Basic.

Stewart, A., Greenfield, S., Hays, R., Wells, K., Rogers, W., Berry, S., McGlynn, E., and Ware, J. (1989). Functional status and well-being of patients with chronic conditions. *Journal of the American Medical Association* 262: 907–13.

Stewart, H. (1989). Technique at the basic fault/regression. *International Journal of Psychoanalysis* 70:221–30.

Stewart, I. (1989). *Does God Play Dice?* New York: Blackwell.

Stigler, S. (1986). *The History of Statistics*. Cambridge: Harvard University Press.

Stiles, W. (1988). Psychotherapy process-outcome correlations may be misleading. *Psychotherapy* 25: 27–35.

Stinson, C., Milbrath, C., Oreidbord, S., and Bucci, W. (1992). Thematic segmentation of psychotherapy transcripts for convergent analysis. Paper presented at the San Francisco Center for the Study of Neurosis.

Stolorow, R. (1990). Converting psychotherapy to psychoanalysis. *Psychoanalytic Inquiry* 10: 119–30.

Stolorow, R., and Atwood, G. (1992). *Contexts of Being: The Intersubjective Foundations of Psychological Life*. Hillsdale, N.J.: Analytic Press.

Stolorow, R., Brandchaft, B., and Atwood, G. (1987). *Psychoanalytic Treatment: An Intersubjective Approach*. Hillsdale, N.J.: Analytic Press.

Stolorow, R., and Lachmann, F. (1980). *Psychoanalysis of Developmental Arrest: Theory and Treatment*. New York: International Universities Press.

Stone, L. (1954). The widening scope of indications for psychoanalysis. *Journal of the American Psychoanalytic Association* 2: 567–94.

Strachey, J. (1934). The nature of the therapeutic action of psychoanalysis. *International Journal of Psychoanalysis* 15: 127–59.

Strozier, C. (1990). Personal communication.

———. (1996). Personal communication.

Strupp, H. (1980a). Success and failure in time-limited psychotherapy: A systematic comparison of two cases (Comparison 1). *Archives of General Psychiatry* 37: 595–603.

——. (1980b). Success and failure in time-limited psychotherapy: A systematic comparison of two cases (Comparison 2). *Archives of General Psychiatry* 37: 708–16.

——. (1980c). Success and failure in time-limited psychotherapy: A systematic comparison of two cases (Comparison 3). *Archives of General Psychiatry* 37: 947–54.

——. (1980d). Success and failure in time-limited psychotherapy: A systematic comparison of two cases (Comparison 4). *Archives of General Psychiatry* 37: 954–74.

Strupp, H., and Binder, J. (1984). *Psychotherapy in a New Key: A Guide to Time-Limited Dynamic Psychotherapy*. New York: Basic.

Strupp, H., and Hadley, S. (1979). Specific vs. nonspecific factors in psychotherapy. *Archives of General Psychiatry* 36: 1125–36.

Strupp, H., Schacht, T., and Henry, W. (1988). Problem-treatment-outcome, congruence: A principle whose time has come. In H. Dahl and H. Thomä (eds.), *Psychoanalytic Process Research Strategies*, 1–14. Berlin: Springer-Verlag.

Suh, C., Strupp, H., and O'Malley, S. (1986). The Vanderbilt process measures: The Psychotherapy Process Scale (VPPS) and the Negative Indicators Scale (VNIS). In L. Greenberg, W. Pinsof, et al. (eds.), *The Psychotherapeutic Process: A Research Handbook*, 285–323. New York: Guilford.

Sullivan, H. (1940). *Conceptions of Modern Psychiatry*. New York: Norton.

——. (1953). *The Interpersonal Theory of Psychiatry*. New York: Norton.

——. (1956). *Clinical Studies in Psychiatry*. New York: Norton.

——. (1964). *The Fusion of Psychiatry and Social Science*. New York: Norton.

Sulloway, S. (1979). *Freud, Biologist of the Mind: Beyond the Psychoanalytic Legend*. New York: Basic.

Sundin, E., Armelius, B., and Nilsson, T. (1994). Reliability studies of scales of psychological capacities: A new method to assess psychological change. *Psychoanalysis and Contemporary Thought* 17 (4): 591–615.

Swerdloff, B. (1963). *The Predictive Value of the Admission Interview*. Ph.D. diss., Columbia University, New York.

Symposium. (1937). Theory of the therapeutic results of psychoanalysis. *International Journal of Psychoanalysis* 18: 125–89.

——. (1950a). On the evaluation of therapeutic results. *International Journal of Psychoanalysis* 31: 200–204.

——. (1950b). On the termination of psycho-analytic treatment. *International Journal of Psychoanalysis* 31: 191–99.

Tanur, J., Mosteller, F., Kruskal, W., Link, R., Pieters, R., Rising, G., and Lehman, E. (1985). *Statistics: A Guide to the Unknown*. Monterey, Calif.: Wadsworth and Brooks/Cole.

Target, M., and Fonagy, P. (1994). The efficacy of psychoanalysis for children: Prediction of outcome in developmental context. *Journal of the American Academy of Child and Adolescent Psychiatry* 33:1134–44.

Task Force on DSM-IV and other committees and work groups of the American Psychiatric Association. (1994). *Diagnostic and Statistical Manual of Mental Disorders (DSM-IV)*. 4th ed. Washington, D.C.: American Psychiatric Association.

Teller, V., and Dahl, H. (1986). The microstructure of free association. *Journal of the American Psychoanalytic Association* 34: 763–98.

Thom, R. (1975). *Structural Stability and Morphogenesis: An Outline of a General Theory of Models*. Reading: Benjamin.

Thomas, R. (1966). Comments on some aspects of self and object representation in a group of psychotic children: An application of Anna Freud's diagnostic profile. *Psychoanalytic Study of the Child* 21: 527–80.

Ticho, E. (1970). Differences between psychoanalysis and psychotherapy. *Bulletin of the Menninger Clinic* 34: 128–38.

———. (1972). Termination of psychoanalysis: Treatment goals, life goals. *Psychoanalytic Quarterly* 41: 315–33.

Torrey, E. (1992). *Freudian Fraud: The Malignant Effect of Freud's Theory on American Thought and Culture*. New York: HarperCollins.

Toulmin, S. (1990). *Cosmopolis: The Hidden Agenda of Modernity*. New York: Free Press.

Tower, L. (1956). Countertransference. *Journal of the American Psychoanalytic Association* 4: 224–65.

Turing, A. (1950). Can a machine think? In J. Newman (ed.), *The World of Mathematics* 4: 2099–2123. New York: Simon and Schuster.

Turkle, S. (1978). *Psychoanalytic Politics*. New York: Basic.

———. (1992). Psychoanalytic culture: Jacques Lacan and the social appropriation of psychoanalysis. In J. Smith and H. Morris (eds.), *Telling Facts: History and Narration in Psychoanalysis,* 220–63. Baltimore: Johns Hopkins University Press.

Tyson, R. (1986). Countertransference evolution in theory and practice. *Journal of the American Psychoanalytic Association* 34: 251–74.

Tyson, R., and Sandler, J. (1971). Problems in the selection of patients for psychoanalysis: Comments on the application of the concepts of "indications," "suitability," and "analysability." *British Journal of Medical Psychology* 44: 211–28.

Vaillant, G. (1975). Sociopathy as a human process: A viewpoint. *Archives of General Psychiatry* 32: 178–83.

———. (1976). Natural history of male psychological health. Part 5, The relation of choice of ego mechanisms of defense to adult adjustment. *Archives of General Psychiatry* 33: 535–45.

———. (1977). *Adaptation to Life*. Boston: Little, Brown.

———. (1986). Comments on Robin Room's "Dependence and society": Deconstruction reconstructed. *British Journal of Addiction* 81: 58.

———. (1987). A developmental view of old and new perspectives of personality disorders. *Journal of Personality Disorders* 1: 146–56.

———. (1992). *Ego Mechanisms of Defense: A Guide for Clinicians and Researchers*. Washington D.C.: American Psychiatric Association Press.

Valenstein, A. (1968). Indications and contraindications for psychoanalytic treatment. *International Journal of Psychoanalysis* 49: 265.

Van Dam, H., Heinicke, C., and Shane, M. (1975). On termination in child analysis. *Psychoanalytic Study of the Child* 30: 443–74.

Vaughan, S., Spitzer, R., Davies, M., and Roose, S. (1997). The definition and assessment of analytic process: Can analysts agree? *International Journal of Psychoanalysis* 78: 959–73.

Veith, I. (1965). *Hysteria: The History of a Disease.* Chicago: University of Chicago Press.

Waelder, R. (1936). On the principle of multiple function. *Psychoanalytic Quarterly* 5: 45–62.

———. (1963). Psychic determinism and the possibility of predictions. *Psychoanalytic Quarterly* 32: 15–42.

Waldhorn, H. (1967). Indications for psychoanalysis. In E. Joseph (ed.), *Monograph Series of the Kris Study Group of the New York Psychoanalytic Institute,* no. 2: 3–51. New York: International Universities Press.

———. (1968). Indications and contraindications: Lessons from the second analysis. *International Journal of Psychoanalysis* 49: 358–62.

Waldron, S. (1976). The significance of childhood neurosis for adult mental health: A follow-up study. *American Journal of Psychiatry* 133: 532–38.

———. (1992). Slips of the analyst. *Psychoanalytic Quarterly* 61: 564–80.

Wallerstein, R. (1964). The role of prediction in theory building in psychoanalysis. *Journal of the American Psychoanalytic Association* 12: 675–91.

———. (1965). The goals of psychoanalysis: A survey of analytic viewpoints. *Journal of the American Psychoanalytic Association* 13: 748–70.

———. (1969). Introduction to panel on psychoanalysis and psychotherapy: The relationship of psychoanalysis to psychotherapy — current issues. *International Journal of Psychoanalysis* 50:117–26.

———. (1981). *Becoming a Psychoanalyst.* New York: International Universities Press.

———. (1986a). *Forty-Two Lives in Treatment: A Study of Psychoanalysis and Psychotherapy.* New York: Guilford.

———. (1986b). Psychoanalysis as a science: A response to the new challenges. *Psychoanalytic Quarterly* 55: 414–51.

———. (1988). One psychoanalysis or many? *International Journal of Psychoanalysis* 69: 5–21.

———. (1989a). Follow-up in psychoanalysis: Clinical and research values. *Journal of the American Psychoanalytic Association* 37: 921–41.

———. (1989b). Psychoanalysis and psychotherapy: An historical perspective. *International Journal of Psychoanalysis* 70: 563–92.

———. (1989c). The psychotherapy research project of the Menninger Foundation: An overview. *Journal of Consulting and Clinical Psychology* 57: 195–205.

———. (1990). Psychoanalysis: The common ground. *International Journal of Psychoanalysis* 71: 3–20.

Wallerstein, R., and Sampson, H. (1971). Issues in research in the psychoanalytic process. *International Journal of Psychoanalysis* 52: 11–50.

Wampold, B. (1992). The intensive examination of social interaction. In T. Kratochwill and J. Levin (eds.), *Single-Case Research Design and Analysis: New Directions for Psychology and Education,* 93–131. Hillsdale, N.J.: Erlbaum.

Weber, J., Bachrach, H., and Solomon, M. (1985a). Factors associated with the outcome of psychoanalysis: Report of the Columbia Psychoanalytic Center Research Project, part 2. *International Review of Psychoanalysis* 12: 127–41.

———. (1985b). Factors associated with the outcome of psychoanalysis: Report of the Columbia Psychoanalytic Center Research Project, part 3. *International Journal of Psychoanalysis* 12: 251–62.

Weber, J., Bradlow, P., Moss, L., and Elinson, J. (1974). Predictions of outcome in psychoanalysis and analytic psychotherapy. *Psychiatric Quarterly* 40: 1–33.

Weber, J., Elinson, J., and Moss, L. (1966). The application of ego strength scales to psychoanalytic clinic records. In G. Goldman and D. Shapiro (eds.), *Developments in Psychoanalysis at Columbia University*. New York: Hatner.

———. (1967). Psychoanalysis and change. *Archives of General Psychiatry* 17: 687–708.

Weber, M. (1905). *The Protestant Ethic and the Spirit of Capitalism*. T. Parsons (trans.). New York: Scribner.

Weinberg, S. (1977). *The First Three Minutes*. New York: Basic.

Weinhardt, L., Forsyth, A., Carey, M., Jaworski, B., and Durant, L. (1998). Realiability and validity of self-report measures of HIV-related sexual behavior: Progress since 1990 and recommendations for research and practice. *Archives of Sexual Behavior* 27: 155–80.

Weinshel, E. (1984). Some observations on the psychoanalytic process. *Psychoanalytic Quarterly* 53: 63–92.

Weisberg, P. (1992). Education and enrichment approaches. In C. Walker and M. Roberts (eds.), *Handbook of Clinical Child Psychology* (2d ed.), 919–32. New York: Wiley.

Weiss, J. (1971). The emergence of new themes: A contribution to the psychoanalytic theory of therapy. *International Journal of Psychoanalysis* 52: 459–67.

Weiss, J., Sampson, H., and Mount Zion Psychotherapy Research Group. (1986). *The Psychoanalytic Process: Theory, Clinical Observation, and Empirical Research*. New York: Guilford.

Weiss, S. (1981). Reflections on the psychoanalytic process, with special emphasis on child analysis and self-analysis. *Annual of Psychoanalysis* 2: 43–56.

Weisz, J., and Weiss, B. (1993). *Effects of Psychotherapy with Children and Adolescence*. Newbury Park, Calif.: Sage.

Wells, K., Stewart, A., Hays, R., Burnham, M., Rogers, W., Daniels, M., Greenfield, S., and Ware, J. (1989). The functioning and well-being of depressed patients: Results from the medical outcome studies. *Journal of the American Medical Association* 262: 914–19.

Wetzler, S. (1985). The historical truth of psychoanalytic reconstructions. *International Review of Psychoanalysis* 12: 187–97.

Wills, D. (1981). Some notes on the application of the diagnostic profile to young blind children. *Psychoanalytic Study of the Child* 36: 217–37.

Windholz, M., and Silberschatz, G. (1988) Vanderbilt Psychotherapy Process Scale: A replication with adult outpatients. *Journal of Consulting and Clinical Psychology* 56: 56–60.

Winnicott, D. (1960). Ego distortion in terms of the true and false self. In *The Maturational Processes and the Facilitating Environment*, 140–52. New York: International Universities Press, 1965.

———. (1962). The aims of psycho-analytic treatment. In *The Maturational Processes and the Facilitating Environment*, 166–70. London: Hogarth, 1965.

———. (1965). *The Maturational Processes and the Facilitating Environment: Studies in the Theory of Emotional Development*. New York: International Universities Press.

———. (1977). *The Piggle: An Account of the Psychoanalytic Treatment of a Little Girl.* New York: International Universities Press.

Wolfe, B. (1993a). Psychotherapy research funding for fiscal years 1986–1991. *Psychotherapy Rehabilitation Research* 1: 7–9.

———. (1993b). Psychosocial treatment and rehabilitation research funding for fiscal year 1991. *Psychotherapy and Rehabilitation Research* 1: 10–11.

Wolpe, J. (1958). *Psychotherapy by Reciprocal Inhibition.* Stanford: Stanford University Press.

Woody, S., and Kihlstrom, L. (1997). Outcomes, quality, and cost: Integrating psychotherapy and mental health services research. *Psychotherapy Research* 7: 365–81.

Wortis, J. (1954). *Fragment of an Analysis with Freud.* New York: McGraw-Hill.

Wyman, Herbert M., and Rittenberg, Stephen M. (1992). The analyzing instrument of Otto Isakower, M.D.: Evolution of a psychoanalytic concept. *Journal of Clinical Psychoanalysis* 1 (2): 165–75.

Yates, B. (1997). From psychotherapy research to cost-outcome research: What resources are necessary to implement which therapy procedures that change what processes to yield which outcomes? *Psychotherapy Research* 7: 345–64.

Yeaton, W., and Seachrest, L. (1981). Critical dimensions in the choice and maintenance of successful treatments, strength, integrity, and effectiveness. *Journal Consulting and Clinical Psychology* 49: 156–67.

Yin, Y. (1994). *Case Study Research Design and Method.* 2d ed. Applied Social Research Series 5. Newbury Park, Calif.: Sage.

Yuille, J., and Wells, G. (1991). Concern about the application of research findings: The issue of ecological validity. In J. Doris (ed.), *The Suggestibility of Children's Recollections: Implications for Eyewitness Testimony,* 118–28. Washington, D.C.: American Psychological Association.

Zetzel, E. (1956). The concept of transference. In *The Capacity for Emotional Growth,* 168–81. New York: International Universities Press, 1970.

———. (1958a). The analytic situation and the analytic process. In *The Capacity for Emotional Growth,* 197–215. New York: International Universities Press, 1970.

———. (1958b). Therapeutic alliance in the analysis of hysteria. In *The Capacity for Emotional Growth,* 182–96. New York: International Universities Press, 1970.

———. (1965). The theory of therapy in relation to a developmental model of the psychic apparatus. *International Journal of Psychoanalysis* 46: 39–52.

———. (1968). The so-called good hysteric. In *The Capacity for Emotional Growth,* 128–42. New York: International Universities Press, 1970.

Zetzel, E., and Meissner, W. (1973). *Basic Concepts of Psychoanalytic Psychiatry.* New York: Basic.

Zilberg, N., Wallerstein, R., DeWitt, K., Hartley, D., et al. (1991). A conceptual analysis and strategy for assessing structural change. *Psychoanalysis and Contemporary Thought* 14: 317–42.

Index